HUNGRY FOR YOU

Joan Smith is a novelist, journalist and critic. She is the author of the highly acclaimed *Misogynies*, which is also also available in Vintage, and five detective novels, two of which have been filmed by BBC television. She lives in London.

BY JOAN SMITH

Non-Fiction

Misogynies
Clouds of Deceit
Hungry for You

Fiction

A Masculine Ending
Why Aren't They Screaming?
Don't Leave Me This Way
What Men Say
Full Stop
Femmes de Siecle (editor)

Joan Smith

HUNGRY FOR YOU

From Cannibalism to Seduction:
A Book on Food

VINTAGE

Published by Vintage 1997

2 4 6 8 10 9 7 5 3 1

Selection, essays and introduction copyright © Joan Smith 1996

The right of Joan Smith to be identified as the author of
this work has been asserted by her in accordance with the
Copyright, Designs and Patents Act, 1988

Pages 387–90 constitute an extension of this copyright
page

First published in Great Britain by
Chatto & Windus Ltd, 1996

Vintage
Random House, 20 Vauxhall Bridge Road, London SW1V 2SA

Random House Australia (Pty) Limited
20 Alfred Street, Milsons Point, Sydney
New South Wales 2061, Australia

Random House New Zealand Limited
18 Poland Road, Glenfield,
Auckland 10, New Zealand

Random House South Africa (Pty) Limited
Endulini, 5A Jubilee Road, Parktown 2193, South Africa

Random House UK Limited Reg. No. 954009

A CIP catalogue record for this book
is available from the British Library

ISBN 0 09 973261 0

Papers used by Random House UK Ltd are natural, recy-
clable products made from wood grown in sustainable
forests. The manufacturing processes conform to the
environmental regulations of the country of origin

Printed and bound in Great Britain by
Cox & Wyman, Reading, Berkshire

CONTENTS

INTRODUCTION

THIS is not a conventional food anthology. Other people have produced those, usually in the form of numerous short sections which cover fascinating but rather narrow aspects of the subject – famous cooks or childhood recollections or shopping for ingredients. What I am interested in is big themes. Because food is central to our existence, the complex role it plays in our lives is frequently overlooked; no matter how much I love cooking and eating, I've long been aware that food has another, equally important function as a means of communicating what people can't put into words or don't even realise they're saying. One of the first things we notice about strangers is their body shape – whether they're fat or thin, how closely they meet our notion of an ideal weight – and this in turn triggers a set of assumptions about them. When we eat for the first time with people we don't know well, we learn a great deal about them from their reactions to what they're served and their table manners; when they invite us to dinner, we get some idea of their feelings towards us from the dishes they've chosen and the care they've taken. What people eat speaks volumes about class, about their attitude to foreigners, about how adventurous they are. But there's more to it than that. Each chapter in this book explores an area – food and sex or anthropophagy or the extraordinary rules and rituals people invent to regulate their intake of food – which demonstrates that hunger cannot be disconnected from our other desires, fears and cravings.

It's no accident that one of the traditional settings for a seduction scene is a restaurant, where the satisfaction of one desire is – at least as far as one of the participants is concerned – only the prelude to indulging another. Lord Byron's dislike of seeing women eat, which developed towards the end of his life into something of a phobia, puzzled his contemporaries but offers post-Freudian readers a startling insight into his anxious feelings about female sexuality. Gertrude Stein's cook conveyed her disapproval of the painter Matisse when he stayed unexpectedly to dinner by serving fried eggs instead of an omelette: 'It takes the same amount of eggs and the same amount of butter,' she said, 'but it shows less respect, and he will understand.' The distinction is so subtle that I can't help wondering whether Matisse got the message instead of savouring the singular pleasure of dipping his bread into a fresh yellow yolk, but perhaps the French are more sensitive in these matters than the British. Food has been used more frequently than the casual observer might suppose as a method of punishment, or even torture: Roman emperors ordered their subjects to provide sumptuous banquets which bankrupted them, while police states in various parts of the world have exploited the peculiar qualities of certain types of vegetable to make people confess to crimes they have not committed.

Stories like these were the starting-point of my inquiry and my assumption that novels, plays, diaries, poems, biographies, newspaper articles, cook books and even slimming manuals would provide many more examples, from the quotidian to the downright bizarre, has been rewarded in ways even I could not have imagined. I hope you will be surprised, amused and shocked by the extracts I've chosen and the conclusions I've drawn from them in the essays which open each chapter. I also hope that when you stop reading you'll sit down to supper with an altered – perhaps a more *wary* – approach to what's about to appear on the table in front of you.

Because the book has a very particular purpose, the extracts have been selected to illustrate its thesis rather than to provide anything approaching a comprehensive survey. The reader will discover that familiar names in the literature of food – Parson Woodforde, for example, whose obsession with his diet relegated the Fall of the Bastille to second place in his diary after the news that he had bought 'a fine Crab' – have been left out in favour of writers whose work is not usually associated with the subject, such as the Roman epigrammist Martial or the French feminist Simone de Beauvoir. Another consideration, and one which obviously falls outside my control, was the question of copyright; there were also occasions when an author or literary agent demanded a fee for an excerpt of previously-published material which put it way beyond the limited budget of an anthology, which is the explanation for several disappointing omissions.

I am, however, grateful to my friends, who have contributed to the enterprise far more directly than they are able to when I am writing a novel. This has been an unusually sociable book, with scribbled suggestions and photocopied extracts arriving regularly in the post; most (with the exception of one or two which I mislaid while moving house or which didn't fit into the book's structure) have been included, and they also stimulated some enormously helpful discussions. Among the people who came up with brilliant examples I would otherwise have missed, or sat patiently through lunch or dinner while I theorised about women's oral impulses or anorexia or the hidden motives behind diets, are: Hanan Al-Shaykh, Mark Bostridge, Jonathan Burnham, Lee Chester, Amanda Craig, Barbara Crossley, Maureen Freely, Anna Gordon, Lelia Green, Barbara Gunnell, Claire Harman, Christopher Hawtree, Lucy Hooberman, Candia McWilliam, Andrea Michell, Neil Philip, Bridget Rosewell, the late Charlie Stramiello in New York, and Peter and Theresa Clark in Damascus.

JOAN SMITH
London, January, 1996

I THE ART OF STARVATION

SHE is long and thin, weak and feeble, with unkempt hair and sunken eyes. Her organs are visible through her skin and 'she seems to have no stomach but only the place where it should be, so deeply hollowed out that the girl's breasts hang from her backbone'. This vivid description of an anorexic, with its uncanny echoes of many first-hand accounts of the disease, is not what it seems. Although it could have been written by the American author Naomi Wolf, who recalled in *The Beauty Myth* how she became so thin in her teens that her doctor could feel her spine through her stomach, it's actually taken from a thirteenth-century text, *Le Roman de la Rose*. One of the most powerful passages in this strange, allegorical account of courtly love, begun by Guillaume de Lorris and completed by Jean de Meun, is an evocation of hunger in which the condition is personified as a starving girl; what's fascinating about it, from a period notable for huge disruptions of the social order which inevitably led to shortages of food, is that Hunger is presented as a figure not so much to be pitied as *feared*. She is the servant of another allegorical female, Poverty, who has 'taught her every kind of malice and made her the governess and nurse of that ugly young fellow Theft'.

What Jean de Meun, who wrote this section of *Le Roman de la Rose*, is suggesting here is a familiar cycle in which poverty is attended by the risk of starvation and a propensity to resort to dishonest methods to cure it. But his underlying theme is more complex and suggestive, from the association of want and attenuation with the female to an instinctive revulsion from both states. This is, in part, because they are an unwelcome reminder of human frailty; what has happened to Jean de Meun's spectral figure of Hunger could happen to anyone, and not just in the thirteenth century.

Starvation exposes what we can rarely bear to think about, which is the skull beneath the skin; unsurprisingly, the Paris-based de Meun chose to banish Hunger to the far north of Scotland, where he left her to scavenge in a stony field, scraping up tufts of grass in a desperate attempt to survive. This place, 'cold as marble' according to the text, also represents the bleak absence of companionship, indeed of any human warmth, which is so often the fate of the starving. Jane Eyre, wandering alone and hungry after her flight from Mr Rochester, meets with more rebuffs than kindness: 'Do not ask me, reader, to give a minute account of that day; as before, I sought work; as before, I was repulsed; as before, I starved; but once did food pass my lips.' All Jane gets to eat is a mess of cold porridge, which she begs from a farmer's daughter as it is about to be thrown to a pig who is too well fed to want it anyway.

Hunger hardens people's hearts; it also anaesthetises the emotions of those who have to endure it. 'We thought only about hunger,' said a woman survivor of the Nazi death camps, explaining how starving inmates stopped worrying about the fate of relatives and friends, about anything but the daily battle to survive. It is clear from such accounts, whether their authors are Auschwitz survivors or Oscar Wilde, complaining about conditions in Wandsworth Gaol in the 1890s, that starvation, far from being an unintended side effect of incarceration, is all too often a deliberate attempt to destroy the humanity of people whose captors hold them in contempt. The Nazis are an extreme example, using the punishment of meagre rations and hard labour to reduce their victims to a physical condition which, in a grotesque way, reflects their bigoted preconception of them. The French novelist Marguerite Duras, describing her husband's return to Paris from the camps at the end of the war in her autobiographical book *La Douleur*, immediately grasped both the horror and the significance of what had been imposed on him: 'He has gone and hunger has taken his place. Emptiness has taken his place.'

Astonishingly, Duras's husband survived. The contrast between the condition described in *La Douleur* and what people mean today when they say 'I'm starving' could hardly be greater; the phrase is colloquially used to describe a mild sensation of hollowness, linked to the pleasurable anticipation of the meal that is safely about to materialise. This shift in meaning says something about the ready availability of food in the developed world in our century, about the way in which hunger has receded as a threat in the rich countries of the northern hemisphere (except, of course, for the minority under-class of the homeless and unemployed). By contrast, a much earlier change in the same verb, which used to mean simply 'to die' but turned into a synonym for dying from hunger, reflects the frequency with which people used to expire from this cause. As late as the 1720s, Daniel Defoe divided the British into seven categories, beginning at the top of society where people lived 'profusely' and moving down through increasing degrees of misery to the bottom two – in which he placed a fifth of the population – where hunger and destitution were a constant threat. The extremes he recorded in the early Georgian period are a salutary reminder that food shortages are far from evenly distributed across populations, falling dispropor-tionately on the poor and dispossessed; even in our own century, deprivation is neither fairly shared nor inevitable. The famines which have ravaged Africa in recent decades have been for the most part a toxic combination of natural disasters and human mismanagement; they occurred in countries like Eritrea, which was embroiled in a lengthy war of secession with Ethiopia, and Kwazulu, the self-governing black homeland where thousands of people were forced to compete for barren scrubland while, over the border in South Africa, white farmers patrolled fertile estates armed with shotguns. 'Hunger', observes the economist Susan George, 'is not a scourge but a scandal.'

Hunger, to put it another way, does not just happen to people; it's *done* to them. The visible effects of starvation are an emblem of disempowerment, an admission that its victims have been reduced to an animal-like state in which nothing matters except food. Another survivor of the camps, the novelist Primo Levi, recalled later that there was no respite even in sleep; waking at night, he could hear the other prisoners moving their jaws as they lay in their bunks, dreaming they were eating. This involuntary obsession is shared, apparently, by anorexic girls and women; describing the complete absence from her school life of the usual teenage fantasies about sex or success, Naomi Wolf explains that 'all the space I had for dreaming was taken up by food'. Why, then, if starvation is not just one of the most lingering and painful ways to die but a calculated punishment imposed by the strong on the weak, would anyone voluntarily inflict it upon herself? The choice of pronoun is deliberate for, with the exception of a handful of fasting saints and political prisoners, voluntary inedia is an overwhelmingly female condition. This feature of the malady has led feminist writers like Susie Orbach to link it with femininity, construing anorexia as a way of rejecting the dramatic (and specifically sexual) changes which affect the female body at puberty – refusing to be a woman, in other words. They also recognise anorexia as a baleful exchange in which food is given up in return for control, but with a crucial difference from the men who undertake it for political reasons: unlike male hunger strikers such as the IRA's Bobby Sands or the Beirut hostage Brian Keenan, the anorexic girl limits her ambition to power over her own body and its cravings. She has, in a sense, internalised the paradoxical beliefs personified in Jean de Meun's starving beggar girl in *Le Roman de la Rose*; in that text, it is implied that Hunger is precisely the opposite of what her haggard appearance suggests, which is to say powerful and wantonly destructive of character.

But of whose character? One of the most famous heroines in English literature, Clarissa Harlowe, is let down by friends and family and eventually raped, dramatically highlighting the plight of a beautiful but almost friendless girl in London in the middle of the eighteenth century; in Richardson's obese novel, Clarissa goes into a prolonged anorexic decline after her assault, exacting a terrible revenge on all those who have abandoned and betrayed her, including the rapist Lovelace, who goes almost mad with grief and remorse as her death draws near. (Richardson's description of Clarissa during her fatal illness, by the way, offers an illustration of the way in which female frailty, when drawn in a way that mitigates the worst ravages of actual self-starvation, carries for some readers a considerable erotic charge.) Her triumph, though, is posthumous and therefore hollow; by the end of the book everyone heartily regrets the way they have behaved but Clarissa is no longer alive to benefit from this change of heart. There is a fuller, if tacit, admission of the self-defeating nature of self-starvation as a strategy in *Wuthering Heights*, the anorexic novel *par excellence*, in which the male anti-hero Heathcliff starves himself to death not because his schemes have succeeded but because they are finally facing defeat. Heathcliff's strange end is a graphic illustration of his inability any longer to control the external world; in the final chapter, when he realises that the dynasty he has worked so hard to destroy is about to be revived through the marriage of Hareton Earnshaw and Catherine Linton, he goes into a feverishly rapid decline. The process takes only four days, hardly a realistic timescale, but the description of his symptoms is painfully familiar: hollow cheeks, glittering eyes, wild talk interrupted by unearthly visions. On the fifth morning, Nelly Dean finds him dead in bed, soaked to the bone, his eyes staring and his lips open in a sneer.

Heathcliff's death marks a dramatic retreat from the masculine violence (sadism is not too strong a word) which has been the cornerstone of his character until the last few pages of the novel; the passivity with which he accepts his fate is almost feminine. It seems fair to assume that Emily Brontë was drawing, perhaps unconsciously, on her own experience here; her most recent biographer, Katherine Frank, has argued that each time Emily was sent away from home to earn her living, her health failed in a manner consistent with a severe bout of anorexia. As soon as Emily was allowed to return to Haworth Parsonage, she resumed her usual position as something of a goddess of the hearth – learning German from a book propped up on the kitchen table while she was kneading the family's bread or making cakes, according to Mrs Gaskell – but she cannot have been unaware that she had let down her impoverished family, which needed the sisters' income to survive. Her victory, such as it was, was gained at the cost of near-total physical and mental breakdown and constituted an admission that she could not cope with the outside world.

Heathcliff's death frees him to rejoin Catherine Earnshaw, another notable anorexic – at key points in the novel, when she has failed to get her own way, Catherine simply stops eating – in a fantasy realm of pure spirit. In real life, the anorexic solution is savagely self-defeating: 'if the mind wins, the body dies', a modern sufferer says starkly. In that sense, the girl or woman who embarks on it places herself in the impossible position of torturer *and* victim. Feverishly attempting to dissociate what goes on in her head from the organism which so obviously supports it, she turns her body into a prison; her only escape routes are death or submission to that very aspect of the human condition she finds intolerable, which is the inextricable symbiosis of mind and body.

Give a Dog a Bone

I was terribly hungry, and I did not know what to do with myself and my shameless appetite. I writhed from side to side on the seat, and bowed my chest right down to my knees; I was almost distracted. When it got dark I jogged along to the Town Hall – God knows how I got there – and sat on the edge of the balustrade. I tore a pocket out of my coat and took to chewing it; not with any defined object, but with dour mien and unseeing eyes, staring straight into space. I could hear a group of little children playing around near me, and perceive, in an instinctive sort of way, some pedestrians pass me by; otherwise, I observed nothing.

All at once, it enters my head to go to one of the meat bazaars underneath me, and beg a piece of raw meat. I go straight along the balustrade to the other side of the bazaar buildings, and descend the steps. When I had nearly reached the stalls on the ground floor, I called up the archway leading to the stairs, and made a threatening backward gesture, as if I were talking to a dog up there, and boldly addressed the first butcher I met.

'Ah, will you be kind enough to give me a bone for my dog?' I said; 'only a bone. There needn't be anything on it; it's just to give him something to carry in his mouth.'

I got the bone, a capital little bone, on which there still remained a morsel of meat, and hid it under my coat. I thanked the man so heartily that he looked at me in amazement.

'Oh, no need of thanks,' said he.

'Oh yes; don't say that,' I mumbled; 'it is kindly done of you,' and I ascended the steps again.

My heart was throbbing violently in my breast. I sneaked into one of the passages, where the forges are, as far in as I could go, and stopped outside a dilapidated door leading to a back-yard. There was no light to be seen anywhere, only blessed darkness all around me; and I began to gnaw at the bone.

It had no taste; a rank smell of blood oozed from it, and I was forced to vomit almost immediately. I tried anew. If I could only keep it down it would, in spite of all, have some effect. It was simply a matter of forcing it to remain down there. But I vomited again. I grew wild, bit angrily into the meat, tore off a morsel, and gulped it down by sheer strength of will; and yet it was of no use. Just as soon as the little fragments of meat became warm in my stomach up they came again, worse luck. I clenched my hands in frenzy, burst into tears from sheer helplessness, and gnawed away as one possessed. I cried, so that the bone got wet and dirty with my tears, vomited, cursed and groaned again, cried as if my heart would break, and vomited anew. I consigned all the powers that be to the lowermost torture in the loudest voice.

From Knut Hamsun, *Hunger* (1888), translated by George Egerton.

Agonies of Emptiness

And now began the latter and fiercer stage of my long sufferings; without using a disproportionate expression I might say, of my agony. For I now suffered, for upwards of sixteen weeks, the physical anguish of hunger in various degrees of intensity; but as bitter, perhaps, as ever any human being can have suffered who has survived it. I would not needlessly harass my reader's feelings by a detail of all that I endured: for extremities such as these, under any circumstances of heaviest misconduct or guilt, cannot be contemplated, even in description, without a rueful pity that is painful to the natural goodness of the human heart. Let it suffice, at least on this occasion, to say, that a few fragments of bread from the breakfast-table of one individual (who supposed me to be ill, but did not know of my being in utter want), and these at uncertain intervals, constituted my whole support. During the former part of my sufferings (that is, generally in Wales, and always for the first two months in London) I was houseless, and very seldom slept under a roof. To this constant exposure to the open air I ascribe it mainly that I did not sink under my torments. Latterly, however, when colder and more inclement weather came on, and when, from the length of my sufferings, I had begun to sink into a more languishing condition, it was, no doubt, fortunate for me, that the same person to whose breakfast-table I had access, allowed me to sleep in a large unoccupied house, of which he was tenant. Unoccupied, I call it, for there was no household or establishment in it; nor any furniture, indeed, except a table, and a few chairs. But I found, on taking possession of my new quarters, that the house already contained one single inmate, a poor, friendless child, apparently ten years old; but she seemed hunger bitten; and sufferings of that sort often make children look older than they are. From this forlorn child I learned, that she had slept and lived there alone for some time before I came: and great joy the poor creature expressed, when she found that I was, in future, to be her companion through the hours of darkness. The house was large; and, from the want of furniture, the noise of the rats made a prodigious echoing on the spacious staircase and hall; and, amidst the real fleshly ills of cold, and, I fear, hunger, the forsaken child had found leisure to suffer still more (it appeared) from the self-created one of ghosts. I promised her protection against all ghosts whatsoever! but, alas! I could offer her no other assistance. We lay upon the floor, with a bundle of cursed law papers for a pillow: but with no other covering than a sort of large horseman's cloak: afterwards, however, we discovered, in a garret, an old sofa-cover, a small piece of rug, and some fragments of other articles, which added a little to our warmth. The poor child crept close to me for warmth, and for security against her ghostly enemies. When I was not more than usually ill, I took her in my arms, so that, in general, she was tolerably warm, and often slept when I could not: for, during the last two months of my sufferings, I slept much in the daytime, and was apt to fall into transient dozings at all hours. But my sleep distressed me more than my watching: for, besides the tumultuousness of my dreams (which were only not so awful as those which I shall have to describe hereafter as produced by opium), my sleep was never more than what is called *dog-sleep*; so that I could hear myself moaning, and was often, as it seemed to me, wakened suddenly by my own voice; and, about this time, a hideous sensation began to haunt me as soon as I fell into a slumber, which has since returned upon me, at different periods of my life, viz. a sort of twitching (I know not where, but apparently about the region of my stomach), which compelled me violently to throw out my feet for the sake of relieving it. This sensation coming on as soon as I began to sleep, and the effort to relieve it constantly awaking me, at length I slept only from exhaustion; and from increasing weakness (as I said before) I was constantly falling asleep, and constantly awaking.

From Thomas de Quincey, *Confessions of an English Opium Eater* (1821).

Starving in Sarajevo

Fehim and Zora Bahor, an elderly Sarajevo couple, ate their last hot meal on April 30. It was provided by the Red Cross, but since then Serb rebels have blocked the humanitarian airlift and food convoys. Now the Bahors look to the Bosnian army to break the siege and put food on their table.

'No one will do it for us,' said Fehim, aged 72, a stick-thin Muslim. 'But it will not be easy. You cannot send men with rifles against tanks.'

Fehim and Zora continue to cultivate their tiny vegetable garden on a strip of earth where flowers and grass once decorated an otherwise bleak city street. Their main meal of the day consists of one of their home-grown spring onions on a piece of bread dipped in water.

'I miss everything,' said Zora, an ethnic Croat who is almost as skeletal as her husband. 'Fruit, vegetables, meat. We used to get some kind of canned meat from the Red Cross, but it was more like a paste. The last time we had real meat, it was a piece of chicken and that was three months ago at least.'

The couple have virtually no other means of support. They have three daughters but none has an income and one is dependent on them. She looks after an infirm distant relative in a house near the frontline. So the Bahors were classed as vulnerable members of the population and Zora had the right to a daily hot dinner from one of 50 food distribution points run by the International Committee of the Red Cross.

But the last Red Cross cargo plane to land in Sarajevo, on March 11, was holed by Serb sniper fire and the airlift suspended.

'Since then we tried to negotiate food convoys into the city, but we only managed to get one in,' said Nina Winquist, the ICRC spokeswoman.

Attempts to get a United Nations wheatflour convoy to supply the bakery failed yesterday when the rebels reneged on an earlier agreement. The only food getting in is being driven over Mount Igman, west of Sarajevo, by Bosnian army drivers and handed over to the UN on the city's outskirts.

'It is pitiful that the only food able to come into Sarajevo at the moment … is being brought in by local trucks under cover of darkness like thieves in the night under Serb gunfire,' said Mark

Cutts, a representative of the UN High Commissioner for Refugees (UNHCR) in Sarajevo.

The city's food warehouses are now empty and the Igman supply line allows only an intermittent trickle of supplies. Yesterday plans to bring about 30 tons of flour on the last few miles of the journey, from the suburbs across the airport and into the city, were aborted when French UN forces failed to bring enough armoured cars to provide an escort.

Many of Sarajevo's 250,000 residents now live on hoarded food stores, but the elderly, sick and those with no relatives abroad to send remittances have nothing.

Aid workers have repeatedly warned that if the international community did not do more to lift Sarajevo's siege it would provoke the Bosnian army into doing the job itself, and so destabilise the military situation rather than keep a lid on it – the declared aim of the UN's passive policy.

'In the end the government is not going to let its people starve,' said Karen Abu Zayd, chief of the UNHCR mission in Sarajevo.

Julian Borger, *Guardian* (14 June 1995).

Something to Get Your Teeth Into

A quite young girl was standing in the open doorway, facing the pallid light of the one small window in Marius's garret, which was opposite the door. She was a lean and delicate-looking creature, her shivering nakedness clad in nothing but a chemise and skirt. Her waistband was a piece of string, and another piece tied back her hair. Bony shoulders emerged from the chemise, and the face above them was sallow and flabby. The light fell upon reddened hands, a stringy neck, a loose, depraved mouth lacking several teeth, bleared eyes both bold and wary: in short, an ill-treated girl with the eyes of a grown woman; a blend of fifty and fifteen; one of those creatures, at once weak and repellent, who cause those who set eyes on them to shudder when they do not weep.

Marius had risen to his feet and was gazing in a sort of stupefaction at what might have been one of those figures of darkness that haunt our dreams. But what was tragic about the girl was that she had not been born ugly. She might even have been pretty as a child, and the grace proper to her age was still at odds with the repulsive premature ageing induced by loose living and poverty. A trace of beauty still lingered in the sixteen-year-old face, like pale sunlight fading beneath the massed clouds of a winter's dawn.

The face was not quite unfamiliar to Marius. He had a notion that he had seen her before.

'What can I do for you, Mademoiselle?'

She answered in her raucous voice:

'I've got a letter for you, Monsieur Marius.'

So she knew his name. But how did she come to know it?

Without awaiting any further invitation she walked in, looking about her with a pathetic boldness at the untidy room with its unmade bed. Long bare legs and bony knees were visible through the vents in her skirt, and she was shivering.

As he took the letter Marius noted that the large wafer sealing it was still damp. It could not have come very far. He read:

My warm-hearted neighbour, most estimable young man!

I have heard of the kindness you did me in paying my rent six months ago. I bless you for it. My elder daughter will tell you that for two days we have been without food, four of us, including my sick wife. If I am not deceived in my trust in humanity I venture to hope that your generous heart will be moved by our affliction and that you will relieve your feelings by again coming to my aid.

I am, with the expression of the high esteem we all owe to a benefactor of humanity,

Yours truly,
Jondrette

P.S. My daughter is at your service, dear Monsieur Marius.

This missive threw an immediate light on the problem that had been perplexing Marius. All was now clear. It came from the same source as the other letters – the same handwriting, the same spelling, the same paper, even the same smell of rank tobacco. He now had five letters, all the work of one author. The Spanish Captain, the unhappy Mère Balizard, the dramatist Genflot, and the aged actor, Fabantou, all were Jondrette – if, indeed, that was his real name.

As we have said, during the time Marius had been living in the tenement he had paid little or no attention even to his nearest neighbours, his thoughts being elsewhere. Although he had more than once encountered members of the Jondrette family in the corridor or on the stairs, they had been to him no more than shadows of whom he had taken so little notice that he had failed to recognize the two daughters when they bumped into him on the boulevard; even now, in the shock of his pity and repugnance, he had difficulty in realizing that this must be one of them.

But now he saw it all. He realized that the business of his neighbour, Jondrette, was the writing of fraudulent begging letters under a variety of names to persons of supposed wealth and benevolence whose addresses he had managed to secure, and that these letters were delivered, at their own peril, by his daughters: for he had sunk so low that he treated the two young girls as counters in his gamble with life. To judge by the episode of the previous evening, their breathless flight and the words he had overheard, the girls were engaged in other sordid pursuits. What it came to was that in the heart of our society, as at present constituted, two unhappy mortals, neither children nor grown women, had been turned by extreme poverty into monsters at once depraved and innocent, drab creatures without name or age or sex, no longer capable of good or evil, deprived of all freedom, virtue, and responsibility; souls born yesterday and shrivelled today like flowers dropped in the street which lie fading in the mud until a cartwheel comes to crush them.

Meanwhile, while Marius watched her in painful astonishment, the girl was exploring the room like an audacious ghost, untroubled by her state of near nakedness in the ragged chemise which at moments slipped down almost to her waist. She moved chairs, examined the toilet-articles on the chest of drawers, fingered Marius's clothes and peered into corners.

'Well, fancy! You've got a mirror,' she said.

She was humming to herself as though she were alone, snatches of music-hall songs, cheerful ditties which her raucous, tuneless voice made dismal. But beneath this show of boldness there was a hint of unease and awkward constraint. Effrontery is an expression of shame. Nothing could have been more distressing than to see her fluttering about the room like a bird startled by the light or with a broken wing. It was plain that in other circumstances of background and education her natural, uninhibited gaiety might have made of her something sweet and charming. In the animal world no creature born to be a dove turns into a scavenger. This happens only among men.

Marius sat pondering while he watched her. She drew near to his writing-table.

'Books!' she said.

A light dawned in her clouded eyes. She announced, with the pride in attainment from which none of us is immune: 'I know how to read.'

Picking up a book that lay open on the table she read, without much difficulty:

'General Bauduin was ordered to seize and occupy, with the five battalions of his brigade, the Château de Hougoumont, which is in the middle of the plain of Waterloo ...'

She broke off and exclaimed:

'Waterloo! I know about that. It's an old battle. My father was there. My father was in the army. We're all real Bonapartists in our family. Waterloo was against the English.' She put the book down and took up a pen. 'I can write, too.' She dipped the pen in the ink and looked at Marius. 'You want to see? I'll write something to show you.'

Before he could say anything she had written on a blank sheet lying on the table: 'Watch out, the bogies are around.' She laid down the pen. 'No spelling mistakes. You can see for yourself. We've had some schooling, my sister and me. We haven't always been what we are now. We weren't brought up to be –'

But here she stopped and gazing with her dulled eyes at Marius she burst out laughing. In a tone in which the extreme of anguish was buried beneath the extreme of cynicism, she exclaimed, 'What the hell!'

She began to hum again and then said:

'Do you ever go to the theatre, Monsieur Marius? I do. I've a young brother who knows one or two actors and he gives me tickets. I don't like the gallery, the benches are uncomfortable and it's too crowded and there are people who smell nasty.'

She fell to examining Marius and said with a coy look:

'Do you know, Monsieur Marius, that you're a very handsome boy?'

The words prompted the same thought in both their minds, causing her to smile and him to blush. Drawing nearer, she laid a hand on his shoulder.

'You never notice me, Monsieur Marius, but I know you by sight. I see you on the stairs, and I've seen you visiting an old man called Père Mabeuf in the Austerlitz quarter when I've been that way. It suits you, you know, having your hair untidy.'

She was striving to make her voice soft but could only make it sound more guttural, and some of the words got lost in their passage from her throat to her lips, as on a piano with some of the notes missing. Marius drew gently away.

'I think, Mademoiselle,' he said with his accustomed cold gravity, 'that I have something belonging to you. Allow me to return it.'

He handed her the wrapping containing the four letters. She clapped her hands and cried:

'We looked for that everywhere!'

Seizing it eagerly, she began to unfold it, talking as she did so:

'Heavens, if you knew how we'd searched, my sister and me! And so you're the one who found it. On the boulevard, wasn't it? It must have been. We were running, and my sister went and dropped it, the silly kid, and when we got home we found it was gone. So because we didn't want to be beaten, because where's the sense in it, what earthly good does it do, it's simply stupid, we said we'd delivered the letters to the people they were written to and they hadn't coughed up anything. And here they are, the wretched letters. How did you know they were mine? Oh, of course, the handwriting. So you're the person we bumped into yesterday evening? It was too dark to see. I said to my sister, "Was it a gentleman?" and she said, "I think it was."'

By now she had fished out the letter addressed to 'The Benevolent Gentleman outside the church of Saint-Jacques-du-Haut-Pas'.

'Ah, this is for the old boy who goes to Mass. Well, it's nearly time so I'd better run along and catch him. Perhaps he'll give me enough for our dinner.' She burst out laughing again. 'And do you know what that will mean? It will be breakfast and dinner for yesterday and the day before – the first meal for three days. Well, who cares? If you don't like it you've got to lump it.'

This reminded Marius of why she had called upon him. He felt in his waistcoat pockets, while she went on talking as though she had forgotten his existence.

'Sometimes I go out at night and don't come home. Last winter, before coming here, we lived under the bridges. You had to huddle together not to freeze and it made my little sister cry. Water's dreadful, isn't it? Sometimes I wanted to drown myself, but then I thought, No, it's too cold. I go off on my own when I feel like it and sleep in a ditch, likely as not. You know, at night when I'm walking along the boulevards the trees look to me like pitchforks, and the houses, they're so tall and black, like the towers of Notre-Dame, and when you come to a strip of white wall it's like a patch of water. And the stars are like street lamps and you'd think they were smoking, and sometimes the wind blows them out and I'm always surprised, as though a horse had come and snorted in my ear; and although it's night-time I think I can hear street-organs and the rattle of looms, all kinds of things. And sometimes I think people are throwing stones at me and I run away and everything goes spinning round me. When you've had nothing to eat it's very queer.'

She was gazing absently at him. Marius, exploring his pockets, had now succeeded in retrieving a five-franc piece and sixteen sous, all the money he possessed at that moment. Enough for today's dinner, he reflected, and as for tomorrow, we'll hope for the best. So he kept the sixteen sous and offered her the five francs.

'The sun's come out at last!' she cried, eagerly accepting the coin; and as though the sun had power to release a torrent of the popular jargon that was her every day speech she declaimed:

'Well, if th' isn't prime! Five jimmy-o'-goblins! Enough to stuff us for two days: You're a true nobleman, mister, and I tips my lid to you. Tripe and sausage and the tipple to wash it down for two whole blooming days.' Hitching up her chemise and making Marius a profound curtsey, she turned with a wave of her hand towards the door. 'Well, good day to you, mister, and your humble servant. I'll be getting back to the gaffer.'

On her way to the door she noticed a crust of stale bread gathering dust on the chest of drawers. She snatched it up and started to devour it.

'It's good, it's tough – something to get your teeth into!'
And she departed.

From Victor Hugo, *Les Misérables* (1862), translated by Norman Denny.

The Hunger Trap

I promise you most truly that if you ever set foot here, you will regret it in the end. No bear, however much he is baited, is so weak and wretched as you will be if you go there. If Poverty can get you into her power, she will make you linger so long on a little straw or hay that she will let you die of Hunger. Hunger used to be her chambermaid and served her so well that, in exchange for her eager and zealous service, Poverty taught her every kind of malice and made her the governess and nurse of that ugly young fellow Theft. She suckled him with her milk, having no other pup to feed him with. And if you want to know about her land, which is neither easy to cultivate nor rich, Hunger lives in a stony field where no corn grows nor any bush or scrub; this field is at the farthest tip of Scotland and is almost as cold as marble. Hunger, who sees neither corn nor trees there, pulls up the very grass with her sharp nails and tough teeth, but finds it very sparse because of the thickly scattered stones. And if I wanted to describe her I could soon do it.

'She is long and thin, weak and feeble, and in great want of oaten bread; her hair is all unkempt, her eyes hollow and deeply sunken, her face pale, with dry lips and cheeks smeared with filth. Anyone who wanted to could see her entrails beneath her hard skin. From her flanks, devoid of every humour, her bones protrude, and she seems to have no stomach but only the place where it should be, so deeply hollowed out that the girl's breasts hang from her backbone. She is so thin that her fingers seem elongated and her knees have lost their roundness, so crushed in the grip of thinness that her heels are high and sharp and prominent, and seem to have no flesh on them. Ceres, goddess of plenty, who causes the corn to grow, does not know the way there, nor does Triptolemus, who guides her dragons. The Fates keep them far away, for they do not want the Goddess of Plenty and weary, suffering Hunger to join together. But if you want to go there where you can be idle as is your habit, Poverty will soon take you, once she has you in her grip, for the road that I am guarding here is not the only one that leads to Poverty; one can come to Poverty through an idle and lazy life. If, in order to attack the fortress, you wished to take the road of which I have just spoken to you, towards weary contemptible Poverty, you might well fail to capture it. But I think it certain that Hunger will be your near neighbour, for Poverty knows that way better by heart than by any parchment map. And you should know that wretched Hunger is still so attentive and courteous towards her mistress (she does not love or esteem her, but is nurtured by her, even though she is weary and naked herself) that she comes to see her and sit with her all day, and takes her by the chin and kisses her, which is uncomfortable and unpleasant. Then, when she sees Theft asleep, she takes him by the ear and wakes him, leaning towards him in her distress and advising and teaching him how to obtain things, whatever he has to endure in order to get them. And Faint Heart agrees with them, although he dreams about the rope, which makes his every hair stand on end in case he should see his trembling son Theft hanged if he is caught stealing. But you may not enter here and must seek your way elsewhere, for you have not served me enough to deserve my love.'

From Guillaume de Lorris and Jean de Meun, *The Romance of the Rose* (1225–78), translated by Frances Horgan.

The Ordeal of Alexander Selkirk, the Real Robinson Crusoe

In the lesser Hutt, at some distance from the other, he dress'd his Victuals, and in the larger he slept, and employ'd himself in reading, singing Psalms, and praying; so that he said he was a better Christian while in this Solitude than ever he was before, or than, he was afraid, he should ever be again. At first he never eat anything till Hunger constrain'd him, partly for grief and partly for want of Bread and Salt; nor did he go to bed till he could watch no longer: the Piemento Wood, which burnt very clear, serv'd him both for Firing and Candle, and refresh'd him with its fragrant Smell.

He might have had Fish enough, but could not eat 'em for want of Salt, because they occasion'd a Looseness; except Crawfish, which are there as large as our Lobsters, and very good: These he sometimes boil'd, and at other times boil'd, as he did his Goats Flesh, of which he made very good Broth, for they are not so rank as ours: he kept an Account of 500 that he kill'd while there and caught as many more, which he mark'd on the Ear and let go. When his Powder fail'd, he took them by speed of foot; for his way of living and continual Exercise of walking and running, clear'd him of all gross Humours, so that he ran with wonderful Swiftness thro the Woods and up the Rocks and Hills, as we perceiv'd when we employ'd him to catch Goats for us. We had a Bull-Dog, which we sent with several of our nimblest Runners to help him in catching Goats; but he distanc'd and tir'd both the Dog and the Men, catch'd the Goats, and brought 'em to us on his back. He told us that his Agility in pursuing a Goat had once like to have cost him his Life; he pursu'd it with so much Eagerness that he catch'd hold of it on the brink of a Precipice, of which he was not aware, the Bushes having hid it from him; so that he fell with the Goat down the said Precipice a great height, and was so stunn'd and bruised with the Fall, that he narrowly escap'd with his Life, and when he came to his Senses, found the Goat dead under him. He lay there about 24 hours, and was scarce able to crawl to his Hutt, which was about a mile distant, or to stir abroad again in ten days.

From Captain Woodes Rogers, *A Cruising Voyage Round the World* (1712).

Stealing to Live

On Monday, January 15th, 1844, two boys appeared before the magistrate at Worship Street police court, London, charged with stealing a half-cooked cow-heel from a shop. They immediately devoured their spoils as they were ravenous. The magistrate felt it necessary to enquire further into the circumstances and was given the following information by the police. The boys were brothers and their mother was a widow. Their father had served in the Army and had later been a policeman. After the death of her husband, the widow was left to struggle along as best she could with nine children. The family lived in dire poverty at no. 2 Pool's Place, Quaker Court, Spitalfields. When visited by a policeman she was found with six of her children. They were all huddled together and the only furniture consisted of two rush-bottomed chairs with seats gone, a little table with two legs broken, one broken cup and one small dish. Hardly a spark of fire came from the hearth and in one corner lay as many rags as would fill a woman's apron. It was on these rags that the whole family slept at night. As they had no blankets they slept in the miserable tatters worn during the daytime. The wretched woman told the policeman that she had had to sell her bed during the previous year in order to buy food. She had pawned her bedding with the grocer for food. Indeed everything had been sold to get bread. The magistrate made her a generous grant from the poor-box.

In February 1844 an application for assistance was made to the Marlborough Street magistrate on behalf of Theresa Bishop, a 60-year-old widow, and her 26-year-old daughter who was ill. She lived at no. 5, Brown Street, Grosvenor Square, in a little back room hardly bigger than a cupboard. The room contained no proper furniture. A chest was used both as table and chair, while a heap of rags in a corner served as a bed for both women. The mother earned a little money as a charwoman. Her landlord stated that she and her daughter had lived in this condition since May 1843. Gradually all their remaining possessions had been sold or pawned, but even so they had been unable to pay any rent. The magistrate allowed them 20s. out of the poor-box.

It is not, of course, suggested that all London workers are so poverty-stricken as these families. There can be no doubt that for every worker who is rendered utterly destitute by society there are ten who are better off. On the other hand it can be confidently asserted that thousands of decent and industrious families – far more deserving of respect than all the rich people in London – live under truly deplorable conditions which are an affront to human dignity. It is equally incontestable that every working man without exception may well suffer a similar fate through no fault of his own and despite all his efforts to keep his head above water.

From Friedrich Engels, *The Condition of the Working Class in England* (1845), translated by W.O. Henderson and W.H. Chaloner.

Too Hungry to Eat

Lord D— placed before me a most magnificent breakfast. It was really so; but in my eyes it seemed trebly magnificent – from being the first regular meal, the first 'good man's table', that I had sat down to for months. Strange to say, however, I could scarcely eat any thing. On the day when I first received my 10*l*. Bank-note, I had gone to a baker's shop and bought a couple of rolls: this very shop I had two months or six weeks before surveyed with an eagerness of desire which it was almost humiliating to me to recollect. I remembered the story about Otway; and feared that there might be danger in eating too rapidly. But I had no need for alarm, my appetite was quite sunk, and I became sick before I had eaten half of what I had bought. This effect from eating what approached to a meal, I continued to feel for weeks: or, when I did not experience any nausea, part of what I ate was rejected, sometimes with acidity, sometimes immediately, and without any acidity. On the present occasion, at Lord D—'s table, I found myself not at all better than usual: and, in the midst of luxuries, I had no appetite.

From Thomas de Quincey, *Confessions of an English Opium Eater* (1821).

No Refuge

Once more I took off my handkerchief – once more I thought of the cakes of bread in the little shop. Oh, for but a crust! for but one mouthful to allay the pang of famine! Instinctively I turned my face again to the village; I found the shop again and I went in; and though others were there besides the woman I ventured the request – 'Would she give me a roll for this handkerchief?'

She looked at me with evident suspicion: 'Nay, she never sold stuff i' that way.'

Almost desperate, I asked for half a cake; she again refused. 'How could she tell where I had got the handkerchief?' she asked.

'Would she take my gloves?'

'No! what could she do with them?'

Reader, it is not pleasant to dwell on these details. Some say there is enjoyment in looking back to painful experience past; but at this day I can scarcely bear to review the times to which I allude: the moral degradation, blent with the physical suffering, form too distressing a recollection ever to be willingly dwelt on. I blamed none of those who repulsed me. I felt it was what was to be expected, and what could not be helped: an ordinary beggar is frequently an object of suspicion; a well-dressed beggar inevitably so. To be sure, what I begged was employment; but whose business was it to provide me with employment? Not, certainly, that of persons who saw me then for the first time, and who knew nothing about my character. And as to the woman who would not take my handkerchief in exchange for her bread, why, she was right, if the offer appeared to her sinister or the exchange unprofitable. Let me condense now. I am sick of the subject.

A little before dark I passed a farmhouse, at the open door of which the farmer was sitting, eating his supper of bread and cheese. I stopped and said –

'Will you give me a piece of bread? for I am very hungry.' He cast on me a glance of surprise; but without answering, he cut a thick slice from his loaf, and gave it to me. I imagine he did not think I was a beggar, but only an eccentric sort of lady, who had taken a fancy to his brown loaf. As soon as I was out of sight of his house, I sat down and ate it.

I could not hope to get a lodging under a roof, and sought it in the wood I have before alluded to. But my night was wretched, my rest broken: the ground was damp, the air cold; besides, intruders passed near me more than once, and I had again and again to change my quarters: no sense of safety or tranquillity befriended me. Towards morning it rained; the whole of the following day was wet. Do not ask me, reader, to give a minute account of that day; as before, I sought work; as before, I was repulsed; as before, I starved; but once did food pass my lips. At the door of a cottage I saw a little girl about to throw a mess of cold porridge into a pig trough. 'Will you give me that?' I asked.

She stared at me. 'Mother!' she exclaimed, 'there is a woman wants me to give her these porridge.'

'Well, lass,' replied a voice within, 'give it her if she's a beggar. T'pig doesn't want it.'

The girl emptied the stiffened mould into my hands and I devoured it ravenously.

From Charlotte Brontë, *Jane Eyre* (1847).

Please Wait Outside

My only consolation, and that a most dismal and solitary one, was in the long expeditions which I made; but I look back upon those as times of acute suffering from poverty and *hunger*, as I never had any allowance and was always sent back to my tutor's with only five shillings in my pocket. Thus, though I walked sometimes twenty-four miles in a day, and was out for eight or ten hours, I never had a penny with which to buy even a piece of bread, and many a time sank down by the wayside from the faintness of sheer starvation, often most gratefully accepting some of their food from the common working-people I met. If I went out with my companions, the utmost mortification was added to the actual suffering of hunger, because, when they went into the village inns to have a good well-earned luncheon, I was always left starving outside, as I never had the means of paying for any food. I believe my companions were very sorry for me, but they never allowed their pity to be any expense to them, and then 'È meglio essere odiato che compatito' is an Italian proverb which means a great deal, especially to a boy. After a time, too, the food at Lyncombe itself became extremely stinted and of the very worst quality – a suet dumpling filled with coarse odds and ends of meat being our dinner on at least five days out of the seven, which of course was very bad for an extremely delicate rapidly-growing youth – and, if I was ill from want of food, which was frequently the case, I was given nothing but rice.

From Augustus Hare, *Story of My Life*, vol. 1 (1896).

Not Enough to Go Round

FOOD BUDGET OF A WORKING-CLASS FAMILY, FEBRUARY, 1921

Total in family: man (labourer = 1.25), wife and four children aged eleven, nine, five years and nine months respectively. These equal 4.38 adult males.

Total calories needed per day: 13,140, or per week, 91,980.

	Food	Protein (oz)	Calories
4 lb 9 oz	Shank of beef	13.20	5,554.6
6 oz	Suet	0.25	1,327.5
1 lb 9 oz	Beef pieces	3.80	1,281.2
24 lb	Bread	31.80	29,033.0
2 qts	Milk	2.60	1,512.0
16 oz	Condensed milk	1.40	1,520.0
8 lb	Potatoes	2.30	2,480.0
1½ lb	Onions	0.30	307.5
½ lb	Margarine	—	1,788.0
½ lb	Lard	—	2,005.0
¼ lb	Butter	—	860.6
½ lb	Bloaters	1.04	341.4
2½ lb	Herrings	5.80	1,608.0
¼ lb	Tea	—	—

2 lb	Sugar	—	3,644.8
¼ lb	Cocoa	0.70	553.6
1¾ lb	Flour	3.10	2,924.9
½ lb	Barley	0.80	763.0
2 lb	Oatmeal	3.90	3,750.0

Totals:

Per week —

Animal protein	28.09	
Vegetable protein	42.90	
Total	70.99 oz	Calories 61,255

Per day	10.14 oz	8,751
Per adult male per day	2.32 oz	1,998
	(or 65.7 grams)	

It is the last line of this budget which is significant. Instead of the 100 grams (3½ oz) of protein, only 65.7 grams (2⅓ oz) are being obtained, of which only 26 grams is animal protein (against a minimum of 30 grams). Instead of the requisite 3,000 great calories per day, only 1,998 are being taken. This summary of the results is tragic. Someone (probably the wife) or everyone in the family is being woefully underfed. There is a 33 per cent deficit in both protein and calories. Such a budget spells disaffection and disease.

From V.H. Mottram, *Food and the Family* (1925).

Unfair Shares

Hunger is not an unavoidable phenomenon like death and taxes. We are no longer living in the seventeenth century when Europe suffered shortages on an average of every three years and famine every ten. Today's world has all the physical resources and technical skills necessary to feed the present population of the planet or a much larger one. Unfortunately for the millions of people who go hungry, the problem is not a technical one – nor was it wholly so in the seventeenth century, for that matter. Whenever and wherever they live, rich people eat first, they eat a disproportionate amount of the food there is and poor ones rarely rise in revolt against this most basic of oppressions unless specifically told to 'eat cake'. Hunger is not a scourge but a scandal.

From Susan George, *How the Other Half Dies* (1976).

Scraps

A short distance from my home a new neighbourhood had sprung up. People lived in six-roomed houses, and some kept little servants. Others who did not keep a girl in the house used to employ girls on Saturdays to clean their steps. A good many girls that I knew were what were called 'step girls' and earned what to me was a small fortune – about 9d – on Saturdays cleaning people's steps. One Saturday I thought I would try my luck and see if I could earn some money, so off I went, unknown to anyone who would be likely to tell my mother. I had not been out long when it began to rain, spoiling all my chances of earning money. I knocked at several doors and asked if they would like the steps cleaned, but not one person would give me a job, so I had to give up in despair. One lady asked me if I was hungry; she said she was sorry she could not have her step cleaned, but if I waited she would give me something to eat. Presently she came to the door with a parcel and gave it to me, telling me not to waste any; what I could not eat I was to take home to my mother. I thanked her and ran off to a sheltered place to open the parcel, expecting to find something I could eat for I was very hungry. But I was doomed to disappointment, for the parcel contained some very dry pieces of bread and some crusts that looked as if they had been nibbled by mice, and a large piece of bacon rind. I could not eat any of it but had promised not to waste it so I gave the bacon rind to a hungry looking dog and carried the crusts to a man who kept a donkey. I had two things fixed in my mind. My mother was constantly telling us if we wanted to waste any of our food that 'wilful waste brings woeful want,' and my father repeatedly told his children never to promise unless they intended to keep their word.

From *Life as We Have Known It*, edited by Margaret Llewelyn Davies (1931).

To Die For

He worked later, he said, as a navvy and a butcher's boy, as an errand boy for a wine shop and in a chocolate factory. He was arrested one day for begging in the streets of Lausanne and another day when he was out of work in Geneva he attacked 'two English women sitting on a bench with their lunch – bread, cheese, eggs. I could not restrain myself,' he confessed. 'I threw myself upon one of the old witches and grabbed the food from her hands. If they had made the slightest resistance I would have strangled them – strangled them, mind you!'

From Christopher Hibbert, *Benito Mussolini: The Rise and Fall of Il Duce* (1962).

Living Hunger

Today is a good day. We look around like blind people who have recovered their sight, and we look at each other. We have never seen each other in sunlight: someone smiles. If it was not for the hunger!

For human nature is such that grief and pain – even simultaneously suffered – do not add up as a whole in our consciousness, but hide, the lesser behind the greater, according to a definite law of perspective. It is providential and is our means of surviving in the camp. And this is the reason why so often in free life one hears it said that man is never content. In fact it is not a question of a human incapacity for a state of absolute happiness, but of an ever-insufficient knowledge of the complex nature of the state of unhappiness; so that the single name of the major cause is given to all its causes, which are composite and set out in an order of urgency. And if the most immediate cause of stress comes to an end, you are grievously amazed to see that another one lies behind; and in reality a whole series of others.

So that as soon as the cold, which throughout the winter had seemed our only enemy, had ceased, we became aware of our hunger; and repeating the same error, we now say: 'If it was not for the hunger! ...'

But how could one imagine not being hungry? The Lager *is* hunger: we ourselves are hunger, living hunger.

On the other side of the road a steam-shovel is working. Its mouth, hanging from its cables, opens wide its steel jaws, balances a moment as if uncertain in its choice, then rushes upon the soft, clayey soil and snaps it up voraciously, while a satisfied snort of thick white smoke rises from the control cabin. Then it rises, turns half around, vomits backwards its mouthful and begins again.

Leaning on our shovels, we stop to watch, fascinated. At every bite of its mouth our mouths also open, our Adam's apples dance up and down, wretchedly visible under the flaccid skin. We are unable to tear ourselves away from the sight of the steam-shovel's meal.

Sigi is seventeen years old and is hungrier than everybody, although he is given a little soup every evening by his probably not disinterested protector. He had begun to speak of his home in Vienna and of his mother, but then he slipped on to the subject of food and now he talks endlessly about some marriage luncheon and remembers with genuine regret that he failed to finish his third plate of bean soup. And everyone tells him to keep quiet, but within ten minutes Béla is describing his Hungarian countryside and the fields of maize and a recipe to make meat-pies with corncobs and lard and spices and ... and he is cursed, sworn at and a third one begins to describe ...

How weak our flesh is! I am perfectly well aware how vain these fantasies of hunger are, but dancing before my eyes I see the spaghetti which we had just cooked, Vanda, Luciana, Franco and I, at the sorting-camp when we suddenly heard the news that we would leave for here the following day; and we were eating it (it was so good, yellow, filling), and we stopped, fools, stupid as we were – if we had only known! And if it happened again ... Absurd. If there is one thing sure in this world it is certainly this: that it will not happen to us a second time.

Fischer, the newest arrival, pulls out of his pocket a bundle, tied together with the painstaking exactitude of the Hungarians, and inside there is a half-ration of bread: half the bread of this morning. It is notorious that only the High Numbers keep their bread in their pockets; none of us old ones are able to preserve our bread for an hour. Various theories circulate to justify this incapacity of ours: bread eaten a little at a time is not wholly assimilated; the nervous tension needed to preserve the bread without touching it when one is hungry is in the highest degree harmful and debilitating; bread which is turning stale soon loses its alimentary value, so that the sooner it is eaten, the more nutritious it is; Alberto says that hunger and bread in one's pocket are terms of opposite sign which automatically cancel each other out and cannot exist in the same individual; and the majority affirm justly that, in the end, one's stomach is the securest safe against thefts and extortions. '*Moi, on m'a jamais volé mon pain!*' David snarls, hitting his concave stomach: but he is unable to take his eyes off Fischer who chews slowly and methodically, 'lucky' enough to still have half-a-ration at ten in the morning: '*Sacré veinard, va!*'

From Primo Levi, *If This Is a Man* (1958), translated by Stuart Woolf.

Robbing the Poor

During the time I worked at that small shop I saw a great deal of the sad side of the lives of the people who lived in the neighbourhood. Men would often come in to buy their dinners – a pennyworth of bread and two ounces of German sausage, or two pennyworths of bread and cheese, and very often a pennyworth of bread with a hole made in it containing a half-pennyworth of treacle. Articles of clothing and household goods were brought and left, something like a pawnshop, only food was given instead of money in return for the goods, which would be redeemed when the poor things were able to pay the money. I had to make out small tickets for a good many of the things. I have seen a pair of children's boots left in pawn for a loaf of bread and a small quantity of butter. Babies' pinafores, frocks, saucepans, candlesticks and all kinds of articles have been brought to hold for food. The practice was illegal, so all articles had to be brought in when no one was about, and I was trained to help to smuggle things in. I was also allowed to serve small articles and was being carefully taught how to weigh bread. I was told when I put a piece of bread on the loaf as a make-weight I was to be sure to press it down, so that the scale went down. I was getting quite expert in the art of cheating in weight, and thought I was very clever, when one day my aunt who had come to see my mother saw me serving in the shop and watched to see how a young girl like me would manage to serve. She soon discovered that I had been taught to weigh bread to the disadvantage of the customer, and when I went home to dinner, she told me she had watched me through the shop window and had seen me cheat a poor woman. When she explained that perhaps I robbed a poor child of a slice of bread I felt so thoroughly ashamed of myself and so sorry that I had not thought of the wrong I was doing, that I was days getting over it. I was too young to tell my mistress about it, but I never gave short weight again.

From *Life as We Have Known It*, edited by Margaret Llewelyn Davies (1931).

Famine in China

I often had to visit the hospital for my teeth at that time. Whenever I went there I had an attack of nausea at the horrible sight of dozens of people with shiny, almost transparent swollen limbs, as big as barrels. The patients were carried to the hospital on flat carts, there were so many of them. When I asked my dentist what was wrong with them, she said with a sigh, 'Edema.' I asked her what that meant, and she mumbled something which I vaguely linked with food.

These people with edema were mostly peasants. Starvation was much worse in the countryside because there were no guaranteed rations. Government policy was to provide food for the cities first, and commune officials were having to seize grain from the peasants by force. In many areas, peasants who tried to hide food were arrested, or beaten and tortured. Commune officials who were reluctant to take food from the hungry peasants were themselves dismissed, and some were physically maltreated. As a result, the peasants who had actually grown the food died in the millions all over China.

I learned later that several of my relatives from Sichuan to Manchuria had died in this famine. Among them was my father's retarded brother. His mother had died in 1958, and when the famine struck he was unable to cope as he would not listen to anyone else's advice. Rations were allotted on a monthly basis, and he ate his within days, leaving nothing for the rest of the month. He soon starved to death. My grandmother's sister, Lan, and her husband, 'Loyalty' Pei-o, who had been sent to the inhospitable countryside in the far north of Manchuria because of his old connection with Kuomintang intelligence, both died too. As food began to run out, the village authorities allocated supplies according to their own, unwritten priorities. Pei-o's outcast status meant that he and his wife were among the first to be denied food. Their children survived because their parents gave their food to them. The father of Yu-lin's wife also died. At the end, he had eaten the stuffing in his pillow and the braids of garlic plants.

One night, when I was about eight, a tiny, very old-looking woman, her face a mass of wrinkles, walked into our house. She looked so thin and feeble it seemed a puff of wind would blow her down. She dropped to the ground in front of my mother and banged her forehead on the floor, calling her 'the savior of my daughter'. She was our maid's mother. 'If it wasn't for you,' she said, 'my daughter would not survive ...' I did not grasp the full meaning of this until a month later, when a letter came for our maid. It said that her mother had died soon after visiting our house, where she had passed on the news that her husband and her younger son were dead. I will never forget the heart-rending sobs of our maid as she stood on the terrace, leaning against a wooden pillar and stifling her moans in her handkerchief. My grandmother sat cross-legged on her bed, weeping as well. I hid myself in a corner outside my grandmother's mosquito net. I could hear my grandmother saying to herself: 'The Communists are good, but all these people are dead ...' Years later, I heard that our maid's other brother and her sister-in-law died soon after this. Landlords' families were placed at the bottom of the list for food in a starving commune.

In 1989 an official who had been working in famine relief told me that he believed that the total number of people who had died in Sichuan was seven million. This would be 10 per cent of the entire population of a rich province. An accepted estimate for the death toll for the whole country is around thirty million.

From Jung Chang, *Wild Swans* (1991).

Sleep Eating

One can hear the sleepers breathing and snoring; some groan and speak. Many lick their lips and move their jaws. They are dreaming of eating; this is also a collective dream. It is a pitiless dream which the creator of the Tantalus myth must have known. You not only see the food, you feel it in your hands, distinct and concrete, you are aware of its rich and striking smell; someone in the dream even holds it up to your lips, but every time a different circumstance intervenes to prevent the consummation of the act. Then the dream dissolves and breaks up into its elements, but it re-forms itself immediately after and begins again, similar, yet changed; and this without pause, for all of us, every night and for the whole of our sleep.

It must be later than 11 p.m. because the movement to and from the bucket next to the night-guard is already intense. It is an obscene torment and an indelible shame: every two or three hours we have to get up to discharge ourselves of the great dose of water which during the day we are forced to absorb in the form of soup in order to satisfy our hunger: that same water which in the evenings swells our ankles and the hollows of our eyes, conferring on all physiognomies a likeness of deformation, and whose elimination imposes an enervating toil on our kidneys.

From Primo Levi, *If This Is a Man* (1958), translated by Stuart Woolf.

Genocide

Year Zero was the dawn of an age in which, *in extremis*, there would be no families, no sentiment, no expression of love or grief, no medicines, no hospitals, no schools, no books, no learning, no holidays, no music: only work and death. 'If our people can build Angkor Wat,' said Pol Pot in 1977, 'they can do anything.' In that year he killed probably more of his people than during all of his reign. Xenophobic and racist, he might have modelled himself on one of the despotic kings who ruled Angkor, the Khmer empire, between the tenth and thirteenth centuries. He was an admirer of Mao Tse-tung and the Gang of Four; and it is not improbable that much as Mao had seen himself as the greatest emperor of China, so Pol Pot saw himself as another Mao, directing his own red guard to purify all elites, subversives and revisionists. In the end he created little more than a slave state.

In my first hours in Phnom Penh I took no photographs; incredulity saw to that. I had no sense of people, of even the remnants of a population; the few human shapes I glimpsed seemed incoherent images, detached from the city itself. On catching sight of me, they would flit into the refuge of a courtyard or a cinema or a filling station. Only when I pursued several, and watched them forage, did I see that they were children. One child about ten years old – although age was difficult to judge – ran into a wardrobe lying on its side which was his or her shelter. In an abandoned Esso station an old woman and three emaciated children squatted around a pot containing a mixture of roots and leaves, which bubbled over a fire fuelled with paper money: thousands of snapping, crackling, brand-new banknotes lay in the gutters, sluiced there by the afternoon rains, from the destroyed Bank of Cambodia.

During the coming weeks one sound remained in my consciousness day and night: the soft, almost lilting sound of starving, sick children approaching death. In the eight months since the Vietnamese liberation, only three relief planes had come from the West – none had been sent by Western governments, the International Red Cross or the United Nations – in spite of appeals from the new regime in Phnom Penh. By the end of October, the tenth month, UNICEF and the Red Cross had sent 100 tons of relief; or as the Red Cross in Geneva preferred to call it, 'more than' 100 tons. In effect, nothing. Few geopolitical games have been as cynical and bereft of civilised behaviour as that which isolated and punished the people of Cambodia, and continues to do so in 1992. It is a game that beckons a second holocaust in Asia.

From John Pilger, 'Return to Year Zero', *Distant Voices* (1992).

Too Hungry to Think

From Stutthof they took us by train to Landsberg. I think it was July 1944. The commandant of our camp was an SS man called Vorster, a beast, who had been in charge of rounding up Jews in the ghettos: a man of power and terror. We left the train – about three thousand women – to enter the camp. He said that when we enter the camp we must not speak. He would shoot anyone who opened her mouth.

I last saw my brother Simcha in 1938 when he was about to have his bar mitzvah. I had not seen him for five years. I did not know if he was alive or dead. I didn't think about him. The Germans did something to us that made us stop thinking.

We thought only about hunger. When you are hungry it is not the stomach that hurts but here [she touches her throat]. There is no

[31]

worse pain in the world. It turns a person into an animal, a beast. We thought only of hunger. We did not think in a logical way.

From Theo Richmond, *Konin: A Quest* (1995).

Starved to Death

We gained a door at last, down some blind alley out of the deafening thoroughfare. She threw herself against it and pulled me up the unlighted stairs. They shook now and then with the violence of our ascent; with my free hand I tried to help myself up by the broad and greasy balustrade. There was little sound in the house. A light shone under the first door we passed, but all was quietness within.

At the very top, from the dense blackness of the passage, my guide thrust me suddenly into a dazzling room. My eyes rejected its array of brilliant light. On a small chest of drawers three candles were guttering, two more stood flaring in the high window ledge, and a lamp upon a table by the bed rendered these minor illuminations unnecessary by its diffusive glare. There were even some small Christmas candles dropping coloured grease down the wooden mantelpiece, and I noticed a fire had been made, built entirely of wood. There were bits of an inlaid workbox or desk, and a chair-rung, lying half burnt in the grate. Some peremptory demand for light had been, these signs denoted, unscrupulously met. A woman lay upon the bed, half clothed, asleep. As the door slammed behind me the flames wavered and my companion released my hand. She stood beside me, shuddering violently, but without utterance.

I looked around. Everywhere proofs of recent energy were visible. The bright panes reflecting back the low burnt candles, the wretched but shining furniture, and some odd bits of painted china, set before the sputtering lights upon the drawers, bore witness to a provincial intolerance of grime. The boards were bare, and marks of extreme poverty distinguished the whole room. The destitution of her surroundings accorded ill with the girl's spotless person and well-tended hands, which were hanging tremulously down.

Subsequently I realised that these deserted beings must have first fronted the world from a sumptuous stage. The details in proof of it I need not cite. It must have been so.

My previous apathy gave place to an exaggerated observation.

Even some pieces of a torn letter, dropped off the quilt, I noticed, were of fine texture, and inscribed by a man's hand. One fragment bore an elaborate device in colours. It may have been a club crest or coat-of-arms. I was trying to decide which, when the girl at length gave a cry of exhaustion or relief, at the same time falling into a similar attitude to that she had taken in the dim church. Her entire frame became shaken with tearless agony or terror. It was sickening to watch. She began partly to call or moan, begging me, since I was beside her, wildly, and then with heartbreaking weariness, 'to stop, to stay'. She half rose and claimed me with distracted grace. All her movements were noticeably fine.

I pass no judgement on her features; suffering for the time assumed them, and they made no insistence of individual claim.

I tried to raise her, and kneeling, pulled her reluctantly towards me. The proximity was distasteful. An alien presence has ever repelled me. I should have pitied the girl keenly perhaps a few more feet away. She clung to me with ebbing force. Her heart throbbed painfully close to mine, and when I meet now in the dark streets others who have been robbed, as she had been, of their great possession, I have to remember that.

The magnetism of our meeting was already passing; and, reason asserting itself, I reviewed the incident dispassionately, as she lay like a broken piece of mechanism in my arms. Her dark hair had come unfastened and fell about my shoulder. A faint white streak of it stole through the brown. A gleam of moonlight strays thus through a dusky room. I remember noticing, as it was swept with her involuntary motions across my face, a faint fragrance which kept recurring like a subtle and seductive sprite, hiding itself with fairy cunning in the tangled maze.

The poor girl's mind was clearly travelling a devious way. Broken and incoherent exclamations told of a recently wrung promise, made to whom, or of what nature, it was not my business to conjecture or inquire.

I record the passage of a few minutes. At the first opportunity I sought the slumberer on the bed. She slept well: hers was a long rest; there might be no awakening from it, for she was dead. Schooled in one short hour to all surprises, the knowledge made me simply richer by a fact. Nothing about the sternly set face invited horror. It had been, and was yet, a strong and, if beauty be not confined to youth and colour, a beautiful face.

Perhaps this quiet sharer of the convulsively broken silence was thirty years old. Death had set a firmness about the finely controlled features that might have shown her younger. The actual years are of little matter; existence, as we reckon time, must have lasted long. It was not death, but life that had planted the look of disillusion there. And romance being over, all goodbyes to youth are said. By the bedside, on a roughly constructed table, was a dearly bought bunch of violets. They were set in a blue bordered teacup, and hung over in wistful challenge of their own diviner hue. They were foreign, and their scent probably unnatural, but it stole very sweetly round the room. A book lay face downwards beside them – alas for parochial energies, not of a religious type – and the torn fragments of the destroyed letter had fallen on the black binding.

A passionate movement of the girl's breast against mine directed my glance elsewhere. She was shivering, and her arms about my neck were stiffly cold. The possibility that she was starving missed my mind. It would have found my heart. I wondered if she slept, and dared not stir, though I was by this time cramped and chilled. The vehemence of her agitation ended, she breathed gently, and slipped finally to the floor.

I began to face the need of action and recalled the chances of the night. When and how I might get home was a necessary question and I listened vainly for a friendly step outside. None since we left it had climbed the last flight of stairs. I could hear a momentary vibration of men's voices in the room below. Was it possible to leave these suddenly discovered children of peace and tumult? Was it possible to stay?

From Charlotte Mew, 'Passed' (1894).

Prison Diets

Paris, 23 March 1898
The food supplied to prisoners is entirely inadequate. Most of it is revolting in character. All of it is insufficient. Every prisoner suffers day and night from hunger. A certain amount of food is carefully weighed out ounce by ounce for each prisoner. It is just enough to sustain, not life exactly, but existence. But one is always racked by the pain and sickness of hunger.

The result of the food – which in most cases consists of weak gruel, badly-baked bread, suet, and water – is disease in the form of incessant diarrhoea. This malady, which ultimately with most prisoners becomes a permanent disease, is a recognised institution in every prison. At Wandsworth Prison, for instance – where I was confined for two months, till I had to be carried into hospital, where I remained for another two months – the warders go round twice or three times a day with astringent medicines, which they serve out to the prisoners as a matter of course. After about a week of such treatment it is unnecessary to say the medicine produces no effect at all. The wretched prisoner is then left a prey to the most weakening, depressing, and humiliating malady that can be conceived; and if, as often happens, he fails, from physical weakness, to complete his required revolutions at the crank or the mill he is reported for idleness, and punished with the greatest severity and brutality. Nor is this all.

Nothing can be worse than the sanitary arrangements of English prisons. In old days each cell was provided with a form of latrine. These latrines have now been suppressed. They exist no longer. A small tin vessel is supplied to each prisoner instead. Three times a day a prisoner is allowed to empty his slops. But he is not allowed to have access to the prison lavatories, except during the one hour when he is at exercise. And after five o'clock in the evening he is not allowed to leave his cell under any pretence, or for any reason. A man suffering from diarrhoea is consequently placed in a position so loathsome that it is unnecessary to dwell on it, that it would be unseemly to dwell on it. The misery and tortures that prisoners go through in consequence of the revolting sanitary arrangements are quite inde-scribable. And the foul air of the prison cells, increased by a system of ventilation that is utterly ineffective, is so sickening and unwhole-some that it is no uncommon thing for warders, when they come in the morning out of the fresh air and open and inspect each cell, to be violently sick. I have seen this myself on more than three occasions, and several of the warders have mentioned it to me as one of the disgusting things that their office entails on them.

The food supplied to prisoners should be adequate and whole-some. It should not be of such a character as to produce the incessant diarrhoea that, at first a malady, becomes a permanent disease.

From *Selected Letters of Oscar Wilde*, edited by Rupert Hart-Davis (1962).

Our Daily Bread

There was no bread in our cell. It was still early morning, and *Shawisha* Nabawiyya had not come with our bread. At first, each of us had been given two loaves per day. We had lodged our protest with the prison administration, and soon we were getting three loaves apiece of bread from outside, the sort that is sold normally, rather than old bread or the regulation prison bread from government bakeries.

The first day, I hadn't eaten a single bit of my bread. When I opened up the pitta loaf, I was treated to the sight of white worms and black termites looking like pinheads stuck into the dough of the bread. On the dish of *ful* – broadbean mash – too, I saw more of those little black and white creatures than I could count, overflowing from the surface of the dish.

That plate of *ful*, and the loaf placed over it, had remained next to the wall all day and all night, until dawn. I opened my eyes to the sound of a young woman, one of the *munaqqabas*, performing her ablutions prior to the dawn prayer. At the foot of the wall I saw the aluminium plate, covered by the loaf, and surrounded by scurrying cockroaches and beetles which disappeared into the cracks of the wall the minute they sensed a foot striking adjacent ground. I saw her leaning over the plate, and I heard her chewing on the bread. Swallowing a bit of water, she whispered to herself, 'Hunger leads to disbelief.'

From Nawal el Sa'adawi, *Memoirs from the Women's Prison* (1983), translated by Marilyn Booth.

Return from the Dead

He wanted to see around the apartment again. We supported him, and he toured the rooms. His cheeks creased, but didn't release his lips; it was in his eyes that we'd seen his smile. In the kitchen he saw the clafoutis we'd made for him. He stopped smiling.

'What is it?' We told him. What was it made with? Cherries – it was the height of the season. 'May I have some?' 'We don't know, we'll have to ask the doctor.' He came back into the sitting room and lay down on the divan. 'So I can't have any?' 'Not yet.' 'Why?'

'There have been accidents in Paris already from letting deportees eat too soon after they got back from the camps.'

He stopped asking questions about what had happened while he was away. He stopped seeing us. A great, silent pain spread over his face because he was still being refused food, because it was still as it had been in the concentration camp. And, as in the camp, he accepted it in silence. He didn't see that we were weeping. Nor did he see that we could scarcely look at him or respond to what he said.

The doctor came. He stopped short with his hand on the door handle, very pale. He looked at us, and then at the form on the divan. He didn't understand. And then he realized: the form wasn't dead yet, it was hovering between life and death, and he, the doctor, had been called in to try to keep it alive. The doctor came into the room. He went over to the form and the form smiled at him. The doctor was to come several times a day for three weeks, at all hours of the day and night. Whenever we were too afraid we called him and he came. He saved Robert L. He too was caught up in the passionate desire to save Robert L. from death. He succeeded.

We smuggled the clafoutis out of the house while he slept. The next day he was feverish and didn't talk about food any more.

If he had eaten when he got back from the camp his stomach would have been lacerated by the weight of the food, or else the weight would have pressed on the heart, which had grown enormous in the cave of his emaciation. It was beating so fast you couldn't have counted its beats, you couldn't really say it was beating – it was trembling, rather, as if from terror. No, he couldn't eat without dying. But he couldn't go on not eating without dying. That was the problem.

The fight with death started very soon. We had to be careful with it, use care, tact, skill. It surrounded him on all sides. And yet there was still a way of reaching him. It wasn't very big, this opening through which to communicate with him, but there was still life in him, scarcely more than a splinter, but a splinter just the same. Death unleashed its attack. His temperature was 104.5° the first day. Then 105°. Then 106°. Death was doing all it could. 106°: his heart vibrated like a violin string. Still 106°, but vibrating. The heart, we thought – it's going to stop. Still 106°. Death deals cruel knocks, but the heart is deaf. This can't go on, the heart will stop. But no.

Gruel, said the doctor, a teaspoonful at a time. Six or seven times a

[37]

day we gave him gruel. Just a teaspoonful nearly choked him, he clung to our hands, gasped for air, and fell back on the bed. But he swallowed some. Six or seven times a day, too, he asked to go to the toilet. We lifted him up, supported him under the arms and knees. He must have weighed between eighty-two and eighty-four pounds: bone, skin, liver, intestines, brain, lungs, everything – eighty-four pounds for a body five feet ten inches tall. We sat him on the edge of the sanitary pail, on which we'd put a small cushion: the skin was raw where there was no flesh between it and the joints. (*The elbows of the little Jewish girl of seventeen from the Faubourg du Temple stick through the skin on her arms. Probably because she's so young and her skin so fragile, the joint is outside instead of in, sticking out naked and clean. She suffers no pain either from her joints or from her belly, from which all her genital organs have been taken out one by one at regular intervals.*) Once he was sitting on his pail he excreted in one go, in one enormous, astonishing gurgle. What the heart held back the anus couldn't: it let out all that was in it. Everything, or almost everything, did the same, even the fingers, which no longer kept their nails, but let them go too. But the heart went on holding back what it contained. The heart. And then there was the head. Gaunt but sublime, it emerged alone from that bag of bones, remembering, relating, recognizing, asking for things. And talking. Talking. The head was connected to the body by the neck, as heads usually are, but the neck was so withered and shrunken – you could circle it with one hand – that you wondered how life could pass through it; a spoonful of gruel almost blocked it. At first the neck was at right angles to the shoulders. Higher up, the neck was right inside the skeleton, joined on at the top of the jaws and winding around the ligaments like ivy. You could see the vertebrae through it, the carotid arteries, the nerves, the pharynx, and the blood passing through: the skin had become like cigarette paper. So, he excreted this dark green, slimy, gushing thing, a turd such as no one had ever seen before. When he'd finished we put him back to bed. He lay for a long time with his eyes half shut, prostrated.

For seventeen days the turd looked the same. It was inhuman. It separated him from us more than the fever, the thinness, the nailless fingers, the marks of SS blows. We gave him gruel that was golden yellow, gruel for infants, and it came out of him dark green like slime from a swamp. After the sanitary pail was closed you could hear the bubbles bursting as they rose to the surface inside. Viscous and slimy,

[38]

it was almost like a great gob of spit. When it emerged the room filled with a smell, not of putrefaction or corpses – did his body still have the wherewithal to make a corpse? – but rather of humus, of dead leaves, of dense undergrowth. It was a somber smell, dark reflection of the dark night from which he was emerging and which we would never know. (*I leaned against the shutters, the street went by below, and as they didn't know what was going on in the room I wanted to tell them that here, in this room above them, a man had come back from the German camps, alive.*)

Of course he'd rummaged in trashcans for food, he'd eaten wild plants, drunk water from engines. But that didn't explain it. Faced with this strange phenomenon we tried to find explanations. We thought that perhaps there, under our very eyes, he was consuming his own liver or spleen. How were we to know? How were we to know what strangeness that belly still contained, what pain?

For seventeen whole days that turd still looks the same. For seventeen days it's unlike anything ever known. Every one of the seven times he excretes each day, we smell it, look at it, but can't recognize it. For seventeen days we hide from him that which comes out of him, just as we hide from him his own legs and feet and whole unbelievable body.

We ourselves never got used to seeing them. You couldn't get used to it. The incredible thing was that he was still alive. Whenever anyone came into the room and saw that shape under the sheets, they couldn't bear the sight and averted their eyes. Many went away and never came back. He never noticed our horror, not once. He was happy, he wasn't afraid any more. The fever bore him up. For seventeen days.

One day his temperature drops.

After seventeen days, death grows weary. In the pail his excretion doesn't bubble any more, it becomes liquid. It's still green, but it smells more human, it smells human. And one day his temperature drops – he's been given twelve liters of serum, and one morning his temperature drops. He's lying on his nine cushions, one for the head, two for the forearms, two for the arms, two for the hands, and two for the feet. For no part of his body could bear its own weight; the weight had to be swathed in down and immobilized.

And then, one morning, the fever leaves him. It comes back, but abates again. Comes back again, not quite so high, and falls again. And then one morning he says, 'I'm hungry.'

Hunger had gone as his temperature rose. It came back when the fever abated. One day the doctor said, 'Let's try – let's try giving him something to eat. We can begin with meat extract. If he can take that, keep on giving it, but at the same time give him all kinds of other food, just small amounts at first, increasing the quantity just a little every three days.'

I spend the morning going around to all the restaurants in Saint-Germain-des-Prés trying to find a meat-juice extractor. I find one in a fashionable restaurant. They say they can't lend it. I say it's for a political deportee who's very ill, it's a matter of life and death. The woman thinks for a minute and says, 'I can't lend it to you, but I can rent it to you for a thousand francs a day.' I leave my name and address and a deposit. The Saint-Benoît restaurant sells me the meat at cost price.

He digested the meat extract without any difficulty, so after three days he began to take solid food.

His hunger grew from what it fed on. It grew greater and greater, became insatiable.

It took on terrifying proportions.

We didn't serve him food. We put the dishes in front of him and left him and he ate. Methodically, as if performing a duty, he was doing what he had to do to live. He ate. It was an occupation that took up all his time. He would wait for food for hours. He would swallow without knowing what he was eating. Then we'd take the food away and he'd wait for it to come again.

He has gone and hunger has taken his place. Emptiness has taken his place. He is giving to the void, filling what was emptied: those wasted bowels. That's what he's doing. Obeying, serving, ministering to a mysterious duty. How does he know what to do about hunger? How does he perceive that this is what he has to do? He knows with a knowledge that has no parallel.

He eats a mutton chop. Then he gnaws the bone, eyes lowered, concentrating on not missing a morsel of meat. Then he takes a second chop. Then a third. Without looking up.

He's sitting in the shade in the sitting room near a half-open window, in an armchair, surrounded by his cushions, his stick beside him. His legs look like crutches inside his trousers. When the sun shines you can see through his hands.

Yesterday he made enormous efforts to gather up the breadcrumbs that had fallen on his trousers and on the floor. Today he lets a few lie.

We leave him alone in the room while he's eating. We don't have to help him now. His strength has come back enough for him to hold a spoon or a fork. But we still cut up the meat for him. We leave him alone with the food. We try not to talk in the adjoining rooms. We walk on tiptoe. We watch him from a distance. He's performing a duty. He has no special preference for one dish over another. He cares less and less. He crams everything down. If the dishes don't come fast enough, he sobs and says we don't understand.

Yesterday afternoon he stole some bread out of the refrigerator. He steals. We tell him to be careful, not to eat too much. Then he weeps.

I used to watch him from the sitting-room door. I didn't go in. For two weeks, three, I watched him eat with unremitting pleasure. I couldn't get used to it either. Sometimes his pleasure made me weep too. He didn't see me. He'd forgotten me.

From Marguerite Duras, *La Douleur* (1985), translated by Barbara Bray.

A Straight Line

As a girl on the brink of adolescence, controlling my body seemed to be my only source of power. Counting calories and plotting my weight loss, pound by pound, on a graph, I was triumphant. The graph began to slant downwards as I lost a pound a day. I was aiming for a straight line and when this was achieved, the neatness pleased me. It was like working steadily and coming top at school. I seemed to have no feelings about it and the refreshing coolness of it pleased me. I had a new sense of order with which to view the outside world and my changing inner self and I latched on to this new system because it distracted me from the disturbing complexities of adult life. At the time, I had no idea why I was doing this, but the illusion of self-mastery quickly became addictive. I had always felt

[41]

that my needs were unacceptable and had tried, repeatedly, to control them. Between the ages of ten and twelve I tried to diet, eating a carton of 98-calorie yoghurt for school lunch, but never lost more than a pound or two.

One day, after a stomach upset, my hunger miraculously vanished. I decided to capitalise on this new development and eat no more than an apple or an egg a day so that my hunger would not return. The illness officially began with this triumph of willpower. I say 'officially' because, as George Eliot says: 'No retrospect can take us back to the true beginning'. Beginnings are always difficult because no story is quite true. I could tell my story another way, beginning in the playground at nursery school. A friend, who later became anorexic, told me you could test for fat by bending in the bath and seeing if your tummy formed a roll. I tried this and discovered I was fat. We set up a problem corner in the classroom and became precocious counsellors.

On the brink of adolescence, turning twelve, I was sent to the house of my grandmother and great-grandmother. My parents returned to my first home in New York that summer; I was in Cape Town, in an apartheid winter, being remodelled. I was angry but I did not know it. During July and August I was coaxed into attendance at opulent suburban tea parties on the grounds that the guests were my People: extended family, friends and fellow descendants of Abraham and Sarah. I could not see that these ladies with their rigid hairdos, their grotesque make up and their mindless colonial chatter had much in common with our patriarchs and matriarchs. My inner life was peopled by prophets and flawed heroes, fed by my grandmother's stories of spiritual trial and awakening. I was quietly contemptuous of the banal world I was supposed to be entering. My favourite heroines were Joan of Arc and Anne Frank, whose diary I read repeatedly. At this time I was preparing for my Barmitzvah, the official coming of age ceremony within the Jewish community, and I chose to read out a passage from the diary which began: 'In spite of everything, I still believe that people are good at heart'.

I admired her resilient innocence. That year I read numerous books by Jewish fighters, victims and martyrs during the Holocaust and remember being half-intrigued, half-repelled by martyrdom. When I complained of tea-party triviality, my grandmother said that most of our talented people had been killed during the war and that these painted ladies were the dregs, but that we should embrace them anyway.

There was a book locked in Gran's cupboard, a book on the Holocaust deemed too shocking for someone of my age to see. Naturally, I waited until she was asleep, extracted the key from her bedside drawer and guiltily turned the pages, eating of the forbidden fruit. I found photographs of people wearing yellow stars. I saw skeletal bodies, faces at gas chambers, faces at mass graves. My people. I tried to hold on to a vision of innocence, to blot out the evidence. I was gripped with horror. Eyes open, I saw that we were naked.

What is defined as anorexia in a secular context can be defined as fasting in a religious one. The religious motive for fasting is typically to purify the body and sharpen the mind: to rise above desire, empty oneself of craving and await a different form of nourishment. Fasting can be an act of atonement. It was something we did, once a year, on Yom Kippur, a ritual response for our collective flaws as humans. To let go of attachment to the body and its cravings felt liberating, but, for me, it was a welcome escape. I did not want to inhabit my body and the disturbing feelings embedded in it. It felt safer to live in the mind and cultivate innocence, as my mother and grandmother seemed to do, to feel pure.

In my family, many of the religious rituals centre around meals. I feared intrusion and indoctrination. Refusing my grandmother's constant pleas to eat (along with those of my great-grandmother) became a covert assertion of my own unvoiced will. This rebellion was so secret that I was scarcely aware of it myself. Externally, I still appeared the perfect granddaughter: gentle, receptive and compliant. As I write, I am again at my grandmother's table in the same formal, shaded dining room with the same electric lights on. Again she urges, 'Eat ... eat ... have some more ... please help yourself ...' Again, my mother and I say, 'Thank you, we *are* helping ourselves', with the slightest edge of irritation in our polite voices. Why does Gran do this? She does it because she mythologises the hostess, the giver. She believes this traditional female role to be a moral duty, according to Our Teachings.

Let me explain Our Teachings to the uninitiated: it is not enough to be generous and to give guests what they want. A hostess must be conspicuously generous, and give more than the guest wants. If the guest is on a diet and wants no potatoes, she'll sneak a couple onto the plate and, if discovered, say 'Oops, too late'. It is her code of love and honour, and it is absolute.

In our family, giving and receiving food was the language of love. What was it then, not to eat? Like many anorexics, I was fiercely individualistic. In rejecting others' food, I rejected what others thought good for me, but I had yet to find my own nourishment. At the same time as I restricted my own calorie intake, I increased that of those around me. The experimental cakes which I baked for others were high in calories but had little nutritional value. Later, I started selling them at school and making money. I became the fantasy mother of my childhood who would not dream of using pre-packaged food, like my mother, or a housekeeper, like my grand-mother. I invented my own recipes and wrote a cookbook. As a child I had a creamy picture I loved: Frances Bear in the kitchen with her mother, who was wearing an apron and baking a cake. That was the kind of mother I was going to be, not a busy career woman like my mother or a lady of tea and visions like my grandmother. Yet, at this stage, I had no idea how to mother even myself.

I wanted control, because I felt I had none. One lapse and it seemed like everything would fall apart; that was the underlying drive behind my rigid regime. Refusing food was both a rejection of self and a fight for self. Mastering the demands of the body gave, at least, the illusion of power and freedom. I remember no hunger pangs. I often ignored my body's knowledge.

When I returned to my parents' house in England, I was found out. Selfishly, I barely noticed their worry. I did not view my behaviour as self-destructive and thought they were over-reacting. My only care was how to continue now that I was being watched. I pretended to eat meals, but hid them in my bottom drawer. I was driven by the thought that if I began to eat, my hunger would return and overwhelm me. I could not trust myself to be moderate. Discipline, it seemed to me, was all or nothing. My meticulously plotted graph crossed below the 60lb mark, which was my goal. Yet still, I kept going (59 lbs ..., 58lbs ...) as an insurance policy against the future. I bought a calorie counting book, calculated an allowance of 100 a day and ate less. I looked at bodyweight charts and imagined perfection. I often sketched my ideal female shape: an hourglass figure with full breasts, a narrow waist and gently curving hips.

At this point my parents were becoming increasingly alarmed, and privacy was becoming more difficult. The worst part was sitting at table with my stern father and crying over two custard creams. I was taken to a faceless grey man behind a desk who weighed me and asked if I wanted to grow up. I pretended that I wished to gain weight, and silently dismissed him. I was offered the chance to go to hospital and turned it down.

At my new school I got cold and clung to radiators. I shied away from others and applied the same rigour to work as I did to dieting. I felt isolated until, at thirteen, I played the part of Lady Macbeth in a school play and gave vent to feelings even more ambitious than my own. My favourite speech was: '... unsex me here ... Stop up th' access and passage to remorse ... That no compunctious visitings of nature ... Shake my fell purpose ...' My mother helped me to understand the lines and perfect each nuance of tone. I loved the thrill of conviction in 'my fell purpose'. Possibly it was the licence of this voicing that made me start socialising and eating.

I said earlier that beginnings are difficult; so are endings. My distorted body image did not really change until my late twenties when I moved to a bleak landscape on the West Coast of Ireland and welcomed the once forbidden feelings. The crucial step was to stay still and let them surface. If Persephone had not eaten the seeds of the underworld, she would have been fully restored to her mother, Demeter. Having eaten the seeds she spends half the year in the upper world with Demeter, and half the year in the underworld, where I seemed to be. For several months I was just falling, falling, like Persephone in the underworld, unable to return to her mother, the Goddess of Grain. It was frightening. It seemed empty, interminable and without sense, but some implicit trust in the unknown process kept me going. I resisted the familiar urge to find distractions (parties, intrigue, drama) and allowed myself to grieve and rage while I chopped vegetables, collected kindling and lit the range. One morning I hit solid ground and awoke feeling more myself than I had ever been. The external world, previously a kaleidoscope of changing patterns and perspectives, seemed to leap into focus. Colours were brighter, shapes more clearly outlined.

This moment of recovery had taken many years from my initial, more superficial, recovery at thirteen. The first stage began with a shift in attitude: my father said that unless I started eating I would have no children. This shocked me into looking in the mirror and drinking a glass of milk. I did, after all, want to grow into a woman.

From 'Pomegranate Seeds' (unpublished ms), Anna Gordon, 1996.

The Store House of the Body

[Rome. A Street]

*Enter a Company of mutinous Citizens, with staves, clubs, and other
weapons.*

1 CIT: Before we proceed any further, hear me speak.

ALL: Speak, speak.

1 CIT: You are all resolved rather to die than to famish?

ALL: Resolved, resolved.

1 CIT: First, you know Caius Martius is chief enemy to the people.

ALL: We know 't, we know 't.

1 CIT: Let us kill him, and we'll have corn at our own price. Is 't a verdict?

ALL: No more talking on 't; let it be done. Away, away!

2 CIT: One word, good citizens.

1 CIT: We are accounted poor citizens, the patricians good. What authority surfeits on would relieve us. If they would yield us but the superfluity, while it were wholesome, we might guess they relieved us humanely; but they think we are too dear: the leanness that afflicts us, the object of our misery, is as an inventory to particularise their abundance; our sufferance is a gain to them. Let us revenge this with our pikes, ere we become rakes: for the gods know I speak this in hunger for bread, not in thirst for revenge.

2 CIT: Would you proceed especially against Caius Martius?

ALL: Against him first: he's a very dog to the commonalty.

2 CIT: Consider you what services he has done for his country?

1 CIT: Very well; and could be content to give him good report for 't, but that he pays himself with being proud.

2 CIT: Nay, but speak not maliciously.

1 CIT: I say unto you, what he hath done famously, he did it to that end: though soft-conscienced men can be content to say it was for his country, he did it to please his mother, and to be partly proud; which he is, even to the altitude of his virtue.

2 CIT: What he cannot help in his nature, you account a vice in him. You must in no way say he is covetous.

1 CIT: If I must not, I need not be barren of accusations: he hath faults, with surplus, to tire in repetition. *Shouts within.* What shouts are these? The other side o' the city is risen: why stay we prating here? to the Capitol!

ALL: Come, come.

1 CIT: Soft! who comes here?

[46]

Enter Menenius Agrippa.

2 CIT: Worthy Menenius Agrippa; one that hath always loved the people.

1 CIT: He's one honest enough: would all the rest were so!

MEN: What work's, my countrymen, in hand? Where go you
With bats and clubs? The matter? Speak, I pray you.

2 CIT: Our business is not unknown to the senate; they have had inkling this fortnight what we intend to do, which now we'll show 'em in deeds. They say poor suitors have strong breaths: they shall know we have strong arms too.

MEN: Why, masters, my good friends, mine honest neighbours,
Will you undo yourselves?

2 CIT: We cannot, sir; we are undone already.

MEN: I tell you, friends, most charitable care
Have the patricians of you. For your wants,
Your suffering in this dearth, you may as well
Strike at the heaven with your staves as lift them
Against the Roman state, whose course will on
The way it takes, cracking ten thousand curbs
Of more strong link asunder than can ever
Appear in your impediment. For the dearth,
The gods, not the patricians, make it, and
Your knees to them, not arms, must help. Alack!
You are transported by calamity
Thither where more attends you; and you slander
The helms o' the state, who care for you like fathers,
When you curse them as enemies.

2 CIT: Care for us! True, indeed! They ne'er cared for us yet: suffer us to famish, and their storehouses crammed with grain; make edicts for usury, to support usurers; repeal daily any wholesome act established against the rich, and provide more piercing statutes daily to chain up and restrain the poor. If the wars eat us not up, they will; and there's all the love they bear us.

MEN: Either you must
Confess yourselves wondrous malicious,
Or be accus'd of folly. I shall tell you
A pretty tale: it may be you have heard it;
But, since it serves my purpose, I will venture
To scale 't a little more.

2 CIT: Well, I'll hear it, sir; yet you must not think to fob off our disgrace with a tale; but, an 't please you, deliver.

MEN: There was a time when all the body's members
Rebell'd against the belly; thus accus'd it:
That only like a gulf it did remain
I' the midst o' the body, idle and unactive,
Still cupboarding the viand, never bearing
Like labour with the rest, where th' other instruments
Did see and hear, devise, instruct, walk, feel,
And, mutually participate, did minister
Unto the appetite and affection common
Of the whole body. The belly answer'd, –
   2 CIT: Well, sir, what answer made the belly?
   MEN: Sir, I shall tell you. – With a kind of smile,
Which ne'er came from the lungs, but even thus –
For, look you, I may make the belly smile
As well as speak – it taintingly replied
To the discontented members, the mutinous parts
That envied his receipt; even so most fitly
As you malign our senators for that
They are not such as you.
   2 CIT: Your belly's answer? What!
The kingly crowned head, the vigilant eye,
The counsellor heart, the arm our soldier,
Our steed the leg, the tongue our trumpeter,
With other muniments and petty helps
In this our fabric, if that they –
   MEN: What then? –
'Fore me, this fellow speaks! what then? what then?
   2 CIT: Should by the cormorant belly be restrain'd,
Who is the sink o' the body, –
   MEN: Well, what then?
   2 CIT: The former agents, if they did complain,
What could the belly answer?
   MEN: I will tell you;
If you'll bestow a small, of what you have little,
Patience a while, you'st hear the belly's answer.
   2 CIT: You're long about it.
   MEN: Note me this, good friend;
Your most grave belly was deliberate,
Not rash like his accusers, and thus answer'd:
'True is it, my incorporate friends,' quoth he,
'That I receive the general food at first,

Which you do live upon; and fit it is,
Because I am the store-house and the shop
Of the whole body: but, if you do remember,
I send it through the rivers of your blood,
Even to the court, the heart, to the seat o' the brain;
And, through the cranks and offices of man,
The strongest nerves and small inferior veins
From me receive that natural competency
Whereby they live. And though that all at once,
You, my good friends,' – this says the belly, mark me, –
  2 CIT: Ay, sir; well, well.
  MEN: 'Though all at once cannot
See what I do deliver out to each,
Yet I can make my audit up, that all
From me do back receive the flour of all,
And leave me but the bran.' What say you to 't?
  2 CIT: It was an answer: how apply you this?
  MEN: The senators of Rome are this good belly,
And you the mutinous members; for, examine
Their counsels and their cares, digest things rightly
Touching the weal o' the common, you shall find
No public benefit which you receive
But it proceeds or comes from them to you,
And no way from yourselves. What do you think,
You, the great toe of this assembly?
  2 CIT: I the great toe? Why the great toe?
  MEN: For that, being one o' the lowest, basest, poorest,
Of this most wise rebellion, thou go'st foremost:
Thou rascal, that art worst in blood to run,
Lead'st first to win some vantage.

From William Shakespeare, *The Tragedy of Coriolanus* (1608–9).

A Starvation Diet

Byron had not damaged his body by strong drinks, but his terror of
getting fat was so great that he reduced his diet to the point of
absolute starvation. He was of that soft, lymphatic temperament
which it is almost impossible to keep within a moderate compass,

particularly as in his case his lameness prevented his taking exercise. When he added to his weight, even standing was painful, so he resolved to keep down to eleven stone, or shoot himself. He said everything he swallowed was instantly converted into tallow and deposited on his ribs.

He was the only human being I ever met with who had sufficient self-restraint and resolution to resist this proneness to fatten: he did so; and at Genoa, where he was last weighed, he was ten stone and nine pounds, and looked much less. This was not from vanity about his personal appearance, but from a better motive; and as, like Justice Greedy, he was always hungry, his merit was the greater. Occasionally he relaxed his vigilance, when he swelled apace.

I remember one of his old friends saying, 'Byron, how well you are looking!' If he had stopped there it had been well, but when he added, 'You are getting fat,' Byron's brow reddened, and his eyes flashed – 'Do you call getting fat looking well, as if I were a hog?' and, turning to me, he muttered, 'The beast, I can hardly keep my hands off him.' The man who thus offended him was the husband of the lady addressed as 'Genevra', and the original of his 'Zuleika', in the *Bride of Abydos*. I don't think he had much appetite for his dinner that day, or for many days, and never forgave the man who, so far from wishing to offend, intended to pay him a compliment.

Byron said he had tried all sorts of experiments to stay his hunger, without adding to his bulk. 'I swelled,' he said, 'at one time to fourteen stone, so I clapped the muzzle on my jaws, and, like the hybernating animals, consumed my own fat.'

He would exist on biscuits and soda-water for days together, then, to allay the eternal hunger gnawing at his vitals, he would make up a horrid mess of cold potatoes, rice, fish, or greens, deluged in vinegar, and gobble it up like a famished dog. On either of these unsavoury dishes, with a biscuit and a glass or two of Rhine wine, he cared not how sour, he called feasting sumptuously. Upon my observing he might as well have fresh fish and vegetables, instead of stale, he laughed and answered:

'I have an advantage over you, I have no palate; one thing is as good as another to me.'

'Nothing,' I said, 'disagrees with the natural man, he fasts and gorges, his nerves and brains don't bother him; but if you wish to live?' –

'Who wants to live?' he replied, 'not I. The Byrons are a short-lived race on both sides, father and mother: longevity is hereditary: I am nearly at the end of my tether. I don't care for death a d—n: it is her sting! I can't bear pain.'

From E.J. Trewlawny, *Recollections of the Last Days of Shelley and Byron* (1858).

A Daughter Gets Her Appetite Back

'And is it *true?*' demanded Caroline, rising on her pillow. 'Is she *really* my mother?'

'You won't cry, or make any scene, or turn hysterical, if I answer Yes?'

'Cry? I'd cry if you said No. It would be terrible to be disappointed now. But give her a name: how do you call her?'

'I call this stout lady in a quaint black dress, who looks young enough to wear much smarter raiment, if she would – I call her Agnes Helstone: she married my brother James, and is his widow.'

'And my mother?'

'What a little sceptic it is! Look at her small face, Mrs Pryor, scarcely larger than the palm of my hand, alive with acuteness and eagerness.' (To Caroline). – 'She had the trouble of bringing you into the world, at any rate: mind you show your duty to her by quickly getting well, and repairing the waste of these cheeks. Heigho! she used to be plump: what she has done with it all, I can't, for the life of me, divine.'

'If *wishing* to get well will help me, I shall not be long sick. This morning, I had no reason and no strength to wish it.'

Fanny here tapped at the door, and said that supper was ready.

'Uncle, if you please, you may send me a little bit of supper – anything you like, from your own plate. That is wiser than going into hysterics – is it not?'

'It is spoken like a sage, Cary: see if I don't cater for you judiciously. When women are sensible – and, above all, intelligible – I can get on with them. It is only the vague, superfine sensations, and extremely wire-drawn notions, that put me about. Let a woman ask me to give her an edible or a wearable – be the same a roc's egg or the breastplate of Aaron, a share of St John's locusts and honey or the leathern girdle about his loins – I can, at least, understand the demand: but when they pine for they know not what – sympathy –

sentiment – some of these indefinite abstractions – I can't do it: I don't know it; I haven't got it. Madam, accept my arm.'

Mrs Pryor signified that she should stay with her daughter that evening. Helstone, accordingly, left them together. He soon returned, bringing a plate in his own consecrated hand.

'This is chicken,' he said; 'but we'll have partridge to-morrow. Lift her up, and put a shawl over her. On my word, I understand nursing. Now, here is the very same little silver fork you used when you first came to the Rectory: that strikes me as being what you may call a happy thought – a delicate attention. Take it, Cary, and munch away cleverly.'

Caroline did her best. Her uncle frowned to see that her powers were so limited: he prophesied, however, great things for the future; and as she praised the morsel he had brought, and smiled gratefully in his face, he stooped over her pillow, kissed her, and said, with a broken, rugged accent –

'Good-night, bairnie! God bless thee!'

From Charlotte Brontë, *Shirley* (1849).

Dreams of Emptiness

Most people know when they are hungry and will eat, more or less, accordingly. Bruch contrasts this fortunate majority with both the anorexic and the obese person, neither of whom knows how to gauge the state of her own stomach or assess what is a reasonable requirement of food for her own bodily needs. The obese person cannot recognise that her stomach is full, nor the anorexic that hers is empty. It is easy enough to see how someone, especially someone who has suffered a childhood of poverty, can be led to a fear of emptiness, of not getting enough to eat, of starvation itself, and so in later life to stave off or compensate for such a fear. And indeed obesity is a disease of the poor rather than the rich. It is perhaps less easy to see how someone from a privileged background can be led to seek emptiness as a physical state, when it is obviously such an unpleasant, even painful, one. Repletion is probably a more pleasurable state for most people than is emptiness, and its metaphorical implications are now widely understood: to be well-fed is to feel safe from poverty and death; it is to engage in an enjoyable activity; and it is to feel loved, if only by oneself. But the metaphorical implications of emptiness are less clear. Because it is both difficult and painful to maintain one's stomach in a state of emptiness, we cannot doubt that there are powerful psychic motivations for sustaining such an activity, which is not only abnormal, but directly contrary to both physiological and social pressures.

From Sheila Macleod, *The Art of Starvation* (1981).

Home Is Where the Appetite Is

On the 29th of July, 1835, Charlotte, now little more than nineteen years old, went as teacher to Miss Wooler's. Emily accompanied her, as a pupil; but she became literally ill from home-sickness, and could not settle to anything, and after passing only three months at Roe Head, returned to the parsonage and the beloved moors.

Miss Brontë gives the following reasons as those which prevented Emily's remaining at school, and caused the substitution of her younger sister in her place at Miss Wooler's:

'My sister Emily loved the moors. Flowers brighter than the rose bloomed in the blackest of the heath for her; – out of a sullen hollow in a livid hill-side, her mind could make an Eden. She found in the bleak solitude many and dear delights; and not the least and best-loved was – liberty. Liberty was the breath of Emily's nostrils; without it she perished. The change from her own home to a school, and from her own very noiseless, very secluded, but unrestricted and unartificial mode of life, to one of disciplined routine (though under the kindest auspices), was what she failed in enduring. Her nature proved here too strong for her fortitude. Every morning, when she woke, the vision of home and the moors rushed on her, and darkened and saddened the day that lay before her. Nobody knew what ailed her but me. I knew only too well. In this struggle her health was quickly broken: her white face, attenuated form, and failing strength, threatened rapid decline. I felt in my heart she would die, if she did not go home, and with this conviction obtained her recall. She had only been three months at school; and it was some years before the experiment of sending her from home was again ventured on.'

This physical suffering on Emily's part when absent from

Haworth, after recurring several times under similar circumstances, became at length so much an acknowledged fact, that whichever was obliged to leave home, the sisters decided that Emily must remain there, where alone she could enjoy anything like good health. She left it twice again in her life; once going as teacher to a school in Halifax for six months, and afterwards accompanying Charlotte to Brussels for ten. When at home, she took the principal part of the cooking upon herself; and did all the household ironing; and after Tabby grew old and infirm, it was Emily who made all the bread for the family; and any one passing by the kitchen-door, might have seen her studying German out of an open book, propped up before her, as she kneaded the dough; but no study, however interesting, interfered with the goodness of the bread, which was always light and excellent. Books were, indeed, a very common sight in that kitchen; the girls were taught by their father theoretically, and by their aunt practically, that to take an active part in all household work was, in their position, woman's simple duty; but, in their careful employment of time, they found many an odd five minutes for reading while watching the cakes, and managed the union of two kinds of employment better than King Alfred.

From Elizabeth Gaskell, *The Life of Charlotte Brontë* (1857).

Skin and Bone

I had but just time in my former to tell you that Colonel Morden was arrived. He was on horseback, attended by two servants, and alighted at the door just as the clock struck five. Mrs Smith was then below in her back shop, weeping, her husband with her, who was as much affected as she; Mrs Lovick having left them a little before, in tears likewise; for they had been bemoaning one another; joining in opinion that the admirable lady would not live the night over. She had told them it was *her* opinion too, from some numbnesses, which she called the forerunners of death, and from an increased inclination to doze.

The colonel, as Mrs Smith told me afterwards, asked with great impatience, the moment he alighted, How Miss Harlowe was? She answered, Alive; but, she feared, drawing on apace. Good God! said he, with his hands and eyes lifted up. Can I see her? My name is

Morden. I have the honour to be nearly related to her. Step up, pray; and let her know [she is sensible, I hope] that I am here. Who is with her?

Nobody but her nurse, and Mrs Lovick, a widow gentlewoman, who is as careful of her as if she were her mother.

And *more* careful too, interrupted he, or she is not careful at all —

Except a gentleman be with her, one Mr Belford, continued Mrs Smith, who has been the best friend she has had.

If Mr Belford be with her, surely I may — but, pray step up and let Mr Belford know that I shall take it for a favour to speak with him first.

Mrs Smith came up to me in my new apartment. I had but just dispatched your servant, and was asking her nurse if I might be again admitted; who answered that she was dozing in the elbow-chair, having refused to lie down, saying she should soon, she hoped, lie down for good.

The colonel, who is really a fine gentleman, received me with great politeness. After the first compliments, My kinswoman, sir, said he, is more obliged to you than to any of her own family. For my part, I have been endeavouring to move so many rocks in her favour; and, little thinking the dear creature so very bad, have neglected to attend her, as I ought to have done the moment I arrived; and *would*, had I known how ill she was, and what a task I should have had with the family. But, sir, your friend has been excessively to blame; and you being so *intimately* his friend has made her fare the worse for your civilities to her. But are there no hopes of her recovery?

The doctors have left her, with the melancholy declaration that there are none.

Has she had good attendance, sir? A skilful physician? I hear these good folks have been very civil and obliging to her —

Who could be otherwise? said Mrs Smith, weeping. She is the sweetest lady in the world!

The character, said the colonel, lifting up his eyes and one hand, that she has from every living creature! Good God! How could your accursed friend —

And how could her cruel parents? interrupted I. We may as easily account for *him* as for *them*.

Too true! returned he, the vileness of the profligates of our sex considered, whenever they can get any of the other into their power.

I satisfied him about the care that had been taken of her; and told him of the friendly and even *paternal* attendance she had had from Dr H. and Mr Goddard.

He was impatient to attend her, having not seen her, as he said, since she was twelve years old; and that then she gave promises of being one of the finest women in England.

She *was* so, replied I, a very few months ago: and, though emaciated, she will appear to you to have confirmed those promises: for her features are so regular and exact, her proportion so fine, and her manner so inimitably graceful that, were she only skin and bone, she must be a beauty.

Mrs Smith, at his request, stepped up, and brought us down word that Mrs Lovick and her nurse were with her; and that she was in so sound a sleep, leaning upon the former in her elbow-chair, that she neither heard her enter the room nor go out. The colonel begged, if not improper, that he might see her, though sleeping. He said that his impatience would not let him stay till she awaked. Yet he would not have her disturbed; and should be glad to contemplate her sweet features, when she saw not him; and asked if she thought he could not go in and come out without disturbing her?

She believed he might, she answered; for her chair's back was towards the door.

He said he would take care to withdraw if she awoke, that his sudden appearance might not surprise her.

Mrs Smith, stepping up before us, bid Mrs Lovick and the nurse not stir when we entered: and then we went up softly together.

We beheld the lady in a charming attitude. Dressed, as I told you before, in her virgin white, she was sitting in her elbow-chair, Mrs Lovick close by her in another chair, with her left arm round her neck, supporting it, as it were; for, it seems, the lady had bid her do so, saying she had been a mother to her, and she would delight herself in thinking she was in her mamma's arms; for she found herself drowsy; perhaps, she said, for the last time she should ever be so.

One faded cheek rested upon the good woman's bosom, the kindly warmth of which had overspread it with a faint, but charming flush; the other paler and hollow as if already iced over by death. Her hands, white as the lily, with her meandering veins more transparently blue than ever I had seen even hers (veins so soon, alas! to be choked up by the congealment of that purple stream which already so languidly creeps rather than flows through them!); her hands hanging lifelessly, one before her, the other grasped by the right hand

of the kind widow, whose tears bedewed the sweet face which her
motherly bosom supported, though unfelt by the fair sleeper; and
either insensibly to the good woman, or what she would not disturb
her to wipe off, or to change her posture: her aspect was sweetly calm
and serene; and though she started now and then, yet her sleep
seemed easy; her breath indeed short and quick; but tolerably free,
and not like that of a dying person.

From Samuel Richardson, *Clarissa or, the History* of *a Young Lady* (1747–8).

Three Steps to Heaven

Heathcliff stood at the open door; he was pale, and he trembled; yet,
certainly, he had a strange joyful glitter in his eyes, that altered the
aspect of his whole face.

'Will you have some breakfast?' I said, 'You must be hungry,
rambling about all night!'

I wanted to discover where he had been; but I did not like to ask
directly.

'No, I'm not hungry,' he answered, averting his head, and
speaking rather contemptuously, as if he guessed I was trying to
divine the occasion of his good humour.

I felt perplexed – I didn't know whether it were not a proper
opportunity to offer a bit of admonition.

'I don't think it right to wander out of doors,' I observed, 'instead
of being in bed: it is not wise, at any rate, this moist season. I dare
say you'll catch a bad cold, or a fever – you have something the
matter with you now!'

'Nothing but what I can bear,' he replied, 'and with the greatest
pleasure, provided you'll leave me alone – get in, and don't annoy
me.'

I obeyed; and, in passing, I noticed he breathed as fast as a cat.

'Yes!' I reflected to myself, 'we shall have a fit of illness. I cannot
conceive what he has been doing!'

That noon, he sat down to dinner with us, and received a heaped-
up plate from my hands, as if he intended to make amends for
previous fasting.

'I've neither cold, nor fever, Nelly,' he remarked, in allusion to my morning's speech. 'And I'm ready to do justice to the food you give me.'

He took his knife and fork, and was going to commence eating, when the inclination appeared to become suddenly extinct. He laid them on the table, looked eagerly towards the window, then rose and went out.

We saw him walking, to and fro, in the garden, while we concluded our meal; and Earnshaw said he'd go, and ask why he would not dine; he thought we had grieved him some way.

'Well, is he coming?' cried Catherine, when her cousin returned.

'Nay,' he answered, 'but he's not angry; he seemed rare and pleased indeed; only, I made him impatient by speaking to him twice; and then he bid me be off to you; he wondered how I could want the company of any body else.'

I set his plate, to keep warm, on the fender: and after an hour or two, he re-entered, when the room was clear, in no degree calmer – the same unnatural – it was unnatural – appearance of joy under his black brows; the same bloodless hue: and his teeth visible, now and then, in a kind of smile; his frame shivering, not as one shivers with chill or weakness, but as a tight-stretched cord vibrates – a strong thrilling, rather than trembling.

I will ask what is the matter, I thought, or who should? And I exclaimed –

'Have you heard any good news, Mr Heathcliff? You look uncommonly animated.'

'Where should good news come from, to me?' he said. 'I'm animated with hunger, and, seemingly, I must not eat.'

'Your dinner is here,' I returned; 'why won't you get it?'

'I don't want it now,' he muttered, hastily. 'I'll wait till supper. And, Nelly, once for all, let me beg you to warn Hareton and the other away from me. I wish to be troubled by nobody – I wish to have this place to myself.'

'Is there some new reason for this banishment?' I inquired. 'Tell me why you are so queer, Mr Heathcliff? Where were you last night? I'm not putting the question through idle curiosity, but –'

'You are putting the question through very idle curiosity,' he interrupted, with a laugh. 'Yet, I'll answer it. Last night, I was on the threshold of hell. To-day, I am within sight of my heaven – I have my eyes on it – hardly three feet to sever me! And now you'd better go – You'll neither see nor hear anything to frighten you, if you refrain from prying.'

Having swept the hearth, and wiped the table, I departed more perplexed than ever.

He did not quit the house again that afternoon, and no one intruded on his solitude, till, at eight o'clock I deemed it proper, though unsummoned, to carry a candle, and his supper to him.

He was leaning against the ledge of an open lattice, but not looking out; his face was turned to the interior gloom. The fire had smouldered to ashes; the room was filled with the damp, mild air of the cloudy evening, and so still, that not only the murmur of the beck down Gimmerton was distinguishable, but its ripples and its gurgling over the pebbles, or through the large stones which it could not cover.

I uttered an ejaculation of discontent at seeing the dismal grate, and commenced shutting the casements, one after another, till I came to his.

'Must I close this?' I asked, in order to rouse him, for he would not stir.

The light flashed on his features, as I spoke. Oh, Mr Lockwood, I cannot express what a terrible start I got, by the momentary view! Those deep black eyes! That smile, and ghastly paleness! It appeared to me, not Mr Heathcliff, but a goblin; and, in my terror, I let the candle bend towards the wall, and it left me in darkness.

'Yes, close it,' he replied, in his familiar voice. 'There, that is pure awkwardness! Why did you hold the candle horizontally? Be quick, and bring another.'

I hurried out in a foolish state of dread, and said to Joseph –

'The master wishes you to take him a light and rekindle the fire.' For I dare not go in myself again just then.

Joseph rattled some fire into the shovel, and went; but he brought it back, immediately, with the supper tray in his other hand, explaining that Mr Heathcliff was going to bed, and he wanted nothing to eat till morning.

We heard him mount the stairs directly; he did not proceed to his ordinary chamber, but turned into that with the panelled bed – its window, as I mentioned before, is wide enough for anybody to get through, and it struck me, that he plotted another midnight excursion, which he had rather we had no suspicion of.

'Is he a ghoul, or a vampire?' I mused. I had read of such hideous, incarnate demons. And then, I set myself to reflect, how I had tended him in infancy; and watched him grow to youth; and followed him almost through his whole course; and what absurd nonsense it was to yield to that sense of horror.

'But where did he come from, the little dark thing, harboured by a good man to his bane?' muttered superstition, as I dozed into unconsciousness. And I began, half dreaming, to weary myself with imaging some fit parentage for him; and repeating my waking meditations, I tracked his existence over again, with grim variations; at last, picturing his death and funeral; of which, all I can remember is, being exceedingly vexed at having the task of dictating an inscription for his monument, and consulting the sexton about it; and, as he had no surname, and we could not tell his age, we were obliged to content ourselves with the single word, 'Heathcliff'. That came true; we were. If you enter the kirkyard, you'll read on his headstone only that, and the date of his death.

Dawn restored me to common sense. I rose, and went into the garden, as soon as I could see, to ascertain if there were any footmarks under his window. There were none.

'He has stayed at home,' I thought, 'and he'll be all right, to-day!'

I prepared breakfast for the household, as was my usual custom, but told Hareton, and Catherine to get theirs, ere the master came down, for he lay late. They preferred taking it out of doors, under the trees, and I set a little table to accommodate them.

On my re-entrance, I found Mr Heathcliff below. He and Joseph were conversing about some farming business; he gave clear, minute directions concerning the matter discussed, but he spoke rapidly, and turned his head continually aside, and had the same excited expression, even more exaggerated.

When Joseph quitted the room, he took his seat in the place he generally chose, and I put a basin of coffee before him. He drew it nearer, and then rested his arms on the table, and looked at the opposite wall, as I supposed, surveying one particular portion, up and down with glittering, restless eyes, and with such eager interest, that he stopped breathing, during half a minute together.

'Come now,' I exclaimed, pushing some bread against his hand. 'Eat and drink that, while it is hot. It has been waiting near an hour.'

He didn't notice me, and yet he smiled. I'd rather have seen him gnash his teeth than smile so.

'Mr Heathcliff! master!' I cried. 'Don't, for God's sake, stare as if you saw an unearthly vision.'

'Don't, for God's sake, shout so loud,' he replied. 'Turn round, and tell me, are we by ourselves?'

'Of course,' was my answer, 'of course, we are!'

Still, I involuntarily obeyed him, as if I were not quite sure.

With a sweep of his hand, he cleared a vacant space in front among the breakfast things, and leant forward to gaze more at his ease.

Now, I perceived he was not looking at the wall, for when I regarded him alone, it seemed, exactly, that he gazed at something within two yards distance. And, whatever it was, it communicated, apparently, both pleasure and pain, in exquisite extremes, at least the anguished, yet raptured expression of his countenance suggested that idea.

The fancied object was not fixed, either; his eyes pursued it with unwearied vigilance; and, even in speaking to me, were never weaned away.

I vainly reminded him of his protracted abstinence from food: if he stirred to touch anything in compliance with my entreaties, if he stretched his hand out to get a piece of bread, his fingers clenched, before they reached it, and remained on the table, forgetful of their aim.

I sat a model of patience, trying to attract his absorbed attention from its engrossing speculation; till he grew irritable, and got up asking, why I would not allow him to have his own time in taking his meals? and saying that, on the next occasion, I needn't wait, I might set the things down, and go.

Having uttered these words, he left the house, slowly sauntered down the garden path, and disappeared through the gate.

The hours crept anxiously by: another evening came. I did not retire to rest till late, and when I did, I could not sleep. He returned after midnight, and, instead of going to bed, shut himself into the room beneath. I listened, and tossed about; and, finally, dressed, and descended. It was too irksome to lie up there, harassing my brain with a hundred idle misgivings.

I distinguished Mr Heathcliff's step, restlessly measuring the floor; and he frequently broke the silence by a deep inspiration, resembling a groan. He muttered detached words, also; the only one I could catch was the name of Catherine, coupled with some wild term of endearment, or suffering; and spoken as one would speak to a person present – low and earnest, and wrung from the depth of his soul.

I had not courage to walk straight into the apartment; but I desired to divert him from his reverie, and, therefore, fell foul of the kitchen fire; stirred it, and began to scrape the cinders. It drew him forth sooner than I expected. He opened the door immediately, and said –

'Nelly, come here – is it morning? Come in with your light.'

'It is striking four,' I answered; 'you want a candle to take upstairs – you might have lit one at this fire.'

'No, I don't wish to go upstairs,' he said. 'Come in, and kindle *me* a fire, and do anything there is to do about the room.'

'I must blow the coals red first, before I can carry any,' I replied, getting a chair and the bellows.

He roamed to and fro, meantime, in a state approaching distraction: his heavy sighs succeeding each other so thick as to leave no space for common breathing between.

'When day breaks, I'll send for Green,' he said; 'I wish to make some legal inquiries of him, while I can bestow a thought on those matters, and while I can act calmly. I have not written my will yet, and how to leave my property, I cannot determine! I wish I could annihilate it from the face of the earth.'

'I would not talk so, Mr Heathcliff,' I interposed. 'Let your will be, a while – you'll be spared to repent of your many injustices, yet! I never expected that your nerves would be disordered – they are, at present, marvellously so, however, and almost entirely, through your own fault. The way you've passed these three last days might knock up a Titan. Do take some food, and some repose. You need only look at yourself, in a glass, to see how you require both. Your cheeks are hollow, and your eyes blood-shot like a person starving with hunger, and going blind with loss of sleep.'

'It is not my fault, that I cannot eat or rest,' he replied. 'I assure you it is through no settled designs. I'll do both, as soon as I possibly can. But you might as well bid a man struggling in the water, rest within arm's length of the shore! I must reach it first, and then I'll rest. Well, never mind, Mr Green: as to repenting of my injustices, I've done no injustice, and I repent of nothing – I'm too happy, and yet I'm not happy enough. My Soul's bliss kills my body, but does not satisfy itself.'

'Happy, master?' I cried. 'Strange happiness! If you would hear me without being angry, I might offer some advice that would make you happier.'

'What is that?' he asked. 'Give it.'

'You are aware, Mr Heathcliff,' I said, 'that from the time you were thirteen years old, you have lived a selfish, unchristian life; and probably hardly had a Bible in your hands, during all that period.

You must have forgotten the contents of the book, and you may not have space to search it now. Could it be hurtful to send for some one – some minister of any denomination, it does not matter which, to explain it, and show you how very far you have erred from its precepts, and how unfit you will be for its heaven, unless a change takes place before you die?'

'I'm rather obliged than angry, Nelly,' he said, 'for you remind me of the manner that I desire to be buried in – It is to be carried to the churchyard, in the evening. You and Hareton may, if you please, accompany me – and mind, particularly, to notice that the sexton obeys my directions concerning the two coffins! No minister need come; nor need anything be said over me – I tell you, I have nearly attained *my* heaven; and that of others is altogether unvalued, and uncoveted by me!'

'And supposing you persevered in your obstinate fast, and died by that means, and they refused to bury you in the precincts of the Kirk?' I said, shocked at his godless indifference. 'How would you like it?'

'They won't do that,' he replied: 'if they did, you must have me removed secretly; and if you neglect it, you shall prove, practically, that the dead are not annihilated!'

As soon as he heard the other members of the family stirring he retired to his den, and I breathed freer – But in the afternoon, while Joseph and Hareton were at their work, he came into the kitchen again, and with a wild look, bid me come, and sit in the house – he wanted somebody with him.

I declined, telling him plainly, that his strange talk and manner frightened me, and I had neither the nerve, nor the will to be his companion, alone.

'I believe you think me a fiend!' he said, with his dismal laugh, 'something too horrible to live under a decent roof!'

Then turning to Catherine, who was there, and who drew behind me at his approach, he added, half sneeringly –

'Will *you* come, chuck? I'll not hurt you. No! to you, I've made myself worse than the devil. Well, there is *one* who won't shrink from my company! By God! she's relentless. Oh, damn it! It's unutterably too much for flesh and blood to bear, even mine.'

He solicited the society of no one more. At dusk, he went into his chamber – through the whole night, and far into the morning, we heard him groaning, and murmuring to himself. Hareton was anxious to enter, but I bid him fetch Mr Kenneth, and he should go in, and see him.

When he came, and I requested admittance and tried to open the door, I found it locked; and Heathcliff bid us be damned. He was better, and would be left alone; so the doctor went away.

The following evening was very wet, indeed it poured down, till day-dawn; and, as I took my morning walk round the house, I observed the master's window swinging open, and the rain driving straight in.

He cannot be in bed, I thought, those showers would drench him through! He must either be up, or out. But, I'll make no more ado, I'll go boldly, and look!

Having succeeded in obtaining entrance with another key, I ran to unclose the panels, for the chamber was vacant – quickly pushing them aside, I peeped in. Mr Heathcliff was there – laid on his back. His eyes met mine so keen, and fierce, I started; and then, he seemed to smile.

I could not think him dead – but his face and throat were washed with rain; the bed-clothes dripped, and he was perfectly still. The lattice, flapping to and fro, had grazed one hand that rested on the sill – no blood trickled from the broken skin, and when I put my fingers to it, I could doubt no more – he was dead and stark!

I hasped the window; I combed his black long hair from his forehead; I tried to close his eyes – to extinguish, if possible, that frightful, life-like gaze of exultation, before any one else beheld it. They would not shut – they seemed to sneer at my attempts, and his parted lips, and sharp, white teeth sneered too! Taken with another fit of cowardice, I cried out for Joseph. Joseph shuffled up, and made a noise, but resolutely refused to meddle with him.

'Th' divil's harried off his soul,' he cried, 'and he muh hev his carcass intuh t' bargin, for ow't Aw care! Ech! what a wicked un he looks girnning at death!' and the old sinner grinned in mockery.

From Emily Brontë, *Wuthering Heights* (1847).

Cold Comfort

But did you feel that you had to maintain the public image of a successful Princess of Wales?
Yes I did, yes I did.

[64]

The depression was resolved, as you say, but it was subsequently reported that you suffered bulimia. Is that true?

Yes, I did. I had bulimia for a number of years. And that's like a secret disease. You inflict it upon yourself because your self-esteem is at a low ebb, and you don't think you're worthy or valuable. You fill your stomach up four or five times a day – some do it more – and it gives you a feeling of comfort. It's like having a pair of arms around you, but it's temporary.

How often would you do that on a daily basis?

Depends on the pressures going on. If I'd been on what I call an awayday, or I'd been up part of the country all day, I'd come home feeling pretty empty, because my engagements at that time would be to do with people dying, people very sick, people's marriage problems, and I'd come home and it would be very difficult to know how to comfort myself having been comforting lots of other people, so it would be a regular pattern to jump into the fridge. It was a symptom of what was going on in my marriage. I was crying out for help but giving the wrong signals and people were using my bulimia as a coat on a hanger: they decided that was the problem – Diana was unstable.

Instead of looking behind the symptom at the cause.

Yes.

What was the cause?

The cause was the situation where my husband and I had to keep everything together because we didn't want to disappoint the public, and yet obviously there was a lot of anxiety.

Do you mean between the two of you?

Yes.

And so you subjected yourself to this phase of bingeing and vomiting?

You could say the word subjected, but it was my escape mechanism, and it worked, for me, at that time.

Did you seek help from any other members of the royal family?

No. When you have bulimia, you're very ashamed of yourself and you hate yourself – and people think you're wasting food – so you don't discuss it with people. And the thing about bulimia is your weight always stays the same, whereas with anorexia you visibly shrink. So you can pretend the whole way through. There's no proof.

When you say people would think you were wasting food, did anybody suggest that to you?

Oh yes, a number of times.

What was said?

Well, it was just, 'I suppose you're going to waste that food later on?' And that was pressure in itself. And of course I would, because it was my release valve.

How long did this bulimia go on for?

A long time, a long time. But I'm free of it now.

Two years, three years?

Mmm. A little bit more than that.

From interview with the Princess of Wales, *Panorama*, 20 November 1995.

Forgetting to Eat

Shelley came of a long-lived race, and, barring accidents, there was no reason why he should not have emulated his forefathers in attaining a ripe age. He had no other complaint than occasional spasms, and these were probably caused by the excessive and almost unremitting strain on his mental powers, the solitude of his life, and his long fasts, which were not intentional, but proceeded from the abstraction and forgetfulness of himself and his wife. If food was near him, he ate it, – if not, he fasted, and it was after long fasts that he suffered from spasms.

From, E. J. Trewlawny, *Recollections of the Last Days of Shelley and Byron* (1858).

Denying the Body

Both anorectics and compulsive eaters binge and starve themselves. However, the anorectic starves for long periods subsisting on as little as an egg and a cookie a day and only occasionally bursting out into a binge which is then purified by even more rigorous fasting or cleansing by laxatives, vomiting or enemas. This bird-like eating is a reflection of a culture that praises thinness and fragility in women. Many women pinpoint the onset of their anorexia as an exaggerated response to dieting and teenage ideals of femininity. As with compulsive eaters, sensing something amiss at adolescence, they sought the answer in their individual biology. Their bodies were changing, becoming curvy and fuller, taking on the shape of a woman. They were changing in a way over which they had no control – they did not know whether they would be small breasted and large hipped or whether their bodies would eventually end up as the teenagers in *Seventeen*.

These upheavals rendered in these young women feelings of confusion, fear and powerlessness. Their changing bodies were associated with a changing position in their worlds at home, at school and with their friends. A curvy body meant the adoption of a teenage girl's sexual identity. This is the time for intense interest in appearance, the time when girls learn the tortuous lesson about not revealing their true selves to boys whether on the tennis court or in school, or in discussing affairs of the heart. These new rules and regulations governing behavior, and the explosive changes taking place are quite out of tune with what has previously been learned and the feelings they generate are enormously complicated. Several women have said on looking back on this time in their lives – a time when they were growing and yet effectively stopped eating – that they felt so out of phase with all that was going on that withdrawal from food was an immensely satisfying way to be in control of the situation. In transcending hunger pangs they were winning in one area of the struggle with their apparently independently developing bodies. They were attempting to gain control over their shapes and their physical needs. They felt their power in their ability to ignore their hunger.

From Susie Orbach, *Fat is a Feminist Issue* (1978).

The Beggar's Banquet

My sixth brother, he who had both his lips cut off, Prince of the Faithful, is called Shakashik.

In his youth he was very poor. One day, as he was begging in the streets of Baghdad, he passed by a splendid mansion, at the gates of which stood an impressive array of attendants. Upon inquiry my brother was informed that the house belonged to a member of the wealthy and powerful Barmecide family. Shakashik approached the door-keepers and solicited alms.

'Go in,' they said, 'and our master will give you all that you desire.'

My brother entered the lofty vestibule and proceeded to a spacious, marble-paved hall, hung with tapestry and over-looking a beautiful garden. He stood bewildered for a moment, not knowing where to turn his steps, and then advanced to the far end of the hall. There, among the cushions, reclined a handsome old man with a long beard, whom my brother recognized at once as the master of the house.

'What can I do for you, my friend?' asked the old man, as he rose to welcome my brother.

When Shakashik replied that he was a hungry beggar, the old man expressed the deepest compassion and rent his fine robes, crying: 'Is it possible that there should be a man as hungry as yourself in a city where I am living? It is, indeed, a disgrace that I cannot endure!' Then he comforted my brother, adding: 'I insist that you stay with me and partake of my dinner.'

With this the master of the house clapped his hands and called out to one of the slaves: 'Bring in the basin and ewer.' Then he said to my brother: 'Come forward, my friend, and wash your hands.'

Shakashik rose to do so, but saw neither ewer nor basin. He was bewildered to see his host make gestures as though he were pouring water on his hands from an invisible vessel and then drying them with an invisible towel. When he finished, the host called out to his attendants: 'Bring in the table!'

Numerous servants hurried in and out of the hall, as though they were preparing for a meal. My brother could still see nothing. Yet his host invited him to sit at the imaginary table, saying: 'Honour me by eating of this meat.'

The old man moved his hands about as though he were touching invisible dishes, and also moved his jaws and lips as though he were chewing. Then said he to Shakashik: 'Eat your fill, my friend, for you must be famished.'

My brother began to move his jaws, to chew and swallow, as though he were eating, while the old man still coaxed him, saying: 'Eat, my friend, and note the excellence of this bread and its whiteness.'

'This man,' thought Shakashik, 'must be fond of practical jokes.' So he said: 'It is, sir, the whitest bread I have ever seen, and I have never tasted the like in all my life.'

'This bread,' said the host, 'was baked by a slave-girl whom I bought for five hundred dinars.' Then he called out to one of his slaves: 'Bring in the meat-pudding, and let there be plenty of fat in it!'

Turning to my brother, the old man continued: 'By Allah, my friend, have you ever tasted anything better than this meat-pudding? Now, on my life, you must eat and not be abashed!'

Presently he cried out again: 'Serve up the stewed grouse!' And again he said to Shakashik: 'Eat your fill, my friend, for you must be very hungry.'

My brother moved his jaws, and chewed, and swallowed, while the old man called for one imaginary dish after another, and pressed his guest to eat. Then the host cried out: 'Serve up the chickens stuffed with pistachio nuts,' and turned to Shakashik, saying: 'Eat, for you have never tasted anything like these chickens!'

'Sir,' replied my brother, 'they are indeed incomparably delicious.'

Thereupon the host moved his fingers as though to pick up a morsel from an imaginary dish, and popped the invisible delicacy into my brother's mouth.

The old man continued to enlarge upon the excellences of the various dishes, while my brother became so ravenously hungry that he would have willingly died for a crust of barley-bread.

'Have you ever tasted anything more delicious,' went on the old man, 'than the spices in these dishes?'

'Never, indeed,' replied Shakashik.

'Eat heartily, then,' said his host, 'and do not be ashamed!'

'I thank you, sir,' answered Shakashik, 'but I have already eaten my fill.'

'Bring in the dessert!' cried the master of the house, and then said to my brother: 'Taste this excellent pastry; eat of these fritters: take this one before the syrup drips out of it!'

Shakashik helped himself to the imperceptible dainty, and, clicking his tongue with delight, remarked upon the abundance of musk in it.

'Yes,' agreed the old man, 'I always insist on a dinar-weight of musk in each fritter, and half that quantity of ambergris.'

My brother continued to move his jaws and lips and to roll his tongue between his cheeks, as though he were enjoying the sumptuous feast.

'Eat of these roasted almonds, and walnuts, and raisins,' said the old man.

'I can eat no more,' replied my brother.

'By Allah,' repeated the host, 'you must eat, and not remain hungry!'

'Sir,' protested Shakashik, 'how can one remain hungry after eating all these dishes?'

My suffering brother considered the manner in which his host was making game of him, and thought: 'By Allah, I will do something that will make him repent of his pranks!'

Presently, however, the old man clapped his hands again and cried: 'Bring in the wine!'

Numerous slaves ran in, moving their hands about as though they were setting wine and cups before their master and his guest. The old man pretended to pour wine into the cups, and to hand one to my brother. 'Take this,' he said, 'and tell me how you like it.'

'Sir,' said Shakashik, 'your generosity overwhelms me!' He lifted the invisible cup to his lips, and made as if to drain it at one gulp.

'Health and joy to you!' exclaimed the old man, as he pretended to pour himself some wine and drink it off. He handed another cup to his guest, and they both continued to act in this fashion until Shakashik, feigning himself drunk, began to roll his head from side to side. Then, taking his bounteous host unawares, he suddenly raised his arm so high that the white of his armpit could be seen, and dealt him a blow on the neck which made the hall echo with the sound. And this he followed by a second blow.

The old man rose in anger and cried: 'What are you doing, vile creature?'

'Sir,' replied my brother, 'you have received your humble slave into your house and loaded him with your generosity; you have fed him with the choicest food and quenched his thirst with the most potent wines. Alas, he became drunk, and forgot his manners! But you are so noble, sir, that you will surely pardon his offence.'

When he heard these words, the old man burst out laughing, and said: 'For a long time I have jested with all types of men, but no one has ever had the patience or the wit to enter into my humours as you have done. Now, therefore, I pardon you, and ask you in truth to eat and drink with me, and to be my companion as long as I live.'

Then the old man ordered his attendants to serve all the dishes which they had consumed in fancy, and when he and my brother had eaten their fill they repaired to the drinking-chamber, where beautiful young women sang and made music. The old Barmecide gave Shakashik a robe of honour and made him his constant companion.

From 'The Tale of Shakashik, the Barber's Sixth Brother', *Tales from the Thousand and One Nights*, medieval, collected late eighteenth century, and translated by N.J. Dawood.

Hunger Strike

The next morning I measured out rice from the sack, picked it over, and cooked it along with the broth, the meat and the vegetables, then had a bath and put on my dress, and my abaya and veil. My throat muscles tightened as they did whenever I rebelled and did what I wanted to do. As I shut the door behind me I called out, 'The food's ready and I'm off to the Institute.' I walked along determinedly in my thick abaya, my throat growing tighter and my palms sweating. Only once I looked back towards the house and saw that its iron door was closed. I didn't notice the heat, or my sweat, or the distance. Instead I concentrated on the obstacles in my path which forced me to cross from one side of the street to the other – heaps of stone and steel beams and mounds of sand left lying about the streets. I couldn't see the Institute building, but it didn't matter. I heard a car horn and stopped myself turning round, drawing my abaya more closely round me and wrapping the black head cover twice round my face. A car horn, and Rashid's voice calling to me. I turned then; he'd opened the back door for me. I stood where I was for a moment but my thoughts were a jumble. I climbed into the back seat and Rashid didn't speak the entire way home. Gradually my throat muscles relaxed, and as I sat in silence I decided to go on hunger strike. When my mother and Batul pleaded with me for the sake of my son Muhammad, I agreed to drink a little tea without sugar, but I ate nothing for three days.

On the fourth day I felt weak and tired. As I lay in bed, I heard my mother saying, 'Are the Institute and books worth getting yourself in this state for?' Batul persuaded Rashid to come in and see me just before the evening prayer and I was confident that my fast must soon be over. In a voice which sounded as if he was making an effort to be kind he said, 'What are you doing to yourself, Tamr?' 'I want to go to the Institute and get educated,' I answered tearfully. His reply was quite unexpected, and I didn't believe it until he repeated it: 'You're not going to the Institute.' 'Then I won't eat,' I said firmly. He went out of the room and I thought I heard him saying, 'As you wish.' I no longer thought about anything. From time to time I opened my eyes. I could hear my mother crying, Batul screaming, and I seemed to see my mother striking her face with the palms of her hands. Batul's children kept asking questions and one of her daughters said, 'Auntie Tamr's going to die!'

Batul appeared annoyed at the strength of my resistance. She came in and made me sit up and tried to force a piece of apple between my teeth without success. I needed all my strength to move my face away and I began turning my head rapidly from one side to the other. My mother eased me back on to the pillow and laid her hand on my forehead reciting prayers. Raised voices echoed off the walls and ceilings. Batul's voice called out, 'Listen to me, Rashid. I swear to God you won't come near me and you're not my lawful husband unless you personally take Tamr to the Institute. Can you hear me, everybody?' My mother walked around with the incense burner in her hand, wailing and crying. She came towards my bed: 'Batul and your brother are fighting and who knows, they might divorce, all because you won't give up the idea of the Institute. Those English have had an effect on you. They must have put a spell on you and poisoned your mind. Tamr, my daughter, get up and ask God's pardon. Batul and your brother are going to get a divorce.'

My muscles went limp and I no longer seemed to have any interest in what the voices were saying. Batul and my mother came to sit me up, so that I'd be able to face in the right direction and say my prayers, but I couldn't. They stayed with me all night long, pleading with me in the name of the Almighty, kissing me then screaming at me, trying to force my jaws open. They managed to get a spoon in but half the soup dribbled down my chin and on to my neck. I shouted at them but my voice came out strangely weak: 'If anybody makes me eat I'll never forgive them and God won't either.' Batul shouted back, 'My God, you don't love anyone except yourself. I thought you and I were like sisters.'

I opened my eyes and I was frightened. The room was in silence. They must have all wearied of trying to convince me. I don't know how much time had gone by but suddenly Batul rushed in kissing me and crying, 'Congratulations,' followed by my mother who was trilling for joy and singing, 'O Tamr, O Tamr, you're going to the Institute by car and you'll come back reading and writing.' I was tired, but even so I struggled into a sitting position, propping myself up with pillows. I opened my mouth to eat without the faintest desire, as if I'd lost my taste for food. Batul reported to me that Rashid had begun to sleep in the sitting-room, took no notice of her, and had stopped speaking to her. Her annoyance had prompted her to march into the sitting-room full of men that afternoon and fling herself at his feet kissing them and weeping. 'Forgive your sister, Rashid; God is forgiving. Knowledge is light. Fatima the Prophet's daughter could express herself eloquently and read and write.'

Rashid had been deeply discomfited. His face became the colour of blood. There and then he found the courage to agree. Everyone in the room knew about his refusal and his sister's fast. In front of them all Batul had knelt at his feet and invoked the Prophet's daughter. He raised her face from his feet and said, 'Be happy, Umm Ashraf. You can tell my sister to stop fasting.'

From Hanan Al-Shaykh, *Women of Sand and Myrrh* (1989), translated by
Catherine Cobham.

Teen Dreams

It is dead easy to become an anorexic. When I was 12 I went to visit an older, voluptuous cousin. 'I try,' she said, to explain the deep-breathing exercises she did before bedtime, 'to visualize my belly as something I can love and accept and live with.' Still compact in a one-piece kid's body, I was alarmed to think that womanhood involved breaking apart into pieces that floated around, since my cousin seemed to be trying to hold herself together by a feat of concentration. It was not a comforting thought. The buds of my breasts hurt already. As she did her exercises I leafed through a copy of *Cosmopolitan*, which had an article demonstrating to women how to undress and pose and move in bed with their partner so as to disguise their fatness.

My cousin looked me over. 'Do you know how much you weigh?' No, I told her. 'Why don't you just hop on the scale?' I could feel how much my cousin wished to inhabit a simple, slight 12-year-old body. That could only mean, I thought, that when I was a woman, I would want to get out of my own body into some little kid's.

A year later, while bent over the drinking fountain in the hall of my junior high school, Bobby Werner, whom I hardly knew, gave me a hard poke in the soft part of my stomach, just below the navel. It would be a decade before I would remember that he was the class fat boy.

That evening I let the juice of the lamb chop congeal on my plate. I could see viscous nodules of fat, a charred outer edge of yellow matter, cooling from liquid to solid, marked USDA CHOICE in edible blue dye. The centre bone, serrated, was cloven with a powerful rotary blade. I felt a new feeling, a nausea wicked with the pleasure of loathing. Rising hungry from the table, a jet of self-righteousness lit up under my oesophagus, intoxicating me. All night long I inhaled it.

The next day I passed the small notepad kept by the dishwasher. I knew what it said, though it was my mother's and private: $1/_2$ *grpfruit. Blk coff. 4 Wheat Thins. 1 popsicle.* A black scrawl: *binge*. I wanted to tear it up. Some memoir.

I had no more patience for the trivial confessions of women. I could taste from my mouth that my body had entered ketosis, imbalanced electrolytes; good. The girl stood on the burning deck. I put the dishes in the sink with a crash of declaration.

At 13, I was taking in the caloric equivalent of the food energy allotted to the famine victims of the siege of Paris. I did my schoolwork diligently and kept quiet in the classroom. I was a wind-up obedience toy. Not a teacher or principal or guidance counsellor confronted me with an objection to my evident deportation in stages from the land of the living.

There were many starving girls in my junior high school, and every one was a teacher's paragon. We were allowed to come and go, racking up gold stars, as our hair fell out in fistfuls and the pads flattened behind the sockets of our eyes. When our eyeballs moved, we felt the resistance. They allowed us to haul our bones around the swinging rope in gym class, where nothing but the force of an exhausted will stood between the ceiling, to which we clung with hands so wasted the jute seemed to abrade the cartilage itself, and the polished wooden floor thirty-five feet below.

An alien voice took mine over. I have never been so soft-spoken. It lost expression and timbre and sank to a monotone, a dull murmur the opposite of strident. My teachers approved of me. They saw nothing wrong with what I was doing, and I could swear they looked straight at me. My school had stopped dissecting alley cats, since it was considered inhumane. There was no interference in my self-directed science experiment: to find out just how little food could keep a human body alive.

The dreams I could muster were none of the adolescent visions that boys have, or free and healthy girls; no fantasies of sex or escape, rebellion or future success. All the space I had for dreaming was taken up by food. When I lay on my bed, in that posture of adolescent reverie, I could find no comfort. My bones pressed sharply into the mattress. My ribs were hooks and my spine a dull blade and my hunger a heavy shield, all I had to stave off the trivialities that would attach themselves like parasites to my body the minute it made a mis-step into the world of women. My doctor put his hand on my stomach and said he could feel my spine. I turned an eye cold with loathing on women who evidently lacked the mettle to suffer as I was suffering.

From Naomi Wolf, *The Beauty Myth* (1990).

Raiding the Fridge

Over the years royal staff and her friends have been puzzled by Diana's appetite, particularly as she always appeared to be so slim. She was frequently found raiding the refrigerator at Highgrove late in the evening and once startled a footman by eating an entire steak and kidney pie when she was staying at Windsor Castle. Her friend Rory Scott remembers her eating a 1lb bag of sweets in short order during a bridge evening while her admission that she ate a bowl of custard before she went to bed added to the perplexity concerning her diet.

In fact virtually from the moment she became the Princess of Wales, Diana has suffered from bulimia nervosa which helps to explain her erratic dietary behaviour. As Carolyn Bartholomew, who has been instrumental in convincing Diana to seek medical help, observes: 'It's been there through her royal career, without a doubt. I hate to say it but I feel that it may erupt when she feels under pressure.' Bulimia, according to a recent Drug and Therapeutics bulletin from the Consumers' Association is suffered by around two per cent of young women in Britain. These women indulge in episodes of massive overeating associated with a sense of loss of control. Between episodes of eating most sufferers fast or induce vomiting. Binges tend to be secret, sometimes pre-planned and are often followed by strong mood swings expressed as guilt, depression, self-hate and even suicidal behaviour. Sufferers usually have a normal body weight but see themselves as being fat, bloated and ugly. This dislike of their bodies leads to fasting between the episodes of overeating and sufferers commonly have a sense of failure, low self-esteem and loss of control. Muscle cramps, kidney and even heart failure are the physical results of prolonged bulimia.

Unlike anorexia nervosa, bulimia survives by disguise. It is a sophisticated illness in as much as sufferers do not admit that they have a problem. They always appear to be happy and spend their lives trying to help others. Yet there is rage beneath the sunny smile, anger which sufferers are afraid to express. Women in the caring professions such as nursing and nannying are particularly prone to the illness. They see their own needs as greed and subsequently feel guilty about caring for themselves. That disgust is translated into violent purging by vomiting or laxatives. As the medical bulletin concludes: 'Bulimia nervosa is a serious, under recognized, potentially chronic and occasionally fatal disorder affecting many young women but rarely men.'

While the roots of both bulimia and anorexia lie in childhood and a disordered family background, uncertainty and anxiety in adult life provide the trigger for the illness. For Diana, the last few months had been an emotional rollercoaster as she had tried to come to terms with her new life as a public figure and the suffocating publicity as well as her husband's ambiguous behaviour towards her. It was an explosive cocktail and it took just one spark to bring on her illness. On one occasion, as the wedding day drew near, Charles put his arm around her waist and commented on what he considered to be her chubby figure. It was an innocent enough remark but it triggered something inside her. Shortly afterwards she made herself sick. It was a profound release of tension and in some hazy way gave her a sense of control over herself and a means of releasing the anger she felt.

From Andrew Morton, *Diana: Her True Story* (1992).

A Civil War

Anorexia is not, of course, a slimmers' disease. It is not a way of starving yourself to death. It is a way of coping with life. It is a means of gaining control in one highly visible area when on every other issue you appear powerless.

You are not only powerless, you are worthless, bad, too demanding. You set standards of perfection at which you constantly fail –

except in the denial of hunger. In a logical extension of the message 'We are what we eat,' the anorexic eats almost nothing.

At 18, and five foot five, I weighed nine and half stone. I was at university. One Saturday, I walked down the street, wearing what I thought was a particularly fetching bum-hugging lime green psyche-delic number. A labourer shouted: 'Fatty!'

A year later, in 1969, I weighed just over five stone. It took about 15 years for me to treat food with less neurosis than my 'normal' friends. Now, I almost trust my appetite. Almost.

What the anorexia is trying to zap, of course, isn't fat, it's her (and his) feelings. Feelings never go away, but they can be subsumed by the struggle to eat less and less.

'What do you remember about the sixties, Mum?' my 10-year-old daughter asks. If honest, I should say: 'Fifty calories in half a banana.'

'Anorexia is civil war,' explains Jill Welbourne. 'A civil war between mind and body. If the mind wins, the body dies.'

Anorexics may suffer from low blood pressure and osteoporosis, coldness, epileptic fits and sores, their periods stop, they risk infertility, they may develop a downy fuzz. Their hearts can fail. Anorexia rarely appears on a death certificate but a very conservative estimate is that 10 per cent of anorexics die.

'I only ever wanted to look nice,' says Diana, 19 and anorexic for seven years. 'Now I look worse than ever. I've got terrible skin, I'm losing my hair. My mother is very critical. She says that it's my own fault and I should hurry up and do something about it. My dad's had enough.'

One assessment of the extent of the problem is that 2 per cent of young women and 0.2 per cent of young men may be anorexic or bulimic. The true numbers are probably far higher since deception is part of the anorexic's repertoire. How many become stable without help, as I did? No one knows. (A number of young sufferers said they'd welcome a telephone hotline to recovered anorexics.)

Anorexia is starved of resources, training, research. It requires better coverage of the issue – not least children affected by the disease.

In my case, my GP suggested I was suffering from diabetes, then lost interest. My mother, with whom I now have a good relationship, was hypercritical and controlling. Food was part of her power. When I starved, I went on strike against her. Stuff your food, was the message.

I gradually realised my mother had been wounded by her own mother's inability to value herself and her children. Anorexia made me acknowledge the chain and try to break it. I would have preferred an easier way.

From Yvonne Roberts, 'Bad to the Bone', *Guardian* (14 August 1995).

A Freak Show

A big circus with its vast numbers of people, animals, and items of equipment forever balancing and supplementing one another can find a use for anybody at any time, even a fasting-artist – if suitably modest in his requirements, of course – on top of which, in this particular instance it was not only the fasting-artist himself who was being engaged but also his long-famous name; indeed, it being a peculiarity of this art that a practitioner's skills do not diminish with advancing age, one could not even say that this was a case of a superannuated artist, past his prime, seeking refuge in a leisurely circus job; on the contrary, the fasting-artist declared – and there was every reason to believe him – that he was fasting as well as ever, in fact he even claimed that, if they let him have his way – as they had no hesitation in promising to do – the day was yet to come when he would really give the world something to wonder at, although in view of the mood of the time, which in his enthusiasm the fasting-artist was prone to overlook, this claim of his provoked no more than a smile from the experts.

Deep down, however, even the fasting-artist retained his sense of proportion, accepting as perfectly natural the fact that he and his cage were not, for example, given star billing and put in the centre of the ring but were placed outside in what was nevertheless a most accessible position in the vicinity of the stables. Large, brightly-painted signs surrounded the cage, announcing what was to be seen there. When during the intervals the audience thronged towards the stables to see the animals it was almost inevitable that they passed the fasting-artist and that people stopped for a moment; they might have stayed with him longer had not the passageway been a narrow one and the pressure of those coming along behind, for whom this constituted an inexplicable hold-up on the way to their desired goal, ruled out a more extended and leisurely look. This was also the

[78]

reason why the fasting-artist, though he looked forward eagerly to these visits as justifying his existence, also trembled at the prospect of them. At first he had hardly been able to wait for interval time; he had feasted his eyes on the advancing throng – only to bow all too soon, since even the most stubborn, almost deliberate self-deception was not proof against the lessons of experience, to the conviction that, every single time, at least as far as intentions were concerned, it was yet another lot *en route* to the stables. Moreover that view of them from a distance was always the most beautiful in memory. Because as soon as they drew level with him his ears were assailed by the shouting and scolding of the two factions that formed and re-formed continually: those on the one hand – for the fasting-artist they were soon the more embarrassing faction of the two – who wished to contemplate him at their ease, not out of any appreciation of what he was doing but out of a spiteful whim, and those who for the moment hankered only after the stables. Once the main body had gone by there came the stragglers, but they, with nothing to prevent them from lingering for as long as they liked, strode rapidly past, almost without a sideways glance, in order to be in time to see the animals. And it was an all-too-infrequent treat when a father chanced along with his children, pointed to the fasting-artist, explained in detail what was involved here, and told them of similar but incomparably more magnificent performances that he had attended years before, and when the children, although as a result of their inadequate preparation both academically and at the hands of life they still stood there uncomprehending – what was fasting to them? – nevertheless revealed in the brightness of their inquisitive eyes a glimpse of fresh, more generous times to come. Possibly it was true, the fasting-artist used then to say to himself sometimes: everything would be that little bit better were his pitch not quite so close to the stables. It made the choice too easy for people, to say nothing of the fact that the smells emanating from the stables, the animals' restlessness during the night, the carrying past of pieces of raw meat for the carnivores, and the cries at feeding-time were all deeply offensive to him and weighed permanently on his mind. To lodge a complaint with the management, however, was more than he dared; after all, it was the animals he had to thank for the vast number of visitors, among whom there might just be the odd one for him, and there was no knowing where he would be hidden away if he attempted to remind them of his existence and consequently of the fact that, when all was said and done, he was no more than an obstacle on the way to the stables.

A minor obstacle, admittedly, and growing smaller all the time. People became accustomed to the strangeness, in this day and age, of anyone's seeking to claim attention for a fasting-artist, and with that his fate was sealed. Fast as he might – and he did so as only he knew how – nothing could save him now; people passed him by. You try explaining fasting to someone! Unless a person feels it he can never be made to understand it. The beautiful signs became soiled and illegible, they were torn down, and no one thought to replace them; the little board showing the number of days fasted, which had at first been kept scrupulously up to date, had for a long time now indicated the same figure, even this small task having become a burden to the staff after the first few weeks; and so, although the fasting-artist fasted on, just as he had once dreamt of doing, and even succeeded without difficulty in accomplishing precisely what he had then said he would accomplish, no one was counting the days, no one, not even the fasting-artist himself, knew the scale of his achievement to date, and his heart grew heavy. And when, as happened at one point, a passing idler stopped in front of the cage, ridiculed the old figure, and spoke of fraud, it was in a sense the stupidest lie that indifference and innate malice could contrive since it was not the fasting-artist who was cheating, he was doing an honest job, it was the world that was cheating him of his reward.

Many more days went by, however, and there came an end to that, too. A foreman, noticing the cage one day, asked the attendants why a perfectly good cage was allowed to stand around unused, full of rotten straw; no one knew the answer until one man, his memory jogged by the little board with the numbers on it, recalled the fasting-artist. They turned the straw over with sticks and found the fasting-artist underneath. 'You still fasting, mate?' the foreman asked. 'Aren't you ever going to stop?' 'Forgive me,' the fasting-artist whispered, addressing them all, though only the foreman, with his ear to the bars, could hear. 'Of course,' the foreman said, putting a finger to his temple to indicate to his men what sort of state the fasting-artist was in. 'Of course we forgive you.' 'I always wanted you to admire my fasting,' the fasting-artist said. 'And so we do,' the foreman said obligingly. 'But you shouldn't admire it,' the fasting-artist said. 'Well, all right, we don't,' said the foreman, 'but why shouldn't we?' 'Because I have to fast, I can't help it,' the fasting-artist said. 'Well, I'm blowed,' said the foreman, 'and why can't you help it?' 'Because,' the fasting-artist began, lifting his head a little and, with lips pursed as if for a kiss, speaking right into the foreman's ear lest anything be lost, 'because I've never been able to find the kind of nourishment I like. If I had found it, believe you me, I'd not have made this fuss but would have eaten my fill the same as you and everyone else.' Those were his last words, but his shattered gaze retained the firm if no longer proud conviction that he was fasting yet.

'All right, deal with this mess!' the foreman said, and they buried the fasting-artist together with the straw. Into the cage they now put a young panther. It was a palpable relief even to the most stolid to see this savage animal thrashing about in the cage that had been bleakly lifeless for so long. He lacked nothing. The food he liked was brought to him by his keepers without a second thought; even freedom he did not appear to miss; that noble body, endowed almost to bursting-point with all it required, seemed to carry its very freedom around with it – somewhere in the teeth, apparently; and sheer delight at being alive made such a torch of the beast's breath that the spectators had difficulty in holding their ground against it. With a conscious effort, however, they crowded round the cage and, once there, would not budge.

From Franz Kafka, 'A Fasting-Artist' (1921–4), translated by J.A. Underwood.

Breaking and Eating

Police in the New York borough of Queens are hunting a serial burglar who they say has pioneered a new crime: breaking and eating.

According to detectives, the famished felon who has struck at least 10 times since April, is more interested in the contents of his victims' refrigerators than their wallets.

'He sits down and eats food while the victims are in their beds,' said Captain Bernard Gillespie, a Queens detective investigating the idiosyncratic crime spree. 'He takes the food right out of their refrigerators.'

The snacking burglar targets mostly older women. He breaks into their second-floor flats while they are sleeping and orders them to cover their heads with pillow-cases or pyjamas before heading for the kitchen.

In at least four of the break-ins, he reportedly made off with provisions. Twice he noshed on the spot, once tucking into a cake he found in a victim's fridge.

Police believe he is a drug addict who steals to finance his habit and satiate his heightened appetite. As well as edible booty, he has made off with jewellery, small electrical appliances and other valuables.

He is described as black, aged between 35 and 45, who usually wears dark clothes and a baseball cap. Police issued a composite sketch of a man looking decidedly well-fed.

In a city which is used to serving as a kind of research and development laboratory for criminal types, the munching burglar has provoked an unusual outcry.

'He's got some nerve stealing from old people,' said Soledad Rodriguez, a 67-year-old resident of Queens, where most of the snack attacks have taken place.

'But what makes matters worse is that he raids their refrigerators. He should be ashamed of himself,' he said.

Police have not said whether the hungry burglar shows a preference for particular foods. But he appears to favour a midnight snack, usually striking between 9pm and 1am at weekends.

Detectives are worried that he may become violent. He has already attacked one of his victims, punching her after she would not keep quiet, then stealing $211 (£135), her food stamps and, of course, dinner.

In Manhattan's smarter eateries, the culinary crime wave has revived painful memories. Last year a 'serial diner' worked his way round the city's best restaurants, refusing to pay when the bill arrived. Police have not linked the two suspects.

Ian Katz, *Guardian* (15 June 1995).

II SEXING THE CHERRY

THE way to a man's heart, teenage girls used to be assured by their mothers and women's magazines, is through his stomach. As a result, even in the late 1960s we were expected to troop obediently into cookery classes each week, clutching Tupperware boxes of ingredients brought from home, to be initiated into the glories of British cuisine – kedgeree, iced ginger cake and other relics of empire. While we were absorbed in replicating the culinary curiosities of an earlier era, our male contemporaries were learning how to put up shelves in the kitchens where, in theory, we would one day slave over a hot stove. Although it was tacitly and reluctantly accepted that what would bring us together in the first place was sex, the idea that girls might have the same appetites as boys wasn't even countenanced. All that was lacking from the title these dreary classes went under at most girls' or mixed secondary schools – domestic science – was the four letters a-t-e-d at the end of the first word.

At home, the notion of an essential difference between men's and women's appetites was enshrined in a pecking order which became the ironic title of one of Margaret Forster's novels: *Have the Men Had Enough?* In my parents' working-class household my father invariably got two lamb chops, my mother and I one each, and when I questioned this arrangement her answer never varied: 'He's a man.' She genuinely didn't mind having less herself and couldn't see what I was getting at. Pointing out that I was a growing girl had no effect, especially as my best friend, who frequently came to tea, was already obsessed with sex and boys and picked at her food as though an inbuilt calorie-counter was at work calibrating every portion. Long before terms like anorexia entered everyday language, it was generally accepted not just that men were bigger, stronger and required more calories but that girls and women were always on diets. I was even told off by one of the teachers at the pretentious girls' high school I attended in Hampshire for eating in the street, a misdemeanour I failed to understand until it was conveyed to me that eating was something the female of the species did in private; she certainly wasn't supposed to be seen enjoying food in a public place, especially if she happened to be wearing school uniform. (I hadn't yet heard of gentlemen's clubs like the Garrick, where men of a certain age and class still gather to lunch in a room where the only female permitted entry is a servant.)

Years later, a possible explanation for this strange prohibition presented itself to me through the unexpected medium of Lord Byron's letters. Writing to his *confidante* Lady Melbourne about a new love affair in 1812, he announced that the object of his affections was Italian and married, which meant that there were no problems about having to take this responsibility on himself; there was one drawback, however, which was that she ate too much. 'Chicken wings, sweetbreads, custards, peaches and port wine,' he listed with barely concealed disgust. 'A woman should never be seen eating or drinking, unless it be *lobster salad* and *champagne*, the only truly feminine and becoming viands.' Years later, when the Irish poet Tom Moore was writing a posthumous biography of Byron, he discovered from a celebrated hostess who had known him in Venice in 1819 that the mild distaste expressed in this letter had subsequently developed into something resembling a phobia. 'He disliked seeing women eat,' she wrote in an unpublished memoir from which she allowed Moore to quote, charitably ascribing this 'extraordinary antipathy' to a fear that his notion of female 'perfection' might be disturbed by the spectacle. It is, at first sight, a puzzling explanation; why should eating, which is a natural function, threaten to degrade women in someone's estimation? The lady added that Byron, having always been 'governed' by women – she meant, I suppose, being dependent, as a serial seducer, on their consent – needed to elevate them in this way in order to find his own submission tolerable; at the same time his nature was so contradictory that he also seemed capable of holding them in contempt. There is a suggestion here, however oblique, that Byron's phobia was to do with sex – that he felt himself so much in thrall to the female sexual appetite that he did not like to be reminded of it by witnessing another form of hunger in the process of satisfying itself. I suspect, though, that Byron also held the view that a woman's function is not to consume but to *be* consumed – a trope so popular in literature that it transcends boundaries of time, place, religion and form.

Heterosexual men, on beholding an attractive female body, insistently divide it into edible parts; for centuries, the female beloved has been subjected to a scrutiny as critical as that of a greengrocer examining the latest crop of apples before deciding whether to buy. Poets and novelists alike seek peaches-and-cream complexions, lips like ripe berries, breasts as round and firm as pomegranates – or, more vulgarly, halved grapefruit. The male voice in the Song of Solomon extols a woman whose lips drip honey: 'thy lips, O my spouse, drop as the honeycomb; honey and milk are under thy tongue'. The sixteenth-century erotic epic *The Perfumed Garden* praises a woman whose flesh is 'mellow like fresh butter'; in our own century, the Sicilian author of *The Leopard*, Giuseppe Tomasi di Lampedusa, gives his seventeen-year-old heroine skin that looks – if one can visualise taste – 'as if it had the flavour of fresh cream'. The female voice in the Song of Solomon is rare in that she responds to her lover in kind: 'As the apple tree among the trees of the wood, so is my beloved among the sons. I sat down under his shadow with great delight, and his fruit was sweet to my taste.' More usually, it is edible women who are served up to delight the tastebuds of their lovers/eulogisers – or to disappoint them, for the bloom of youth, perishable as the fragrant skin of a peach, wears off and the lover's languorous delight with it. Parolles warns Helena in *All's Well That Ends Well* that 'your virginity, your old virginity, is like one of our French withered pears; it looks ill, it eats drily'. Gracie Fields, the down-to-earth Rochdale girl who became a popular icon in the 1930s and 1940s, mocks an imaginary lover on a cracked old 78 rpm record: 'Will you love me when I'm mutton as you love me when I'm lamb?', dramatising the point with a satirical chorus in the quavering voice of sheep/older woman. Several decades later, in her novel *The Edible Woman*, the Canadian writer Margaret Atwood invents a conventional heroine who gradually comes to regard her fiancé as someone who will gobble her up like an icing-sugar figure on a wedding cake; women, according to this classic late sixties feminist view, are sugary icons in perpetual danger of being devoured.

The obvious explanation of this theme is that the mouth is itself a sexual organ, the one with which human beings generally make their first sexual contact with each other. Freud wrote dismissively of the oral phase of sexuality as one in which 'sexual activity has not yet been separated from the ingestion of food', even though the two activities are so closely linked as to make a nonsense of the notion that separating them is a defining element of mature sexuality. But while his theory does not explain why the theme of love-object-as-food in literature should be quite so gender-specific, his focus on that phase in human development when the baby takes nourishment and pleasure from the mother's breast is a useful clue: the infant's earliest experience of the human female defines her as literally *consumable*. In reality, the hungry child is not necessarily male but for centuries there has been an elision of child/boy in Western culture; who is in any doubt that the Madonna and child, our most pervasive iconic image, represents mother and *son* rather than mother and daughter? It's also interesting that this image is conventionally represented in terms of the utmost tranquillity, leaving it to a twentieth-century woman psychoanalyst, Melanie Klein, to identify the tumultuous emotions – pleasure, fear of loss, anger – which have been censored out of it. Yet if the notion of the edible woman derives from this early experience, setting up a paradigm of male predator/female prey which adult heterosexual men find so hard to shake off, where does that leave adult women whose childish experience of hunger and satisfaction has been ruthlessly repressed?

One answer is that it produces an ambivalence in them about appetite, a guilty apprehension that it is inappropriate in beings whose function is to assuage hunger, not feel it themselves. This self-denying ordinance may go some way to explain the readiness of women, whatever their weight and body shape, to embark on diets; by contrast, until very recently, most celebrated chefs and gour-mands, from the Roman Apicius to Brillat-Savarin, Escoffier, Ray-mond Blanc and Marco Pierre White, have been male. The difficulty women have in admitting their desire for oral gratification sometimes results in a collusive (and masochistic) acquiescence in the idea of themselves as food/object; a disturbing exposition of this theme can be found in *The Butcher*, Alina Reyes's erotic novella in which a young woman who works in a butcher's shop is sexually aroused by her identification with the slabs of dead meat her boss handles daily. (Madonna's song 'Where Life Begins', a rapturous celebration of *cunnilingus*, is unusual in that the woman/meal is for once very much alive and in charge of the experience.) If, though, women are conventionally allowed only two strategies for dealing with their appetites, denial or self-objectification, what happens to their repressed hunger? One of the consequences is anger and Lord Byron's unease on seeing women eat reflects a commonly expressed male fear that, once the feminine appetite has been liberated, it will be voracious. This fear is compounded by anatomy, which encourages comparisons between the mouth and the female sexual organ; the spectre at Byron's feast, so to speak, is the *vagina dentata*, in which two taboo female appetites, hunger and desire, inhabit one toothy cavity. Women, according to this fearful scenario, experience them even more powerfully and destructively than men; they are out for revenge and the male organ is vulnerable to symbolic castration in a way the female pudenda are not.

It's a striking feature of men's imagery of woman-as-food that it's frequently vegetarian, transforming the object of desire into luscious fruit like figs and cherries. Men are also happy to think of their female lovers as tender birds of prey (hence 'birds', the dismissive sixties' slang term for women) but not as creatures with hooves, teeth and a predatory appetite of their own. Whoever heard of a fig – or indeed an oyster, which belongs to that sub-group of crude comparisons inspired by an apparent similarity in shape or smell to the female genitalia – biting back? This is not entirely wishful thinking, for it's clear that women have as tortured a relation to food as they do to sex, especially when it comes to admitting a craving for it. The one type of enthusiastic consumption most of them will admit to is eating for comfort, especially when a love affair has gone wrong; they console themselves with the notion that food is a substitute for love or sex, as though only the loss of one entitles them to the other, and fail to ask: What exactly is this female hunger that can express itself only in a context of anger and despair? Henry Fielding wrote in *Tom Jones* about 'what is commonly called love, namely the desire of satisfying a voracious appetite with a certain quantity of delicate white human flesh'; in a carnivorous world, women are only just beginning to get their share.

Figs

The proper way to eat a fig, in society,
Is to split it in four, holding it by the stump,

And open it, so that it is a glittering, rosy, moist, honied, heavy-
petalled four-petalled flower.

Then you throw away the skin
Which is just like a four-petalled calex,
After you have taken off the blossom with your lips.

But the vulgar way
Is just to put your mouth to the crack, and take out the flesh in
one bite.

Every fruit has its secret.

The fig is a very secretive fruit.
As you see it standing growing, you feel at once it is symbolic:
And it seems male.
But when you come to know it better, you agree with the
Romans, it is female.

The Italians vulgarly say, it stands for the female part; the fig-
fruit:
The fissure, the yoni,
The wonderful moist conductivity towards the centre.

Involved,
Inturned,
The flowering all inward and womb-fibrilled;
And but one orifice.

The fig, the horse-shoe, the squash-blossom.
Symbols.

There was a flower that flowered inward, womb-ward;

Now there is a fruit like a ripe womb.
It was always a secret.
That's how it should be, the female should always be secret.

There never was any standing aloft and unfolded on a bough
Like other flowers, in a revelation of petals;
Silver-pink peach, venetian glass of medlars and sorb-apples,
Shallow wine-cups on short, bulging stems
Openly pledging heaven:
Here's to the thorn in flower! Here is to Utterance!
The brave, adventurous rosaceae.

Folded upon itself, and secret unutterable,
And milk-sapped, sap that curdles milk and makes *ricotta*,
Sap that smells strange on your fingers, that even goats won't
    taste it;
Folded upon itself, enclosed like any Mohammedan woman,
Its nakedness all within-walls, its flowering forever unseen,
One small way of access only, and this close-curtained from the
    light;
Fig, fruit of the female mystery, covert and inward,
Mediterranean fruit, with your covert nakedness,
Where everything happens invisible, flowering and fertilisation,
    and fruiting
In the inwardness of your you, that eye will never see
Till it's finished, and you're over-ripe, and you burst to give up
    your ghost.

Till the drop of ripeness exudes,
And the year is over.

That's how the fig dies, showing her crimson through the purple
    slit
Like a wound, the exposure of her secret, on the open day.
Like a prostitute, the bursten fig, making a show of her secret.

That's how women die too.

The year is fallen over-ripe,
The year of our women.
The year of our women is fallen over-ripe.

The secret is laid bare.
And rottenness soon sets in.
The year of our women is fallen over-ripe.

When Eve once knew *in her mind* that she was naked
She quickly sewed fig-leaves, and sewed the same for the man.
She'd been naked all her days before,
But till then, till that apple of knowledge, she hadn't had the fact
  on her mind.

She got the fact on her mind, and quickly sewed fig-leaves.
And women have been sewing ever since.
But now they stitch to adorn the bursten fig, not to cover it.
They have their nakedness more than ever on their mind,
And they won't let us forget it.

Now, the secret
Becomes an affirmation through moist, scarlet lips
That laugh at the Lord's indignation.

What then, good Lord! cry the women.
We have kept our secret long enough.
We are a ripe fig.
Let us burst into affirmation.

They forget, ripe figs won't keep.
Ripe figs won't keep.

Honey-white figs of the north, black figs with scarlet inside, of
  the south.
Ripe figs won't keep, won't keep in any clime.
What then, when women the world over have all bursten into
  self-assertion?
And bursten figs won't keep?

D.H. Lawrence (1923).

A Bread Roll

Looking at the spread I've laid out on the table, I begin to feel wary of the competition. I go back to the bathroom and dab on more perfume and inspect my face for spots with increasing dismay.

But later I'm reassured by the thought of the bite-size filo-pastry pouches filled with camembert and cranberries, the spinach and salmon mousse, the tomato I found almost ready to burst that now reclines in slices, on a bed of fresh marjoram lapped by raspberry vinegar, the apple tarts with slices spread open like legs and the champagne, all left hardly touched as we fuck, bare and forked, on the floor.

He cups my cunt in his hand like a bread-roll, nudges the halves apart, and fills me.

Hull, pod, shell, bone, fillet.

From Lucy Ellmann, *Sweet Desserts* (1988).

Blood and Roses

The quail must be dry-plucked because putting them in boiling water affects their flavour. That is just one of many cooking secrets that can only be learned through practice. Ever since she had burned her hands on the griddle, Rosaura wanted nothing to do with any kind of culinary activity, so she was ignorant of that and many other gastronomical secrets. But whether she did it to impress her husband Pedro or to compete with Tita in her own territory – who can say? – there was one day when Rosaura did attempt to cook. When Tita tried nicely to give her some advice, Rosaura became irritated and asked Tita to leave her alone in the kitchen.

The rice was obviously scorched, the meat dried out, the dessert burnt. But no-one at the table dared display the tiniest hint of displeasure, not after Mama Elena had pointedly remarked, 'As the first meal that Rosaura has cooked it isn't bad. Don't you agree, Pedro?'

Making a real effort not to insult his wife, Pedro replied, 'No, for her first time, it's not too bad.'

Of course, that afternoon the entire family felt sick to their stomachs.

That had been a tragedy, but nothing like the one that shook the ranch this time. Tita's blood and the roses from Pedro proved quite an explosive combination.

Everyone was a little tense as they sat down at the table, but that's as far as it went until the quail were served. It wasn't enough he'd made his wife jealous earlier, for when Pedro tasted his first mouthful, he couldn't help closing his eyes in voluptuous delight and exclaiming, 'It's a dish for the gods!'

Mama Elena knew that the quail was exquisite; none the less, Pedro's remark did not sit well with her, and she replied, 'It's too salty.'

Rosaura, saying she was feeling sick and getting nauseous, barely took three bites. But something strange was happening to Gertrudis.

On her the food seemed to act as an aphrodisiac; she began to feel an intense heat pulsing through her limbs. An itch in the centre of her body kept her from sitting properly in her chair. She began to sweat, imagining herself on horseback with her arms clasped around one of Pancho Villa's men: the one she had seen in the village plaza the week before, smelling of sweat and mud, of dawns that brought uncertainty and danger, smelling of life and of death. She was on her way to market in Piedras Negras with Chencha, the servant, when she saw him coming down the main street, riding in front of the others, obviously the captain of the troop. Their eyes met and what she saw in his made her tremble. She saw all the nights he'd spent staring into the fire and longing to have a woman beside him, a woman he could kiss, a woman he could hold in his arms, a woman like her. She got out her handkerchief and tried to wipe these sinful thoughts from her mind as she wiped away the sweat.

But it was no use, something strange had happened to her. She turned to Tita for help, but Tita wasn't there, even though her body was sitting up quite properly in her chair; there wasn't the slightest sign of life in her eyes. It was as if a strange alchemical process had dissolved her entire being in the rose petal sauce, in the tender flesh of the quails, in the wine, in every one of the meal's aromas. That was the way she entered Pedro's body, hot, voluptuous, totally sensuous.

With that meal it seemed they had discovered a new system of communication, in which Tita was the transmitter, Pedro the receiver, and poor Gertrudis the medium, the conducting body through which the singular sexual message was passed.

Pedro didn't offer any resistance. He let Tita penetrate to the farthest corners of his being, and all the while they couldn't take their eyes off each other. He said, 'Thank you, I have never had anything so exquisite.'

It truly is a delicious dish. The roses give it an extremely delicate flavour.

From Laura Esquivel, *Like Water for Hot Chocolate* (1989), translated by
Carol Christensen and Thomas Christensen.

A Feast for Four

Once upon a time there lived in the city of Baghdad a young bachelor who was by trade a porter.

One day, as he sat in the market-place leaning idly against his basket, a young woman, dressed in rare silks and cloaked in a gold-embroidered mantle of Mosul brocade, stopped before him and gently raised her veil. Beneath it there showed dark eyes with long lashes and lineaments of perfect beauty.

'Lift up your basket, porter,' she said in a sweet voice, 'and follow me.'

At once the porter took up his basket and followed her, thinking to himself: 'This is indeed a blessed day!' until she stopped at the door of a house and knocked. The door was opened by a Christian, who gave her, in return for a piece of gold, a measure of olives and two casks of wine. These she put into the basket and said to the porter: 'Follow me.'

'By Allah,' thought the porter, 'this is surely my lucky day!'

He took up his basket and followed her until she stopped at a fruiterer's, where she bought Syrian apples and Othmani quinces, Omani peaches, cucumbers from the Nile, Egyptian lemons and Sultani citrons, sweet-scented myrtle and henna flowers, camomile, anemones, violets, sweet-briar, and pomegranate-blossom. All these she put into the basket and again said to the porter: 'Follow me.'

She stopped at a butcher's stall and said to him: 'Cut me ten pounds of meat.' She wrapped the meat in a large banana-leaf and, putting it into the basket, ordered the porter to follow her. She next made her way to a grocer's shop, where she bought pistachios, nuts and raisins, and thence to a confectioner's, where she chose a platter of dainty sweetmeats stuffed with almonds and flavoured with musk, lemon cakes, pastry crescents, Zainab's combs, and honey tarts. And all these she placed into the porter's basket.

'Had you told me,' observed the porter, 'I would have brought a mule to carry all these things!'

The young woman smiled at the porter's remark and, bidding him hold his tongue, stopped at a perfume-seller's and bought ten different essences, rose-water, willow-water and musk-rose dew, two loaves of sugar, a sprinkling-bottle, frankincense, aloe-wood, amber-gris, and candles of Alexandrine wax. Again the porter took up his basket and followed her until she came to a magnificent lofty house facing a great courtyard. Its doors were of ebony plates with red gold.

Here the young woman unveiled her face and knocked, and the door was opened by a girl of surpassing beauty. Her forehead was white as a lily and her eyes were more lustrous than a gazelle's. Her brows were crescent moons, her cheeks anemones, and her mouth like the crimson ruby on King Solomon's ring. Her teeth were whiter than a string of pearls, and like twin pomegranates were her breasts.

At the sight of this girl the porter was so overwhelmed with wonder that the basket nearly fell off his head.

'Surely this is the most auspicious day of my life!' he thought.

'Pray come in, sister,' said the girl who had opened the door, 'and let this weary porter put down his burden.'

The porter followed the two girls into a spacious and nobly vaulted hall. The ceiling was wondrously carved in patterns of elaborate design, and the walls were hung with tapestry of silk and rich brocade. In the centre of the hall a fountain played in a pool of crystal water, and near the far side stood a couch of alabaster inlaid with diamonds and covered with a red silken quilt embroidered with pearls. A third girl, slim and exquisitely beautiful, was reclining on the couch. Her face was radiant as the full moon and all the witchcraft of Babylon was in her eyes. A paragon of Arabian grace, she was like a star twinkling in a cloudless sky or a golden dome shimmering in the night.

The girl, who was the oldest of the three, rose from her couch and, walking slowly to the middle of the hall, said to her sisters: 'Why are you standing idly by? Come, let us take down this heavy basket from the porter's head.'

The three girls helped the porter put down his basket, and when they had taken out the contents and arranged them in their proper places, they handed him two pieces of gold, saying: 'Take this, and go your way.'

The porter looked at the young girls and marvelled at the perfection of their beauty; never in all his days had he seen the like. He noticed that there was no man in the house, and stood hesitant before them, gazing in wonderment at the plentiful drinks, fruits, and flowers.

'Why do you not go?' asked the eldest of the girls, the mistress of the house. 'Do you find your payment too little?' Then, turning to her sisters, she said: 'Give him another dinar.'

'By Allah, sweet ladies,' replied the porter, 'you have paid me well enough; my ordinary pay is but a few coppers. It is about you that my heart is troubled. How is it that you live alone in this house with no man to attend you? Do you not know that a feast cannot be merry with fewer than four companions, and that women cannot be truly happy without men? Now you are only three, my ladies. You need a fourth, a man of discretion who can be trusted with secrets.'

'But, porter,' replied the eldest, laughing, 'do you not see that we are young girls and should therefore be wary of confiding in strangers? "A secret shared," says the proverb, "is a secret lost."'

'I swear by your dear life,' he replied, 'that I am a discreet and honest man, lacking neither in wisdom nor in learning. Your secrets, ladies, shall be safe with me.'

'You must know,' said the second with a mischievous smile, 'that we have spent a large fortune on this house. Have you anything with which to pay us? We shall not allow you to sit in our midst and be our drinking-companion unless you contribute a sum of money. Does not the proverb say: "Friendship without gold is worth no more than a pip"?'

'Have you a well-lined purse, young man?' put in the youngest. 'If you have nothing, be off with nothing!'

But the mistress of the house cut short her sisters' pleasantry.

'By Allah,' she said, 'this man has not failed us today: another might have lost his patience. I myself will undertake to pay for him.'

'Stay with us, then, good porter,' cried her sisters, 'and be welcome in this house.'

At this the porter rejoiced. He thanked them and kissed the ground before them. Presently the eldest rose and, tying a girdle round her waist, began to make ready for the evening. She strained and poured out the wine, arranged the fruit and flowers, and set places for the feast beside the fountain. The three girls sat down with their delighted guest. The mistress of the house poured wine for herself and for her sisters, and then handed a cup to the porter.

'Drink this,' she said, 'and may it bring you joy!'

The porter quickly drained his cup. He kissed his hostesses' hands and recited verses in their praise, his head swaying from side to side. The three girls again filled their cups, and so did the porter.

'My lady,' he said, bowing low before the eldest, 'I am your servant, your bondsman.'

'Drink,' she cried, 'and may your wine be sweet and wholesome!'

When they had drained their cups a second time, they rose and danced round the fountain, singing and clapping their hands in unison. They went on drinking until the wine took possession of their senses and overcame their reason, and, when its sovereignty was fully established, the first girl got up and cast off all her clothes, letting down her long hair to cover her nakedness. She jumped into the fountain, frolicking and washing her body, filling her mouth with water and squirting it at the porter. At length she came out of the pool and threw herself into the porter's lap. Then she pointed down to that which was between her thighs and said: 'Darling master, what do you call that?'

'The gateway to heaven,' the porter answered.

'Are you not ashamed?' cried the girl, and, taking him by the neck, began to beat him.

'Then it is your crack.'

'Villain!' cried the girl, and slapped him on his thigh.

'It is your thing!'

'No, no,' she cried, shaking her head.

'Then it is your hornets' nest,' said the porter.

All three slapped him, laughing, until his flesh was red.

'Then tell me what *you* call it!' he shouted.

'The Buttercup,' the girl replied.

'At last,' cried the porter. 'Allah keep you safe and sound O Buttercup.'

They passed the wine round and round again. Presently the second girl took off her clothes and threw herself onto the porter's lap. Pointing to that which was between her thighs, she said: 'Light of my eyes, what is the name of this?'

'The thing!' he answered.

'A naughty word,' she cried. 'Have you no shame?' And she slapped him so hard that the hall echoed to the sound.

'Then it must be the Buttercup.'

'No, no,' she cried, and slapped him on the neck.

'Well, what do you call it, my sister?'

'Sesame,' the second girl replied.

After the wine had gone round once more, and the porter had somewhat recovered from his beatings, the last girl, the fairest of the three, got up and threw off her clothes. The porter began to stroke his neck, saying, 'Allah save me from yet another beating!' as he watched her descend, utterly naked, into the fountain. She washed her limbs, and sported in the water. He marvelled at the beauty of her face, which resembled the full moon rising in the night sky, at the roundness of her breasts, and her graceful, quivering thighs. Then she came out of the water and laid herself across his lap.

'Tell me the name of this,' she said, pointing to her delicate parts.

The porter tried this name and that, and finally begged her to tell him and stop beating him.

'The Inn of Abu Mansoor,' the girl replied.

'Allah preserve you,' cried the porter, 'O Inn of Abu Mansoor.'

The girls dressed themselves and resumed their seats. Now the porter got up, undressed, and went down into the fountain. The girls watched him as he sported in the water and washed as they had done. Eventually he came out of the fountain, threw himself into the lap of the first girl, and rested his feet on the knees of the second. Pointing to his rising organ, he demanded of the first girl, 'And what do you call this, my queen?'

The girls laughed till they fell over on their backs. To every guess they hazarded he answered 'No', biting each one in turn, and kissing, pinching, and hugging them, which made them laugh all the more. Finally they cried, 'Brother, what is its name, then?'

'Know that this,' the porter replied, 'is my sturdy mule which feeds on buttercups, delights in sesame, and spends the night in the Inn of Abu Mansoor.'

At these words the girls collapsed with laughter.

The four amused themselves till nightfall, when the girls said to the porter: 'In the name of Allah, our friend, rise, put on your clothes, and get out of this house.'

'By Allah,' replied the porter, 'my soul would more willingly leave my body than I your company. Pray let us join the night with the day, and when tomorrow comes we will bid each other farewell.'

Finding him a pleasant, witty rogue, the eldest of the girls said to her sisters: 'By my life, let him stay with us, so that we may beguile the night with his drollery.'

The others agreed, and said to the porter: 'You may pass the night here on one condition: that you obey us strictly and ask no questions about anything you see.'

'I agree to that, my mistresses,' he answered.

'Rise, then,' they said, 'and read the writing on the door.'

The porter went to the door, on which he found these words inscribed in letters of gold: 'He who speaks of that which does not concern him shall hear what will displease him.'

'Bear witness, my mistresses,' he said, 'that I will never speak of that which does not concern me.'

Presently the eldest of the girls set before them meat and drink, and when they had finished eating they lit lamps and candles and burned incense in the braziers. Then they moved to the other side of the hall and sat down to another bout, telling stories and reciting verses.

From 'The Porter and the Three Girls of Baghdad', *Tales from the Thousand and One Nights*, medieval, collected late eighteenth century, translated by N.J. Dawood.

Low Fat Love

Flaccus, the sort of girl I hate
Is the scrawny one, with arms so thin
My rings would fit them, hips that grate,
Spine like a saw, knee like a pin
And a coccyx like a javelin.
But all the same I don't go in
For sheer bulk. I appreciate
Good meat, not blubber, on my plate.

From Martial, *The Epigrams*, first century AD, translated by James Michie.

Little Bird

Though Mr Blifil was not of the complexion of Jones, nor ready to eat every woman he saw, yet he was far from being destitute of that appetite which is said to be the common property of all animals. With this he had likewise that distinguishing taste which serves to direct men in their choice of the objects, or food, of their several appetites; and this taught him to consider Sophia as a most delicious morsel, indeed to regard her with the same desires which an ortolan inspires into the soul of an epicure. Now, the agonies which affected the mind of Sophia rather augmented than impaired her beauty; for her tears added brightness to her eyes, and her breasts rose higher with her sighs. Indeed no one hath seen beauty in its highest lustre who hath never seen it in distress. Blifil therefore looked on this human ortolan with greater desire than when he had viewed her last, nor was his desire at all lessened by the aversion which he discovered in her to himself.

From Henry Fielding, *Tom Jones* (1749).

To a Young Lady, with Some Lampreys

With lovers 'twas of old the fashion
By presents to convey their passion;
No matter what the gift they sent,
The Lady saw that love was meant.
Fair *Atalanta*, as a favour,
Took the boar's head her Hero gave her;
Nor could the bristling thing affront her,
'Twas a fit present from a hunter.
When Squires send woodcocks to the dame,
It serves to show their absent flame:
Some by a snip of woven hair,
In posied lockets bribe the fair;
How many mercenary matches
Have sprung from Di'mond-rings and watches!
But hold – a ring, a watch, a locket
Would drain at once a Poet's pocket;
He should send songs that cost him nought,
Nor ev'n be prodigal of thought.
   Why then send Lampreys? fye, for shame!
'Twill set a virgin's blood on flame.
This to fifteen a proper gift!
It might lend sixty-five a lift.
   I know your maiden Aunt will scold,

And think my present somewhat bold.
I see her lift her hands and eyes.
   'What, eat it, Niece? eat *Spanish* flies!
Lamprey's a most immodest diet:
You'll neither wake nor sleep in quiet.
Should I to night eat Sago cream,
'Twould make me blush to tell my dream;
If I eat Lobster, 'tis so warming,
That ev'ry man I see looks charming.
Wherefore had not the filthy fellow
Laid *Rochester* upon your pillow?
I vow and swear, I think the present
Had been as modest and as decent.
   'Who has her virtue in her power?
Each day has its unguarded hour;
Always in danger of undoing,
A prawn, a shrimp, may prove our ruin!
   'The shepherdess, who lives on sallad,
To cool her youth, controuls her palate;
Should *Dian*'s maids turn liqu'rish livers,
And of huge lampreys rob the rivers,
Then all beside each glade and Visto,
You'd see Nymphs lying like *Calisto*.
   'The man who meant to heat your blood,
Needs not himself such vicious food' –
   In this, I own, your Aunt is clear,
I sent you what I might well spare:
For when I see you (without joking)
Your eyes, lips, breasts, are so provoking,
They set my heart more cock-a-hoop,
Than could whole seas of craw-fish soupe.

John Gay (1720).

Goose Girl

Often in the theatre, too, in full view of all the people Theodora
would throw off her clothes and stand naked in their midst, having
only a girdle about her private parts and her groins – not, however,

because she was ashamed to expose these also to the public, but because no one is allowed to appear there absolutely naked: a girdle round the groins is compulsory. With this minimum covering she would spread herself out and lie face upwards on the floor. Servants on whom this task had been imposed would sprinkle barley grains over her private parts, and geese trained for the purpose used to pick them off one by one with their bills and swallow them. Theodora, so far from blushing when she stood up again, actually seemed to be proud of this performance. For she was not only shameless herself, but did more than anyone else to encourage shamelessness.

From Procopius, *The Secret History*, (c. 500–65 AD), translated by
G.A. Williamson.

Rôti sans pareil

Take a large olive, stone it and stuff it with a paste made of anchovy, capers and oil.

Put the olive inside a trussed and boned bec-figue (garden warbler).

Put the bec-figue inside a fat ortolan.

Put the ortolan inside a boned lark.

Put the stuffed lark inside a boned thrush.

Put the thrush inside a fat quail.

Put the quail, wrapped in vine-leaves, inside a boned lapwing.

Put the lapwing inside a boned golden plover.

Put the plover inside a fat, boned, red-legged partridge.

Put the partridge inside a young, boned, and well-hung woodcock.

Put the woodcock, rolled in bread-crumbs, inside a boned teal.

Put the teal inside a boned guinea-fowl.

Put the guinea-fowl, well larded, inside a young and boned tame duck.

Put the duck inside a boned and fat fowl.

Put the fowl inside a well-hung pheasant.

Put the pheasant inside a boned and fat wild goose.

Put the goose inside a fine turkey.

Put the turkey inside a boned bustard.

Having arranged your roast after this fashion, place it in a saucepan of proper size with onions stuffed with cloves, carrots, small squares of ham, celery, mignonette, several strips of bacon well seasoned, pepper, salt, spice, coriander seeds, and two cloves of garlic.

Seal the saucepan hermetically by closing it with pastry. Then put it for ten hours over a gentle fire, and arrange it so that the heat penetrates evenly. An oven moderately heated would suit better than the hearth.

Before serving, remove the pastry, put your roast on a hot dish after having removed the grease, if there is any, and serve.

From Norman Douglas, *Venus in the Kitchen or Love's Cookery Book* (1952).

Love Bites (i)

The details ... O God! ... I cannot find words to paint them. It was as if the villain, the most libertine of the four, though seemingly the least removed from the views of Nature, was prepared to tread her path and put a smaller degree of nonconformity into his order of worship, only by compensating for a semblance of lesser depravity by inflicting the highest degree of outrage upon my person ... Alas, if in imagination I had on occasion strayed to thoughts of such pleasures, I always believed them to be as chaste as the God who inspired them: they were given to humankind by Nature as a consolation and were born of love and decency. Foreign to me was the notion that man, like the beasts of the field, could pleasure himself only by making his partners suffer. But this I now discovered, and with such a degree of violence that the natural pain of the loss of my virginity was the least of the agonies which I was required to bear during his terrifying onslaught. But Antonin marked the moment of paroxysm with such furious whoopings and bellowings, with such murderous assaults on every part of my body, and not least with bites which were like the tiger's bloody caress, that for a moment I believed I had fallen prey to some wild animal which would not be sated until it had devoured me whole. When these horrors ended, I collapsed upon the altar where I had been sacrificed, motionless and almost unconscious.

From the Marquis de Sade, *Justine, or the Misfortunes of Virtue* (1791),
translated by David Cowerd.

Food and the Sexual Impulse

This is not going to be about aphrodisiacs, as the reader might expect, but about another connection between the two great impulses of mankind, in dealing with which we can follow the Freudian line of thought. The mouth, where food enters, and through which nearly all sensations and feelings connected with food, besides the satisfaction of hunger, are transmitted to us, has, in man, sexual functions as well, at least the lips have. This simple fact makes the mouth suspect. In other words, the investigator cannot help suspecting that the two groups of sensations and feelings which originate there may not always be distinguishable. This idea is strengthened by the fact, well known to all psychologists who study eating sensations, that it is not always possible in ordinary life to separate the different kinds of sensations, like taste and smell. It may well be the same with the two great impulses of food and sex.

From this point of view, Freud has investigated the behaviour of the newborn child, and it is asserted that the sucking of the infant is the first sexual act of a human being. It is believed that this sexual pleasure is first bound up with the action of feeding at the mother's breast but that the child soon learns to separate this pleasure, so that later on when the child is weaned the pleasure becomes transferred to parts of his own body such as the thumb and the tongue, or to the now condemned dummy teat. This is called autoeroticism, and the lips erogenous zones.

Opponents of Freud, to whom the idea of sucking babies having a sexual life was horrible, asked why this pleasure in sucking for its own sake should be connected with sex; to consider it simply as an organ-pleasure would, they suggested, be sufficient, in which case the skin of the lips would represent the organ. From our point of view it would be all the same whether the pleasure in sucking for its own sake were called sexual or not, but this does seem to the author to explain the hitherto undiscovered origin of this action, and as this book is devoted to detecting the causes of habits of nutrition and of actions connected with them, we cannot afford to ignore a possible explanation like this.

From H.D. Renner, *The Origin of Food Habits* (1944).

Pale Face

He's healthy – yet he's deathly pale;
Seldom drinks wine and has a hale
Digestion – but looks white and ill;
Sunbathes, rouges his cheeks – and still
Has a pasty face; licks all the cunts
In Rome – and never blushes once.

From Martial, *The Epigrams*, first century AD, translated by James Michie.

Love Bites (ii)

So there was in my impulse toward Zylphia, not only the drive to
have all the ocean for us, but also the drive to lose it, the ocean, to
annihilate ourselves in the ocean, to destroy ourselves, to torment
ourselves, or rather – as a beginning – to torment her, Zylphia my
beloved, to tear her to pieces, to eat her up. And with her it's the
same: what she wanted was to torment me, devour me, swallow me,
nothing but that. The orange stain of the sun seen from the water's
depths swayed like a medusa, and Zylphia darted among the
luminous filaments devoured by the desire to devour me, and I
writhed in the tangles of darkness that rose from the depths like long
strands of seaweed beringed with indigo glints, raving and longing to
bite her.

From Italo Calvino, *t-zero* (1984), translated by William Weaver.

Flesh

The blade plunged gently into the muscle then ran its full length in
one supple movement. The action was perfectly controlled. The slice
curled over limply onto the chopping block.

The black meat glistened, revived by the touch of the knife. The
butcher placed his left hand flat on the broad rib and with his right
hand began to carve into the thick meat once again. I could feel that
cold elastic mass beneath the palm of my own hand. I saw the knife

enter the firm dead flesh, opening it up like a shining wound. The steel blade slid down the length of the dark shape. The blade and the wall gleamed.

The butcher picked up the slices one after the other and placed them side by side on the chopping block. They fell with a flat slap – like a kiss against the wood.

With the point of the knife the butcher began to dress the meat, cutting out the yellow fat and splattering it against the tiled wall. He ripped a piece of greaseproof paper from the wad hanging on the iron hook, placed a slice in the middle of it, dropped another on top. The kiss again, more like a clap.

Then he turned to me, the heavy packet flat on his hand he tossed it onto the scales.

The sickly smell of raw meat hit my nostrils. Seen close up, in the full summer morning light which poured in through the long window, it was bright red, beautifully nauseating. Who said that flesh is sad? Flesh is not sad, it is sinister. It belongs on the left side of our souls, it catches us at times of the greatest abandonment, carries us over deep seas, scuttles us and saves us; flesh is our guide, our dense black light, the well which draws our life down in a spiral, sucking it into oblivion.

The flesh of the bull before me was the same as that of the beast in the field, except that the blood had left it, the stream which carries life and carries it away so quickly, of which there remained only a few drops like pearls on the white paper.

And the butcher who talked to me about sex all day long was made of the same flesh, only warm, sometimes soft sometimes hard; the butcher had his good and inferior cuts, exacting and eager to burn out their life, to transform themselves into meat. And my flesh was the same, I who felt the fire light between my legs at the butcher's words.

From Alina Reyes, *The Butcher* (1988), translated by David Watson.

All on a Plate

Evelyn is talking but I'm not listening. Her dialogue overlaps her own dialogue. Her mouth is moving but I'm not hearing anything and I can't listen, I can't really concentrate, since my rabbit has been cut to look ... just ... like ... a ... star! Shoestring french fries surround it and chunky red salsa has been smeared across the top of the plate – which is white and porcelain and two feet wide – to give the appearance of a sunset but it looks like one big gunshot wound to me and shaking my head slowly in disbelief I press a finger into the meat, leaving the indentation of one finger, then another, and then I look for a napkin, not my own, to wipe my hand with. Evelyn hasn't broken her monologue – she talks and chews exquisitely – and smiling seductively at her I reach under the table and grab her thigh, wiping my hand off, and still talking she smiles naughtily at me and sips more champagne. I keep studying her face, bored by how beautiful it is, flawless really, and I think to myself how strange it is that Evelyn has pulled me through so much; how she's always been there when I needed her most. I look back at the plate, thoroughly unhungry, pick up my fork, study the plate hard for a minute or two, whimper to myself before sighing and putting the fork down. I pick up my champagne glass instead.

From Bret Easton Ellis, *American Psycho* (1991).

A DIY Dinner

Fabullus, if the gods are kind,
In a few days you'll be wined and dined
At my house – if it's understood
You bring the feast with you: good food,
Good wine, a pretty girl, salt wit,
And lots of laughs to garnish it.
Those are the terms of my fine dinner,
Sweet friend, for the old cobweb-spinner
Is busy in my purse. My side
Of the bargain will be to provide
The most delicious of all presents
Imaginable, love's pure essence –
The ointment which was my girl's gift
From Venus and the Loves. Once sniffed,
You'll beg the gods to metamorphose
Fabullus into one huge nose!

Catullus 'Poem 13', (c. 84–54 BC), translated by James Michie (1969).

Pot Luck

Denise was soon made aware of the situation and accepted it; it was entirely normal for Simenon to have regular sexual connections with the maids. Denise wrote later that one new maid, on learning of the situation, asked a colleague: '*On passe toutes à la casserole?*' She was told that it was not compulsory, but she would certainly be asked.

From Patrick Marnham, *The Man Who Wasn't Maigret: A Portrait of Georges Simenon* (1992).

A Food Molester

CLIFF: Stop yelling. I'm trying to read.

JIMMY: Why do you bother? You can't understand a word of it.

CLIFF: Uh huh.

JIMMY: You're too ignorant.

CLIFF: Yes, and uneducated. Now shut up, will you?

JIMMY: Why don't you get my wife to explain it to you? She's educated. (*To her.*) That's right, isn't it?

CLIFF: (*Kicking out at him from behind his paper*) Leave her alone, I said.

JIMMY: Do that again, you Welsh ruffian, and I'll pull your ears off. (*He bangs* CLIFF's *paper out of his hands.*)

CLIFF: (*Leaning forward*) Listen – I'm trying to better myself. Let me get on with it, you big, horrible man. Give it me. (*Puts his hand out for paper.*)

ALISON: Oh, give it to him, Jimmy, for heaven's sake! I can't think!

CLIFF: Yes, come on, give me the paper. She can't think.

JIMMY: Can't think! (*Throws the paper back at him.*) She hasn't had a thought for years! Have you?

ALISON: No.

JIMMY: (*Picks up a weekly*) I'm getting hungry.

ALISON: Oh no, not already!

CLIFF: He's a bloody pig.

JIMMY: I'm not a pig. I just like food – that's all.

CLIFF: Like it! You're like a sexual maniac – only with you it's food. You'll end up in the *News of the World*, boyo, you wait. James

Porter, aged twenty-five, was bound over last week after pleading guilty to interfering with a small cabbage and two tins of beans on his way home from the Builder's Arms. The accused said he hadn't been feeling well for some time, and had been having black-outs. He asked for his good record as an air-raid warden, second class, to be taken into account.

JIMMY: (*Grins*) Oh, yes, yes, yes. I like to eat. I'd like to live too. Do you mind?

CLIFF: Don't see any use in your eating at all. You never get any fatter.

JIMMY: People like me don't get fat. I've tried to tell you before. We just burn everything up. Now shut up while I read. You can make me some more tea.

From John Osborne, *Look Back in Anger* (1957).

The Way to a Man's Heart

It was past their bedtime but their mother hadn't noticed yet. She was perched on a stool in the kitchen, reading a cookbook and munching one of the drumsticks Grandma Bedloe had left on the counter. 'Beef Goulash,' she read out. 'Beef with Pearl Onions. Beef Crescents. Agatha, what was that beef dish Grandma Bedloe told us about?'

'I don't remember,' Agatha said, switching to a yellow crayon.

'It was rolled up in Bisquick dough.'

'I remember she talked about it but I don't remember the name.'

'Bisquick dough sprinkled with herbs of some kind. She had it at their neighbors'.'

'Maybe you could call and ask her.'

'I can't do that. She'd want to know who I was making it for.'

Her mother set down the drumstick and wiped her fingers on a paper towel before turning another page. 'Beef à la Oriental,' she read out.

'Couldn't you just say you were making it for the typewriter man?'

'These things are touchy,' her mother said. 'You wouldn't understand.'

That hurt Agatha's feelings a little. She scowled and kicked her feet out. By mistake, she kicked Thomas. He was drowsing over a plastic cup of grapefruit juice. He opened his eyes and said, 'Stop.'

'Always serve a man red meat,' her mother told Agatha. 'Remember that for the future.'

'Red meat,' Agatha repeated dutifully.

'It shows you think of them as strong.'

'What if you served them fish?'

'Men don't like fish.'

'They like chicken, though.'

'Well, yes.'

'If you served them chicken, would they think you thought they were scared?'

'Hmm?' her mother said.

Thomas said, 'Mama, Agatha kicked me.' But his eyes were closing again.

'Well, here goes,' their mother said, and she reached for the phone.

'You're calling Grandma Bedloe?' Agatha asked.

'No, silly, I'm calling Mr Rumford.'

From Anne Tyler, *Saint Maybe* (1991).

Sins of the Flesh

THOMASINA: Septimus, what is carnal embrace?

SEPTIMUS: Carnal embrace is the practice of throwing one's arms around a side of beef.

THOMASINA: Is that all?

SEPTIMUS: No ... a shoulder of mutton, a haunch of venison well hugged, an embrace of grouse ... *caro, carnis*; feminine; flesh.

THOMASINA: Is it a sin?

SEPTIMUS: Not necessarily, my lady, but when carnal embrace is sinful it is a sin of the flesh, QED. We had *caro* in our Gallic Wars – 'The Britons live on milk and meat' – '*lacte et carne vivunt*'. I am sorry that the seed fell on stony ground.

From Tom Stoppard, *Arcadia* (1993).

A Feminine Diet

As to Annabella, she requires time and all the cardinal virtues, and in the interim I am a little verging towards one who demands neither, and saves me besides the trouble of marrying, by being married already. She besides does not speak English, and to me nothing but Italian – a great point, for from certain coincidences the very sound of that language is music to me, and she has black eyes, and *not* a very white skin, and reminds me of many in the Archipelago I wished to forget, and makes me forget what I ought to remember, all which are against me. I only wish she did not swallow so much supper – chicken wings, sweetbreads, custards, peaches and port wine; a woman should never be seen eating or drinking, unless it be *lobster salad* and *champagne*, the only truly feminine and becoming viands. I recollect imploring one lady not to eat more than a fowl at a sitting, without effect, and I have never yet made a single proselyte to Pythagoras.

Lord Byron to Lady Melbourne, 25 September 1812, from *Byron: A Self-Portrait in His Own Words*, edited by Peter Quennell.

Too Perfect to Eat

Very little food sufficed him; and he preferred fish to flesh for this extraordinary reason, that the latter, he said, rendered him ferocious. He disliked seeing women eat; and the cause of this extraordinary antipathy must be sought in the dread he always had, that the notion he loved to cherish of their perfection and almost divine nature might be disturbed. Having always been governed by them, it would seem that his very self-love was pleased to take refuge in the idea of their excellence, – a sentiment which he knew how (God knows how) to reconcile with the contempt in which, shortly afterwards, almost with the appearance of satisfaction, he seemed to hold them. But contradictions ought not to surprise us in characters like Lord Byron's; and then, who does not know that the slave holds in detestation his ruler?

Account of Lord Byron in Italy, quoted in *Letters and Journals of Lord Byron*, vol. II, Thomas Moore (1830).

Love Bites (iii)

We shall give the name of 'pregenital' to organizations of sexual life in which the genital zones have not yet taken over their predominant part. We have hitherto identified two such organizations, which almost seem as though they were harking back to early animal forms of life.

The first of these is the *oral* or, as it might be called, *cannibalistic* pregenital sexual organization. Here sexual activity has not yet been separated from the ingestion of food; nor are opposite currents within the activity differentiated. The *object* of both activities is the same; the sexual *aim* consists in the *incorporation* of the object – the prototype of a process which, in the form of *identification*, is later to play such an important psychological part. A relic of this constructed phase of organization, which is forced upon our notice by pathology, may be seen in thumb-sucking, in which the sexual activity, detached from the nutritive activity, has substituted for the extraneous object one situated in the subject's own body.

From Sigmund Freud, *Three Essays on the Theory of Sexuality* (revised edition, 1915) translated by James Strachey.

Dona Flor's Recipe for Marinated Crab

INGREDIENTS (*for 8 servings*)

1 *cup of coconut milk, without water*	*a shallot*
	2 *onions*
1 *cup of dendê oil*	$^1/_2$ *cup of olive oil*
2 *pounds of tender crabs*	*a red pepper*
	1 *pound of tomatoes*

SAUCE

3 *cloves of garlic*	
salt to taste	**GARNISH**
juice of one lemon	4 *tomatoes*
a pinch of coriander	1 *onion*
a sprig of parsley	1 *red pepper*

PROCEDURE

Grate two onions, crush garlic in mortar;
Onion and garlic do not smell badly, ladies,

They are fruits of the earth, perfumed.
Mince the coriander, the parsley, several tomatoes,
The shallot and half the pepper.
Mix all with the olive oil
And set aside this sauce
Of aromatic flavour.
(Those silly women who dislike the smell of onion,
What do they know about pure smells?
Vadinho liked to eat raw onion
And his kisses were like fire.)
Wash the crabs whole in lemon juice,
Wash them well, and then a little more,
To get out all the sand without taking away the taste of the sea.
Then season them, dipping them, one by one,
In the sauce, and put them in the skillet,
Each separate, with its seasoning.
Spread the remaining sauce over them
Slowly, for this is a delicate dish!
(Alas, it was Vadinho's favourite dish!)
Select four tomatoes, one pepper, one onion,
And slice them over the crabs
As a garnish.
Let them stand at room temperature for two hours
To absorb the flavour. Then put the skillet on the stove.
(He went to buy the crabs himself,
He was an old customer at the Market ...)

When almost done, and only then,
Add the coconut milk, and at the very end
The dendê oil, just before removing from the stove.
(He used to go and taste the seasoning every minute,
Nobody had a more delicate palate.)

There you have that exquisite dish, of the finest cuisine,
Whoever can make it can rightfully boast
Of being a first-rate cook.
But, lacking the skill, it is better not to try it,
For everyone was not born a kitchen artist.
(It was Vadinho's favourite dish,
I will never again serve it at my table.
His teeth bit into the crab,

His lips were yellow with the dendê oil,
Alas, never again his lips,
His tongue, never again
His mouth burning with raw onion!)

From Jorge Amado, *Dona Flor and her Two Husbands* (1969), translated by
Federico de Onis.

Cakes and Male

The passion came up in him, stroke after stroke, like the ringing of a
bronze bell, so strong and unflawed and indomitable. His knees
tightened to bronze as he hung above her soft face, whose lips parted
and whose eyes dilated in a strange violation. In the grasp of his hand
her chin was unutterably soft and silken. He felt strong as winter, his
hands were living metal, invincible and not to be turned aside. His
heart rang like a bell clanging inside him.

He took her up in his arms. She was soft and inert, motionless. All
the while her eyes, in which the tears had not yet dried, were dilated
as if in a kind of swoon of fascination and helplessness. He was
superhumanly strong, and unflawed, as if invested with supernatural
force.

He lifted her close and folded her against him. Her softness, her
inert, relaxed weight lay against his own surcharged, bronze-like
limbs in a heaviness of desirability that would destroy him, if he were
not fulfilled. She moved convulsively, recoiling away from him. His
heart went up like a flame of ice, he closed over her like steel. He
would destroy her rather than be denied.

But the overweening power of his body was too much for her. She
relaxed again, and lay loose and soft, panting in a little delirium. And
to him, she was so sweet, she was such bliss of release, that he would
have suffered a whole eternity of torture rather than forego one
second of this pang of unsurpassable bliss.

'My God,' he said to her, his face drawn and strange, transfigured,
'what next?'

She lay perfectly still, with a still, child-like face and dark eyes,
looking at him. She was lost, fallen right away.

'I shall always love you,' he said, looking at her.

But she did not hear. She lay, looking at him as at something she could never understand, never: as a child looks at a grown-up person, without hope of understanding, only submitting.

He kissed her, kissed her eyes shut, so that she could not look any more. He wanted something now, some recognition, some sign, some admission. But she only lay silent and child-like and remote, like a child that is overcome and cannot understand, only feels lost. He kissed her again, giving up.

'Shall we go down and have coffee and Kuchen?' he asked.

The twilight was falling slate-blue at the window. She closed her eyes, closed away the monotonous level of dead wonder, and opened them again to the every-day world.

'Yes,' she said briefly, regaining her will with a click. She went again to the window. Blue evening had fallen over the cradle of snow and over the great pallid slopes. But in the heaven the peaks of snow were rosy, glistening like transcendent, radiant spikes of blossom in the heavenly upper-world, so lovely and beyond.

Gudrun saw all their loveliness, she *knew* how immortally beautiful they were, great pistils of rose-coloured, snow-fed fire in the blue twilight of the heaven. She could *see* it, she knew it, but she was not of it. She was divorced, debarred, a soul shut out.

With a last look of remorse, she turned away, and was doing her hair. He had unstrapped the luggage, and was waiting, watching her. She knew he was watching her. It made her a little hasty and feverish in her precipitation.

They went downstairs, both with a strange other-world look on their faces, and with a glow in their eyes. They saw Birkin and Ursula sitting at the long table in a corner, waiting for them.

'How good and simple they look together,' Gudrun thought, jealously. She envied them some spontaneity, a childish sufficiency to which she herself could never approach. They seemed such children to her.

'Such good Kranzkuchen!' cried Ursula greedily. 'So good!'

'Right,' said Gudrun. 'Can we have Kaffee mit Kranzkuchen?' she added to the waiter.

And she seated herself on the bench beside Gerald. Birkin, looking at them, felt a pain of tenderness for them.

'I think the place is really wonderful, Gerald,' he said; 'prachtvoll and wunderbar and wunderschön and unbeschreiblich and all the other German adjectives.'

Gerald broke into a slight smile.

'*I* like it,' he said.

The tables, of white scrubbed wood, were placed round three sides of the room, as in a Gasthaus. Birkin and Ursula sat with their backs to the wall, which was of oiled wood, and Gerald and Gudrun sat in the corner next them, near to the stove. It was a fairly large place, with a tiny bar, just like a country inn, but quite simple and bare, and all of oiled wood, ceilings and walls and floor, the only furniture being the tables and benches going round three sides, the great green stove, and the bar and the doors on the fourth side. The windows were double, and quite uncurtained. It was early evening.

The coffee came – hot and good – and a whole ring of cake.

'A whole Kuchen!' cried Ursula. 'They give you more than us! I want some of yours.'

From D.H. Lawrence, *Women in Love* (1920).

The Morning After

They were sitting in a grimy coffee-shop around the corner from the hotel. Duncan was counting the rest of his money to see what they could afford to have for breakfast. Marian had undone the buttons of her coat, but was holding it together at the neck. She didn't want any of the other people to see her red dress: it belonged too obviously to the evening before. She had put Ainsley's ear-rings in her pocket.

Between them on the green arborite-surfaced table was an assortment of dirty plates and cups and crumbs and splashes and smears of grease, remnants of the courageous breakfasters who had pioneered earlier into the morning when the arborite surface was innocent as a wilderness, untouched by the knife and fork of man, and had left behind them the random clutter of rejected or abandoned articles typical of such light travellers. They knew they would never pass that way again. Marian looked at their waste-strewn trail with distaste, but she was trying to be casual about breakfast. She didn't want her stomach to make a scene. I'll just have coffee and toast, maybe with jelly; surely there will be no objections to that, she thought.

A waitress with harassed hair appeared and began to clear the table. She flapped a dog-eared menu down in front of each of them.

[115]

Marian opened hers and looked at the column headed 'Breakfast Suggestions'.

Last night everything had seemed resolved, even the imagined face of Peter with its hunting eyes absorbed into some white revelation. It had been simple clarity rather than joy, but it had been submerged in sleep; and waking to the sound of water sighing in the pipes and loud corridor voices, she could not remember what it was. She had lain quietly, trying to concentrate on it, on what it might possibly have been, gazing at the ceiling, which was blotched with distracting watermarks; but it was no use. Then Duncan's head had emerged from beneath the pillow where he had placed it during the night for safe-keeping. He stared at her for a moment as though he didn't have the least idea who she was or what he was doing in that room. Then 'Let's get out of here,' he said. She had leaned over and kissed him on the mouth, but after she had drawn back he had merely licked his lips, and as though reminded by the action said, 'I'm hungry. Let's go for breakfast. You look awful,' he had added.

'You're not exactly the picture of health yourself,' she replied. His eyes were heavily circled and his hair looked like a raven's nest. They got out of bed and she examined her own face briefly in the yellowed wavery glass of the bathroom mirror. Her skin was drawn and white and strangely dry. It was the truth: she did look awful.

She had not wanted to put those particular clothes back on but she had no choice. They dressed in silence, awkward in the narrow space of the room whose shabbiness was even more evident in the grey daylight, and furtively descended the stairs.

She looked at him now as he sat hunched over across the table from her, muffled again in his clothes. He had lit a cigarette and his eyes were watching the smoke. The eyes were closed to her, remote. The imprint left on her mind by the long famished body that had seemed in the darkness to consist of nothing but sharp crags and angles, the memory of its painfully-defined almost skeletal ribcage, a pattern of ridges like a washboard, was fading as rapidly as any other transcient impression on a soft surface. Whatever decision she had made had been forgotten, if indeed she had ever decided anything. It could have been an illusion, like the blue light on their skins. Something had been accomplished in his life though, she thought with a sense of weary competence; that was a small comfort; but for her nothing was permanent or finished. Peter was there, he hadn't vanished; he was as real as the crumbs on the table, and she would have to act accordingly. She would have to go back. She had missed the morning bus but she could get the afternoon one, after talking to Peter, explaining. Or rather avoiding explanation. There was no real reason to explain because explanations involved causes and effects and this event had been neither. It had come from nowhere and it led nowhere, it was outside the chain. Suddenly it occurred to her that she hadn't begun to pack.

She looked down at the menu. 'Bacon and Eggs, Any Style,' she read. 'Our Plump Tender Sausages.' She thought of pigs and chickens. She shifted hastily to 'Toast.' Something moved in her throat. She closed the menu.

'What do you want?' Duncan asked.

'Nothing, I can't eat anything,' she said, 'I can't eat anything at all. Not even a glass of orange juice.' It had finally happened at last then. Her body had cut itself off. The food circle had dwindled to a point, a black dot, closing everything outside … She looked at the grease-spot on the cover of the menu, almost whimpering with self-pity.

'You sure? Oh well then,' said Duncan with a trace of alacrity, 'that means I can spend it all on me.'

From Margaret Atwood, *The Edible Woman* (1969).

Cupboard Love

I loved a lass, a fair one,
    As fair as e'er was seen;
She was indeed a rare one,
    Another Sheba queen.
But fool as then I was,
    I thought she loved me too;
But now, alas, she's left me,
    Falero, lero, loo.

Her hair like gold did glister,
    Each eye was like a star;
She did surpass her sister,
    Which passed all others far.
She would me honey call;
    She'd, oh she'd kiss me too;

But now, alas, she's left me,
    Falero, lero, loo.

In summer time to Medley
    My love and I would go;
The boatmen there stood ready,
    My love and I to row.
For cream there would we call,
    For cakes, and for prunes too;
But now, alas, she's left me,
    Falero, lero, loo.

Many a merry meeting
    My love and I have had;
She was my only sweeting,
    She made my heart full glad.
The tears stood in her eyes,
    Like to the morning dew;
But now, alas, she's left me,
    Falero, lero, loo.

And as abroad we walkèd,
    As lovers' fashion is,
Oft as we sweetly talkèd
    The sun should steal a kiss.
The wind upon her lips
    Likewise most sweetly blew;
But now, alas, she's left me,
    Falero, lero, loo.

Her cheeks were like the cherry,
    Her skin as white as snow;
When she was blithe and merry,
    She angel-like did show.
Her waist exceeding small,
    The fives did fit her shoe;
But now, alas, she's left me,
    Falero, lero, loo.

In summer time or winter
    She had her heart's desire;

I still did scorn to stint her
    From sugar, sack, or fire.
The world went round about,
    No cares we ever knew;
But now, alas, she's left me,
    Falero, lero, loo.

From George Wither, *A Description of Love*, (1620).

Potatoes and Love: Some Reflections

The beginning

I have friends who begin with pasta, and friends who begin with rice, but whenever I fall in love, I begin with potatoes. Sometimes meat and potatoes and sometimes fish and potatoes, but always potatoes. I have made a lot of mistakes falling in love, and regretted most of them, but never the potatoes that went with them.

Not just any potato will do when it comes to love. There are people who go on about the virtues of plain potatoes – plain boiled new potatoes with a little parsley or dill, or plain baked potatoes with crackling skins – but my own feeling is that a taste for plain potatoes coincides with cultural antecedents I do not possess, and that in any case, the time for plain potatoes – if there is ever a time for plain potatoes – is never at the beginning of something. It is also, I should add, never at the end of something. Perhaps you can get away with plain potatoes in the middle, although I have never been able to.

All right, then: I am talking about crisp potatoes. Crisp potatoes require an immense amount of labor. It's not just the peeling, which is one of the few kitchen chores no electric device has been invented to alleviate; it's also that the potatoes, once peeled, must be cut into whatever shape you intend them to be, put into water to be systematically prevented from turning a loathsome shade of bluish-brownish-black, and then meticulously dried to ensure that they crisp properly. All this takes time, and time, as any fool can tell you, is what true romance is about. In fact, one of the main reasons why you must make crisp potatoes in the beginning is that if you don't make them in the beginning, you never will. I'm sorry to be so cynical about this, but that's the truth.

There are two kinds of crisp potatoes that I prefer above all others. The first are called Swiss potatoes, and they're essentially a large potato pancake of perfect hash browns; the flipping of the pancake is so wildly dramatic that the potatoes themselves are almost beside the point. The second are called potatoes Anna; they are thin circles of potato cooked in a shallow pan in the oven and then turned onto a plate in a darling mound of crunchy brownness. Potatoes Anna is a classic French recipe, but there is something so homely and old-fashioned about them that they can usually be passed off as either an ancient family recipe or something you just made up.

For Swiss potatoes: Peel 3 large (or 4 small) russet potatoes (or all-purpose if you can't get russets) and put them in cold water to cover. Start 4 tablespoons butter and 1 tablespoon cooking oil melting in a nice heavy large frying pan. Working quickly, dry the potatoes and grate them on the grating disk of the Cuisinart. Put them into a colander and squeeze out as much water as you can. Then dry them again on paper towels. You will need more paper towels to do this than you ever thought possible. Dump the potatoes into the frying pan, patting them down with a spatula, and cook over medium heat for about 15 minutes, until the bottom of the pancake is brown. Then, while someone is watching, loosen the pancake and, with one incredibly deft motion, flip it over. Salt it generously. Cook 5 minutes more. Serves two.

For potatoes Anna: Peel 3 large (or 4 small) russet potatoes (or Idahos if you can't get russets) and put them in water. Working quickly, dry each potato and slice into $\frac{1}{16}$-inch rounds. Dry them with paper towels, round by round. Put 1 tablespoon clarified butter into a cast-iron skillet and line the skillet with overlapping potatoes. Dribble clarified butter and salt and pepper over them. Repeat twice. Put into a 425° oven for 45 minutes, pressing the potatoes down now and then. Then turn up the oven to 500° and cook 10 more minutes. Flip onto a round platter. Serves two.

The middle (I)

One day the inevitable happens. I go to the potato drawer to make potatoes and discover that the little brown buggers I bought in a large sack a few weeks earlier have gotten soft and mushy and are sprouting long and quite uninteresting vines. In addition, one of them seems to have developed an odd brown leak, and the odd brown leak appears to be the cause of a terrible odor that in only a few seconds has permeated the entire kitchen. I throw out the potatoes and look in the cupboard for a box of pasta. This is the moment when the beginning ends and the middle begins.

The middle (II)
Sometimes, when a loved one announces that he has decided to go on a low-carbohydrate, low-fat, low-salt diet (thus ruling out the possibility of potatoes, should you have been so inclined), he is signaling that the middle is ending and the end is beginning.

The end
In the end, I always want potatoes. Mashed potatoes. Nothing like mashed potatoes when you're feeling blue. Nothing like getting into bed with a bowl of hot mashed potatoes already loaded with butter, and methodically adding a thin cold slice of butter to every forkful. The problem with mashed potatoes, though, is that they require almost as much hard work as crisp potatoes, and when you're feeling blue the last thing you feel like is hard work. Of course, you can always get someone to make the mashed potatoes for you, but let's face it: the reason you're blue is that there *isn't* anyone to make them for you. As a result, most people do not have nearly enough mashed potatoes in their lives, and when they do, it's almost always at the wrong time.

(You can, of course, train children to mash potatoes, but you should know that Richard Nixon spent most of his childhood making mashed potatoes for his mother and was extremely methodical about getting the lumps out. A few lumps make mashed potatoes more authentic, if you ask me, but that's not the point. The point is that perhaps children should not be trained to mash potatoes.)

For mashed potatoes: Put 1 large (or 2 small) potatoes in a large pot of salted water and bring to a boil. Lower the heat and simmer for at least 20 minutes, until tender. Drain and place the potatoes back in the pot and shake over low heat to eliminate excess moisture. Peel. Put through a potato ricer and immediately add 1 tablespoon heavy cream and as much melted butter and salt and pepper as you feel like. Eat immediately. Serves one.

From Nora Ephron, *Heartburn* (1983).

Manandwomanatmidnight

(formula by the Futurist art critic P.A. Saladin)
Pour some red zabaglione onto a round plate so as to form a large
pool.

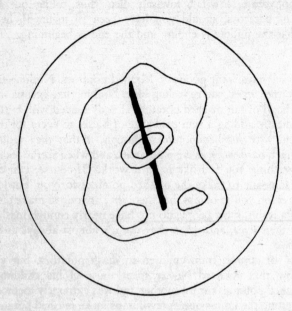

In the middle of this place a nice big onion ring transfixed by a stalk
of candied angelica. Then lay out two candied chestnuts, as shown in
the illustration, and serve one plate per couple.

From F.T. Marinetti, *The Futurist Cookbook* (1932),
translated by Suzanne Brill

Love and Death

The cook had spent three days over that dish. And she must take
great care, Mrs Ramsay thought, diving into the soft mass, to choose
a specially tender piece for William Bankes. And she peered into the
dish, with its shiny walls and its confusion of savoury brown and

yellow meats, and its bay leaves and its wine, and thought, This will celebrate the occasion – a curious sense rising in her, at once freakish and tender, of celebrating a festival, as if two emotions were called up in her, one profound – for what could be more serious than the love of man for woman, what more commanding, more impressive, bearing in its bosom the seeds of death; at the same time these lovers, these people entering into illusion glittering eyed, must be danced round with mockery, decorated with garlands.

'It is a triumph,' said Mr Bankes, laying his knife down for a moment. He had eaten attentively. It was rich; it was tender. It was perfectly cooked. How did she manage these things in the depths of the country? he asked her. She was a wonderful woman. All his love, all his reverence had returned; and she knew it.

'It is a French recipe of my grandmother's,' said Mrs Ramsay, speaking with a ring of great pleasure in her voice. Of course it was French. What passes for cookery in England is an abomination (they agreed). It is putting cabbages in water. It is roasting meat till it is like leather. It is cutting off the delicious skins of vegetables. 'In which,' said Mr Bankes, 'all the virtue of the vegetable is contained.' And the waste, said Mrs Ramsay. A whole French family could live on what an English cook throws away.

From Virginia Woolf, To The Lighthouse (1927).

Second Helpings

Dear Ipsitilla, my sweetheart,
My darling, precious, beautiful tart,
Invite me round to be your guest
At noon. Say yes, and I'll request
Another favour: make quite sure
That no one latches the front door,
And don't slip out for a breath of air,
But stay inside, please, and prepare
A love-play with nine long acts in it,
No intervals either! Quick, this minute,
Now, if you're in the giving mood;
For lying here, full of good food,

I feel a second hunger poke
Up through my tunic and my cloak.

Catullus, 'Poem 32' (c. 84–54 BC), translated by James Michie (1969).

Frogs' Legs

Put three dozen frogs' legs in a saucepan with a dozen chopped mushrooms, four shallots also chopped, and two ounces of butter. Toss them on a fire for five minutes; then add a tablespoon of flour, a little salt and pepper, grated nutmeg; and moisten with a glass of white wine and a teacupful of consommé.

Boil for ten minutes, meanwhile mix the yolks of four eggs with two tablespoonfuls of cream. Now remove the frogs' legs and the other ingredients from the fire, then add the eggs and cream, stirring continually until thoroughly mixed, and serve.

A noble aphrodisiac.

From Norman Douglas, *Venus in the Kitchen or Love's Cookery Book* (1952).

One Thing Leads to Another

Let us now examine the system of our senses taken as a whole. We shall see that the Author of Creation had two aims, one of which is the consequence of the other, namely the preservation of the individual and the continuation of the species.

Such is the destiny of man, considered as a sensitive being; it is towards this dual goal that all his activities are directed.

The eye perceives external objects, reveals the marvels with which man is surrounded, and teaches him that he is part of a great whole.

Hearing perceives sounds, not only as an agreeable sensation, but also as a warning of the movement of potentially dangerous bodies.

Feeling, in the form of pain, gives immediate notice of all bodily wounds.

The hand, that faithful servant, not only prepares man's withdrawal from danger, and protects him on his way, but also lays hold by choice of those objects which instinct tells it are most suitable for making good the losses caused by the maintenance of life.

Smell investigates those objects: for noxious substances almost always have an evil odour.

Then taste makes its decision, the teeth are set to work, the tongue joins with the palate in savouring, and soon the stomach begins its task of assimilation.

And now a strange languor invades the body, objects lose their colour, the body relaxes, the eyes close, everything disappears, and the senses are in absolute repose.

When he awakes, man sees that nothing has changed in his surroundings, but a secret fire is aflame in his breast, a new faculty has come into play; he feels an urge to share his existence with another being.

This disturbing and imperious urge is common to both sexes; it brings them together, and unites them; and when the seed of a new existence has been sown, they can sleep in peace; they have just fulfilled their most sacred duty, by ensuring the perpetuation of the species.

From Jean-Anthelme Brillat-Savarin, *The Physiology of Taste* (1825), translated
by Anne Drayton.

Last Orders

Sunday, 29 January 1860
Saw Barrière who told us this striking anecdote. On the Place de Grève he had seen a condemned man whose hair had visibly stood on end when he had been turned to face the scaffold. Yet this was the man who, when Dr. Pariset had asked him what he wanted before he died, had answered: 'A leg of mutton and a woman.'

From the *Goncourt Journals*, by Edmond (1822–96) and Jules (1830–70)
Goncourt, translated by Robert Baldick.

Gentleman's Relish

Mr. John Dounce was returning one night from the Sir Somebody's

[125]

Head, to his residence in Cursitor Street – not tipsy, but rather excited, for it was Mr. Jennings's birthday, and they had had a brace of partridges for supper, and a brace of extra glasses afterwards, and Jones had been more than ordinarily amusing – when his eyes rested on a newly-opened oyster shop, on a magnificent scale, with natives laid, one deep, in circular marble basins in the windows, together with little round barrels of oysters directed to Lords and Baronets, and Colonels and Captains, in every party of the habitable globe.

Behind the natives were the barrels, and behind the barrels was a young lady of about five-and-twenty, all in blue, and all alone – splendid creature, charming face, and lovely figure! It is difficult to say whether Mr. John Dounce's red countenance, illuminated as it was by the flickering gas-light in the window before which he paused, excited the lady's risibility, or whether a natural exuberance of animal spirits proved too much for that staidness of demeanour which the forms of society rather dictatorially prescribe. But certain it is that the lady smiled: then put her finger upon her lip, with a striking recollection of what was due to herself; and finally retired, in oyster-like bashfulness, to the very back of the counter. The sad-dog sort of feeling came strongly upon John Dounce; he lingered – the lady in blue made no sign. He coughed – still she came not. He entered the shop.

'Can you open me an oyster, my dear?' said Mr. John Dounce.

'Dare say I can, sir,' replied the lady in blue with playfulness. And Mr. John Dounce ate one oyster, and then looked at the young lady; and then ate another, and then squeezed the young lady's hand as she was opening the third, and so forth, until he had devoured a dozen of those at eightpence in less than no time.

'Can you open me half a dozen more, my dear?' inquired Mr. John Dounce.

'I'll see what I can do for you, sir,' replied the young lady in blue, even more bewitchingly than before; and Mr. John Dounce ate half a dozen more of those at eightpence.

From Charles Dickens, Sketches by 'Boz' (1836–7).

Snails à la C.C.C.

Boil the snails for about twenty minutes in salt water. Then take them out of the shells.

Chop some rosemary, an onion, garlic, and parsley, and put them to fry in olive oil in a saucepan; place the snails in it and season with pepper and salt. After a few minutes add a handful of fresh or dry mushrooms, half a cup of broth, and a little tomato sauce dissolved in water.

Let them boil for about a quarter of an hour and then pour in a glass of strong red wine and let the snails cook.

An old friend ate this dish in Bolgidinga when he was there, and declares that he found himself at least ten years younger!

From Norman Douglas, *Venus in the Kitchen or Love's Cookery Book* (1952).

A Tasty Dish

Good manners apart, though, the aspect of those monumental dishes of macaroni was worthy of the quivers of admiration they evoked. The burnished gold of the crusts, the fragrance of sugar and cinnamon they exuded, were but preludes to the delights released from the interior, when the knife broke the crust; first came a smoke laden with aromas, then chicken livers, hard boiled eggs, ham, chicken and truffles in masses of piping hot, glistening macaroni, to which the meat juice gave an exquisite hue of suède.

The beginning of the meal, as happens in the provinces, was quiet. The arch-priest made the sign of the Cross and plunged in without a word. The organist absorbed the succulent dish with closed eyes; he was grateful to the Creator that his ability to shoot hare and woodcock could bring him ecstatic pleasures like this, and the thought came to him that he and Teresina [his dog] could exist for a month on the cost of one of these dishes; Angelica, the lovely Angelica, forgot her Tuscan affectations and part of her good manners and devoured her food with the appetite of her seventeen years and the vigour given by grasping her fork half-way up the handle. Tancredi, in an attempt to link gallantry with greed, tried to imagine himself tasting, in the aromatic forkfuls, the kisses of his neighbour Angelica, but he realised at once that the experiment was disgusting and suspended it, with a mental reserve about reviving this fantasy with the pudding; the Prince, although rapt in the contemplation of Angelica sitting opposite him, was the only one at table able to notice that the *demi-glace* was overfilled, and made a mental note to tell the cook so next day; the others ate without thinking of anything, and without realising that the food seemed so delicious because sensuality was circulating in the house.

From Giuseppe Tomasi di Lampedusa, *The Leopard* (1958), translated by Archibald Colquhoun.

The Fruit of Love (i)

How beautiful are thy feet with shoes, O prince's daughter! the joints of thy thighs are like jewels, the work of the hands of a cunning workman.

2 Thy navel is like a round goblet, which wanteth not liquor: thy belly is like an heap of wheat set about with lilies.

3 Thy two breasts are like two young roes that are twins.

4 Thy neck is as a tower of ivory; thine eyes like the fishpools in Heshbon, by the gate of Bath-rabbin: thy nose is as the tower of Lebanon which looketh toward Damascus.

5 Thine head upon thee is like Carmel, and the hair of thine head like purple; the king is held in the galleries.

6 How fair and how pleasant art thou, O love, for delights!

7 This thy stature is like to a palm tree, and thy breasts to clusters of grapes.

8 I said, I will go up to the palm tree, I will take hold of the boughs thereof: now also thy breasts shall be as clusters of the vine, and the smell of thy nose like apples;

9 And the roof of thy mouth like the best wine for my beloved, that goeth down sweetly, causing the lips of those that are asleep to speak.

10 I am my beloved's, and his desire is toward me.

11 Come, my beloved, let us go forth into the field; let us lodge in the villages.

12 Let us get up early to the vineyards; let us see if the vine flourish, whether the tender grape appear, and the pomegranates bud forth: there will I give thee my loves.

13 The mandrakes give a smell, and at our gates are all manner of pleasant fruits, new and old, which I have laid up for thee, O my beloved.

From the Song of Solomon: II, Authorised Version.

Butter Wouldn't Melt ...

I was in love with a woman who was all grace and perfection, beautiful of shape, and gifted with all imaginable charms. Her cheeks were like roses, her forehead lily white, her lips like coral; she had teeth like pearls, and breasts like pomegranates. Her mouth opened round like a ring; her tongue seemed to be incrusted with precious gems; her eyes, black and finely slit, had the languor of slumber, and her voice the sweetness of sugar. With her form pleasantly filled out, her flesh was mellow like fresh butter, and pure as the diamond.

As to her vulva, it was white, prominent, round as an arch; the centre of it was red, and breathed fire, without a trace of humidity; for, sweet to the touch, it was quite dry. When she walked it showed in relief like a dome or an inverted cup. In reclining it was visible between her thighs, looking like a kid couched on a hillock.

From Sheikh Umar Ibn Muhammed al-Nefzawi, *The Perfumed Garden: The History of Djoâidi and Fadehat el Djemal*, sixteenth century, translated by Sir Richard Burton.

Shaken not Stirred

Escape into books. When he asks what you're reading, hold it up without comment. The next day look across to the brown chair and you will see him reading it too. A copy from the library that morning. He has seven days. He will look over the top and wink, saying: Beat you.

He will seem to be listening to the classical music station, glancing quickly at you for approval.

At the theater he will chomp Necco wafers loudly and complain about the head in front of him.

He will ask you what *supercilious* means.

He will ask you who Coriolanus is.

He might want to know where Sardinia is located.

What's a *croissant*?

Begin to plot your getaway. Envision possibilities for civility. These are only possibilities.

A week, a month, a year: Tell him you've changed. You no longer like the same music, eat the same food. You dress differently. The two of you are incongruous together. When he tells you that he is changing too, that he loves your records, your teas, your falafel, your shoes, tell him: See, that's the problem. Endeavor to baffle.

Pace around in the kitchen and say that you are unhappy.

But I love you, he will say in his soft, bewildered way, stirring the spaghetti sauce but not you, staring into the pan as if waiting for something, a magic fish, to rise from it and say: That is always enough, why is that not always enough?

From Lorrie Moore, 'How', *Self-Help* (1985).

Bed and Bored

SIMO: That was the best meal I've had in this house this year. I don't know when I've enjoyed my food so much. My wife has just given me a capital lunch, and told me to go and have a sleep. Huh! I don't think! There's more to it than that. It isn't just by accident that she gives me a better lunch than usual. She wants to get me into bed, that's what the old lady wants. I don't think I care for bed just after lunch; no, thank you, so I've slipped out quietly. I know she's waiting for me, in a high old temper.

TRANIO: So there's trouble in store for the old man before the day's out. He's in for a bad dinner and a rough night.

SIMO: The more I think of it, the more sure I am: to have an old wife and a rich one is to say good-bye to slumber. It's a positive torture to go to bed. That's why I have now decided to take a walk into town rather than have a nap at home. I don't know how it is with you; I know how it is with me all right – or rather all wrong – and it'll get worse.

From Plautus, *The Ghost* (c. 254–184 BC), translated by E.F. Watling.

Just a Little Neck

The candles had all burned down, and the only light was that of the moon and the street. I could see his iced and gleaming profile as he set the child down on the pillow. 'Come here, Louis, you haven't fed enough, I know you haven't,' he said with that same calm, convincing voice he had used skillfully all evening. He held my hand in his, his own warm and tight. 'See her, Louis, how plump and sweet she looks, as if even death can't take her freshness; the will to live is too strong! He might make a sculpture of her tiny lips and rounded hands, but he cannot make her fade! You remember, the way you wanted her when you saw her in that room.' I resisted him. I didn't want to kill her. I hadn't wanted to last night. And then suddenly I remembered two conflicting things and was torn in agony: I remembered the powerful beating of her heart against mine and I hungered for it, hungered for it so badly I turned my back on her in the bed and would have rushed out of the room had not Lestat held me fast; and I remembered her mother's face and that moment of horror when I'd dropped the child and he'd come into the room. But he wasn't mocking me now; he was confusing me. 'You want her, Louis. Don't you see, once you've taken her, then you can take whomever you wish. You wanted her last night but you weakened, and that's why she's not dead.' I could feel it was true, what he said. I could feel again that ecstasy of being pressed to her, her little heart going and going. 'She's too strong for me ... her heart, it wouldn't give up,' I said to him. 'Is she so strong?' he smiled. He drew me close to him. 'Take her, Louis, I know you want her.' And I did. I drew close to the bed now and just watched her. Her chest barely moved with her breath, and one small hand was tangled in her long, gold hair. I couldn't bear it, looking at her, wanting her not to die and wanting her; and the more I looked at her, the more I could taste her skin, feel my arm sliding under her back and pulling her up to me, feel her soft neck. Soft, soft, that's what she was, so soft. I tried to tell myself it was best for her to die – what was to become of her? – but these were lying thoughts. I wanted her! And so I took her in my arms and held her, her burning cheek on mine, her hair falling down over my wrists and brushing my eyelids, the sweet perfume of a child strong and pulsing in spite of sickness and death. She moaned now, stirred in her sleep, and that was more than I could bear. I'd kill her before I'd let her wake and know it. I went into her throat and heard Lestat saying to me strangely, 'Just a little tear. It's just a little throat.' And I obeyed him.

From Anne Rice, *Interview with the Vampire* (1976).

Venison

Paul set the bags down, told how they had split
the deer apart, the ease of peeling it
simpler than skinning a fruit, how the buck
lay on the worktable, how they sawed
an anklebone off, the smell not rank.
The sun slipped into night.

Where are you I wondered as I grubbed
through cupboards for noodles at least.
Then came venison new with blood,
stray hair from the animal's fur.
Excited, we cooked the meat.

Later, I dreamt against your human chest,
you cloaked me in your large arms, then
went for me the way you squander food sometimes.
By then, I was eating limbs in my sleep, somewhere
in the snow alone, survivor of a downed plane,
picking at the freshly dead. Whistles
of a far-off flute – legs, gristle, juice.
I cracked an elbow against a rock, awoke.
Throughout the night, we consumed and consumed.

Karen Chase, *New Yorker* (27 November 1995).

Declaration of Love Dinner

A shy lover yearns to express his feelings to a beautiful and intelligent woman. The following Declaration of Love Dinner served on the terrace of a grand hotel in the twinkling night of the city will help him to achieve this aim.

I Desire You: antipasto composed of a myriad selection of exquisite tid-bits, which the waiter will only let them admire, while She contents herself with bread and butter.

Flesh Adored: A big plate made from a shining mirror. In the centre, chicken slices perfumed with amber and covered with a thin layer of cherry jam. She, while eating, will admire her reflection in the plate.

This is How I'll Love You: Little tubes of pastry filled with many different flavours, one of plums, one of apples cooked in rum, one of potatoes drenched in cognac, one of sweet rice, etc. She, without batting an eyelid, will eat them all.

Super Passion: A very compact cake of sweet pastry with small cavities on the top filled with anise, glacier mints, rum, juniper and Amaro.

Tonight With Me: A very ripe orange enclosed in a large hollowed-out sweet pepper, embedded in a thick zabaglione flavoured with juniper and salted with little bits of oyster and drops of sea water.

Formula by the Futurist Aeropainter,
FILLÌA

From F.T. Marinetti, *The Futurist Cookbook* (1932), translated by Suzanne Brill.

The Woman Who Loved to Cook

If no man appeared who would love her
(her face moist with cooking,
her breasts full of apple juice
or wine),
she would whip one up:
of gingerbread,
with baking powder
to make him rise.

Even her poems
were recipes.
'Hunger,' she would write, 'hunger.'
The magic word to make it go away.
But nothing filled her up
or stopped that thump.
Her stomach thought it was a heart.

Then one day she met a man,
his cheeks brown as gingerbread,
his tongue a slashed pink ham
upon a platter.
She wanted to eat him whole
& save his eyes.
Her friends predicted he'd eat her.

How does the story end?
You know it well.

She's getting fatter
& she drinks too much.

Her shrink has read her book
& heard her tale.

'Oral,' he says,
& coughs
& puffs his pipe.

'Oral,'
he says,
& now
'time's up.'

Looking for love, she read cookbooks,
She read recipes for *tartlettes*,
terrines de boeuf, timbales,
& Ratatouille.
She read cheese fondue
& Croque Monsieur,
& Hash High Brownies
& Lo Mein.

Erica Jong, *Half-Lives* (1973).

The Edible Man

She turned to him. 'Where's the kitchen?' but she didn't wait for an answer. Instead she followed the trail of cooking smells, sniffing them out like a bloodhound, letting her senses lead her there.

She pulled open the fridge. Milk, cheese, butter. In the freezer compartment: vanilla ice-cream. She took out these things and went back to Connor, who was still in his bedroom, bare-chested, immobile. She opened the carton of milk, pulled at the waist-band of his trousers and poured the milk down inside. The milk was cold.

'Stop!' He tried to move away. 'Stop that!'

She laughed at him. 'I can't!'

She threw down the empty carton and picked up the tub of ice-cream, ripped off its lid and pushed a handful of it into her mouth.

Connor's trousers were wet and heavy. He began to unbutton them, but couldn't help noticing as he did so how the skin on her chest and neck seemed even redder and angrier. He stopped what he was doing and instead took the carton of ice-cream from her, put in his hand and scooped some out. He applied it to her throat and her chest.

She enjoyed this sensation: the coldness of the ice and the warmth of his skin underneath it. She pulled him to her. He still smelled of oranges. She pushed her face on to his neck, into his hair and smelled him properly. What did he really smell of?

She felt his hands on her breasts, her back, but they held no ice now, were simply touching her. She whispered, close to his ear, 'What do you taste like?' and took a tentative nibble.

'Christ!'

He jerked his head away, slapping a hand on to the spot she'd bitten. He checked his fingers to see if she had drawn blood. The expression on her face implied that she had. He frowned at her. 'That's dangerous.'

'You taste like tomatoes.'

He couldn't help smiling. 'You've still got bean-juice all over your face, it's probably that you can taste.'

He put out his hand and gently wiped some of the mess from her cheek. She grabbed his fingers and pushed them into her mouth, sucking them, tasting salt and garlic and resin. The feel of her mouth excited him. His trousers felt strange, though, as if prematurely full of creamy semen. He wanted to take them off but was embarrassed by his sudden state of arousal.

She sucked his fingers and then his hand, covering it in speculative licks and nibbles. He was being savaged by an irrepressible toy dog. She ran her nose from his wrist to his armpit, savouring him, chewing at his underarm hair and tasting the nasty bitter taste of his deodorant. She spat and screwed up her face. To quell the taste she grabbed hold of the pat of butter and bit into it. He said, 'Don't eat that! It's butter! Don't eat butter like that,' while he tried, at the same time, to pull off his trousers. She watched this and laughed when she saw the head of his penis jutting out from the opening in his boxer shorts. Roughly she shoved him backwards, on to the bed. Her mind was crammed full of buttery things, yellow things, oil and excess.

He lay on the bed, at once hopeful and hopeless. She knocked the remnants of the tray on to the floor, picking up some mushrooms in the process, one of which she pushed into his navel, then straddled him, low down, squatting either side of his knees and staring at his manhood.

She had never seen a penis before and was both fascinated and amused by what she saw. He looked like a pink leek, a radish, a red asparagus. He smelled milky.

His eyes widened as she leaned forward and took the tip of him into her mouth. She said, her mouth now full, 'You taste like an oyster, like a prawn.'

She was not overly impressed by the taste, but it seemed a natural enough flavour so she pressed down her teeth, ever so slightly. He sat bolt upright – 'Don't bite it! Please God!' – and jerked her head away.

He saw her face, so stupid, so child-like, so full of impulse, and wondered what they were doing, what they could do. At the back of his mind he knew that he would make love with her, if he could, but he didn't know, couldn't be sure, that she wouldn't change her mind half-way through, get bored or get angry. She wasn't emotionally consistent.

He pulled her closer to him and touched the redness on her chest and neck, then took her nipple into his mouth as she sat astride him. She pulled it away. 'That's my job.'

Is she joking? he wondered.

Her face was serious. 'If we have sex now ...' she frowned, 'will it be interesting? Will it taste of anything? I mean, what would we do?'

Even as she spoke, he felt himself diminishing. He said, 'I suppose the point is that you do it because you want to be close to another person.'

She pulled back slightly and stared at him. His face was covered by his hair, his body was lean. Like the bacon, she thought, not too much fat on it.

She pushed his hair away from his face. Underneath it, his eyes were uncertain. She liked that. She felt herself warming inside, bubbling a little, like milk before it boils. She pushed him gently down again and pulled off his shorts.

This is a real, live, proper man, she thought, delighted.

She pulled the covers over him, as though tucking him up for the night, scooped another mittful of ice-cream from the tub, and then slipped in beside him. She pushed down her creamy hands and took hold of his now somewhat flabby member. He gasped at the coldness of her touch.

'Where does this go?' she asked quietly. Then added, 'Don't tell me, I'll guess.'

From Nicola Barker, *Reversed Forecast* (1994).

Second Helpings

'Every Debit must have its corresponding Credit,' explained Christie, 'Perhaps every bad must have its corresponding good. An extension might be called Moral Double-Entry. In eating these beef olives, which is very good for us, we are at the same time preventing someone else from eating them; which is undoubtedly bad for them.'

'We had beef olives over today,' said the Shrike, 'that's why we're eating them.'

'Not in Cawnpore,' said Christie.

'Eh?' said the Shrike. 'Mr Cameron took some home, too, we had so many over.'

'Did he pay for them?' asked Christie.

'No, of course not. It's his business,' said the Shrike, without offence.

'That's an added complication,' said Christie. 'Who do we Debit? And who Credit?'

'Christ knows,' said the Shrike.

'I'm uncertain, too,' said Christie.

Here is Heisenberg's Principle of Uncertainty:

Accurate measurement of an observable quantity necessarily produces uncertainties in one's knowledge of the values of other observables.

'I think he'll give up the beef olives soon,' said the Shrike, 'no one seems to want them very much any more. Only the old people buy them now. The housewives don't know what they are.'

'Why should they?' said Christie, 'Debit beef olives, Credit housewives.'

'Can't you leave your work at work?' said the Shrike, gently.

Christie nearly asked her what his work was; but he realised he might go too far. No one must know of his Great Idea, not even the Shrike.

The Shrike was a kindly, warm girl of about twenty-nine whom Christie had met at the Hammersmith Palais (venerated for the visit of the Original Dixieland Jazz Band) the night after doing his accounts. The Shrike had picked on Christie for a Ladies' Invitation, and that was that. Christie was not unwilling, for the Shrike was nice, nice was the word that applied nicely to the Shrike. Soon Christie knew that the Shrike had an Old Mum up in Islington, that she was not trying to find a husband like all the other girls were, that she had a modest flat of her own in Brook Green, near splendid Lyons' (Tapper's opposition), and that she would quite like to see Christie again, if it suited him, she would not want to impose but she did like his average kind face, and the way he dressed, and the way he held her properly, and this was a Ladies' Invitation after all, wasn't it?

'Yes,' Christie had said, generally, to everything, and thought to himself that if he could satisfactorily stabilise his sexual arrangements then he could the more efficiently concentrate on his Great Idea. And so it was to be: nothing happens by accident in this novel. Or almost nothing.

The occasion of the beef olives above was the second visit that Christie had made to the Shrike's flat. The first had been after the encounter at the Palais, when the Shrike had made it clear (in the same breath as she had suggested a second) that she never let anyone on the first occasion: it was one of her little rules.

After dinner on this second occasion, then, Christie having expressed proper gratitude for the provender provided, the Shrike asked him if he would care to recline on the moderately elegant sofa which helped to fill her living-room. Christie did so care, and the Shrike accordingly went to fetch her Goblin cylinder vacuum cleaner which was an old model but recently serviced and creating an excellent suction at its nozzle. The Shrike removed Christie's clothing, article by article, whilst at the same time giving him a good going over with the Goblin, using the full range of accessories as well as simply the end of the tube or pipe. Christie was enchanted: he quickly had one ejaculation, and another came after about twenty minutes. He was only eighteen. Then the Shrike took her own clothes off, very unashamedly and naturally, of course, and performed an unsophisticated but infinitely alluring dance for Christie, especially for him, solely for him. This spontaneous dance brought her closer and closer to Christie over a period of about fifteen minutes until it was being performed on top of him with extremely pleasurable results for both of them: and in the pleasantest course of time Christie and the Shrike were able to enjoy almost simultaneous orgasms of unforgettable proportions and intensities.

From B.S. Johnson, *Christie Malry's Own Double-Entry* (1973).

The Fruit of Love (ii)

No white nor red was ever seen
So am'rous as this lovely green.
Fond lovers, cruel as their flame,
Cut in these trees their mistress' name.
Little, alas, they know, or heed,
How far these beauties hers exceed!
Fair trees! wheres'e'er your barks I wound,
No name shall but your own be found.

When we have run our passion's heat,
Love hither makes his best retreat.
The gods, that mortal beauty chase,
Still in a tree did end their race.
Apollo hunted Daphne so,
Only that she might laurel grow:
And Pan did after Syrinx speed,
Not as a nymph, but for a reed.

What wondrous life in this I lead!
Ripe apples drop about my head;
The luscious clusters of the vine
Upon my mouth do crush their wine;
The nectarine and curious peach
Into my hands themselves do reach;
Stumbling on melons, as I pass,
Ensnared with flowers, I fall on grass.

From Andrew Marvell, 'The Garden' (1681).

Cunt

The misogynist said 'Fish'
he lacked the appetite for it.
Of myself I would say,
a slight starchiness, the juice of raw potato,
the scent of unripe camembert,
oystery seaweed soup, sometimes with a hint of miso,
a funky fermented richness.
My favourite is cream and baby's breath,
that magic week or so
that is all warm albumen,
an almost salty moreishness.
Of course it always ends in violence
in blood and liverish gore,
a metallic tang that appeals
mainly to Tartars who eat their meat raw.
I cannot cook, don't offer up
metaphors of my devotion
marinated, baked or fried.
But here, I've a marvellous truffle season,
at this very moment, in my underpants.
You be the diner I'll be the dinner.
Don't hold back after the ripe and runny entree.
Treat yourself to desert:
nibble on, right through the gristle,
offal, muscle to the scrape of bone.

Consume me, until the wound
that some claim it is, is all that's left.
Eat it up, swallow the presentiment
that it is cunty who will chew on you.

Alev Adil (unpublished, 1994)

III EATING SHIT

WHEN the Irish writers Somerville and Ross embarked on a tour of the Medoc in the 1890s, one of their first visits was to the church of St Michel in Bordeaux. The church was famous for its gruesome relics – a set of mummies, accidentally preserved by soil conditions in the subterranean cavern in which they had been interred. A cheerful guide interrupted her breakfast to lead the two women into the cavern, where she held up a candle and illuminated a group of skeletons with strips of leathery brown skin still attached: '*Voici la famille empoisonnée!*' she exclaimed dramatically. 'Observe the morsel still in the mouth of the little one! Mosh-rhume! *Hein?*' The entire family, the guide insisted, had been found dead after eating poisonous fungi, a story which Somerville and Ross did not entirely credit, although their spirits were considerably dampened by the grisly tableau. A few days later, when their carriage broke down on a country road, they were given a bed for the night by their driver's cousin, who honoured her unexpected guests by serving up wild mushrooms fried in oil.

'There rose before us', the cousins wrote in their account of the journey, 'a vision of *La Famille empoisonnée* among the mummies of St Michel, and the dusty bits of fungus that they still retained in their jaws'. They took a couple of mouthfuls and, to their hostess's obvious incomprehension, refused the rest. Yet it is the very detail which both writers remembered – the fragments of mushroom in the mummies' jaws – which makes the story so unlikely. Mushroom poisoning is not instantaneous; in the case of the most toxic mushroom of all, the Death Cap or *Amanita phalloides*, there is a deceptive period of remission during which the unfortunate sufferers think they are getting better, only to be felled by a second and invariably fatal onset of symptoms. If the mummies of St Michel really had pieces of mushroom stuck to their teeth, the most plausible explanation is that someone – perhaps an early exponent of the heritage industry – had put them there to impress gullible foreign tourists. Wild mushrooms – chanterelles, *pieds de mouton, trompettes de mort, morels, cèpes* or *porcini* – are one of the glories of Mediterranean cooking and an experienced cook is unlikely to use a poisonous variety by mistake. Admittedly the difference between the heavenly *Boletus edulis* and its mildly poisonous relatives (such as the alarmingly named Devil's Bolete) isn't completely obvious to the untutored eye; I once picked a cluster of luscious yellow chanterelles in an English hedgerow, only to discover when I got home that they also looked quite a lot like the *false* chanterelle, which causes 'digestive complaints' according to the mushroom expert and chef, Antonio Carluccio. But the horrified reaction to fungi of Somerville and Ross, in a region where wild mushrooms are habitually picked and eaten, demonstrates the power of cultural difference and the ease with which an existing prejudice can be reinforced. People have fixed ideas about what is and isn't edible, and some are more easily persuaded out of them than others.

Travellers' tales are full of these misunderstandings, in which intention and effect are almost comically far apart. Harold McGee argues in *On Food and Cooking: The Science and Lore of the Kitchen* that almost all our likes and dislikes are learned; our attitude to smells and tastes, he says, 'is moulded by social custom, opportunity, and often private associations with pleasant or painful moments'. Yet Lady Macartney's account of having to force herself to eat sea slugs, a particular delicacy in Chinese Turkestan, shows that some cultural barriers are impossible to cross. It is also a reminder that bad experiences with food are not always caused by malice, although they are sometimes the result of practical jokes. I've always been puzzled by the peculiar English custom of inserting hard, inedible objects into one of the courses at a celebratory meal and laughing immoderately when someone cracks a tooth; the fact that the victim then has to hand the offending object back, because the silver threepenny bits traditionally placed in Christmas puddings are now a collectors' item, adds insult to injury. My own family went in for a cheaper variant: sausage rolls stuffed with cotton-wool or clothes pegs in place of meat, which were a standard practical joke at parties during my childhood. One explanation which suggests itself is that the oral drives, being infantile in origin (as Freud suggests), never quite shake off their association with infantile behaviour. Another is that women, on whom the burden of preparing food tends to fall, simply get tired of their nurturing role and can't resist getting their own back. It's a striking fact that women's fiction, cutting across cultural and temporal boundaries, identifies the endless preparation of meals for husbands or fathers who take their effort entirely for granted as the kind of drudgery which prompts female discontent and rebellion.

Of course every child who's been sent to bed without supper knows that food, or the absence of it, can make you very miserable indeed; one of the most mortifying memories of my own childhood involves, of all apparently innocuous objects, a Jaffa cake. We were visiting my father's oldest friend, who came from the same north-eastern English town but had progressed rapidly up the social scale to become headmaster of a boys' school in Hertfordshire; these visits were always rather stilted affairs and, even at the age of seven, I knew that they were replete with the risk of social gaffes. On this occasion I innocently bit into the Jaffa cake, realised I didn't like it, and was left with a dreadful dilemma: my mother would, I knew, accuse me of 'showing her up' in front of my father's posh friends if I failed to finish it. I settled for concealing it in my right palm and sitting completely still for the rest of the visit, in the vain hope that I might spot a place to conceal it. The Jaffa cake, however, did not enter a reciprocal condition of stasis and oozed stickily through my fingers when we got up to leave, precipitating the scene I had attempted to avoid.

Even food you enjoy can make you sick in sufficient quantities, especially when it is accompanied by generous amounts of alcohol. This is a lesson Samuel Pepys seems to have been reluctant to learn; during a typically convivial evening in the summer of 1660, he ate 'a fine collation of collar of beef, &c', washed down with Rhenish wine, and was ill throughout the night. A day later, he was forced to admit that his illness did not have an organic cause, writing in his diary: 'I rose today without any pain, which makes me think that my pain yesterday was nothing but from my drinking too much the day before.' His diary continues, however, to record spectacular episodes of nocturnal vomiting and stupendous hangovers. Most people's bad experiences with food remain within this register but the explorer Captain Scott, during his doomed expedition to the South Pole, unintentionally wrecked his slender chance of survival by blending a concoction of curry powder and melted pemmican – dried pounded meat mixed with fat and sometimes with currants – when food stocks ran low. The final pages of his diary contain one harrowing entry after another, recording in detail how a violent bout of indigestion made him so ill that he failed to realise that frostbite had set in to his right foot, destroying his toes. Scott's suffering was accidental but secret policemen in disparate parts of the world have long understood the potential of food to make people do what they want – not just by withholding it but as an instument of torture.

'This leaflet will bring tears to your eyes' announces a recent campaign by Amnesty International, the organisation which works on behalf of torture victims and political prisoners throughout the world. The picture below the lettering is innocuous enough: three long slender red chillies, one of them slit open so its seeds are spilling out. Inside, the leaflet explains that the pods were used as an instrument of torture on a bus conductor, Antony Ginting, in the town of Deli Tue in North Sumatra. The police who abducted him suspected him of theft, according to Amnesty, 'so to make him confess they beat him, then rubbed chillies into his eyes'. Anyone who has chopped up chillies while cooking and accidentally rubbed his or her eyes knows how painful even a small amount of their juice can be; contact-lens wearers have to wash their hands repeatedly to avoid the residue getting on their lenses when they take them out, or experience agonies when they insert them the following day. The idea that anyone should deliberately inflict such a punishment on another human being is startling but the practice is not as recondite as it sounds; another form of the same torture, this time inserting chillies into the anus, is said to have been practised in parts of the Indian sub-continent.

Roman writers occasionally mention a variant as a punishment for male homosexuality, although the context suggests they are referring to a gay in-joke rather than a genuine threat: the bisexual poet Catullus, warning a friend not to seduce a young man with whom he is in love, threatens to drag his feet apart and push slices of radish or mullet into his anus if he touches the boy. Radish, like chillies, is famously hot; mullet are bony. A fisherman made the mistake of approaching the Emperor Tiberius, who had retired to the island of Capri in fear of assassination attempts, and offering him a fine example of the same fish; furious at this breach in his security, Tiberius ordered his guards to rub it in the man's face. But then the Romans, as we know from the surviving recipes of the cooks who bore the name Apicius, were endlessly curious and inventive about food. Perhaps this means, as John Lanchester hints in *The Debt to Pleasure*, his witty novel about a murderous gourmet, that the more *haute* the *cuisine*, the more likely that its practitioners will be tempted to put food to other, less benign uses?

A Fly in My Soup

In that house everything was disgusting, not only the sleeping arrangements but the food. Concetta was slovenly, dirty, always in a hurry, always slapdash, and her kitchen was a black corner in which pans and dishes had the dirt of years upon them and there was never any water and nothing was ever washed and the cooking was always done in a headlong, happy-go-lucky style. Always, every day, Concetta cooked the same food, the dish that in Ciociaria is called *minestrina*: a number of thin slices cut from a home-made loaf and placed one on top of another, enough to fill a *spasetta*, which is a shell-shaped earthenware dish; and then, poured over the bread, a small potful of bean soup. This dish is eaten cold, after the bean soup has soaked thoroughly into the whole of the bread, reducing it to a mush. I never did think *minestrina* a good dish: but in Concetta's house, partly owing to the dirt, which meant that there were always a few dead flies or caterpillars to be found in it, partly because she was unable to make even this very simple dish properly, it positively turned my stomach. Besides, they ate it in the real peasant way, without bowls, dipping into the dish all together with their spoons, putting their spoons in their mouths and then plunging them into the mush again. And would you believe it? One day I made a remark to her on the subject of the large number of dead flies I found mixed up among the bread and the beans, and she, like the boorish creature she was, answered: 'Never mind, eat them up, eat them up! What's a fly, after all? It's meat, isn't it? – just as much as veal.' In the end, seeing that Rosetta could no longer bring herself to eat this filth, I took to going with Concetta, every now and then, out of the orange-grove on to the main road. This was where the market was now held; it was no longer in the town, where, what with the air raids and the Fascists and their requisitionings, nothing was now safe. On the main road you could find peasant-women selling new-laid eggs, fruit, a few bits of meat and even, on occasion, fish. The prices of all these things were crazily high, but if anyone tried to argue and get the price reduced, they would say: 'All right then, you can eat the money and I'll eat the eggs.' They too, of course, knew that there was a food shortage and that money in a time of food shortage is useless, and

[148]

they made my blood boil. However, I always bought something or other; and thus I ended up by providing things to eat for Concetta's family as well, to such an extent that my money melted away like water and this in itself became another cause for uneasiness.

From Alberto Moravia, *Two Women* (1957), translated by Angus Davidson.

Why Are You Serving This Shit?

'The worst thing was college food. Absolute disaster. I couldn't eat it. There was only one Indian restaurant in Oxford at the time, the Taj Mahal. It was terrible, so I called for the manager. "Why are you serving this shit?" He said it was for English students who knew no better. In the end I found a little old Indian lady in Cowley and for three years I used to go to her house for Sunday lunch.'

Tariq Ali, *Independent* (22 February 1994).

Don't Say Cheese

Uccello also did some work in *terra verde* and colour in the cloister of San Miniato outside Florence. He painted scenes from the lives of the Fathers of the Church, in which he ignored the rule of consistency in colouring, for he made the fields blue, the cities red, and the buildings in various colours as he felt inclined. He was wrong to do so, because something which is meant to represent stone cannot and should not be coloured with another tint. It is said that while Paolo was at work on this painting the abbot gave him for his meals hardly anything but cheese. Paolo grew sick of this, but being a mild-mannered man he merely decided not to go there any more. The abbot sent to look for him, but whenever Paolo heard the friars asking for him he arranged not to be at home. And if he happened to meet a pair of them in Florence he took to his heels as fast as he could in the opposite direction. Seeing this, two of them who were more curious than the rest (and could run faster) caught him up one day and demanded why he never returned to finish the work he had started and why he always ran away when he caught sight of a friar. Paolo said:

> You've brought me to such a sorry state that I not only run away from the sight of you, I can't even go where there are carpenters working. This is all the fault of your dim-witted abbot. What with his cheese pies and his cheese soups, he's stuffed me so full of cheese that I'm frightened they'll use me to make glue. If he went on any more I wouldn't be Paolo Uccello, I'd be pure cheese.

The friars roared with laughter and went and told the abbot what Uccello said; and then the abbot persuaded him to come back and gave him something else for his meals.

From Giorgio Vasari, Lives of the Artists, vol. I (1550), translated by
George Bull.

Shock Treatment

I woke warm and placid in my white cocoon. A shaft of pale, wintry sunlight dazzled the mirror and the glasses on the bureau and the metal doorknobs. From across the hall came the early morning clatter of the maids in the kitchen, preparing the breakfast trays.

I heard the nurse knock on the door next to mine, at the far end of the hall. Mrs Savage's sleepy voice boomed out, and the nurse went into her with the jingling tray. I thought, with a mild stir of pleasure, of the steaming blue china coffee pitcher and the blue china breakfast cup and the fat blue china cream jug with the white daisies on it.

I was beginning to resign myself.

If I was going to fall, I would hang on to my small comforts, at least, as long as I possibly could.

The nurse rapped on my door and, without waiting for an answer, breezed in.

It was a new nurse – they were always changing – with a lean, sand-coloured face and sandy hair, and large freckles polka-dotting her bony nose. For some reason the sight of this nurse made me sick at heart, and it was only as she strode across the room to snap up the green blind that I realized part of her strangeness came from being empty-handed.

I opened my mouth to ask for my breakfast tray, but silenced myself immediately. The nurse would be mistaking me for somebody else. New nurses often did that. Somebody in Belsize must be having shock treatments, unknown to me, and the nurse had, quite understandably, confused me with her.

I waited until the nurse had made her little circuit of my room, patting, straightening, arranging, and taken the next tray in to Loubelle one door farther down the hall.

Then I shoved my feet into my slippers, dragging my blanket with me, for the morning was bright, but very cold, and crossed quickly to the kitchen. The pink-uniformed maid was filling a row of blue china coffee pitchers from a great, battered kettle on the stove.

I looked with love at this line-up of waiting trays – the white paper napkins, folded in their crisp, isosceles triangles, each under the anchor of its silver fork, the pale domes of the soft-boiled eggs in the blue egg cups, the scalloped glass shells of orange marmalade. All I had to do was reach out and claim my tray, and the world would be perfectly normal.

'There's been a mistake,' I told the maid, leaning over the counter and speaking in a low, confidential tone. 'The new nurse forgot to bring in my breakfast tray today.'

I managed a bright smile, to show there were no hard feelings.

'What's the name?'

'Greenwood. Esther Greenwood.'

'Greenwood, Greenwood, Greenwood.' The maid's warty index finger slid down the list of names of the patients in Belsize tacked up on the kitchen wall. 'Greenwood, no breakfast today.'

I caught the rim of the counter with both hands.

'There must be a mistake. Are you sure it's Greenwood?'

'Greenwood,' the maid said decisively as the nurse came in.

The nurse looked questioningly from me to the maid.

'Miss Greenwood wanted her tray,' the maid said, avoiding my eye.

'Oh,' the nurse smiled at me, 'you'll be getting your tray later on this morning, Miss Greenwood. You ...'

But I didn't wait to hear what the nurse said. I strode blindly out into the hall, not to my room, because that was where they would come to get me, but to the alcove, greatly inferior to the alcove at Caplan, but an alcove, nevertheless, in a quiet corner of the hall, where Joan and Loubelle and DeeDee and Mrs Savage would not come.

I curled up in the far corner of the alcove with the blanket over my head. It wasn't the shock treatment that struck me, so much as the bare-faced treachery of Doctor Nolan. I liked Doctor Nolan, I loved her, I had given her my trust on a platter and told her everything, and she had promised, faithfully, to warn me ahead of time if ever I was to have another shock treatment.

From Sylvia Plath, *The Bell Jar* (1963).

Entertaining Guests

Steventon, 1 December 1798

My mother made her *entrée* into the dressing-room through crowds of admiring spectators yesterday afternoon, and we all drank tea together for the first time these five weeks. She has had a tolerable night, and bids fair for a continuance in the same brilliant course of action to-day … Mr Lyford was here yesterday; he came while we were at dinner, and partook of our elegant entertainment. I was not ashamed at asking him to sit down to table, for we had some pease-soup, a sparerib, and a pudding. He wants my mother to look yellow and to throw out a rash, but she will do neither.

From *Jane Austen's Letters* (1995), edited by Deidre Le Faye.

A Scrambled Message

Hélène had her opinions; she did not, for instance, like Matisse. She said a Frenchman should not stay unexpectedly to a meal, particularly if he asked the servant beforehand what there was for dinner. She said foreigners had a perfect right to do these things but not a Frenchman, and Matisse had once done it. So when Miss Stein said to her, 'Monsieur Matisse is staying for dinner this evening,' she would say, 'In that case I will not make an omelette but fry the eggs. It takes the same number of eggs and the same amount of butter but it shows less respect, and he will understand.'

From Elizabeth David, *Mediterranean Food* (1950).

Kitchen Dreams

Kalloo the cook had worked for the family for more years than he could remember. He had started as the cook's help, washing dishes, grinding the spices and running errands. When the old cook died of an overdose of opium Kalloo inherited both his job and his taste for opium. His inherent laziness fed by the enervating influence of the drug kept him working for his inadequate pay, because he lacked the energy and the courage to give notice and look for work elsewhere. Moreover, his emotions had grown roots through the years, and he was emotionally attached to the family. He had watched with affectionate interest the birth, childhood, youth and manhood of the sons of the house and felt he was an elder brother.

Of his own age he was uncertain but felt young enough when opium-inspired. Eyes outlined with powdered 'soorma', tiny attar-soaked bit of cotton hidden in his ear, his cotton embroidered cap set at an angle, he went of an evening to the Street of the Moon.

The morning after he would be slower of movement than usual, and when he weighed the flour, the lentils, the rice and fat for the day his hands would shake, and Mughlani, who had charge of the stores, would shake her grey head and wheeze asthmatically: 'You men, you are all animals even when your feet hang in the grave. What you need, Kalloo Mian, is a wife to keep you at home.'

'What I need is someone to help me in the kitchen. It is hard work that makes my hands shake and my head grow heavy,' he would grumble. But the repeated suggestion took root in his mind and he brooded over the need to find himself a wife. He had been married once when very young, but his wife had died and left him a son who had been nothing but a source of trouble.

Young Munnay lived with his mother's people and every now and again appeared saying he had lost his job and needed money. Kalloo would storm: 'Where do you think I can find the money? Dig it from the ground? Pluck it from the trees? Wait for it to rain from heaven? Why do you not work, you shiftless wretch? Work here with me and I'll teach you to be a cook. I could get you three or four rupees a month as my help. That is how I started.'

'Oh no,' the boy mocked. 'Start as your help and end as you have done! What great fortune have you piled up? I know the Collector Sahib's khansama who gets sixty rupees a month, and has a help, and you get twenty rupees like a plain barvarchi. I'll find work in a shop again, and be able to give you three or four rupees a month myself.'

'Much you have given me already. Get away from here you lazy son of an owl,' he raged, but he felt the sting of the taunts. He was not a plain 'barvarchi' who knew only how to cook Indian food, he was a 'khansama' who could serve the best English dishes too. Twenty rupees a month – why he could get sixty rupees too. He counted the number of people for whom he cooked – Khan Sahib one, Begum Sahib two, the two sons, guests, any number, say at least three or four a day, that made seven or eight. Then the servants … there was Mughlani one, and the widow Naseera who helped her, two – no one to help him – Nuru the bearer, three – Khan Sahib's bearer, four – his son Husnoo who worked for the master's two sons, five, himself, six, and of course the guests brought servants. That was much over twelve people – might be twice twelve meals a day for twenty rupees a month. One day he would ask for more pay or say, 'I can find work anywhere, I can cook English food –'

But the day was not today, not tomorrow …

From Attia Hosain, 'The Street of the Moon', *Phoenix Fled* (1953).

A Fishy Tale

'You see, *mon ami*, where you went wrong was over your fundamental assumption.' Hercule Poirot, beaming placidly across the table at his friend, waved an expository hand. 'A man under severe mental stress doesn't choose that time to do something that he's never done before. His reflexes just follow the track of least resistance. A man who is upset about something *might* conceivably come down to dinner dressed in his pyjamas – but they will be his *own* pyjamas – not somebody else's.

'A man who dislikes thick soup, suet pudding, and blackberries suddenly orders all three one evening. *You* say, because he is thinking of something else. But *I say that a man who has got something on his mind will order automatically the dish he has ordered most often before.*

'*Eh bien*, then, what other explanation could there be? I simply could not think of a reasonable explanation. And I was worried! The incident was all wrong. It did not fit! I have an orderly mind and I like things to fit. Mr Gascoigne's dinner order worried me.

'Then you told me that the man had disappeared. He had missed a Tuesday and a Thursday the first time for years. I liked that even less. A queer hypothesis sprang up in my mind. If I were right about it *the man was dead*. I made inquiries. The man *was* dead. And he was very neatly and tidily dead. In other words the bad fish was covered up with the sauce!

'He had been seen in the King's Road at seven o'clock. He had had dinner here at seven-thirty – two hours before he died. It all fitted in – the evidence of the stomach contents, the evidence of the letter. Much too much sauce! You couldn't see the fish at all!

From Agatha Christie, 'Four-and-Twenty Blackbirds' (1960).

Rubbing His Face in It

A few days after [Tiberius] came to Capreae a fisherman suddenly intruded on his solitude by presenting him with an enormous mullet, which he had lugged up the trackless cliffs at the rear of the island. Tiberius was so scared that he ordered his guards to rub the fisherman's face with the mullet. The scales skinned it raw, and the poor fellow shouted in his agony: 'Thank Heaven, I did not bring Caesar that huge crab I also caught!' Tiberius sent for the crab and had it used in the same way.

From Suetonius (born c. 70 AD), *The Twelve Caesars*, translated by Robert Graves (1957).

Learning Her Place

That day Yamina and Fatiha were preparing an ousbane couscous. Yamina, squatting, scraped the tripes in an enamel basin under the faucet. Fatiha chopped the vegetables and was having fun with her sister-in-law while she was peeling onions which made her cry and had driven the little ones away.

'Look, Yamina, if you want to be an excellent cook you have to do things in the right order, like my mother always said! Otherwise it will be spoiled! You start with the garlic, then the onion, then the spinach stems, forget about the leaves; after that you mix it with harissa and throw a fistful of raw rice in the mixture; here, help me stuff the tripe; do you see how clean it is? Come on, let's go, stuff, stuff!'

They broke into laughter just as Aïcha came into the kitchen.

'Come, Yamina, come, I have something else for you to do; Fatiha can finish by herself.'

Yamina regretfully obeyed her mother while Fatiha, who understood clearly that her mother-in-law did not like to see them together, having fun and not knowing what it was all about, continued her work without showing the least reaction. This only irritated Aïcha more, as she hated this attitude of indifference that she saw as a bit devious. She had been separating them so much lately that it could only have been intentional. Fatiha went on working as if nothing had happened. Dusting, putting things away, washing, ironing, cooking; all these things passed the time which strangely did not really seem to be her own any more. The feeling of something temporary and, at times, the certainty that the future would be different from the present (because this was not what she expected from life), clashed against its opposite: the feeling of immutability, powerlessness to change things at all, the sensation of impassable obstacles, of walls.

Aïcha was seated in the courtyard, sewing. Hocine came home. She held her arms out to him. He came to her and she made him sit under the fig tree. She looked at him with such love it was impossible to resist her; the sun wasn't any warmer than her eyes!

'My son, your father has gone to City Hall. Come, my son, sit down ... do you want some coffee?'

'Yes, thank you.'

Aïcha turned and called Fatiha.

'Fatiha, my daughter, make us a coffee.'

The mother and son remained silently next to each other under the fig tree. Then, no longer able to hold it back, she asked him the question that had been plaguing her for days.

'My son, are you happy?'

Hocine smiled.

'A wife is the reflection of her husband, my son; if you are happy, she is happy.'

Hocine said nothing and Aïcha dared not break the worrisome silence.

Fatiha served the coffee and went back to the kitchen.

From Ali Ghalem, *A Wife for My Son* (1979), translated by G. Kazolias.

Nero's Orgies

Gradually Nero's vices gained the upper hand: he no longer tried to laugh them off, or hide, or deny them, but openly broke into more serious crime. His feasts now lasted from noon till midnight, with an occasional break for diving into a warm bath, or if it were summer, into snow-cooled water. Sometimes he would drain the artificial lake in the Campus Martius, or the other in the Circus, and hold public dinner parties there, including prostitutes and dancing-girls from all over the city among his guests. Whenever he floated down the Tiber to Ostia, or cruised past the Gulf of Baiae, he had a row of temporary brothels erected along the shore, where married women, pretending to be inn-keepers, solicited him to come ashore. He also forced his friends to provide him with dinners; one of them spent 40,000 gold pieces on a turban party, and another even more on a rose banquet.

From Suetonius (born c. 70 AD), *The Twelve Cæsars*, translated by Robert Graves (1957).

A Real Job

'And what part of housework do you like the best?' the girl persisted.

Mrs Bell smiled again, wanly. 'Seems to me sometimes as if I couldn't tell what part I like the least!' she answered. Then with sudden heat: 'Oh, my child! Don't you marry till Ross can afford at least one servant for you!'

Diantha put her small, strong hands behind her head and leaned back in her chair. 'We'll have to wait some time for that, I fancy,' she said ... 'Now sit still for once, Mother dear; read or lie down. Don't stir till supper's ready.'

And from pantry to table she stepped, swiftly and lightly, setting out what was needed, greased her pans and set them before her, and proceeded to make biscuit.

Her mother watched her admiringly. 'How easy you do it!' she said. 'I never could make bread without getting flour all over me. You don't spill a speck!'

Diantha smiled. 'I ought to do it easy by this time. Father's got to have hot bread for supper – or thinks he has! – and I've made it every night when I was at home for these ten years back.'

'I guess you have,' said Mrs Bell proudly. 'You were only eleven when you made your first batch. I can remember just as well! I had one of my bad headaches that night – and it did seem as if I couldn't sit up! But your father has to have his biscuit whether or no. And you said, "Now, Mother, you lie right still on that sofa and let me do it! I can!" And you could. You did! They were better'n mine that first time – and your father praised 'em – and you've been at it ever since.'

'Yes,' said Diantha, with a deeper note of feeling that her mother caught, 'I've been at it ever since.'

'Except when you were teaching school,' pursued her mother ...

'I've got something to tell you presently, Mother.'

'I do hope you and Ross haven't quarrelled.'

'No, indeed we haven't, Mother. Ross is splendid. Only –'

'Only what, Diantha?'

'Only he's so tied up!' said the girl, brushing every chip from the hearth. 'He's perfectly helpless there, with that mother of his – and those four sisters.'

'Ross is a good son,' said Mrs Bell, 'and a good brother. I never saw a better. He's certainly doing his duty. Now if his father'd lived, you two could have got married by this time maybe, though you're too young yet.'

Diantha washed and put away the dishes she had used, saw that the pantry was in its usual delicate order, and proceeded to set the table, with light steps and no clatter of dishes.

'I'm twenty-one,' she said.

'Yes, you're twenty-one,' her mother allowed. 'It doesn't seem possible, but you are. My first baby!' She looked at her proudly.

'If Ross has to wait for all those girls to marry – and to pay his father's debts – I'll be old enough,' said Diantha grimly.

Her mother watched her quick assured movements with admiration, and listened with keen sympathy. 'I know it's hard, dear child. You've only been engaged six months – and it looks as if it might be some years before Ross'll be able to marry. He's got an awful load for a boy to carry alone.'

'I should say he had!' Diantha burst forth. 'Five helpless women! – or three women and two girls. Though Cora's as old as I was when I began to teach. And not one of them will lift a finger to earn her own living.'

'They weren't brought up that way,' said Mrs Bell. 'Their mother doesn't approve of it. She thinks home is the place for a woman, and so does Ross – and so do I,' she added rather faintly.

Diantha put her pan of white puff-balls into the oven, sliced a quantity of smoked beef in thin shavings, and made white sauce for it, talking the while as if those acts were automatic. 'I don't agree with Mrs Warden on that point, nor with Ross, nor with you, Mother,' she said. 'What I have to tell you is this: I'm going away from home – to work.'

From Charlotte Perkins Gilman, 'What Diantha Did' (1912).

How It Should Be Done

The true emptiness beneath the American housewife's routine has been revealed in many ways. In Minneapolis recently a schoolteacher named Maurice K. Enghausen read a story in the local newspaper about the long work week of today's housewife. Declaring in a letter to the editor that 'any woman who puts in that many hours is awfully slow, a poor budgeter of time, or just plain inefficient,' this thirty-six-year-old bachelor offered to take over any household and show how it could be done.

Scores of irate housewives dared him to prove it. He took over the household of Mr. and Mrs. Robert Dalton, with four children, aged two to seven, for three days. In a single day, he cleaned the first floor, washed three loads of clothes and hung them out to dry, ironed all the laundry including underwear and sheets, fixed a soup-and-sandwich lunch and a big backyard supper, baked two cakes, prepared two salads for the next day, dressed, undressed, and bathed the children, washed woodwork and scrubbed the kitchen floor. Mrs. Dalton said he was even a better cook than she was. 'As for cleaning,' she said, 'I am more thorough, but perhaps that is unnecessary.'

From Betty Friedan, *The Feminine Mystique* (1963).

A Woman's Work

If I tell you how hard my mother worked! For example, she used to make *challah* for the Jews to eat on *shabbes*. We had a baker opposite our house. His name was Bekker [Yiddish for baker] and he *was* a baker – *der shtimer bekker* we called him – the dumb baker – because there was something wrong with him and he couldn't speak. We make an arrangement with him so he allows us to use his wood oven.

My mother starts Thursday at noon. She takes flour, eggs, sugar, yeast and she makes a big dough. Late in the evening it was ready, so she wakes up both my sisters – one was eight years older than me, one five years older. They were rolling the dough and making the strips, and my mother did the plaiting. She was the specialist at plaiting, and so quick. This room with the big table was like a little factory. At eleven, twelve o'clock at night the girls finish their job and go back to bed. Then you have to wait till the dough rises.

At about one o'clock in the morning, we take a big metal tray and carry it across the street to the baker, and we wait. When he finishes baking his bread, the oven is ready for the *challas*, which do not need so much heat. We wait and then we push the *challas* in the oven. After about an hour we bring home the bread. When the oven is cold, the baker is left with charcoal, which he sells to the tailors, who use it in their pressing irons.

At seven o'clock on Friday morning our grocery opens and people come to buy. My mother has had about one hour's sleep. She has swollen legs from standing. Because she works day and night, we have a Polish woman who used to come in every day to clean and look after the children when they were small. I loved this woman very much. Every *shabbes* I went to her home and brought her a pot of coffee and Jewish cake, which my mother sent her. My mother brought us up to help people. I remember as a child some poor Poles from a village near Konin used to buy at our grocery. They said: 'We have no money to pay.' So my mother said: 'Okay, bread I will give you without money, and when you have, you will pay back.' She had a big book for people who paid with credit.

She could not make a living just from making bread. She sold other things, for example, pickled herrings which she made, and pickled cucumber. My father helps with the cucumbers. We buy wooden barrels and repair them so they don't leak. In summertime, in June, there are one or two weeks when all the cucumbers come out. They ripen overnight in the fields. Then you buy cheap. You make an arrangement with the farmer and he brings a wagon with cucumbers. You buy them by the *shok*. A *shok* was sixty. I think it was a measure from old Tsarist Russia.

We have a little courtyard, where we clean the barrels, wash the cucumbers and put them in the barrels. You put in salt, water, garlic and also dill. When the barrel was filled with water it was very heavy. We rolled the barrels down a plank into our cellar and it stays there for several months. The cellar had an iron key about nine inches long.

In October we buy cabbage from the farmers. We had a hand machine – a *hubl*, a kind of plane, which fits over the open barrel. The *hubl* has a little box. You put the cabbage inside, and you move it back and forth, back and forth, so the cabbage is sliced and falls into the barrel. Then you have a big wooden stick and push it down to flatten the cabbage. I did it with my father – it is strong work. Then you put in salt, some apples, but no vinegar – just a little water, because the cabbage gives water.

In winter, when there are no fresh vegetables, a customer comes to buy a cucumber or some cabbage to make sour soup. Everything is preserved for the winter. The farmers dig a big hole in the ground, put in the potatoes and cover it. The same with carrots and beetroot. In the cellar we had a lot of straw where we kept onions and apples.

By government rules you were allowed to open the shop at seven in the morning and must close at seven in the evening. A good rule, but rules are not for Jews. If a customer wants to buy at eight o'clock at night, he goes to the door at the back. If a policeman catches you, you have a fine. The police knew this was going on. Some took bribes, some didn't.

From Theo Richmond, *Konin: A Quest* (1995).

Sweet Death

James Möllendorpf, the oldest of the merchant senators, died in a grotesque and horrible way. The instinct of self-preservation became very weak in this diabetic old man; and in the last years of his life he fell a victim to a passion for cakes and pastries. Dr Grabow, as the Möllendorpf family physician, had protested energetically, and the distressed relatives employed gentle constraint to keep the head of the family from committing suicide with sweet bake-stuffs. But the old Senator, mental wreck as he was, rented a room somewhere, in some convenient street, like Little Groping Alley, or Angelswick, or Behind-the-Wall – a little hole of a room, whither he would secretly betake himself to consume sweets. And there they found his lifeless body, the mouth still full of half-masticated cake, the crumbs upon his coat and upon the wretched table. A mortal stroke had supervened, and put a stop to slow dissolution.

From Thomas Mann, *Buddenbrooks* (1902), translated by H.T. Lowe-Porter.

You've Been Warned

Aurelius, I'm entrusting you with all
I love most, with my boy. I ask a small
Favour. If you have ever pledged your soul
To keep some cherished object pure and whole,
Then guard him – I don't mean from any stranger
Walking the streets on business bent: the danger
I fear is you yourself and that great spike
That ruins good and naughty boys alike.
When you're outside the house, wave your erection
At any one you like, in what direction
You please, but (I'm not asking much, I trust)
Make him the one exception. If, though, lust
And sheer perversity unhinge your reason
And drive you to the abominable treason
Of plotting against me, a grisly fate
Awaits you. Feet chained, through the open gate
Of your own flesh you'll suffer, for your sins,
The thrust of radishes and mullets' fins.

Catullus, Poem 15, (c.84–c.54 BC), translated by James Michie (1969).

Getting Your Own Back

'I should call it reconstructing the punishment,' said Mrs. Thackenbury; 'and, anyhow, I don't see how you could introduce a system of primitive school-boy vengeance into civilized adult life. We haven't outgrown our passions, but we are supposed to have learned how to keep them within strictly decorous limits.'

'Of course the thing would have to be done furtively and politely,' said Clovis; 'the charm of it would be that it would never be perfunctory like the other thing. Now, for instance, you say to yourself: ' "I must show the Webleys some attention at Christmas, they were kind to dear Bertie at Bournemouth," and you send them a calendar, and daily for six days after Christmas the male Webley asks the female Webley if she has remembered to thank you for the calendar you sent them. Well, transplant that idea to the other and more human side of your nature, and say to yourself: "Next Thursday is Nemesis Day; what on earth can I do to those odious people next door who made such an absurd fuss when Ping Yang bit their youngest child?" Then you'd get up awfully early on the allotted day and climb over into their garden and dig for truffles on their tennis court with a good gardening fork, choosing, of course, that part of the court that was screened from observation by the laurel bushes. You wouldn't find any truffles but you would find a great peace, such as no amount of present-giving could ever bestow.'

'I shouldn't,' said Mrs. Thackenbury, though her air of protest sounded a bit forced, 'I should feel rather a worm for doing such a thing.'

'You exaggerate the power of upheaval which a worm would be able to bring into play in the limited time available,' said Clovis; 'if you put in a strenuous ten minutes with a really useful fork, the result ought to suggest the operations of an unusually masterful mole or a badger in a hurry.'

'They might guess I had done it,' said Mrs. Thackenbury.

'Of course they would,' said Clovis; 'that would be half the satisfaction of the thing, just as you like people at Christmas to know what presents or cards you've sent them. The thing would be much easier to manage, of course, when you were on outwardly friendly terms with the object of your dislike. That greedy little Agnes Blaik, for instance, who thinks of nothing but her food, it would be quite simple to ask her to a picnic in some wild woodland spot and lose her just before lunch was served; when you found her again every morsel of food could have been eaten up.'

'It would require no ordinary human strategy to lose Agnes Blaik when luncheon was imminent: in fact, I don't believe it could be done.'

'Then have all the other guests, people whom you dislike, and lose the luncheon. It could have been sent by accident in the wrong direction.'

'It would be a ghastly picnic,' said Mrs. Thackenbury.

'For them, but not for you,' said Clovis; 'you would have had an early and comforting lunch before you started, and you could improve the occasion by mentioning in detail the items of the missing banquet – the lobster Newburg and the egg mayonnaise, and the curry that was to have been heated in a chafing-dish. Agnes Blaik would be delirious long before you got to the list of wines, and in the long interval of waiting, before they had quite abandoned hope of the lunch turning up, you could induce them to play silly games, such as that idiotic one of "the Lord Mayor's dinner-party", in which every one has to choose the name of a dish and do something futile when it is called out. In this case they would probably burst into tears when their dish is mentioned. It would be a heavenly picnic.'

From Saki (H.H. Munro), 'The Feast of Nemesis', from *Beasts and Superbeasts* (1914).

A Hangover

27 December 1660

With my wife to Sir W. Batten's to dinner, where much and good company. Good and much entertainment. My wife, not very well, went home. I stayed late there, seeing them play at cards; and so home and to bed. This afternoon there came in a strange lord to Sir W. Batten's by a mistake and enters discourse with him, so that we could not be rid of him till Sir Arn. Brames and Mr. Bens and Sir Wm. fell a-drinking to him till he was drunk, and so sent him away. About the middle of the night I was very ill, I think with eating and drinking too much; and so I was forced to call the mayde (who pleased my wife and I in her running up and down so innocently in her smock) and vomited in the bason; and so to sleep, and in the morning was pretty well – only got cold and so have pain in pissing, as I used to have.

From *The Diary of Samuel Pepys*, edited by Robert Latham and
William Matthews (1985).

Leaving Without Paying

It is not long since two young men – mere youths – entered a *restaurant*, and bespoke a dinner of unusual luxury and expense, and afterwards arrived punctually at the appointed hour to eat it. They did so, apparently with all the zest of youthful appetite and youthful glee. They called for champagne, and quaffed it hand in hand. No symptom of sadness, thought, or reflection of any kind was observed to mix with their mirth, which was loud, long, and unremitting. At last came the *café noir*, the cognac, and the bill: one of them was seen to point out the amount to the other, and then both burst out afresh into violent laughter. Having swallowed each his cup of coffee to the dregs, the *garçon* was ordered to request the company of the *restaurateur* for a few minutes. He came immediately, expecting perhaps to receive his bill, minus some extra charge which the jocund but economical youths might deem exorbitant.

Instead of this, however, the elder of the two informed him that the dinner had been excellent, which was the more fortunate as it was decidedly the last that either of them should ever eat: that for his bill, he must of necessity excuse the payment of it, as in fact they neither of them possessed a single sou: that upon no other occasion would they thus have violated the customary etiquette between guests and landlord; but that finding this world, its toils and its troubles, unworthy of them, they had determined once more to enjoy a repast of which their poverty must forever prevent the repetition, and then – take leave of existence for ever! For the first part of this resolution, he declared that it had, thanks to his cook and his cellar, been achieved nobly; and for the last, it would soon follow – for the *café noir*, besides the little glass of his admirable cognac, had been medicated with that which would speedily settle all their accounts for them.

The *restaurateur* was enraged. He believed no part of the rhodomontade but that which declared their inability to discharge

[165]

the bill, and he talked loudly, in his turn, of putting them into the hands of the police. At length, however, upon their offering to give him their address, he was persuaded to let them depart.

On the following day, either the hope of obtaining his money, or some vague fear that they might have been in earnest in the wild tale that they had told him, induced this man to go to the address they had left with him; and there he heard that the two unhappy boys had been that morning found lying together hand in hand, on a bed hired a few weeks before by one of them. When they were discovered, they were already dead and quite cold.

From Fanny Trollope, Paris and the Parisians (1835).

A Promise He Won't Keep

30 December 1661

At the office about this Estimate. And so with my wife and Sir. W. Penn to see our pictures – which do not much displease us. And so back again; and I stayed at the Miter, whither I had invited all my old acquaintance of the Exchequer to a good Chine of beefe – which with three barrels of oysters and three pullets and plenty of wine and mirth, was our dinner. There was about twelve of us. Among others, Mr. Bowyer the old man, and Mr. Faulconberge, Shadwell, Taylor, Spicer, Woodruffe, Servington, &c.; and here I made them a foolish promise to give them one this day twelvemonth, and so for ever while I live. But I do not entend it.

From The Diary of Samuel Pepys, edited by Robert Latham and
William Matthews (1985).

Dinner Miseries

I. You are a bachelor; you return home to dress to go to town to dine; you find out you have lost the key of the street door, and then are obliged to call in the aid of the locksmith or to break in the *porte*.

II. To wash and shave with cold water, when the thermometer stands at the freezing point.

III. Dressing by candlelight – at the moment you are tying your cravat, out goes the last inch of candle in the house, and to be obliged to finish dressing in the dark.

IV. To be obliged to pass by the servant at the moment she is sweeping the staircase, and to get all over dust, because you have not time to wait.

V. To take a hackney-coach, that you may keep yourself clean, and on getting out of the coach, to place your foot in a heap of mud, which covers your shoes, and then to be reduced to the necessity of wiping them with your pocket handkerchief.

VI. Having arrived in a hurry, although a little too late, and as hungry as a hunter, in the expectation of finding the guests already seated at table, to pass the dining-room, and see that the cloth is not even laid.

VII. On arriving in the saloon, where all the guests are assembled, you salute the host, and, after paying a well-turned compliment to the mistress of the house, you sit down precipitately upon an arm chair, and almost kill the cat she but a few minutes before had been smothering with caresses.

VIII. To have forgotten your snuff-box when one cannot do without it, and no one present takes snuff.

IX. To come out without a pocket handkerchief, on a cold winter's day, when you have a violent cold in the head.

X. At table, to be placed at one end between two little boys, about the age of ten, whilst the most cheerful guests are sitting at the other end, among beautiful ladies.

XI. To be regaled during the dinner with the agreeable and polite noise of the master and the mistress of the house alternately scolding their servants, calling them names, and being called upon to be the judge between them.

XII. After having been as hungry as a hawk the whole morning, you perceive, as you are about to sit down to table, that your appetite has all at once disappeared.

XIII. To be forced to eat potatoes or piecrust, when you are no longer hungry.

XIV. To be suddenly informed, by your palate, instead of owing the discovery to the olfactory nerves, that the last oyster you swallowed was *rather too far gone* to recall it.

XV. To eat too fast, and without thinking to use the knife instead of the fork (*à l'Anglaise*), lose the road to your mouth, and wound your cheek with a sharp-pointed knife (*à la Française*).

XVI. To break a tumbler or wine glass, with the end of the bottle or decanter, while you are in the act of replacing the latter.

XVII. In taking soup, to feel a hair in your mouth, which, in proportion as you draw it out, it lengthens, and tickles your lips.

XVIII. Eating a poached egg, feel your bread meet with a certain resistance in the interior of the shell, in consequence of its containing a little half-formed and half-cooked chicken.

XIX. To detect, in a mouthful of leg of mutton, a clove of garlic, when you loathe this vegetable.

XX. A small pebble having got itself incrusted in a piece of soft bread, and which you have not perceived, to cranch it between your teeth with so much violence, that it causes the most excruciating pain, and extorts from you, at the same time, some horrid oath.

XXI. The small bone of a herring, or of a carp, sticking in your palate, you try all you can to get it up by coughing and spitting; at length your stomach revolts, and you serve up your dinner again in rather an unusual way.

XXII. After having officiously offered to carve a fowl, to see yourself obliged to acknowledge that you don't know how, and that before twenty witnesses, whose eyes, during your awkward efforts, are continually fixed upon you.

XXIII. After having eaten, if not swallowed, a cherry, a black-heart, or a strawberry, to discover by the taste that you have unfortunately been unintentionally the death of some poor unhappy maggot that had been shut up in it.

XXIV. A pear, which, after being peeled, seems as if it would melt in your mouth, deceives you, and breaks one of your teeth, because you did not take the necessary precaution to prelude upon it with a knife, instead of biting it.

XXV. Having discoursed during dinner with well-informed people, and to recollect, at tea-time, that you made two grammatical errors in combatting their assertions.

XXVI. After having risen from table, to stoop with too much precipitancy to pick up a lady's glove, you knock your head against the arm of the chair, on which she is seated; and, on getting up again, you give another a blow on the stomach with your head, after having felt your tight pantaloons give way, when you have no drawers on.

From Dick Humelbergius Secundus, *Apician Morsels; or Tales of the Table, Kitchen, and Larder* (1829).

When the ladies went upstairs that misery was over for a time, but Mr. Wharton was still not happy. Dick came round and took his wife's chair, so that he sat between the lord and his brother. Lopez and Happerton fell into city conversation, and Sir Damask tried to amuse himself with Mr. Wharton. But the task was hopeless, – as it always is when the elements of a party have been ill-mixed. Mr. Wharton had not even heard of the new Aldershot coach which Sir Damask had just started with Colonel Buskin and Sir Alfonso Blackbird. And when Sir Damask declared that he drove the coach up and down twice a week himself, Mr. Wharton at any rate affected to believe that such a thing was impossible. Then when Sir Damask gave his opinion as to the cause of the failure of a certain horse at Northampton, Mr. Wharton gave him no encouragement whatever. 'I never was at a racecourse in my life,' said the barrister. After that Sir Damask drank his wine in silence.

'You remember that claret, my lord?' said Dick, thinking that some little compensation was due to him for what had been said about the champagne.

But Lord Mongrober's dinner had not yet had the effect of mollifying the man sufficiently for Dick's purposes. 'Oh, yes, I remember the wine. You call it '57, don't you?'

'And it is '57 – '57, Leoville.'

'Very likely, – very likely. If it hadn't been heated before the fire—'

'It hasn't been near the fire,' said Dick.

'Or put into a hot decanter—'

'Nothing of the kind.'

'Or treated after some other damnable fashion, it would be very good wine, I dare say.'

'You are hard to please, my lord, to-day,' said Dick, who was put beyond his bearing.

'What is a man to say? If you will talk about your wine I can only tell you what I think. Any man may get good wine, – that is if he can afford to pay the price, – but it isn't one out of ten who knows how to put it on the table.' Dick felt this to be very hard. When a man pays 110s. a dozen for his champagne, and then gives it to guests like Lord Mongrober who are not even expected to return the favour, then that man ought to be allowed to talk about his wine without fear of rebuke. One doesn't have an agreement to that effect written down on parchment and sealed; but it is as well understood and ought to be as faithfully kept as any legal contract. Dick, who could on occasions be awakened to a touch of manliness, gave the bottle a shove and threw himself back in his chair. 'If you ask me, I can only tell you,' repeated Lord Mongrober.

'I don't believe you ever had a bottle of wine put before you in better order in all your life,' said Dick. His lordship's face became very square and very red as he looked round at his host. 'And as for talking about my wine, of course I talk to a man about what he understands. I talk to Monogram about pigeons, to Tom there about politics, to 'Apperton and Lopez about the price of consols, and to you about wine. If I asked you what you thought of the last new book, your lordship would be a little surprised.' Lord Mongrober grunted and looked redder and squarer than ever; but he made no attempt at reply, and the victory was evidently left with Dick, – very much to the general exaltation of his character. And he was proud of himself. 'We had a little tiff, me and Mongrober,' he said to his wife that night. ''E's a very good fellow, and of course he's a lord and all that. But he has to be put down occasionally, and, by George, I did it to-night. You ask Lopez.'

From Anthony Trollope, *The Prime Minister* (1871).

Dining with Disappointment

Patricia's knife and fork and plate policy worked out much as Rose had anticipated. The regulars, trained by Gerard, resented the innovation and ignored the pie and curry and trifle arrangement, eating up the sandwiches and canapés, and thereafter, scorning the plates and utensils, making their own impromptu sandwiches by tearing open rolls and jamming in lettuce leaves and bits of ham and tomato which then fell out onto the carpet. Gerard's little cakes, discovered in the larder, were popular too, so was the cheese which Rose had provided. One or two guests out of politeness (Jenkin) or because they were genuinely interested in the steak and kidney pie (Gulliver) or because the whole thing had been their own idea (Patricia) fussily found a place to sit and some piece of furniture to sit at and uncomfortably, while the others strolled about, sat down to a pretence of ordinary dinner. Gideon, to Patricia's annoyance and chagrin, defected to the strollers. Claret was now provided, and the fruit cup was still available. The gin and whisky were not in demand at the early stages, even by Duncan who was the last to arrive and startled his friends by asking for Perrier, then drinking the cup, then only at a later stage the whisky. By then Gulliver and Lily were also on whisky. Lily, who had earlier discovered the gin-laced glass abandoned by Violet and drunk it up, was by now distinctly tipsy. Tamar caused distress by eating nothing; at last she accepted a plate of trifle which was discovered next morning, untouched, upon a window ledge behind a curtain. She also, for a while, disappeared, and was found by Rose upstairs in Gerard's bedroom in the dark, sitting at the window and, she said, watching the children next door who had been capering round the garden in their night clothes. By the time coffee was served it was getting very late and the evening was in danger of being wrecked by what Gerard subsequently called 'that simulacrum of a dinner party'.

From Iris Murdoch, *The Book and the Brotherhood* (1987).

Hot Stuff

Now we have heard how Mrs Sedley had prepared a fine curry for her son, just as he liked it, and in the course of dinner a portion of this dish was offered to Rebecca. 'What is it?' said she, turning an appealing look to Mr Joseph.

'Capital,' said he. His mouth was full of it; his face quite red with the delightful exercise of gobbling. 'Mother, it's as good as my own curries in India.'

'Oh, I must try some, if it is an Indian dish,' said Miss Rebecca. 'I am sure everything must be good that comes from there.'

'Give Miss Sharp some curry, my dear,' said Mr Sedley, laughing.

Rebecca had never tasted the dish before.

'Do you find it as good as everything else from India?' said Mr Sedley.

'Oh, excellent!' said Rebecca, who was suffering tortures with the cayenne pepper.

'Try a chili with it, Miss Sharp,' said Joseph, really interested.

'A chili,' said Rebecca, gasping. 'O yes!' She thought a chili was something cool, as its name imported, and was served with some. 'How fresh and green they look!' she said, and put one into her mouth. It was hotter than the curry; flesh and blood could bear it no longer. She laid down her fork. 'Water, for Heaven's sake, water!' she cried. Mr Sedley burst out laughing (he was a coarse man, from the Stock Exchange, where they love all sorts of practical jokes). 'They are real Indian, I assure you,' said he. 'Sambo, give Miss Sharp some water.'

The paternal laugh was echoed by Joseph, who thought the joke capital. The ladies only smiled a little. They thought poor Rebecca suffered too much. She would have liked to choke old Sedley, but she swallowed her mortification as well as she had the abominable curry before it, and as soon as she could speak, said, with a comical, good-humoured air –

'I ought to have remembered the pepper which the Princess of Persia puts in the cream-tarts in the *Arabian Nights*. Do you put cayenne into your cream-tarts in India, sir?'

Old Sedley began to laugh, and thought Rebecca was a good-humoured girl. Joseph simply said – 'Cream-tarts, Miss? Our cream is very bad in Bengal. We generally use goats' milk; and, 'gad, do you know, I've got to prefer it!'

'You won't like *everything* from India now, Miss Sharp,' said the old gentleman; but when the ladies had retired after dinner, the wily old fellow said to his son, 'Have a care, Joe; that girl is setting her cap at you.'

From William Thackeray, *Vanity Fair* (1848).

Showing Off

Pera, Constantinople, 10 March 1718

[The Sultana] gave me a dinner of fifty dishes of meat, which, after their fashion, was placed on the table but one at a time, and was extremely tedious, but the magnificence of her table answered very well to that of her dress. The knives were of gold, the hafts set with diamonds, but the piece of luxury that grieved my eyes was the table cloth and napkins, which were all tiffany, embroidered with silks and gold in the finest manner in natural flowers. It was with the utmost regret that I made use of these costly napkins, as finely wrought as the finest handkerchiefs that ever came out of this country. You may be sure that they were entirely spoilt before dinner was over. The sherbet, which is the liquor they drink at meals, was served in china bowls, but the covers and salvers massy gold. After dinner water was brought in a gold basin and towels of the same kind of the napkins, which I very unwillingly wiped my hands upon, and coffee was served in china with gold soûcoupes.

From Lady Mary Wortley Montagu, *The Turkish Embassy Letters*, edited by
Malcolm Jack (1993).

Too Many Cooks

Brumana, 22 February 1928

Poor Mrs. Manasseh is nearly exhausted because two men came to her on Saturday and said that one of them was going to marry her cook next day. A pretty girl, and she had no particular wish to marry the man, who squints. Argument was vain, however, and as it was the last day before Lent and no marrying for two months, there was nothing for it: they spent a hectic day sewing the essential underwear: the bridegroom sent a white frock and old silver shoes: there were streams of relatives all day drinking coffee and eating cakes: and finally Mrs. Manasseh took the bride and bride's mother to the church at 8 p.m. on a gusty evening. The priest seemed to have forgotten all about it, and couldn't be found till someone had the bright idea of tolling the church bell for him. Luckily everyone carried a candle, so the ceremony was not performed in pitch darkness. Mrs. Manasseh returned exhausted to her cookless home, and is now being assisted by the bride's family, who are full of gratitude, and only ignorant of cookery.

From Freya Stark, *Letters from Syria* (1942).

Dead Scared

We were most careful to copy our hosts in all things. We put salt in our soup with the blades of our knives; we absorbed the rich sauce of our delicious *ragoût* with pieces of bread, being indeed pressed to do so by M. Marcault; we cleaned our knives on rinds of leathery crust;

in fact, we conformed, as we thought, admirably. Everything was going on velvet, when, after the *ragoût*, the smell of fried oil became apparent, and from a covered-in pan Suzanne helped us each to a large piece of something that resembled sweetbread, and cut rather like a tough custard pudding. It was fried bright brown, but the inside was yellowish white, and the whole thing was swimming in hot oil. We asked nervously what it was.

'*Mais, mangez le donc,*' responded Suzanne, as she reversed the frying-pan to let the last drops of oil run on to our plates. '*C'est biang bong! C'est du cépe – du champignong, vous savez,*' seeing that we did not seem much enlightened. Here was local colour with a vengeance! There rose before us in a moment the brown, contorted visages of *La Famille empoisonnée* among the mummies of St. Michel, and the dusty bits of fungus that they still retained in their jaws. The situation, however, did not admit of retreat. And we attempted none. The mushroom, or fungus, whatever it was, had a dreadful taste, as though rotten leaves and a rusty knife had been fried together in fat. Moreover, it was patent to the meanest intelligence that, whatever its taste might be, no digestion save that of a native or an ostrich could hope to compete with it. We each swallowed two lumps of it whole, and then my cousin looked wanly at me and said, 'One more, and I shall be sick.'

From E.Œ. Somerville and Martin Ross, *In The Vine Country* (1893).

An Unusual Excursion

Early mornings are my favourite time of the day in Provence. The sensation of slightly *mouvementé* air, of the preliminary to a full breeze, and the sight of dew on the plants by kitchen, patio and pool, like the crystalline cerulean sky that so often accompanies daybreak, never fails to lift the spirits.

That morning I padded downstairs at an impressive five minutes to six. There was a degree of ambient crispness in the kitchen (stone-flagged, I think I may have forgotten to say, and challengingly cool to bare feet all year round). I put the kettle on and stood leafing through my much-stained paperback reprint of Reboul's *La Cuisinière provençale* (1895). As the kettle boiled, and was ultra-politely removed from the hob before starting to whistle, I made a large pot of Twining's English Breakfast, which I decanted into my capacious thermos. Then I headed for the door, pausing only to pocket a banana and an orange from the fruit bowl as I went; all these preparations having acquired the agreeably staid pattern of a ritual from the fact that I repeat them on each and every one of the late summer and autumn mornings on which I choose to go mushroom hunting.

The car – my car this time, a thrifty Volkswagen, resident at St-Eustache all the year around, rather than any of the hire models mentioned hitherto, the last of which had been returned to the franchise concession at Avignon several days previously – had been parked an earshot-defying hundred yards or so from the honeymooners' bedroom. It started first time and I bumped along the unmetalled lane to the main road before roaring off in the direction of the Lubéron hills. On the seat beside me were my wicker basket, my Sherlock Holmesian magnifying glass (hardly ever used or needed) and my copy of *Champignons de nos pays* by Henri Romagnesi (ditto, though I also keep all six volumes of *Champignons du Nord et du Midi* by André Marchand back at the house).

In the following account, the alert reader will notice that I am being a little bit coy about the geographical specifics. Forgive me: but we amateur mycologists, especially amateur mycologists of a culinary bent, passionately guard our favoured patches of land – a promising batch of *cèpes*-yielding beeches here, a cropped roadside thronging with ink caps there, yonder a patch of nettles known to feature spectacular examples of *Langermannia gigantea* or the giant puffball, and somewhere else a field with a healthy quantity of cow excrement conducive to the fructation of the nasty-tasting but currently popular hallucinogen *Psilocybe semilanceata*, appropriately known in English as the Liberty Cap. (This, by the way, is not, as it is sometimes taken to be, the hallucinogen used by the notorious shamans of the Koryk tribe in far Siberia, the *Amanita muscaria* or fly agaric, ingestible via reindeer or indeed human urine, most often popularly reproduced in the image of a red-capped-white-dotted toadstool, providing a convenient seat for any momentarily resting elf or fairy. The shamen call that mushroom the *wapag*, after a body of magical beings who inhabit the fungi with a view to passing on secrets from the realm of the spirits.) We mushroom hunters are a secretive and wary breed, and it is through ingrained force of habit that I confine my account of the site of my labours to the description *a patch of land somewhere in the south of France.* As evidence of the need for caution, the first car I encountered belonged to M. Robert, the local schoolmaster and a noted fungi enthusiast whose especial passion, he had once divulged to me when we bumped into each other at Mme Cottison's stall in Cavaillon market, was the *cèpe*. His *deux chevaux* was heading, interestingly and provocatively, in the opposite direction from mine. As our vehicles passed each other the teacher and I both raised a hand in cautious fraternal salutation.

It's fascinating to remark how different are these excursions, undertaken in Provence and in Norfolk. Partly this is to do with dress: my multiply layered and woolly-hatted autumnal East Anglian self could be taken for no relation to my linen-shirted *méridionale* alter ego. In England I am a freak, participating in a bizarre act of voluntary self-endangerment; in France I am the intelligent *homme moyen sensuel* rationally maximizing the use of the earth's resources and my pleasure, and also saving a few francs in the process. The air in Provence (when the *mistral* is not blowing, of course, a phenomenon which makes the practice, indeed the very thought, of mycology impossible) carries the scent of wild herbs, of the *garrigue*; in Norfolk, on some days, before plunging into the deep English silence of the woods, I fancy I can catch the faintest tang of the sea. Please imagine here a passage which evokes the comparative experiences of mushroom hunting all over Europe, with many new metaphors and interesting facts.

I parked the car in a passing place and state-approved picnic spot some ten kilometres away from home – a hilly site (though not *too* hilly). Seizing basket and knife and leaving my other equipment – this being a specific quest rather than a generalized exploratory expedition, more like Captain Bligh's voyage than Captain Cook's – set off boldly upwards, my breath not even, at that hour, starting to steam as it would begin to in the next few weeks (and as it probably would already be doing had I been on a comparable expedition in Norfolk). The faint path wound along and up a rocky way through patchy conifers in the direction of a grove of Mediterranean oak and beech, not directly visible from the roadside. Later in the year this would become a popular location for *la chasse*, especially for the massacre of those songbirds which always make disappointingly unmeaty eating. For the moment I had the landscape to myself. In the distance I could see the hill town of – –.

The walk took about twenty minutes. Mushroom hunting is an

agreeable mixture of the active and the contemplative: on the one hand is the fresh air, the promise of the early day, the walk, the sudden bends and stoops; on the other, the intellectual activity of identification and of what military strategists – in one of these euphemisms which often seem more compellingly sanguinary than the terms they replace – call 'target acquisition'. The atmosphere was described with a false jollity by Tolstoy in *Anna Karenina*: in truth it involves an anxious concentration on one's own performance, a determination to come back with one's mushroom or on it, a silent free-floating mixture of boredom and anxiety of the sort familiar to hunters and psychoanalysts. So much looking down can induce a vertigo when one finally looks up and realizes where one is, who one is. Comically, on this occasion I straight away came across a robust clump of *cèpes* under the first two trees I examined – M. Robert would have been doing very well indeed if he had found anything remotely comparable. I enjoyed one of the pleasures of mycology, a brief, silent, rapturous gloat. On a different day with a different purpose I would have been delighted to find my mission accomplished so rapidly (I might even have shared some of my harvest with Pierre and Jean-Luc). Not today, though. I pressed on. At the edge of the clump I found a patch of *Entoloma sinuatum*, the toxic field-mushroom look-alike known as Le Grand Empoisonneur de la Côte d'Or, not a fungus you often see in the United Kingdom. Again I pressed on.

I found what I was looking for almost exactly where I had thought I would.

From John Lanchester, *The Debt to Pleasure* (1996).

Pecking Order

The mother carried in the large tray of food and placed it on the cloth. She withdrew to the side of the room near a table on which stood a water jug. She waited there, ready to obey any command. In the center of the gleaming copper tray was a large oval dish filled with fried beans and eggs. On one side hot loaves of flat bread were piled. On the other side were arranged small plates with cheese, pickled lemons and peppers, as well as salt and cayenne and black pepper. The brothers' bellies were aflame with hunger, but they restrained themselves and pretended not to see the delightful array, as though it meant nothing to them, until their father put out his hand to take a piece of bread. He split it open while muttering, 'Eat.' Their hands reached for the bread in order of seniority: Yasin, Fahmy, and then Kamal. They set about eating without forgetting their manners or reserve.

Their father devoured his food quickly and in great quantities as though his jaws were a mechanical shredding device working non-stop at full speed. He lumped together into one giant mouthful a wide selection of the available dishes – beans, eggs, cheese, pepper and lemon pickles – which he proceeded to pulverize with dispatch while his fingers prepared the next helping. His sons ate with deliberation and care, no matter what it cost them and how incompatible it was with their fiery temperaments. They were painfully aware of the severe remark or harsh look they would receive should one of them be remiss or weak and forget himself and thus neglect the obligatory patience and manners.

Kamal was the most uneasy, because he feared his father the most. The worst punishment either of his two brothers would receive was a rebuke or a scolding. The least he could expect was a kick or a slap. For this reason, he consumed his food cautiously and nervously, stealing a glance from time to time at what was left. The food's quick disappearance added to his anxiety. He waited apprehensively for a sign that his father was finished eating. Then he would have a chance to fill his belly. Kamal knew that although his father devoured his food quickly, taking huge helpings selected from many different dishes, the ultimate threat to the food, and therefore to him, came from his two brothers. His father ate quickly and got full quickly. His two brothers only began the battle in earnest once their father left the table. They did not give up until the plates were empty of anything edible.

Therefore, no sooner had his father risen and departed than Kamal rolled up his sleeves and attacked the food like a madman. He employed both his hands, one for the large dish and the other for the small ones. All the same, his endeavor seemed futile, given his brothers' energetic efforts. So Kamal fell back on a trick he resorted to when his welfare was threatened in circumstances like these. He deliberately sneezed on the food. His two brothers recoiled, looking at him furiously, but left the table, convulsed with laughter. Kamal's dream for the morning was realized. He found himself alone at the table.

From Naguib Mahfouz, *Palace Walk* (1956), translated by William Maynard Hutchins and Olive E. Kenny.

Chips with Everything

The Ashok, with its polished empty spaces and its inconsequential happenings, reminded me of one of the old Marx Brothers films. A whiff of institutional austerity was diluted with outbursts of a poetic impulse by which surfaces of the lobby furniture were freshly decorated every morning with patterns of frangipani blossom. Service was well-meaning but muddled, and to attempt to put through a long-distance telephone call was to expose oneself to unpredictabilities of success or failure rivalling those of the gaming table.

At dinner a menu decorated like an illuminated manuscript promised fish under eleven guises, each described in hyperbolical terms. The Chef's Choice was grilled pomfret, 'flown to you specially from the Goan sea'.

'Today we are not serving pomfret,' the waiter said.

'In that case I'll take the snapper.'

The waiter shook his head. 'No snapper, sir.'

'What fish have you then?'

'On this day we have no fish, reason being that all fish in Indian sea severely infected by disease.'

The menu listed nine chicken dishes. I ran my finger down the list and the waiter butted in, 'Tonight the Chef is recommending fried chicken, sir.'

'With chips?'

'Oh yes, sir. Always we are serving chips.'

'Can I have some beer?' I asked.

'Beer only served in bar, sir.'

The bar was immediately behind, its open frontier a yard from where I sat. It was permanently tenanted by silent and lugubrious German technicians separated from each other by an empty stool, and seeking oblivion in Indian whisky. I went into the bar, ordered a beer and stood it on a table in the bar area within reach of my arm, hoping that the waiter would go away, but this, as he had no other customers to serve, he clearly had no intention of doing.

From Norman Lewis, *A Goddess in the Stones* (1991).

Lee Ho Fook's

What brought the Chinaman down to the building-site? Ah, it was Fate;
And Fate in the scaffolding kicked from its cradle the vat,
Thirty foot over his dithering head, of boiling and thunderous tea.
Who was on hand, though, to rush from his post and manhandle the fellow
(Then of a frightened, diminutive, immigrant state of fragility)
Into a sheltering barrow, the moment the day's brew exploded
Exactly where seconds before he'd been staring and dreaming of mountains
And seagulls and sails in the harbour? Charlie Wood.

The building-site is buildings now, the Cannon Street Office
Of the Hong Kong and Cantonese Bank – and all would be buried beneath
Were it not for the Chinaman's blur of cross-cultural gratitude:
'You have saved my life. The least I can do in return
Is to ask you to dine as my guest in my fabulous restaurant
Whenever you will.' 'Well thanks very much,' says Charlie –
'I might take you up on that offer.' – Back to the grit and the grind;
Thinking, though, *Tell you what, Charlie Boy, could be a bit of a bonus*!

Indeed, while the mind of this builder was normally dark,
And dripping with flesh, and unwholesome, infested, and spotty, a shaft
Of purest sunshine scored suddenly over the tracks as he pondered his luck;
And a sluice and an avalanche opened of rice and prawns like the coins in *The Golden Shot*
Churning and pouring forever and all of it aimed at his lap;
Which drew him away from the mix of cement he was feeding

And up in a daze to the Works hut, and on through a dozen or more
Inscrutable *Yellow Pages* – well, it would take him a couple of tea-
 breaks ...

Years pass. And the tiny impulse of distaste Lee had felt
At his saviour's first beaming appearance and chirpy request for a
 knife and fork
Has swollen; of late it resembles a sort of unsociable illness
That has to be kept in check by a sidling withdrawal to the stairs
Whenever his own lucky star, with its multiple coatings of yester-
 day's earth,
Comes rollicking in for the freebies – as often as three times a week.
(Something is fouling the lock in the door to his dream of new
 premises;
Something as fixed as the bambooey bulge in Charlie Wood's cheek.)

So Charlie is left to chew over the Chinaman's lapses of honour
And nibble at rightful reprisals: *When his highness emerges at last*
To slide me as ever the ready-paid bill on a saucer
(Disguising by this, he supposes, his part of the bargain)
What if I dashed this half-cup of their pissy tea at him –
Out of the blue, to remind him why Woodsy is here?
– Or when they've been keeping me waiting an hour for the soup, to
 come out with it –
Oy, son, I had you in a barrow once – *instead of my usual?*

                                   Mick Imlah, *Birthmarks* (1988).

Second Helpings?

To the Chinese guests the dinner was most recherché. Many of the
things had come from China and were very costly. But I found it
difficult to swallow some of them, in spite of the mustard and salt
Jafar Ali had provided. Any very dainty tidbit my hostess insisted on
my eating, conveying the choicest bits from the bowl with her own
chopsticks to my mouth. I managed pretty well till the sea slugs came
along; if they had been minced or disguised in some way, they might
not have been so bad, but they were served boiled whole, and when I
saw these huge black slugs, covered with lumps, wobbling about in

front of me, I wondered how I should live through the ordeal of swallowing one. But there was no getting out of it and I was faced with the choice of eating it or giving offence. So I covered one well with mustard, shut my eyes and swallowed it whole. The ladies were so pleased with me that they insisted on me eating another; and three or four times I had to go through the awful ordeal. It was many days before I forgot those sea slugs, for eating the tough, gelatinous things whole like that made me horribly ill afterwards.

From Lady Macartney, *An English Lady in Chinese Turkestan* (1931).

Oral Rape

They flung me on my back on the bed, and held me down firmly by shoulders and wrists, hips, knees, and ankles. Then the doctors came stealing in. Someone seized me by the head and thrust a sheet under my chin. My eyes were shut. I set my teeth and tightened my lips over them with all my strength. A man's hands were trying to force open my mouth; my breath was coming so fast that I felt as though I should suffocate. His fingers were striving to pull my lips apart – getting inside. I felt them and a steel instrument pressing around my gums, feeling for gaps in my teeth. I was trying to jerk my head away, trying to wrench it free. Two of them were holding it, two of them dragging at my mouth. I was panting and heaving, my breath quicker and quicker, coming now with a low scream which was growing louder. 'Here is a gap,' one of them said. 'No, here is a better one. This long gap here!' A steel instrument pressed my gums, cutting into the flesh. I braced myself to resist that terrible pain. 'No, that won't do' – that voice again. 'Give me the pointed one!' A stab of sharp, intolerable agony. I wrenched my head free ... Then something gradually forced my jaws apart as a screw was turned; the pain was like having the teeth drawn. They were trying to get the tube down my throat, I was struggling madly to stiffen my muscles and close my throat. They got it down, I suppose, though I was unconscious of anything then save a mad revolt of struggling, for they said at last: 'That's all!' and I vomited as the tube came up. They left me on the bed exhausted, gasping for breath and sobbing convulsively.

From Sylvia Pankhurst, *The Suffragette Movement* (1931).

Table Talk

Gradually he exhausted his store of talk, that he had thought was limitless. Muriel moved about all the time, laying the table and listening, only looking now and again across the barren garden of his talk into his windows. But he hardened his heart and turned his head from her. The boys had stripped to their waists, and had knelt on the hearth-rug and washed themselves in a large tin bowl, the mother sponging and drying their backs. Now they stood wiping themselves, the firelight bright and rosy on their fine torsos, their heavy arms swelling and sinking with life. They seemed to cherish the firelight on their bodies. Benjamin, the younger, leaned his breast to the warmth, and threw back his head, showing his teeth in a voluptuous little smile. Mersham watched them, as he had watched the peewits and the sunset.

Then they sat down to their dinners, and the room was dim with the steam of food. Presently the father and the eldest brother were in from the cow-sheds, and all assembled at table. The conversation went haltingly; a little badinage on Mersham's part, a few questions on politics from the father. Then there grew an acute, fine feeling of discord. Mersham, particularly sensitive, reacted. He became extremely attentive to the others at table, and to his own manner of eating. He used English that was exquisitely accurate, pronounced with the Southern accent, very different from the heavily-sounded speech of the home folk. His nicety contrasted the more with their rough, country habit. They became shy and awkward, fumbling for something to say. The boys ate their dinners hastily, shovelling up the mass as a man shovels gravel. The eldest son clambered roughly with a great hand at the plate of bread-and-butter. Mersham tried to shut his eyes. He kept up all the time a brilliant tea-talk that they failed to appreciate in that atmosphere. It was evident to him; without forming the idea, he felt how irrevocably he was removing them from him, though he had loved them. The irony of the situation appealed to him, and added brightness and subtlety to his wit. Muriel, who had studied him so thoroughly, confusedly understood. She hung her head over her plate, and ate little. Now and again she would look up at him, toying all the time with her knife – though it was a family for ugly hands – and would address him some barren question. He always answered the question, but he invariably disregarded her look of earnestness, lapped in his unbreakable armour of light irony. He acknowledged, however, her power in the flicker of irritation that accompanied his reply. She quickly hid her face again.

They did not linger at tea, as in the old days. The men rose, with an 'Ah well!' and went about their farm-work. One of the lads lay sprawling for sleep on the sofa; the other lighted a cigarette and sat with his arms on his knees, blinking into the fire. Neither of them ever wore a coat in the house, and their shirt-sleeves and their thick bare necks irritated the stranger still further by accentuating his strangeness. The men came tramping in and out to the boiler. The kitchen was full of bustle, of the carrying of steaming water, and of draughts. It seemed like a place out of doors. Mersham shrank up in his corner, and pretended to read the 'Daily News'. He was ignored, like an owl sitting in the stalls of cattle.

'Go in the parlour, Cyril. Why don't you? It's comfortable there.'

Muriel turned to him with this reproach, this remonstrance, almost chiding him. She was keenly aware of his discomfort, and of his painful discord with his surroundings. He rose without a word and obeyed her.

From D.H. Lawrence, 'A Modern Lover' (1934).

Boiling Point

In the large kitchen, which occupied most of the middle of the house, a sullen fire burned, the smoke of which wavered up the blackened walls and over the deal table, darkened by age and dirt, which was roughly set for a meal. A snood full of coarse porridge hung over the fire, and standing with one arm resting upon the high mantel, looking moodily down into the heaving contents of the snood, was a tall young man whose riding-boots were splashed with mud to the thigh, and whose coarse linen shirt was open to his waist. The firelight lit up his diaphragm muscles as they heaved slowly in rough rhythm with the porridge.

He looked up as Judith entered, and gave a short, defiant laugh, but said nothing. Judith crossed slowly over until she stood by his side. She was as tall as he. They stood in silence, she staring at him, and he down into the secret crevasses of the porridge.

'Well, mother mine,' he said at last, 'here I am, you see. I said I would be in time for breakfast, and I have kept my word.'

His voice had a low, throaty, animal quality, a sneering warmth that wound a velvet ribbon of sexuality over the outward coarseness of the man.

Judith's breath came in long shudders. She thrust her arms deeper into her shawl. The porridge gave an ominous leering heave; it might almost have been endowed with life, so uncannily did its movements keep pace with the human passions that throbbed above it.

'Cur,' said Judith, levelly, at last. 'Coward! Liar! Libertine! Who were you with last night? Moll at the mill or Violet at the vicarage? Or Ivy, perhaps, at the ironmongery? Seth – my son ...' Her deep, dry voice quivered, but she whipped it back, and her next words flew out at him like a lash.

'Do you want to break my heart?'

'Yes,' said Seth, with an elemental simplicity.

The porridge boiled over.

From Stella Gibbons, *Cold Comfort Farm* (1932).

An Egg Shortage

5 Cheyne Row, Chelsea

Oh, little woman! you will come to our aid, if possible; but if impossible, what on earth are we to do for eggs? At this present Mr C. is breakfasting on shop-eggs, and doesn't know it; and I am every morning expecting to hear in my bed an explosion over some one too far gone for his making himself an illusion about it. All the people who kept fowls round about have, the maids say, during my absence ceased to keep them, and the two eggs from Addiscombe three times a week are not enough for us both; I, 'as one solitary individual' needing three in the day – one for breakfast, one in hot milk for luncheon, and one in my small pudding at dinner. When I left Holm Hill, Mrs Russell was in despair over her hens; thirty of them yielded but three eggs a day. Yours, too, may have struck work; and in that case never mind. Only if you could send us some, it would be a mercy.

18 October 1864.

From *I Too Am Here: Selections from the Letters of Jane Welsh Carlyle* (1977),
edited by Alan and Mary McQueen Simpson.

Careless Talk

'How good, how kind, *how* thoughtful!' said Mary Dash. 'I can't tell you what a difference they will make! And you brought them like this all the way from Shepton Mallet in the train?' She looked helpless. 'Where do you think I had better put them? This table's going to be terribly small for four, and *think*, if one of Eric Farnham's sweeping gesticulations ...' She signalled a waiter. 'I want these put somewhere for me till the end of lunch. *Carefully*,' she added. 'They are three eggs.' The waiter bowed and took the parcel away. 'I do hope they will be all right,' said Mrs Dash, looking suspiciously after him. 'But at least they'll be quieter with the hats, or something. I expect you see how crowded everywhere is?'

Joanna looked round the restaurant and saw. The waiters had to melt to get past the backs of the chairs; between the net-curtained windows, drowsy with August rain, mirrors reflected heads in smoke and electric light and the glitter of buttons on uniforms. Every European tongue struck its own note, with exclamatory English on top of all. As fast as people went wading out people came wading in, and so many greeted each other that Joanna might easily have felt out of it. She had not lunched in London for four months and could not resist saying so to her friend.

'Honestly, you haven't deteriorated,' said Mary. Herself, she was looking much as ever, with orchids pinned on to her last year's black. 'Then how lucky I caught you just today! And I'm glad the others will be late. The only men one likes now are always late. While it's still just you and me, there's so much to say. I don't know what I've done without you, Joanna.' She fixed enraptured eyes on Joanna's face. 'For instance, can *you* tell me what's become of the Stones?'

'No, I'm afraid I can't. I ...'

'And Edward and I were wondering if you could tell us about the Hickneys. I know they are somewhere in Dorset or Somerset. They're not by any chance anywhere near you? ... Well, never mind. Tell me about yourself.'

But at this point Eric Farnham joined them. 'You don't know how sorry I am,' he said. 'I was kept. But you found the table all right. Well, Joanna, this couldn't be nicer, could it?'

'Isn't she looking radiant?' said Mary Dash. 'We have been having the most tremendous talk.'

Eric was now at the War Office, and Joanna, who had not seen him in uniform before, looked at him naively, twice. He reminded her of one of the pictures arrived at in that paper game when, by drawing on folded-over paper, you add to one kind of body an intriguingly wrong kind of head. He met her second look kindly through his shell-rimmed glasses. 'How do you think the war is going?' she said.

'Oh, we mustn't ask him things,' said Mary quickly. 'He's doing most frightfully secret work.' But this was lost on Eric, who was consulting his wrist watch. 'As Ponsonby's later than I am,' he said, 'that probably means he'll be pretty late. Though God knows what they do at that Ministry. I propose not waiting for Ponsonby. First of all, what will you two drink?'

'Ponsonby?' Joanna said.

'No, I don't expect you'd know him. He's only been about lately,' said Mary. 'He's an expert; he's very interesting.'

'He could be,' said Eric. 'He was at one time. But he's not supposed to be interesting just now.' The drinks came; then they got together over the *cartes du jour*. Ponsonby did not arrive till just after the potted shrimps. 'This is dreadful,' he said. 'I do hope you'll forgive me. But things keep on happening, you know.' He nodded rapidly round to several tables, then dropped exhausted into his place. 'Eat?' he said. 'Oh, really, anything – shrimps. After that, whatever you're all doing.'

'Well, Mary's for grouse,' said Eric. Ponsonby, after an instant of concentration, said, 'In that case, grouse will do me fine.'

'Now you must talk to Joanna,' said Mary Dash. 'She's just brought me three eggs from the country and she's longing to know about everything.'

Ponsonby gave Joanna a keen, considering look. 'Is it true,' he said, 'that in the country there are no cigarettes at all?'

'I believe there are sometimes some. But I don't –'

'There are. Then that alters everything,' said Ponsonby. 'How lucky you are!'

'I got my hundred this morning,' said Eric, 'from my regular man. But those will have to last me to Saturday. I can't seem to cut down, somehow. Mary, have you cut down?'

'I've got my own, if that's what you mean,' said she. 'I just got twenty out of my hairdresser.' She raised her shilling-size portion of butter from its large bed of ice and spread it tenderly over her piece of toast. 'Now, what is your news?' she said. 'Not that I'm asking anything, of course.'

'I don't think anything's happened to me,' said Eric, 'or that anything else has happened that you wouldn't know about. When I say happened I mean *happened*, of course. I went out of London for one night; everywhere outside London seemed to me very full. I must say I was glad to be home again.' He unlocked his chair from the chair behind him, looked at the grouse on his plate, then took up his knife and fork.

'Eric,' said Mary, after a minute, 'the waiter's trying to tell you there's no more of that wine *en carafe*.'

'Bring it in a bottle then. I wonder how much longer –'

'Oh, my dear, so do *I*,' said Mary. 'One daren't think about that. Where we were dining last night they already had several numbers scratched off the wine list. Which reminds me. Edward sent you his love.'

'Oh, how *is* Edward?' Joanna said. 'What is he doing?'

'Well, I'm not strictly supposed to say. By the way, Eric, I asked Joanna, and she doesn't know where the Stones *or* the Hickneys are.'

'In the case of the Hickneys, I don't know that it matters.'

'Oh, don't be inhuman. You know you're not!'

'I must say,' said Eric, raising his voice firmly, 'I do like London now a lot of those people have gone. Not *you*, Joanna; we all miss you very much. Why don't you come back? You've no idea how nice it is.'

Joanna, colouring slightly, said, 'I've got no place left to come back to. Belmont Square –'

'Oh, my Lord, yes,' he said. 'I did hear about your house. I was so sorry. Completely? ... Still, you don't want a house, you know. None of us live in houses. You could move in on someone. Sylvia has moved in on Mona –'

'That's not a good example,' said Mary quickly. 'Mona moved out almost at once and moved in on Isobel, but the worst of that is that now Isobel wants her husband back, and meanwhile Sylvia's taken up with a young man, so Mona can't move back to her own flat. But what would make it difficult for Joanna is having taken on all those hens. Haven't you?'

'Yes, and I have evacuees –'

'But we won't talk about those, will we?' said Mary quickly. 'Any more than you would want to hear about bombs. I think one great rule is never to bore each other. Eric, *what's* that you are saying to Ponsonby?'

Eric and Ponsonby had seized the occasion to exchange a few

rapid remarks. They stopped immediately. 'It was quite boring,' Ponsonby explained.

'I don't believe you,' said Mary. 'These days everything's frightfully interesting. Joanna, you must be feeling completely dazed. Will everyone ask you things when you get home?'

'The worst of the country these days,' said Joanna, 'is everyone gets so wrapped up in their own affairs.'

'Still, surely they must want to know about us? I suppose London is too much the opposite,' said Mary. 'One lives in a perfect whirl of ideas. Ponsonby, who was that man I saw you with at the Meunière? I was certain I knew his face.'

'That was a chap called Odgers. Perhaps he reminded you of somebody else? We were talking shop. I think that's a nice place, don't you? I always think they do veal well. That reminds me, Eric. Was your friend the other evening a Pole, or what?'

'The fact is I hardly know him,' said Eric. 'I'm never quite sure of his name myself. He's a Pole all right, but Poles aren't really my thing. He was quite interesting, as a matter of fact; he had quite a line of his own on various things. Oh, well, it was nothing particular ... No, I can't do you Poles, Mary. Warrington's really the man for Poles.'

'I know he is, but he keeps them all up his sleeve. You do know about Edward and the Free French? I hope it didn't matter my having told you that, but Edward took it for granted that you already knew.'

Ponsonby recoiled from his wrist-watch. 'Good heavens,' he said, 'it *can't* be as late as this? If it is, there's someone waiting for me.'

'Look,' said Eric, 'I'll hurry on coffee.'

'You know,' Mary added anxiously, 'you really can't concentrate without your coffee. Though I know we mustn't be difficult. It's like this all the time,' she said to Joanna. 'Have *you* got to hurry, Eric?'

'I needn't exactly hurry. I just ought to keep an eye on the time.'

'I'll do that for you,' Mary said. 'I'd love to. You see you've hardly had a word with Joanna, and she's wanting so much to catch up with life. I tell you one thing that *is* worrying me: that waiter I gave Joanna's lovely eggs to hasn't been near this table again. Do you think I put temptation right in his way? Because, do you know, all the time we've been talking I've been thinking up a new omelette I want to make. One's mind gets like that these days,' she said to Joanna. 'One seems able to think of twenty things at one time. Eric, do you think you could flag the *maître d'hôtel*? I don't know how I'd feel if I lost three eggs.'

From Elizabeth Bowen, *The Demon Lover and Other Stories* (1945).

The Bare Necessities

Then at Fuller's. A fat, smart woman, in red hunting cap, pearls, check skirt, consuming rich cakes. Her shabby dependant also stuffing. Hudson's van unloading biscuits opposite. The fat woman had a louche large white muffin face. T'other was slightly grilled. They ate & ate. Talked about Mary. But if she's very ill, you'll have to go to her. Youre the only one ... But why should she be? ... I opened the marmalade but John doesnt like it – And we have two pounds of biscuits in the tin upstairs ... Something scented, shoddy, parasitic about them. Then they totted up cakes. And passed the time o' day with the waitress. Where does the money come to feed these fat white slugs? Brighton a love corner for slugs. The powdered the pampered the mildly improper. I invested them in a large house in Sussex Sqre. We cycled. Irritated as usual by the blasphemy of Peacehaven. Helen has fallen through, I mean the house I got her with Enid Jones, the day Enid lunched here, with Vita; & I felt so untidy yet cool; & she edgy & brittle. No walks for ever so long. People daily. And rather a churn in my mind. And some blank spaces. Food becomes an obsession. I grudge giving away a spice bun. Curious – age, or the war? Never mind.

Entry for Wednesday, 26 February 1941, from *The Diary of Virginia Woolf*, Vol. 5, 1936–41, edited by Anne Olivier Bell, assisted by Andrew McNeillie.

Green with Embarrassment

[My mother] could never have believed it possible that it was out of uncontrollable panic that I upset a whole dish of spinach into my lap, at one of the first dinner-parties I ever went to. I was about eighteen, and I had on my best green satin evening dress, very smart and tight and shiny. I mopped away at the mess with my long white kid gloves, and made it much worse. The kind parlour-maid tried to help me; but my neighbours, instead of making a joke of it, pretended that they did not see; no doubt from the best of motives, but it was not the right treatment. Oh dear, Oh dear, how I did wish to fall down dead that very instant! But it was a horrible dress anyhow; I had been allowed no choice in colour or make; and I was glad when it was found to be spoilt for ever.

From Gwen Raverat, *Period Piece* (1952).

Secrets of the Menu

... Yesterday there was a storm that lasted all day until nearly midnight. Most of the day I stood up front, under the bridge, on a protected and elevated spot, and admired the magnificent spectacle as the mountainous waves rolled up and poured a whirling cloud of foam over the ship. The ship began to roll fearfully, and several times we were soaked by a salty shower. It turned cold, and we went in for a cup of tea. Inside, however, the brain flowed down the spinal canal and tried to come out again from under the stomach. Consequently I retired to my bed, where I soon felt fine again and later was able to consume a pleasant supper. Outside from time to time a wave thundered against the ship. The objects in my cabin had all come to life: the sofa cushion crawled about on the floor in the semidarkness; a recumbent shoe sat up, looked around in astonishment, and then shuffled quietly off under the sofa; a standing shoe turned wearily on its side and followed its mate. Now the scene changed. I realised that the shoes had gone under the sofa to fetch my bag and brief case. The whole company paraded over to join the big trunk under the bed. One sleeve of my shirt on the sofa waved longingly after them, and from inside the chests and drawers came rumbles and rattles. Suddenly there was a terrible crash under my floor, a rattling, clattering, and tinkling. One of the kitchens is underneath me. There, at one blow, five hundred plates had been awakened from their deathlike torpor and with a single bold leap had put a sudden end to their dreary existence as slaves. In all the cabins round about, unspeakable groans betrayed the secrets of the menu. I slept like a top, and this morning the wind is beginning to blow from another side ...

C.G. Jung to Emma Jung, 25 September 1909, from *Memories, Dreams, Reflections: C.G. Jung*, edited by Aniela Jaffe (translated by Richard and Clara Winston) (1963).

Seeds of Disapproval

There was a deadly feud between Sir John Conroy and Baroness Lehzen. But that was not all. The Duchess had grown too fond of her major-domo. There were familiarities, and one day the Princess Victoria discovered the fact. She confided what she had seen to the Baroness, and to the Baroness's beloved ally, Madame de Späth. Unfortunately, Madame de Späth could not hold her tongue, and was actually foolish enough to reprove the Duchess; whereupon she was instantly dismissed. It was not so easy to get rid of the Baroness. That lady, prudent and reserved, maintained an irreproachable demeanour. Her position was strongly entrenched; she had managed to secure the support of the King; and Sir John found that he could do nothing against her. But henceforward the household was divided into two camps. The Duchess supported Sir John with all the amplitude of her authority; but the Baroness, too, had an adherent who could not be neglected. The Princess Victoria said nothing, but she had been much attached to Madame de Späth, and she adored her Lehzen. The Duchess knew only too well that in this horrid embroilment her daughter was against her. Chagrin, annoyance, moral reprobation, tossed her to and fro. She did her best to console herself with Sir John's affectionate loquacity, or with the sharp remarks of Lady Flora Hastings, one of her maids of honour, who had no love for the Baroness. The subject lent itself to satire; for the pastor's daughter, with all her airs of stiff superiority, had habits which betrayed her origin. Her passion for caraway seeds, for instance, was uncontrollable. Little bags of them came over to her from Hanover, and she sprinkled them on her bread and butter, her cabbage, and even her roast beef. Lady Flora could not resist a caustic observation; it was repeated to the Baroness, who pursed her lips in fury; and so the mischief grew.

From Lytton Strachey, *Queen Victoria* (1921).

Dinner by Firelight

4 September 1666

Up by break of day to get away the remainder of my things, which I did by a lighter at the Iron gate; and my hands so few, that it was the afternoon before we could get them all away. Sir W. Penn and I to Tower street, and there met the fire Burning three or four doors beyond Mr. Howells; whose goods, poor man (his trayes and dishes, Shovells &c., were flung all along Tower street in the kennels, and people working therewith from one end to the other), the fire coming on in that narrow street, on both sides, with infinite fury. Sir W. Batten, not knowing how to remove his wind, did dig a pit in the garden and laid it in there; and I took the opportunity of laying all the papers of my office that I could not otherwise dispose of. And in the evening Sir W. Penn and I did dig another and put our wine in it, and I my parmazan cheese as well as my wine and some other things. The Duke of York was at the office this day at Sir W. Penn's, but I happened not to be within. This afternoon, sitting melancholy with Sir W. Penn in our garden and thinking of the certain burning of this office without extraordinary means, I did propose for the sending up of all our workmen from Woolwich and Deptford yards (none whereof yet appeared), and to write to Sir W. Coventry to have the Duke of York's permission to pull down houses rather then lose this office, which would much hinder the King's business. So Sir W. Penn he went down this night, in order to the sending them up tomorrow morning; and I wrote to Sir W. Coventry about the business, but received no answer.

This night Mrs. Turner (who, poor woman, was removing her goods all this day – good goods, into the garden, and knew not how to dispose of them) – and her husband supped with my wife and I at night in the office, upon a shoulder of mutton from the cook's, without any napkin or anything, in a sad manner but were merry. Only, now and then walking into the garden and saw how horridly the sky looks, all on a fire in the night, was enough to put us out of our wits; and endeed it was extremely dreadfull – for it looks just as if it was at us, and the whole heaven on fire. I after supper walked in the dark down to Tower street, and there saw it all on fire at the Trinity house on that side and the Dolphin tavern on this side, which was very near us – and the fire with extraordinary vehemence.

From *The Diary of Samuel Pepys*, edited by Robert Latham and William Matthews (1985).

Teeth Money

Adrianople, 1 April 1717

You see that I am very exact in keeping the promise you engaged me to make but I know not whether your curiosity will be satisfied with the accounts I shall give you, though I can assure you that the desire I have to oblige you to the utmost of my power has made me very diligent in my enquiries and observations. 'Tis certain we have but very imperfect relations of the manners and religion of these people, this part of the world being seldom visited but by merchants, who mind little but their own affairs, or travellers who make too short a stay to be able to report anything exactly of their own knowledge. The Turks are too proud to converse familiarly with merchants etc., who can only pick up some confused informations, which are generally false, and can give no better account of the ways here, than a French refugee lodging in a garret in Greek Street, could write of the court of England. The journey we have made from Belgrade hither by land cannot possibly be passed by any out of a public character. The desert woods of Serbia are the common refuge of thieves who rob fifty in a company, that we had need of all our guards to secure us, and the villages so poor that only force could exort from them necessary provisions. Indeed the janissaries had no mercy on their poverty, killing all the poultry and sheep they could find without asking who they belonged to, while the wretched owners durst not put in their claim for fear of being beaten. Lambs just fallen, geese and turkeys big with egg all massacred without distinction! I fancied I heard the complaints of Moelibeus for the hope of his flock. When the pashas travel 'tis yet worse. Those oppressors are not content with eating all that is to be eaten belonging to the peasants; after they have crammed themselves and their numerous retinue they have the impudence to exact what they call teeth money, a contribution for the use of their teeth, worn with doing them the honour of devouring their meat. This is a literal, known truth, however extravagant it seems; and such is the natural corruption of a military government, their religion not allowing of this barbarity any more than our does.

From Lady Mary Wortley Montagu, *The Turkish Embassy Letters*, edited by Malcolm Jack (1993).

Scotland v. Italy

It was not without great delight that I came to some lofty plane-trees, forming a kind of irregular avenue to a miserable house, and under the shade of these trees I took shelter from the heat of the sun, which was now beginning to be oppressive. The edifice had the appearance of what might be supposed to be a farm-house, but had all the gloom of desolation around it. It was a pretty spot, however, and might have been made a delightful residence. I saw no signs of human existence, and I felt no inclination to disturb the repose of the inhabitants, though I began to feel the effects of my sausage breakfast. I determined to stop at the first repectable house that I met, and try how far the hospitality of the country was likely to go.

It was not long before I was able to put this intention into effect, for I reached a house which was in a tolerable state of repair, and to which the proprietor was making some further additions. This augured well, and I walked up to the door, where a good-looking girl appeared, yet before I could reach her she had vanished, and immediately afterwards a man came forward, to whom I addressed a petition for wine, for which I was prepared to pay, and if they had none, water would be a very valuable commodity in my eyes. I told him that I had come from a distant land to admire the beauties of his country. He required, however, no incitement to give me all and more than I required. He called for chairs, and we sat down under the shade of a tree, while he directed the servant to bring out some refreshment. It was indeed scanty, and of very coarse quality, but it was evidently given with good will, and that would far more than have compensated for even less luxurious fare. The bread was coarse and old, the cheese I could scarcely make any impression upon, and if this may be taken as a sample of their mode of diet, I would back Scotland against Italy, even with her oat-cakes and porridge.

From Crauford Tait Ramage, *The Nooks and By-Ways of Italy* (1868).

They called the meat-balls *klops*. An orderly went round and ladled out two grey pellets on each thick white plate. The cadets did not take up their forks. They tried not to look at the food, they tried not to look at each other; they did not know where to look. They did not know what to do with their hands. Then the prefect, *Stubenältester* was the unprepossessing term, went off like a firecracker. The sound was something like *Klawp/sah RHOWFF!* and it was an order. Twenty-three white china disks flew up, changed hands, whirled through the air, tilted on the same angle at the head, flew on – It was a dazzling manoeuvre, executed like a variety turn. Johannes sat up, friendly and captivated.

The prefect rapped *RrrrhALT!* and the plates grounded smoothly. There was a plate once more in front of every boy and about ten of them were empty; and there was now before the prefect's place a neat mound of meat-balls. He shovelled, fast as fast, a *klops* at a time. The boys kept their poses. Then he put down the fork and cracked his sound. The plates circled; six more were cleared. They landed with Johannes's full one conspicuous in their middle.

'You there, pass up your plate,' said the prefect. 'And mind you know how to next week. Tonight you may take it up to me yourself.'

Johannes did not budge.

'Did you hear me?' said the prefect. He did not speak, he shouted.

'Yes,' said Johannes.

'Bring up your plate!'

'No,' said Johannes.

The walls did not come down.

'Oh it isn't that I want to eat it,' said Johannes. Then, fearing he'd been rude about the food in someone's house, he said, 'You see, I'm not hungry,' and began to weep again. Johannes's German was deplorable, full of wrong inflections and French words, and he spoke it with the buzzing slur of the Baden peasants.

The cadets acted sniggers.

Johannes turned to a boy of twelve, 'Have mine,' he said, 'won't you?'

The boy recoiled but knew it was too late. He had looked at the new monster's plate; he was included in his doom.

'I am waiting,' said the prefect.

'You had enough,' said Johannes. 'It is disgusting to eat up other people's dinners. They look as if they wanted them themselves.'

There was a swell of embarrassment.

'Stand up when you speak to me,' said the prefect.

'*Pourquoi donc?*' said Johannes.

'STAND UP.'

'This is very silly,' said Johannes.

There was a stiffening – the captain on the round stood by Johannes's chair. 'Get up,' he said.

Johannes got up.

'Name?'

'We already met, *Monsieur l'Officier*, you very kindly showed me upstairs this afternoon.'

The captain was the physics master. The masters at Benzheim were Army officers, and a tricky lot; men whose physique was too poor for soldiering and whose talents or connexions had failed to get them a staff appointment. 'Name?' the captain said.

'Johannes von Felden.'

'Cadet von Felden,' said the captain, leaning on his stick, 'I must remind you, One: your *Stubenältester* is your immediate superior; Two: your display of civilian humour is out of place at Benzheim, and will not be tolerated.'

'Do I have to do everything he tells me, sir?' said Johannes.

'You heard me. In future you will address me as *Herr Hauptmann*.'

'Yes, *Herr Hauptmann*.'

'We have had enough of your Yes's and No's, Cadet von Felden. The correct form is "At your orders, *Herr Hauptmann*." That is all. Cadets, you may finish your supper.'

Johannes picked up his plate and took it to the head of the table. He put it before the prefect with a slight bow. '*Monsieur, vous me dégoûtez,*' he said, and returned to his chair.

The prefect resumed command; the plates circulated – four untouched lots remained. As he chewed he pulled out his watch, laid it on the table, then went, *Faaahll/T TSOOH!* and the four boys before whom full plates happened to have come down, ate. It was forty seconds to go till grace, they had long finished their bread and mug of cocoa, and the wretched minced meat was stone cold.

From Sybille Bedford, *A Legacy* (1956).

Garlic Breath

He whose impious hand has strangled
his agèd father deserves to eat it. It is
more harmful than hemlock. Garlic.
Peasants must have iron guts.
What venom rages in my gizzard?
Have these roots been stewed
in vipers' blood without my knowledge?
Has Canidia handled this evil dish?
Medea infatuate with the Argonauts' captain
(more fair than all his crew)
when he tried to yoke the unbroken bulls
anointed her Jason with this;
and before she fled on the great winged worm
she took revenge on his mistress
by making her gifts besmeared with this.
Never did such a fiery, stifling heat
settle on drought-parched Apulia.
Nessus' shirt did not sear
more swelteringly into
resourceful Hercules' shoulders.
If ever you are tempted this way again,
my humorous Maecenas, I devoutly hope
that your girl will push away your face
and retreat to the very edge of the bed.

Horace, Epode 3, (68–5 BC), translated by W.G. Shepherd.

Shopping Fever

And here I must observe again, that this necessity of going out of our
houses to buy provisions was in a great measure the ruin of the
whole city, for the people catched the distemper on these occasions
one of another, and even the provisions themselves were often
tainted; at least I have great reason to believe so; and therefore I
cannot say with satisfaction what I know is repeated with great
assurance, that the market-people and such as brought provisions to

town were never infected. I am certain the butchers of Whitechapel, where the greatest part of the flesh-meat was killed, were dreadfully visited, and that at least to such a degree that few of their shops were kept open, and those that remained of them killed their meat at Mile End and that way, and brought it to market upon horses.

However, the poor people could not lay up provisions, and there was a necessity that they must go to market to buy, and others to send servants or their children; and as this was a necessity which renewed itself daily, it brought abundance of unsound people to the markets, and a great many that went thither sound brought death home with them.

It is true people used all possible precaution. When any one bought a joint of meat in the market they would not take it off the butcher's hand, but took it off the hooks themselves. On the other hand, the butcher would not touch the money, but have it put into a pot full of vinegar, which he kept for that purpose. The buyer carried always small money to make up any odd sum, that they might take no change. They carried bottles of scents and perfumes in their hands, and all the means that could be used were used; but then the poor could not do even these things, and they went at all hazards.

From Daniel Defoe, *A Journal of the Plague Year* (1722).

Bad Manners

Alice glanced nervously along the table, as she walked up the large hall, and noticed that there were about fifty guests, of all kinds: some were animals, some birds, and there were even a few flowers among them. 'I'm glad they've come without waiting to be asked,' she thought: 'I should never have known who were the right people to invite!'

There were three chairs at the head of the table; the Red and White Queens had taken two of them, but the middle one was empty. Alice sat down, rather uncomfortable at the silence, and longing for someone to speak.

At last the Red Queen began. 'You've missed the soup and fish,' she said. 'Put on the joint!' And the waiters set a leg of mutton before

Alice, who looked at it rather anxiously, as she had never had to carve one before.

'You look a little shy; let me introduce you to that leg of mutton,' said the Red Queen. 'Alice – Mutton; Mutton, Alice.' The leg of mutton got up in the dish and made a little bow to Alice; and she returned the bow, not knowing whether to be frightened or amused.

'May I give you a slice?' she said, taking up the knife and fork, and looking from one Queen to the other.

'Certainly not,' the Red Queen said, very decidedly: 'it isn't etiquette to cut any one you've been introduced to. Remove the joint!' And the waiters carried it off, and brought a large plum-pudding in its place.

'I won't be introduced to the pudding, please,' Alice said rather hastily, 'or we shall get no dinner at all. May I give you some?'

But the Red Queen looked sulky, and growled 'Pudding – Alice; Alice – Pudding. Remove the pudding!' and the waiters took it away before Alice could return its bow.

However, she didn't see why the Red Queen should be the only one to give orders, so, as an experiment, she called out 'Waiter! Bring back the pudding!' and there it was again in a moment like a conjuring trick. It was so large that she couldn't help feeling a *little* shy with it, as she had been with the mutton; however, she conquered her shyness by a great effort, and handed a slice to the Red Queen.

'What impertinence!' said the Pudding. 'I wonder how you'd like it, if I were to cut a slice out of *you*, you creature!'

Alice could only look at it and gasp.

'Make a remark,' said the Red Queen: 'it's ridiculous to leave all the conversation to the pudding!'

From Lewis Carroll, *Through the Looking-Glass and What Alice Found There* (1871).

Swan Song

Olim lacus colueram,
olim pulcher exstiteram,
dum cygnus ego fueram ...

Once I had lakes to live upon:
in glory I would swim along –
once, when I was still a swan.

Poor thing, poor thing –
not a raw thing
but done like anything!

Once I was whiter than the snow,
finer than any bird I know:
now see me – blacker than a crow!

Poor thing ...

Cook on the spit is curving me,
flames sear through every nerve in me –
now here's a waiter *serving* me!

Poor thing ...

I'd rather be in the fresh air
out on a lake – or anywhere
but peppered up as gourmet's fare.

Poor thing ...

Here in this serving dish I lie
where I have no strength to fly
as grinding molars greet the eye ...

Poor thing ...

From the *Carmina Burana*, thirteenth century, translated by David Parlett.

A Close Shave

This is what happened. One of our host's country tenants had
presented him with a haunch of venison from a tall, plump stag that
he had killed himself. Hephaestion the cook carelessly hung it rather

too low on the kitchen door and a stray hound was able to pull it down and carry it off. When Hephaestion discovered his loss, for which he had only himself to blame, he began to cry miserably. There seemed to be nothing he could do, and what would happen when his master called for his supper he dared not imagine. He worked himself up into such a state of terror that he called his little son to him, kissed him a tender goodbye, picked up a rope and went off to hang himself. His wife, who loved him dearly, heard the dreadful news just in time. She wrenched the rope from his hands and asked him: 'Are you blind, my sweet Hephaestion? Has this accident so unbalanced you that you can't see the door that Providence has kept open for your escape? If you still have any sense left after your awful discovery, please, please use it and listen to me! You know the priests' ass which was brought in today? Take it to some lonely spot and cut its throat. Then carve off a haunch, like the one you have lost, stew it till tender, disguise the flavour with the most savoury sauce you can invent, and serve it up as venison at the master's table.'

The rogue of a cook, overjoyed at the prospect of saving his life at the price of mine, called his wife the cleverest woman in the world and began sharpening his kitchen knives.

Time pressed. I could not afford to stay where I was and concoct a plan for saving myself. I decided to escape from the knife which I felt so close to my throat, by running away at once. I broke my halter and galloped off as fast as my legs would carry me, not forgetting to kick out my heels as I went. I shot across the first portico and, without hesitating for a moment, dashed into the dining-room where the master of the house was banqueting with the priests on sacrificial meats. I knocked down and smashed a great part of the dinner service and some of the tables, too. He was greatly annoyed by my irreverent entry and the damage I had caused. 'Take away this frisky brute,' he told one of his slaves. 'Shut him up in a safe place where his pranks won't disturb the peace of my guests.' Rescued from the knife by my own cleverness, I was glad indeed to be locked up securely in my cell.

From Apuleius, *The Golden Ass* (c. AD 120–180), translated by Robert Graves (1950).

A Case of Hamicide

Care was taken to hang the hams well away from places where people sat, and certainly never above the table and the benches around it. I knew of a case in which a ham committed homicide. An old grandfather on a farm had placed his armchair underneath the hams, and one of them fell on him; the old gentleman died of a fractured skull. The locals concluded that it was the pig's revenge.

From Henriette Dussourt, *Les Secrets des fermes au coeur de la France* (1982), translated by Anthea Bell.

Turtle Soup

When Victor got upstairs, his mother was still in the kitchen. Eggs were boiling and she had put a big pot of water on a back burner. 'You took it out again!' Victor said, seeing the terrapin's box on the counter.

'Yes. I prepare the stew tonight,' said his mother. 'That is why I need the cream.'

Victor looked at her. 'You're going to – you have to kill it tonight?'

'Yes, my little one. Tonight.' She jiggled the pot of eggs.

'Mama, can I take it downstairs to show Frank?' Victor asked quickly. 'Just for five minutes, Mama. Frank's down there now.'

'Who is Frank?'

'He's that fellow you asked me about today. The blond fellow we always see. *Please*, Mama.'

His mother's black eyebrows frowned. 'Take the *terrapène* downstairs? Certainly not. Don't be absurd, my baby! The *terrapène* is not a toy!'

Victor tried to think of some other lever of persuasion. He had not removed his coat. 'You wanted me to get acquainted with Frank –'

'Yes. What has that got to do with the *terrapène*?'

The water on the back burner began to boil.

'You see, I promised him I'd –' Victor watched his mother lift the terrapin from the box, and as she dropped it into the boiling water his mouth fell open. '*Mama!*'

'What is this? What is this noise?'

Victor, open-mouthed, stared at the terrapin whose legs were now

[203]

racing against the steep sides of the pot. The terrapin's mouth opened, its eyes looked right at Victor for an instant, its head arched back in torture, then the open mouth sank beneath the seething water – and that was the end.

Victor blinked. The terrapin was dead. He came closer, saw the four legs and the tail stretched out in the water. He looked at his mother.

She was drying her hands on a towel. She glanced at him, then said, 'Ugh!' She smelled her hands, then hung the towel back.

'Did you have to kill it like that?'

'How else? The same way you kill a lobster. Don't you know that? It doesn't hurt them.'

He stared at her. When she started to touch him, he stepped back. He thought of the terrapin's wide open mouth, and his eyes suddenly flooded with tears. Maybe the terrapin had been screaming and it hadn't been heard over the bubbling of the water. The terrapin had looked at him, wanting him to pull it out, and he hadn't moved to help it. His mother had tricked him, acted so fast that he couldn't save it. He stepped back again. 'No, don't touch me!'

From Patricia Highsmith, 'The Terrapin', *Ellery Queen's Mystery Magazine* (1962).

Clear Mock Turtle Soup
(Fr. Potage de Tortue Fausse Clair)

$^{1}/_{2}$ a calf's head
5 quarts of clear second stock (or water)
2 onions
1 turnip
1 strip of celery
bouquet-garni (parsley, basil, marjoram, thyme, bay-leaf)
12 peppercorns

4 cloves
2 blades of mace
2 glasses of sherry
1 tablespoonful of lemon-juice
$^{1}/_{2}$ a lb. of lean beef
$^{1}/_{2}$ a lb. of lean veal
the whites and shells of 2 eggs
salt

Method. – Soak the head 24 hours in salt and water, changing it frequently. Then bone the head (the brains and tongue may be used for some other purpose), tie the meat in a thin cloth and break the bones into small pieces; put them into a stewpan, cover with cold water, add a tablespoonful of salt, let it boil up, strain, and wash the head in cold water. Return the meat and bones to the stewpan, put in the stock and a dessertspoonful of salt, boil up and skim well. Now add the prepared vegetables, herbs, peppercorns, cloves and mace, and when boiling, remove the scum, put on the cover and cook slowly for about 3 hours, according to the size of the head. Strain, put the meat aside, and when the stock is cold remove the fat, and clarify with the coarsely chopped beef and veal, and whites of eggs, see recipe No. 10. Return to the saucepan, with the sherry, the lemon-juice and a little of the meat of the head, cut into small pieces. Add necessary seasoning, boil up and serve.

This recipe may be thickened with a tablespoonful of arrowroot when a thicker soup is required.

The remainder of the calf's head can be used for an entrée.

Time. – To prepare the stock, $3\frac{1}{2}$ to 4 hours. To clarify and re-heat, 40 to 60 minutes. **Average Cost.** 5s. 9d. with stock. **Seasonable** at any time. **Sufficient** for 12 or 14 persons.

MARJORAM (Fr. *marjolaine*). – The common marjoram is indigenous to Britain, and grows on chalky soils. Its flowers are reddish in colour, growing in clustered spikes. It possesses balsamic, aromatic and bitter properties, and from the plant is obtained 'oil of thyme.' Sweet and pot marjoram, natives of southern Europe, are cultivated in gardens for culinary use; the young tops and leaves, both green and dried, are used for seasoning.

From *Mrs Beeton's Book of Household Management*, new edition.

A Woman's Work Is Never Done

Hamad took off his iqal and ghutra and placed them as usual on the coffee table. Drunkenness never affected his spruceness. Almost every night he came home under the influence of drink but never did he come home with his dress disorderly or his hair dishevelled. Sometimes he came home staggering from the effects of liquor but he would take off his clothes in his usual methodical way and place them on the coffee table by the television set. She wished he would eat out for she was in no mood to cook. He looked at her, smiled and said, 'I want some macaroni'.

She had hoped not to have this labour imposed on her. She would have to take the mince meat out of the fridge and soak it in water. The macaroni would have to be washed and boiled. Preparing the gravy with the necessary care and attention would demand enormous effort. Should she refuse on the grounds that it was too late? Should she feign illness and offer a light alternative? Egg and onion or cheese and tomato sandwiches? She had tried this once before and he had been furious with her. The effects lasted for some time. But she surrendered to the macaroni pot. She got up and took Hamad's iqal and ghutra to the bedroom. He put a wrestling tape on the video. André the Giant was being menaced by Hulk Hogan. As his wife went from the bedroom to the kitchen he called out, 'Who do you think is going to win, Hulk Hogan or André the Giant?'

She said crossly, 'Wrestling is a complete farce.'

'What about the chairs they smash over their heads and the blood that pours down their faces?'

'It's a complete and utter farce.'

'But it's great entertainment.'

She was tempted to reply that it was entertainment for idiots and fools but she refrained. She knew that Hamad was extra touchy when he was drunk and would twist anything she said and flare up. As she went into the kitchen she said, 'Each to his taste.'

She took out a packet of mince meat and poured some hot water over it. She took out the macaroni and measured some out into a small pot. What was it she loved in Hamad that led her to marry him? His bushy moustache? His thick sensuous lips? His roving eyes? His generosity? She did not know! Sometimes he got on her nerves so much that she wished she had been a Christian nun who never got married at all. She once complained to her friend Ulya about his inconsiderate way of demanding a hot meal after midnight. Ulya guffawed, 'Thank God he only demands a hot dinner and not something else,' she said.

She wanted to ask about the something else that other husbands demanded of their wives but did not do so because Ulya could at time be very direct and extremely frank.

Her sister, Fatma, was married to a man who was very domestic. He never stayed up late, never got drunk and never went out at night. He was fast asleep at ten and up at five. He went on trips only with her and never went shopping or on any outing without her. In spite of all this she never heard a word from her sister in praise of her husband or of gratitude to the fates for having sent her such a paragon. Hamad came into the kitchen and sniffed noisily at the cooking smells, 'Did you know that my mum used to call me the kitchen cat?'

She smiled through her anger and annoyance. He took some olives out of a bottle in the fridge.

'I used to eat everything in the kitchen,' he said, 'vegetables fruit, stale food, bread and sweets. I used to be crazy about sweets.'

Her irritation returned. She frowned. She took some onions and started to chop them up. Hamad laughed.

'You'll cry,' he said.

She glared at him as he laughed.

'Don't get cross. Psychologists tell us that there is something positive about crying. It releases tension and is a safety valve for pressures so people do not explode.'

He took a tomato from the table as he left the kitchen chuckling.

'If I suffered from nervous tension I would take a dozen onions and cut them up with you so I could cry and get relief, but the stories and jokes of the lads this evening were so good that I do not feel any anxiety or tension.'

Under her breath Hamad's wife cursed psychologists, her husband, his friends and the wretched luck that had bound her to a man with such stupid sentiments. As she chopped the onions she cut a finger of her left hand. She opened a drawer, took out a bottle of iodine and dabbed her wound. It stang. She started to cry and the tears of grief mingled with the tears caused by chopping the onions.

From Muhammad al Murr, 'A Late Dinner' in *Dubai Tales* (1991), translated by Peter Clark.

Frozen to Death

Her first instinct was not to believe any of it, to reject it all. It occurred to her that perhaps he hadn't even spoken, that she herself had imagined the whole thing. Maybe, if she went about her business and acted as though she hadn't been listening, then later, when she sort of woke up again, she might find none of it had ever happened.

'I'll get the supper,' she managed to whisper, and this time he didn't stop her.

When she walked across the room she couldn't feel her feet touching the floor. She couldn't feel anything at all – except a slight nausea and a desire to vomit. Everything was automatic now – down the stairs to the cellar, the light switch, the deep freeze, the hand inside the cabinet taking hold of the first object it met. She lifted it out, and looked at it. It was wrapped in paper, so she took off the paper and looked at it again.

A leg of lamb.

All right then, they would have lamb for supper. She carried it upstairs, holding the thin bone-end of it with both her hands, and as she went through the living-room, she saw him standing over by the window with his back to her, and she stopped.

'For God's sake,' he said, hearing her, but not turning round. 'Don't make supper for me. I'm going out.'

At that point, Mary Maloney simply walked up behind him and without any pause she swung the big frozen leg of lamb high in the air and brought it down as hard as she could on the back of his head.

She might just as well have hit him with a steel club.

She stepped back a pace, waiting, and the funny thing was that he remained standing there for at least four or five seconds, gently swaying. Then he crashed to the carpet.

From Roald Dahl, 'Lamb to the Slaughter', *Someone Like You* (1954).

Verbal Bulimia

Jools sipped her glass of red wine. She was in an unusually reflective mood and wasn't saying much. I get very nervous when there are long silences so I started reading the menu out loud.

'Lamb steak with a rosemary *jus*,' I read. 'Have you noticed that everything comes with a *jus* these days? Whatever happened to gravy, that's what I'd like to know? First of all it became *coulis*, or should I say *a coulis*, because some time in the late eighties a law was passed saying that you couldn't describe anything on a menu without the use of the indefinite article, then it became *a salsa*, and now it's called *a jus*. You know, I wouldn't mind betting that sometime quite soon there will be a rehabilitation of gravy. One of the Sundays will run an article called 'Come back comfort food' and there'll be *a gravy* on every menu south of Watford, just like bangers and mash, except it's now called Toulouse sausages and potato purée, with *an onion jus*, of course ...'

'God, you don't half go on,' said Jools. 'I've never heard anyone go on about food like you do.'

'Well, I've never seen anyone eat as much as you,' I countered. 'I don't know why I'm so obsessed with reading menus. It's a kind of verbal bulimia, I think. I get my kicks from reading about food, then spitting all the words out. Sad, isn't it?'

Jools looked at me oddly, then laughed, but her heart obviously wasn't in it. We ate our meal in virtual silence.

From Imogen Parker, *Something Funny* (1995).

What Women Are Made For

Georges looked at the ladies as he listened, dazed and excited by the brutal judgements being whispered in his ear, while behind him the waiters kept repeating in respectful tones:

'*Poulardes à la maréchale ... Filets de sole sauce ravigote ...*'

'My dear fellow,' said Daguenet, giving him the benefit of his experience, 'don't take that fish: it's no good at all at this time of night ... And have the Léoville: it's less treacherous than the other.'

Waves of heat were rising from the candelabra, from the dishes being handed round, and from the whole table round which thirty-eight people were suffocating; and the waiters kept forgetting themselves and running across the carpet, so that it was spotted with grease. Yet the supper failed to get any livelier. The ladies toyed with their meat, leaving half of it uneaten. Tatan Néné alone helped herself greedily to every dish. At that advanced hour of the night, the guests' appetites were only nervous cravings, the capricious desires of disordered stomachs. The old gentleman next to Nana refused every dish offered him; he had only taken a spoonful of soup, and now he sat in front of his empty plate gazing silently around him. There were some discreet yawns, and occasionally eyelids closed, and faces turned haggard. It was a dreadful bore – as it always was, according to Vandeuvres. This sort of supper ought to be a naughty affair, he said, if it was to be amusing. Otherwise, if it was too decent and respectable, you might as well eat in good society, where it wasn't any more boring. If it hadn't been for Bordenave, who was still bawling away, everybody would have fallen asleep. Bordenave himself, with his leg duly stretched out on its chair, was letting his neighbours, Lucy and Rose, wait on him as if he were a sultan. They were giving him their entire attention, looking after him, pampering him, and watching over his glass and plate; but that did not prevent him from complaining.

'Who's going to cut up my meat for me? ... I can't, the table's miles away.'

Every few minutes Simonne got up and stood right behind him to cut his meat and his bread. All the women took a great interest in what he was eating. The waiters were constantly recalled, and he was stuffed to suffocation. When Simonne wiped his mouth, while Rose and Lucy were changing his plate, he found this a charming attention, and condescending at last to express his appreciation, he said:

'That's right, my girl, that's as it should be ... That's what all women are made for!'

From Emile Zola, *Nana* (1880), translated by George Holden.

Last Days of the Raj

The Comet-Danes were the senior Qui-Hais of the station, the Brigadier having retired some years before, at which time they decided to live on in India rather than return to an England with which they had long since lost touch.

Their narrow driveway had been designed for carriages, so we were obliged to leave our motor and Ramaswami at the main gate. A ragged chokidar (watchman) holding a butthi (oil lantern) was stationed there. In Hindustani (for no good Qui-Hai would dream of employing an English-speaking servant) he warned us to guard against all things that crawl, and led us at a mournful pace to his master's bungalow, where we were welcomed by our hosts. Mrs Comet-Dane was resplendent in an ancient and voluminous black satin gown. A broad strap of the same material was looped over her left wrist, the other end of which was sewn to the hem of her train. The Brigadier, a rather frail but still handsome old gentleman, was tall and thin with white wavy hair which he wore longer than the present day fashion. His high turned-up collar was secured by a well-tied black silk stock.

There were eight other guests, six of them men, and when the last had arrived cocktails were served – mixed vermouth with an excess of Italian. For some curious reason the rims of the glasses had been dampened and subsequently dipped in bright red granulated sugar, a portion of which was immediately transferred to our faces.

When we had completed this sanguinary transformation we were led to the dining room where we were confronted by a long table in the centre of which was a fantastic arrangement of coloured rice. Thousands of small grains, dyed the most flagrant hues conceivable, were laid on the white cloth in the pattern of a flower basket, from which sprang in ricey splendour exotic blue roses, green zinnias, black corn flowers and pink golden rod.

When I could tear my reluctant eyes from this startling master-piece, I observed at the place of each guest a small dish containing a raw egg removed from its shell. I was consumed with curiosity to know its purport and glanced furtively at Philip, who harbours an intense aversion to an uncooked egg. As the meal progressed I learned that it was to be turned into one's hot soup. I congratulated my husband on his poker face as he gallantly fell into line. When the fish arrived each piece appeared as a brown and arid island, segregated from its sister by a red and turbulent sea. We shortly discovered this body of water to be mashed potatoes dyed in beet juice!

By the time I had eaten purple carrots and red brussels sprouts I felt prepared for any eventuality, but the arrival of the iced pudding left me shaken and exhausted of surprise. It was served on a tray in what appeared to be a large blue Wedgwood china bowl of the most delicate texture and exquisite colouring. To my alarm, Mrs Comet-Dane took a fork and spoon and, raising them simultaneously a few inches into the air, brought them smartly down into the sides of the bowl breaking it into several pieces. That it was made of spun sugar had not occurred to me!

When the coffee was brought I was inured against anything that might present itself and was not surprised to see that, instead of being contained in a pot or percolator, it was spread on a wooden tray! The coffee beans were laid in a little pile; near them were a few cloves, twelve lumps of sugar, a glass of Kümmel, one of brandy, one of Benedictine, and one filled with the juice of half an orange. Our

Qui-Hais had apparently forgotten, or perhaps ignored, the fact that three of their guests were total abstainers from alcohol. Mrs Comet-Dane, without consulting the tastes of anyone, tossed all these ingredients together with a quantity of water into a chafing dish which stood over a spirit lamp, and we were given no option to drinking the resulting mixture.

From Elizabeth Crawford Wilkin, *Dekho! The India That Was* (1958).

A Fatal Mixture

Friday, March 16 or Saturday 17. – Lost track of dates, but think the last correct. Tragedy all along the line. At lunch, the day before yesterday, poor Titus Oates said he couldn't go on; he proposed we should leave him in his sleeping-bag. That we could not do, and we induced him to come on, on the afternoon march. In spite of its awful nature for him he struggled on and we made a few miles. At night he was worse and we knew the end had come.

Should this be found I want these facts recorded. Oates' last thoughts were of his Mother, but immediately before he took pride in thinking that his regiment would be pleased with the bold way in which he met his death. We can testify to his bravery. He has borne intense suffering for weeks without complaint, and to the very last was able and willing to discuss outside subjects. He did not – would not – give up hope till the very end. He was a brave soul. This was the end. He slept through the night before last, hoping not to wake; but he woke in the morning – yesterday. It was blowing a blizzard. He said, 'I am just going outside and may be some time.' He went out into the blizzard and we have not seen him since.

I take this opportunity of saying that we have stuck to our sick companions to the last. In case of Edgar Evans, when absolutely out of food and he lay insensible, the safety of the remainder seemed to demand his abandonment, but Providence mercifully removed him at this critical moment. He died a natural death, and we did not leave him till two hours after his death. We knew that poor Oates was walking to his death, but though we tried to dissuade him, we knew it was the act of a brave man and an English gentleman. We all hope to meet the end with a similar spirit, and assuredly the end is not far.

I can only write at lunch and then only occasionally. The cold is intense, −40° at midday. My companions are unendingly cheerful, but we are all on the verge of serious frostbites, and though we constantly talk of fetching through I don't think any one of us believes it in his heart.

We are cold on the march now, and at all times except meals. Yesterday we had to lay up for a blizzard and to-day we move dreadfully slowly. We are at No 14 pony camp, only two pony marches from One Ton Depôt. We leave here our theodolite, a camera, and Oates' sleeping-bags. Diaries, &c., and geological specimens carried at Wilson's special request, will be found with us or on our sledge.

Sunday, March 18. – To-day, lunch, we are 21 miles from the depôt. Ill fortune presses, but better may come. We have had more wind and drift from ahead yesterday; had to stop marching; wind N.W., force 4, temp. −35°. No human being could face it, and we are worn out *nearly*.

My right foot has gone, nearly all the toes – two days ago I was proud possessor of best feet. These are the steps of my downfall. Like an ass I mixed a small spoonful of curry powder with my melted pemmican – it gave me violent indigestion. I lay awake and in pain all night; woke and felt done on the march; foot went and I didn't know it. A very small measure of neglect and have a foot which is not pleasant to contemplate. Bowers takes first place in condition, but there is not much to choose after all. The others are still confident of getting through – or pretend to be – I don't know! We have the last *half* fill of oil in our primus and a very small quantity of spirit – this alone between us and thirst. The wind is fair for the moment, and that is perhaps a fact to help. The mileage would have seemed ridiculously small on our outward journey.

Monday, March 19. – Lunch. We camped with difficulty last night, and were dreadfully cold till after our supper of cold pemmican and biscuit and a half a pannikin of cocoa cooked over the spirit. Then, contrary to expectation, we got warm and all slept well. To-day we started in the usual dragging manner. Sledge dreadfully heavy. We are 15½ miles from the depôt and ought to get there in three days. What progress! We have two days' food but barely a day's fuel. All our feet are getting bad – Wilson's best, my right foot worst, left all right. There is no chance to nurse one's feet till we can get hot food into us. Amputation is the least I can hope for now, but will the trouble spread? That is the serious question. The

weather doesn't give us a chance – the wind from N. to N.W. and
–40° temp. to-day.

Wednesday, March 21. – Got within 11 miles of depôt Monday
night; had to lay up all yesterday in severe blizzard. To-day forlorn
hope, Wilson and Bowers going to depôt for fuel.

Thursday, March 22 and 23. – Blizzard bad as ever – Wilson and
Bowers unable to start – to-morrow last chance – no fuel and only
one or two of food left – must be near the end. Have decided it shall
be natural – we shall march for the depôt with or without our effects
and die in our tracks.

Thursday, March 29. – Since the 21st we have had a continuous
gale from W.S.W. and S.W. We had fuel to make two cups of tea
apiece and bare food for two days on the 20th. Every day we have
been ready to start for our depôt *11 miles* away, but outside the door
of the tent it remains a scene of whirling drift. I do not think we can
hope for any better things now. We shall stick it out to the end, but
we are getting weaker, of course, and the end cannot be far.

It seems a pity, but I do not think I can write more.

R. SCOTT

Last entry.
For God's sake look after our people.

From *Scott's Last Expedition*: *The Personal Journals of Captain R.F. Scott, CVO,
RN, on His Journey to the South Pole* (1913).

IV FINE YOUNG CANNIBALS

EVERYONE knows the same stories about cannibalism. They remember the Uruguayan rugby team whose plane crashed in the Andes in 1972, although they also know that the players weren't *real* cannibals, just desperate young men who did what they had to in order to stay alive – it isn't as though they actually *wanted* to eat their dead friends. Then there's Hannibal the Cannibal, the psychologist turned serial killer who eats people in the stylish film of Thomas Harris's thriller, *The Silence of the Lambs*. Anthony Hopkins won an Oscar for his performance as the gastronomic ghoul who strings along plucky little Jodie Foster, portraying Lecter as a chic criminal with far more brains than the FBI agents desperately trying to extract information from him. The fictional Lecter is much more charismatic than that pathetic little man who turned out to have a freezer full of human body parts – real body parts, that is – when police raided his apartment in Milwaukee in July 1991.

Who else? Well, Polynesia is famous for its cannibals and there's Sweeney Todd, the demon barber of Fleet Street, who robbed his customers and passed their corpses to Mrs Lovett next door to turn into her famous meat pies. And Sawney Beane, the Scottish brigand whose wife suspended human arms and legs from the roof of their cave as you or I might hang game. But Sweeney Todd is a character in a story by the little-known Tom Prest, a bogeyman who scares and thrills at the same time, and Sawney Beane might as well be fictional, given the unreliability of the sources for his exploits. If real, live, twentieth-century cannibals exist, it's surely in equatorial islands like Borneo or New Guinea where the natives still wear bones through their noses and stew their victims in big pots over an open fire – just like those cartoons the *Daily Mirror* still ran in the 1960s.

Remember? The ones where two big-game hunters in pith helmets exchange doubtful looks as the water starts to bubble and make nervous jokes about Old Carruthers saying the natives were always keen to have Englishmen for dinner. Hmm, getting into dangerous territory here ...

Cannibalism, in other words, makes people vague and nervous – so much so that it's constantly being turned into a joke. People shrug off their anxiety by remarking airily that human flesh tastes sweet, like veal or pork, but they're uncertain where this assertion actually comes from. There *are* descriptions in *Alive*, Piers Paul Read's book about the Andes air crash, but it sticks in the mind precisely because so few accounts of cannibalism tell the reader what the meat tastes like, concentrating instead on the diners' reactions: lip-smacking relish if they fall into the 'savage' category, horror and nausea if the consumption of human flesh has been unwitting or involuntary. An added *frisson* in many supposedly factual accounts comes from the cannibals' alleged order of preference for different nationalities, with some tribes swearing that the French or English are more delicious than, say, the Spanish. What makes these claims so unreliable, as Reay Tannahill observes in her history of cannibalism, *Flesh and Blood*, is that the preferences 'seem to have depended largely on the fancy of the chronicler'; some authors, curious as it may seem, give the impression of being flattered by the suggestion that their flesh is sweeter than the inhabitants of some neighbouring country.

Tannahill was writing about the supposed habits of the Caribs, the people who lived on several West Indian islands and whose practice of eating enemies who had been captured or killed in battle horrified the invading Spanish; their name, in a corrupt Spanish transliteration, is the source of the word cannibalism. The derivation is telling: anthropophagy, the neutral term preferred by anthropologists, comes from the conjunction of a Greek noun and verb (*anthropos*, a human being, and *phagein*, to eat); cannibalism, the popular word, associates the practice with a racial group who were regarded by Europeans from Captain Cook onwards (he landed there in 1492) as a bunch of painted savages. This being so, the European invaders felt little compunction in forcing them to change their customs by converting them to Christianity or wiping them out, using highly coloured accounts of human sacrifice and flesh-eating as a justification. A striking feature of cannibal narratives is their similarity to one another, the repetition of familiar scenarios in which demonic figures, scarcely recognisable as human, fall upon their victims and tear lumps out of barely dead or still-breathing flesh. One particularly rich source of such stories, the vegetarian polemicist Joseph Ritson – he believed that eating animals inevitably led to eating human flesh – claimed in a tract published in 1802 that there were cannibal tribes all over the non-European world who devoured their victims raw. Ritson listed Peruvian hunters who ignored sheep and cattle in favour of gobbling up their shepherds and 'negros' from Africa who 'bite large pieces out of the arms or legs of their neighbours, and fellow-slaves, which they swallow with great avidity'.

What emerges from these credulous narratives is greater evidence of a prurient curiosity within *developed* cultures about cannibalism than of its widespread practice outside them. This is not to argue that cannibalism does not exist, especially in circumstances of desperate food shortages such as in the Nazi concentration camps, but to suggest that it has always had an unacknowledged function as an index of savagery – a distancing mechanism used to enforce a dubious hierarchy of racial superiority. As a result, the most outlandish and unlikely tales have, throughout history, found an eager audience who did not stop to question unlikely details such as the supposed cannibal preference for biting off and eating raw chunks of flesh; readers who would laugh at the notion of tribes devouring animals in this way have been remarkably uncritical when the meat in question is human. If cannibal narratives are a form of disguised self-justification for colonial cultures, it explains their popularity in the literature of empire-building peoples from the ancient Romans to Victorian England; cannibals pop up regularly in the *Thousand and One Nights*, fictional product of an expansionist medieval Muslim culture, and the memoirs of Marco Polo, thirteenth-century apologist for the Mongol emperor of China. The binary oppositions they represent – nature/culture, savagery/civilisation – are neatly expressed by the French anthropologist Claude Lévi-Strauss in the title of his celebrated study of myth and ritual, *Le Cru et le cuit* (*The Raw and the Cooked*); the cooking metaphor is peculiarly apposite given that many accounts of cannibalism stress the failure of the savage 'other' to cook their victims. (The Roman satirist Juvenal, describing a supposedly recent outbreak of cannibalism in Rome's traditional enemy, Egypt, comments disapprovingly on the Egyptians' failure to turn their human fodder into a stew.)

The smugness with which 'civilised' people regard cannibal natives is summed up in Joseph Ritson's casual remark about the fate of the

Caribs: 'They are now nearly extirpated by the Christians.' A much later author, Lewis Robert Wolberg, took a paternalistic line in his book *The Psychology of Eating* (1937), observing that 'ecclesiastical pressure has forced the savage to restrain his appetite and to give up his tasty human dishes'. Wolberg does not seem to have stopped to consider the irony of so-called savages being persuaded out of their supposed cannibal habits by emissaries of a religion itself so firmly rooted in anthropophagous ritual. For, as Mark's Gospel recounts, Jesus laid down the form of the Church's central act of worship in terms that are overtly cannibalistic; in case anyone was in any doubt about what he meant when he gave the disciples bread and said 'Take, eat: this is my body', the Fourth Lateran Council in 1215 rejected symbolic interpretations in favour of the doctrine of transubstantiation. Subsequently, the slippage between metaphor and reality was so great that in the late Middle Ages, churches all over southern Europe had to be locked against *religieuses* who obsessively consumed communion wafers, refusing other forms of sustenance in favour of what they genuinely believed to be the body of Christ.

The fourteenth-century saint, Catherine of Siena, felt a need to substitute 'the filth of disease and the blood of Christ's agony' for ordinary food, on two occasions forcing herself to suck the putrefying breast of a dying woman or to drink pus. (The response of the sick to these saintly ministrations has not been recorded.) The curious aftermath was a vision in which Christ uncovered the wound in his side and urged Catherine to drink from it, which she did rapturously – a swift transition from anthropophagous imagery to something resembling *fellatio*. The scene is a salutary reminder of the extent to which our sexual practices mimic the act of eating another human being, a truth hinted at in love-talk like 'I could eat you up'. Lévi-Strauss made the same point, and hinted at the existence of a parallel set of taboos, when he described cannibalism as 'alimentary incest'.

This raises the intriguing possibility that cannibal narratives fascinate developed cultures not only because they validate notions of racial superiority but because they embody our darkest urges and fears about sex. Cannibalism involves the literal incorporation of the other, that fusing of two into one which is at the heart of so many sexual fantasies; at a crude level, it appears to defy the precipitous return to isolation that follows orgasm and is the origin of the sensation of *petite mort*. Few novelists have reflected this cannibalistic element of the erotic impulse so graphically as Italo Svevo, whose protagonist in *The Confessions of Zeno* dreams of devouring his beloved's neck; another Italian, Italo Calvino, creates a love scene in his novel *Under the Jaguar Sun* in which his characters recognise the 'universal cannibalism that leaves its imprint on every amorous relationship', momentarily erasing the distinction between themselves and dinner; for a few seconds, people who understand themselves to be 'cooked' in the metaphorical sense are able to flirt with the notion that they might literally become so – and eaten.

For most of us, 'cannibalism is metaphorised' in Gian-Paolo Biasin's striking phrase from his book *The Flavours of Modernity* – or ironised, as in *A Modest Proposal*, Swift's caustic satire on the attitude of the English towards the Irish, and Byron's blackly humorous account of a shipwreck in *Don Juan*. Yet there are occasional contemporary cases of voluntary anthropophagy whose details appear, at first sight, to defy understanding. One of these is Jeffrey Dahmer, whose bizarre housekeeping habits were revealed by an obituary in the *Guardian* after he was beaten to death in a Wisconsin prison in 1994: 'Prosecutors believed that Jeffrey Dahmer was serious about his cannibalism. Besides the contents of his freezer they found no food in apartment 213 – only condiments.' The familiar detail, hinting that Dahmer liked to eat his victims with just a sprinkling of salt and pepper, suggests that he is already being mythologised. This is borne out by Brian Masters's precise if repellent account in *The Shrine of Jeffrey Dahmer*, in which he relates that Dahmer once 'ate a bicep which he had fried in a skillet, tenderized and sprinkled with sauce'; in all, he prepared six meals using body parts from his seventeen victims.

This is horrific enough but it does not add up to the exclusively anthropophagous diet implied in the *Guardian* – more a stylised and deliberate flouting of taboo. But the really sensational and revealing aspect of Dahmer's crimes lies in the racial profile of his victims, the vast majority of whom were black or South-East Asian – very different physical specimens from the weedy, fair-haired Dahmer. Ever since they were brought to the American South from Africa as slaves, black men have been invested with mythic attributes of physical strength and sexual potency; in killing and eating them, Dahmer may have been ritually acting out fantasies of subjugating and incorporating the feared and desired 'other' – even, perhaps, hoping to confer some of their potency on himself.

After his arrest, Dahmer inquired plaintively of his doctors, 'whether there was anyone in the world like him, or was he the only one?' The final phrase is ambiguous, implying 'special' as well as 'isolated' and turning Dahmer into a quasi-heroic figure, treading a solitary path that would have been familiar to our common tribal ancestors. Yet the reality behind the image of the lonely cannibal, cursed inheritor of a savage tradition that can no longer be understood by his deracinated peers, is far more gruesome. What motivates people like Dahmer is a catastrophic failure of the imagination, an inability to think metaphorically which compels them to act out the symbolic order regardless of the cost, to themselves and others, in horror and degradation. Unlike the rest of us, they either don't know or don't care that, except in dire emergencies, eating people is wrong.

A Perversion

In the *Proceedings of the Royal Institute of Anthropophagy*
(last year's Spring number, page 132),
there is a most unusual instance recorded
of a man and woman who conspired to eat each other –
and would have done so, had not the laws of nature prevented it.
I heartily agree with the writer of the article
who denounces the whole affair as a 'flagrant travesty',
a 'perversion of the established rites' and a 'half-baked stunt'.

From Christopher Reid, *In The Echoey Tunnel* (1991).

Roasted Stranger

We lay down upon the sand and fell asleep. Next morning we rose and, striking inland, came after a few hours in sight of a lofty building among the trees. As we drew nearer, a number of naked and wild-looking men emerged from the door, and without a word took hold of my companions and myself and led us into the building, where we saw their King seated upon a throne.

The King bade us sit down, and presently his servants set before us dishes of such meats as we had never seen before in all our lives. My famished companions ate ravenously; but my stomach revolted at the sight of this food and, in spite of my hunger, I could not eat a single mouthful. As things turned out, however, my abstinence saved my life. For as soon as they had swallowed a few morsels my comrades began to lose their intelligence and to act like gluttonous maniacs, so that after a few hours of incessant guzzling they were little better than savages.

Whilst my companions were thus feeding, the naked men brought in a vessel filled with a strange ointment, with which they anointed their victims' bodies. The change my companions suffered was astonishing; their eyes sank into their heads and their bellies grew horribly distended, so that the more they swelled the more insatiable their appetites became.

My horror at this spectacle knew no bounds, especially when I soon discovered that our captors were cannibals who fattened their victims in this way before slaughtering them. The King feasted every day on a roasted stranger; his men preferred their diet raw.

When my transformed companions had thus been robbed entirely of all their human faculties, they were committed to the charge of a herdsman, who led them out every day to pasture in the meadows. I myself was reduced to a shadow by hunger and fear and my skin shrivelled upon my bones. Therefore the savages lost all interest in me and no longer cared even to watch my movements.

One day I slipped out of my captors' dwelling and made off across the island. On reaching the distant grasslands I met the herdsman with his once-human charges. But instead of pursuing me or ordering me to return he appeared to take pity on my helpless condition, and pointing to his right made signs to me which seemed to say: 'Go this way: have no fear.'

I ran on and on across the rolling plains in the direction he indicated. When evening came I ate a scanty meal of roots and herbs and lay down to rest upon the grass; but fear of the cannibals had robbed me of all desire to sleep, and at midnight I rose again and trudged painfully on.

From 'The Fourth Voyage of Sinbad the Sailor', *Tales from the Thousand and One Nights*, medieval, collected late eighteenth century, and translated by N.J. Dawood.

The Only Way to Survive

For some days several of the boys had realized that if they were to survive they would have to eat the bodies of those who had died in the crash. It was a ghastly prospect. The corpses lay around the plane in the snow, preserved by the intense cold in the state in which they had died. While the thought of cutting flesh from those who had been their friends was deeply repugnant to them all, a lucid appreciation of their predicament led them to consider it.

Gradually the discussion spread as these boys cautiously mentioned it to their friends or to those they thought would be sympathetic. Finally, Canessa brought it out into the open. He argued forcefully that they were not going to be rescued; that they would have to escape themselves, but that nothing could be done without food; and that the only food was human flesh. He used his knowledge of medicine to describe, in his penetrating, high-pitched voice, how their bodies were using up their reserves. 'Every time you move,' he said, 'you use up part of your own body. Soon we shall be so weak that we won't have the strength even to cut the meat that is lying there before our eyes.'

Canessa did not argue just from expediency. He insisted that they had a moral duty to stay alive by any means at their disposal, and because Canessa was earnest about his religious belief, great weight was given to what he said by the more pious among the survivors.

'It is meat,' he said. 'That's all it is. The souls have left their bodies and are in heaven with God. All that is left here are the carcasses, which are no more human beings than the dead flesh of the cattle we eat at home.'

Others joined the discussion. 'Didn't you see,' said Fito Strauch, 'how much energy we needed just to climb a few hundred feet up the mountain? Think how much more we'll need to climb to the top and then down the other side. It can't be done on a sip of wine and a scrap of chocolate.'

The truth of what he said was incontestable.

A meeting was called inside the Fairchild, and for the first time all twenty-seven survivors discussed the issue which faced them – whether or not they should eat the bodies of the dead to survive. Canessa, Zerbino, Fernández, and Fito Strauch repeated the arguments they had used before. If they did not they would die. It was their moral obligation to live, for their own sake and for the sake of their families. God wanted them to live, and he had given them the means to do so in the dead bodies of their friends. If God had not wished them to live, they would have been killed in the accident; it would be wrong now to reject this gift of life because they were too squeamish.

'But what have we done,' asked Marcelo, 'that God now asks us to eat the bodies of our dead friends?'

There was a moment's hesitation. Then Zerbino turned to his captain and said, 'But what do you think *they* would have thought?'

Marcelo did not answer.

'I know,' Zerbino went on, 'that if my dead body could help you to stay alive, then I'd certainly want you to use it. In fact, if I do die and you don't eat me, then I'll come back from wherever I am and give you a good kick in the ass.'

This argument allayed many doubts, for however reluctant each boy might be to eat the flesh of a friend, all of them agreed with Zerbino. There and then they made a pact that if any more of them were to die, their bodies were to be used as food.

Marcelo still shrank from a decision. He and his diminishing party of optimists held onto the hope of rescue, but few of the others any longer shared their faith. Indeed, a few of the younger boys went over to the pessimists – or the realists, as they considered themselves – with some resentment against Marcelo Pérez and Pancho Delgado. They felt they had been deceived. The rescue they had been promised had not come.

The latter were not without support, however. Coche Inciarte and Numa Turcatti, both strong, tough boys with an inner gentleness, told their companions that while they did not think it would be wrong, they knew that they themselves could not do it. Liliana Methol agreed with them. Her manner was calm as always but, like the others, she grappled with the emotions the issue aroused. Her instinct to survive was strong, her longing for her children was acute, but the thought of eating human flesh horrified her. She did not think it wrong; she could distinguish between sin and physical revulsion, and a social taboo was not a law of God. 'But,' she said, 'as long as there is a chance of rescue, as long as there is *something* left to eat, even if it is only a morsel of chocolate, then I can't do it.'

Javier Methol agreed with his wife but would not deter others from doing what they felt must be done. No one suggested that God might want them to choose to die. They all believed that virtue lay in survival and eating their dead friends would in no way endanger their souls, but it was one thing to decide and another to act.

Their discussions had continued most of the day, and by mid-afternoon they knew that they must act now or not at all, yet they sat inside the plane in total silence. At last a group of four – Canessa, Maspons, Zerbino, and Fito Strauch – rose and went out into the snow. Few followed them. No one wished to know who was going to cut the meat or from which body it was to be taken.

Most of the bodies were covered by snow, but the buttocks of one protruded a few yards from the plane. With no exchange of words Canessa knelt, bared the skin, and cut into the flesh with a piece of broken glass. It was frozen hard and difficult to cut, but he persisted until he had cut away twenty slivers the size of matchsticks. He then stood up, went back to the plane, and placed them on the roof.

Inside there was silence. The boys cowered in the Fairchild. Canessa told them that the meat was there on the roof, drying in the sun, and that those who wished to do so should come out and eat it. No one came, and again Canessa took it upon himself to prove his resolution. He prayed to God to help him do what he knew to be right and then took a piece of meat in his hand. He hesitated. Even with his mind so firmly made up, the horror of the act paralysed him. His hand would neither rise to his mouth nor fall to his side while the revulsion which possessed him struggled with his stubborn will. The will prevailed. The hand rose and pushed the meat into his mouth. He swallowed it.

He felt triumphant. His conscience had overcome a primitive, irrational taboo. He was going to survive.

From Piers Paul Read, *Alive: The Story of the Andes Survivors* (1974).

What Did You Say Your Last Name Was?

'Do you spook easily, Starling?'

'Not yet.'

'See, we've tried to interview and examine all the thirty-two known serial murderers we have in custody, to build up a database for psychological profiling in unsolved cases. Most of them went along with it – I think they're driven to show off, a lot of them. Twenty-seven were willing to cooperate. Four on death row with appeals pending clammed up, understandably. But the one we want the most, we haven't been able to get. I want you to go after him tomorrow in the asylum.'

Clarice Starling felt a glad knocking in her chest and some apprehension too.

'Who's the subject?'

'The psychiatrist – Dr Hannibal Lecter,' Crawford said.

A brief silence follows the name, always, in any civilized gathering.

Starling looked at Crawford steadily, but she was too still. 'Hannibal the Cannibal,' she said.

From Thomas Harris, *The Silence of the Lambs* (1988).

Baby Killers

One day in 1960, the three-year-old daughter of my aunt Jun-ying's next-door neighbor in Yibin went missing. A few weeks later the neighbor saw a young girl playing in the street wearing a dress that looked like her daughter's. She went up and examined it: it had a mark which identified it as her daughter's. She reported this to the police. It turned out that the parents of the young girl were selling wind-dried meat. They had abducted and murdered a number of babies and sold them as rabbit meat at exorbitant prices. The couple were executed and the case was hushed up, but it was widely known that baby killing did go on at the time.

Years later I met an old colleague of my father's, a very kind and capable man, not given to exaggeration. He told me with great emotion what he had seen during the famine in one particular commune. Thirty-five percent of the peasants had died, in an area where the harvest had been good – although little was collected, since the men had been pulled out to produce steel, and the commune canteen had wasted a large proportion of what there was. One day a peasant burst into his room and threw himself on the floor, screaming that he had committed a terrible crime and begging to be punished. Eventually it came out that he had killed his own baby and eaten it. Hunger had been like an uncontrollable force driving him to take up the knife. With tears rolling down his cheeks, the official ordered the peasant to be arrested. Later he was shot as a warning to baby killers.

From Jung Chang, *Wild Swans* (1991).

Living on the Family

In Alesia, however, they knew nothing of these preparations; the time by which they had expected relief was past and their corn was exhausted. So they summoned an assembly and considered what their fate was to be. Among the various speeches that were made – some advising capitulation, others recommending a sortie while they still had the strength – the speech of Critognatus, a noble Arvernian whose opinion commanded great respect, deserves to be recorded for its unparalleled cruelty and wickedness.

'I do not intend,' he said, 'to make any comment on the views of those who advise "capitulation" – the name they give to the most shameful submission to enslavement; in my opinion they ought not to be regarded as citizens or allowed in the assembly. I will concern myself only with those who advocate a sortie. You all approve their suggestion, as showing that we have not forgotten our traditional courage. But it is not courage, it is weakness, to be unable to endure a short period of privation. It is easier to find men who will voluntarily risk death than men who will bear suffering patiently. Even so, I would support their proposal – so much do I respect their authority – if it involved no loss beyond that of our own lives. But in making our decision we must consider all our fellow countrymen, whom we have called to our aid. If eighty thousand of us are killed in one battle, what heart do you suppose our relatives and kinsmen will have when they are compelled to fight almost over our corpses? Do not leave them to continue the struggle alone when for your sakes they have counted their own danger as nothing, and do not by folly and rashness, or by lack of resolution, ruin all Gaul and subject it to perpetual servitude. Because they have not come on the appointed day, do you doubt their loyalty or constancy to our cause? What? Do you suppose the Romans are working day after day on those outer fortifications to amuse themselves? Since our countrymen cannot get messengers through the cordon that is drawn round us, to assure you that they are coming soon, believe what the enemy are telling you by their actions: for it is the fear of their coming that keeps the Romans hard at work night and day.

'What counsel, then, have I to offer? I think we should do what our ancestors did in a war that was much less serious than this one [109–102 BC]. When they were forced into their strongholds by the Cimbri and Teutoni, and overcome like us by famine, instead of surrendering they kept themselves alive by eating the flesh of those who were too old or too young to fight. Even if we had no precedent for such an action, I think that when our liberty is at stake it would be a noble example to set to our descendants. For this is a life and death struggle, quite unlike the war with the Cimbri, who, though they devastated Gaul and grievously afflicted her, did eventually evacuate our country and migrate elsewhere, and left us free men, to live on our own land under our own laws and in possession of our rights. The Romans, we know, have a very different purpose. Envy is the motive that inspires them. They know that we have won renown by our military strength, and so they mean to install themselves in our lands and towns and fasten the yoke of slavery on us for ever. That is how they have always treated conquered enemies. You do not know much, perhaps, of the condition of distant peoples; but you need only look at the part of Gaul on your own borders that has been made into a Roman province, with new laws and institutions imposed upon it, ground beneath the conqueror's iron heel in perpetual servitude.'

At the conclusion of the debate it was decided to send out of the town those whom age or infirmity incapacitated for fighting. Critognatus' proposal was to be adopted only as a last resort – if the reinforcements still failed to arrive and things got so bad that it was a choice between that and surrendering, or accepting dictated peace terms.

From Julius Caesar, *De Bello Gallico* (c. 100–44 BC), translated by
S.A. Handford, revised by Jane F. Gardner.

Vampire Soldiers

On quitting the kingdom of Kinsai and entering that of Fu-chau the traveller journeys south-eastwards for six days through mountains and valleys, passing cities and towns and homesteads in plenty. The people are idolaters subject to the Great Khan and are all under the government of Fu-chau, with which we have now begun to deal. They live by trade and industry and are amply provided with the means of life. There is abundance of game here, both beast and bird, besides lions of great size and ferocity. Ginger and galingale are superabundant: indeed for a Venetian groat you could buy a quantity of fresh ginger equivalent to 80 lb. There is a fruit here that resembles saffron; though it is actually nothing of the sort, it is quite as good as saffron for practical purposes. Furthermore, you must know that the natives eat all sorts of brute beast. They even relish human flesh. They do not touch the flesh of those who have died a natural death; but they all eat the flesh of those who have died of a wound and consider it a delicacy. Among soldiers and men at arms the following practice prevails: they have their hair close-cropped as far back as the ears, and in the middle of their faces they paint in blue what looks like the blade of a sword. They all march on foot except their captain. They carry lances and swords and are the most blood-thirsty lot in the world. For I assure you that they go about every day killing men and drink the blood and then devour the whole body. This is their daily occupation – to go about killing men in order to drink their blood and then devour their flesh.

From *The Travels* of *Marco Polo*, early thirteenth century, translated by
R.E. Latham (1958).

Hungry but High-Minded

Foreseeing that if the boat lived through the stormy weather the time must come, and soon come, when we should have absolutely no morsel to eat, I had one momentous point often in my thoughts. Although I had, years before that, fully satisfied myself that the instances in which human beings in the last distress have fed upon each other are exceedingly few, and have very seldom indeed (if ever) occurred when the people in distress, however dreadful their extremity, have been accustomed to moderate forbearance and restraint – I say, though I had, long before, quite satisfied my mind on this topic, I felt doubtful whether there might not have been in former cases some harm and danger from keeping it out of sight and pretending not to think of it. I felt doubtful whether some minds, growing weak with fasting and exposure, and having such a terrific idea to dwell upon in secret, might not magnify it until it got to have an awful attraction about it. This was not a new thought of mine, for it had grown out of my reading. However, it came over me stronger than it had ever done before – as it had reason for doing – in the boat, and on the fourth day I decided that I would bring out into the light that uniformed fear which must have been more or less darkly in every brain among us. Therefore, as a means of beguiling the time and inspiring hope, I gave them the best summary in my power of Bligh's voyage of more than three thousand miles, in an open boat, after the Mutiny of the *Bounty*, and of the wonderful preservation of that boat's crew. They listened throughout with great interest, and I concluded by telling them that, in my opinion, the happiest circumstances in the whole narrative was that Bligh, who was no delicate man either, had solemnly placed it on record therein that he was sure and certain that under no conceivable circumstances whatever would that emaciated party, who had gone through all the pains of famine, have preyed on one another. I cannot describe the visible relief which this spread through the boat, and how the tears stood in every eye. From that time I was as well convinced as Bligh himself that there was no danger and that this phantom, at any rate, did not haunt us.

From Charles Dickens and Wilkie Collins, *The Wreck* of *the Golden Mary* (1856).

Desperate Measures

In the Warsaw ghetto (and others) as well as in the concentration camps of Belsen, Buchenwald and Auschwitz, human flesh was sometimes all that there was to sustain those who would not release their hold on life. On March 21, 1942 the Warsaw propaganda division of the *Generalgouvernement* curtly reported that: 'The death figure in the ghetto still hovers around 5000 per month. A few days ago, the first case of hunger-cannibalism was recorded. In a Jewish family the man and his three children died within a few days. From the flesh of the child who died last – a twelve-year-old boy – the mother ate a piece. To be sure, this could not save her either, and she herself died two days later.' In Belsen, a former British internee engaged on clearing away dead bodies gave evidence that 'as many as one in ten had a piece cut from the thigh or other part of the body … On my very next visit to the mortuary I actually saw a prisoner whip out a knife, cut a portion out of the leg of a dead body and put it quickly into his mouth.'

From Reay Tannahill, *Flesh and Blood* (1975).

Becoming More Desperate

At the same time as the boys dug into the snow in search of the buried bodies, the corpses that they had preserved nearer the surface began to suffer from the stronger sun which melted the thin layer of snow which covered them. The thaw had truly set in – the level of the snow had fallen far below the roof of the Fairchild – and the sun in the middle of the day became so hot that any meat left exposed to it would rot quickly. Added, then, to the labours of digging, cutting, and snow melting was that of covering the bodies with snow and then shielding them from the sun with sheets of cardboard or plastic.

As the supplies grew short, an order went out from the cousins that there was to be no more pilfering. This edict was no more effective than most others which seek to upset an established practice. They therefore sought to make what food they had last longer by eating parts of the human body which previously they had left aside. The hands and feet, for example, had flesh beneath the skin which could be scraped off the bone. They tried, too, to eat the tongue off one corpse but could not swallow it, and one of them once ate the testicles.

On the other hand they all took to the marrow. When the last shred of meat had been scraped off a bone it would be cracked open with the axe and the marrow extracted with a piece of wire or a knife and shared. They also ate the blood clots which they found around the hearts of almost all the bodies. Their texture and taste were different from that of the flesh and fat, and by now they were sick to death of this staple diet. It was not just that their senses clamoured for different tastes; their bodies too cried out for those minerals of which they had for so long been deprived – above all, for salt. And it was in obedience to these cravings that the less fastidious among the survivors began to eat those parts of the body which had started to rot. This had happened to the entrails of even those bodies which were covered with snow, and there were also the remains of previous carcasses scattered around the plane which were unprotected from the sun. Later everyone did the same.

What they would do was to take the small intestine, squeeze out its contents onto the snow, cut it into small pieces, and eat it. The taste was strong and salty. One of them tried wrapping it around a bone and roasting it in the fire. Rotten flesh, which they tried later, tasted like cheese.

The last discovery in their search for new tastes and new sources of food were the brains of the bodies which they had hitherto discarded. Canessa had told them that, while they might not be of particular nutritional value, they contained glucose which would give them energy; he had been the first to take a head, cut the skin across the forehead, pull back the scalp, and crack open the skull with the axe. The brains were then either divided up and eaten while still frozen or used to make the sauce for a stew; the liver, intestine, muscle, fat, heart and kidneys, either cooked or uncooked, were cut up into little pieces and mixed with the brains. In this way the food tasted better and was easier to eat. The only difficulty was the shortage of bowls suitable to hold it, for before this the meat had been served on plates, trays, or pieces of aluminium foil. For stew Inciarte used a shaving bowl, while others used the top halves of skulls. Four bowls made from skulls were used in this way – and some spoons were made from bones.

The brains were inedible when putrid, so all the heads which remained from the corpses they had consumed were gathered together and buried in the snow. The snow was also combed for other parts which had previously been thrown away. Scavenging took on an added value – especially for Algorta, who was the chief scavenger among them. When he was not digging holes or helping the cousins cut up the bodies, his bent figure could be seen hobbling around the plane, poking into the snow with an iron stick. He looked so much like a tramp that Carlitos gave him the nickname of Old Vizcacha – but his dedication was not without its rewards, because he found many pieces of old fat, some with a thin strip of flesh. These he would place on his part of the roof. If they were waterlogged, they would dry out in the sun, forming a crust which made them more palatable. Or, like the others, he would put them on a piece of metal which caught the sun and in this way warm what he was eating; once, when the sun was exceptionally strong, he actually cooked them.

From Piers Paul Read, *Alive: The Story of the Andes Survivors* (1974).

In Defence of An English Gentleman

In 1818, [Sir John] Franklin, who had fought at Trafalgar with Nelson, commanded a ship in an expedition searching for the Northwest Passage. From 1819 to 1821, he had commanded his own expedition, exploring the area to the east of Hudson Bay. In 1825, he left his dying wife, at her own urging, in a third futile attempt to find the Passage. He returned to England in 1827, remarried in 1828, and was knighted in 1829. After serving as Governor of Van Diemen's Land for several years, he began planning his final expedition in 1843. On May 19, 1845, the fifty-nine-year-old Franklin sailed in command of this expedition, consisting of 129 men and officers equipped with supplies for three years. The expedition was last seen on July 26, 1845. About the time in 1848 that the supplies would have been exhausted, search expeditions were formed, eventually involving hundreds of men and dozens of ships, including two from America. The British government offered a reward of £10,000 for either the rescue of the expedition or the discovery of its fate.

This reward was claimed by Dr. John Rae, Chief Factor of the Hudson's Bay Company. While exploring the region north of Repulse Bay in April 1854, Rae met a group of Eskimos who had heard that a party of white men had died a great distance to the west. Investigating, he found other Eskimos who possessed articles bearing Franklin's crest and who claimed to have obtained the articles from another group of Eskimos who had seen the bodies of thirty-five to forty white men. These bodies were reported to have been mutilated and the cooking pots near them to have contained human flesh. After a brief, unsuccessful search for this last group of Eskimos and for the bodies, Rae sailed for England. Relying on the hearsay evidence and the Franklin relics, which he had purchased, he announced to the public that the Franklin expedition had met a fate 'as terrible as the imagination can conceive'. He asserted, unequivocally, that 'our wretched countrymen had been driven to the last resource – cannibalism – as a means of prolonging existence'. The assertion created a general stir and greatly disturbed part of the public. *The Times* refused to accept his report as final. An editorial writer argued that if Eskimos could live through 'starving times', it would be 'strange indeed that the white men should not have been able to accomplish the same feat.' He urged that steps be taken as soon as possible 'for solving one of the most painful problems of our times.' Hendrik van Loon remarks that as long as his father lived, his father remembered the 'shock of horror that had swept across the civilized world' as the news of Rae's report spread.

Dickens may not have read the report when it was first printed, for on November 20, he wrote to W. H. Wills:

It has occurred to me that I am rather strong on Voyages and Cannibalism, and might do an interesting little paper for the next No. on that part of Dr. Rae's report, taking the arguments against its probabilities. Can you get me a newspaper cutting containing his report? If not will you have it copied for me and sent up to Tavistock House straight way.

The 'interesting little paper' was printed as two *Household Words* lead articles. Dickens apparently was agitated after he read the report and judged that the evidence was weak for the kind of conclusion Rae had drawn from it. He thought that Rae might have made a more careful investigation before hurrying back to England and that he might have been more hesitant about accepting hearsay testimony from Eskimo witnesses, who, in Dickens' opinion, were 'covetous, treacherous, and cruel' savages. Expressing concern for 'those who take the nearest and dearest interest in the fate of that unfortunate expedition,' Dickens became Franklin's public defender.

Dickens based his defense on two grounds – the character of the Eskimo witnesses and the character of Franklin himself. Dickens attacked the credibility of the Eskimos in general, saying that savages were natural liars, but spent much of his scorn on Rae's interpreter:

> Ninety-nine interpreters out of a hundred, whether savage, half-savage, or wholly civilized, interpreting to a person of superior station and attainments, will be under a strong temptation to exaggerate. This temptation will always be strongest precisely where the person interpreted to is seen to be the most excited and impressed by what he hears; for in proportion as he is moved, the interpreter's importance is increased.

This attack on the Eskimos was only incidental to the second defense, which Dickens called 'analogy.' He argued that because Franklin had resisted terrible stresses on previous expeditions, Franklin had proved himself a type of hero for whom cannibalism would have been virtually a moral impossibility. When Franklin and his men previously had descended 'far into the valley of the shadow of Death,' they had lain 'down side by side, calmly and even cheerfully awaiting their release from this world.' Franklin, as commander of the expedition, had played a special role, 'infusing into it, as such a man necessarily must, the force of his character and discipline, patience and fortitude.' Dickens concluded his defense in the first article thus:

> Heaven forbid that we, sheltered and fed, and considering this question at our warm hearth, should audaciously set limits to any extremity of desperate distress! It is in reverence for the brave and enterprising, in admiration for the great spirits who can endure even unto the end, in love for their names, and in tenderness for their memory, that we think

of the specks, once ardent men, 'scattered about in different positions' on the waste of ice and snow, and plead for their lightest ashes ... as the citadel of the position, that the better educated the man, the better disciplined the habits, the more reflective and religious the tone of thought, the more gigantically improbable the 'last resource' becomes.

The defense on the ground of 'analogy' ended as an appeal to the faith in the British gentleman and hero.

The second article, devoted entirely to distinguishing the British hero from ordinary men, continued this appeal. Dickens cited several instances of cannibalism, chiefly among foreign seamen. In part, his citations attempt to show that the men who resorted to the 'last resource' were in more desperate situations than Franklin's men. Dickens' comments, however, emphasize two points, that such men were degraded before they were placed under stress, and that while under stress the men lacked the support of such heroic commanders as Bligh and Franklin. Dickens ended his long series of citations with a homily:

In weighing the probabilities and improbabilities of the 'last resource,' the foremost question is – not the nature of the extremity; but the nature of the men. We submit that the memory of the lost Arctic voyagers is placed, by reason and experience, high above the taint of this so easily-allowed connection; and that the noble conduct and example of such men, and of their great leader himself, under similar endurances, belies it, and outweighs by the weight of the whole universe the chatter of a gross handful of uncivilized people, with a domesticity of blood and blubber. Utilitarianism will protest 'they are dead; why care about this?' Our reply shall be, 'Because they ARE dead, therefore we care about this. Because they served their country well, and deserved well of her, and can ask, no more on this earth, for her justice or her loving-kindness; give them both, full measure, pressed down, running over. Because no Franklin can come back, to write the honest story of their woes and resignation, read it tenderly and truly in the book he has left us. Because they lie scattered on those wastes of snow ... therefore cherish them gently, even in the breasts of children. Therefore, teach no one to shudder without reason, at the history of their end. Therefore, confide with their own firmness, in their fortitude, their lofty sense of duty, their courage, and their religion.

From Robert Louis Brannan (ed.), *Under the Management of Mr Charles Dickens, His Production of 'The Frozen Deep'* (1966).

The Milwaukee Cannibal

Jeffrey Dahmer was 15 when he began showing the obsessions which would make him one of the world's best-known serial killers.

It was then that neighbours discovered the mutilated carcass of a dog close to the Dahmer family house in a small town in Ohio. The dog's head was mounted on a stick next to a wooden cross; the body was skinned and filleted and nailed to a tree.

It was also at this time that young Jeffrey's chemistry teachers reported the boy's keen interest in the effects of acid on flesh.

Americans were recollecting such details of the grisly Dahmer biography last night, as officials confirmed that the multiple murderer had himself been murdered in prison in Portage, Wisconsin.

Dahmer was beaten to death by a fellow prisoner, and found in a pool of blood. It was an end that mirrored a life spent awash in blood.

In the 13 years before his arrest and confession in 1991, Jeffrey Dahmer killed 17 gay men or young boys. The former soldier and chocolate-factory employee lured most of them to his apartment for paid photo-sessions, before drugging and killing them.

Dahmer then usually had sex with the corpse, before chopping it up and eating chunks of the flesh and the internal organs.

Despite an overpowering smell – which Dahmer ascribed to a broken freezer and spoiled meat – and the sounds of a chain-saw late at night, the killer's neighbours in Milwaukee never suspected what lay within the now notorious apartment 213.

When police finally came to the address in the centre of the city, they needed oxygen masks and protective clothing to handle what they found.

All around were Polaroid photos of Dahmer having sex with naked men, some of them mutilated and dismembered. One picture showed a corpse eaten away by acid from the nipples down.

There was a human head in the refrigerator, and three others in the chest-freezer. Five skulls – polished clean – were in a filing cabinet.

The search took hours, and unearthed five full skeletons, human remains in a chemical drum in the bedroom, and even a pickled penis.

He had stored lungs, intestines, a kidney and a liver in his freezer. Pointing out the heart of one victim, an athlete called Oliver Lacy, Dahmer told police he was saving the organ 'to eat later'. Prosecutors believed that Jeffrey Dahmer was serious about his cannibalism.

Besides the contents of his freezer, they found no food in apartment 213 – only condiments.

At least 11 men had been killed in the apartment. Later, he confessed that he had murdered another three in his grandmother's house.

Dahmer committed his first murder in 1978, when he was 18 years old. He picked up a hitch-hiker, Steven Hicks, shared a few beers with him and then bludgeoned him with a barbell.

He cut the corpse into 50 pieces and scattered them in a nearby wood. The remains were discovered only years later, when Dahmer told police where to look.

Like Britain's Dennis Nilsen, Dahmer avoided suspicion by picking his prey carefully, lighting on drifters and homeless men who would not be missed.

Despite taking chances, Dahmer repeatedly escaped the attention of the police.

In May 1991, police were alerted after a Laotian boy aged 14 was seen fleeing from Dahmer's flat. He was naked and there was blood flowing from his buttocks. Dahmer told police that he and the boy were gay lovers who had had a tiff – and the boy was promptly handed over. Dahmer killed him that night.

Detectives found his body in the Dahmer apartment – along with the corpse of the boy's brother, whom Dahmer had killed three years earlier.

After he was convicted and sentenced to 16 consecutive life sentences, Dahmer overtook John Wayne Gacy and Charles Manson as the central figure in America's growing serial killer industry. He was the subject of TV interviews and literary memoirs.

Most of the attention focussed on the question of motive. Dahmer's family claimed he was the victim of a child molestor when he was eight.

Others said he had always been a loner who was unable to connect with other human beings.

High school friends told how Dahmer would fake epileptic fits and simulate animal sounds in class.

He was also a severe alcoholic, and often arrived drunk at school.

He was discharged from the army, where he served in Germany, for being drunk on duty too often.

His penchant for black victims seemed to have been due to an experience in prison in 1989, after a conviction for child molestation.

'Something happened to him that he would never talk about,' said

Dahmer's stepmother, Shari, who noted that, after his release, 'he hated black people'.

Dahmer also frequently expressed his loathing for homosexuals.

Yesterday Shari Dahmer said she hoped her stepson's death might now bring some peace to the relatives of those he had murdered.

Jonathan Freedland, *Guardian* (29 November 1994).

A Bad Reputation

At three o'clock a moderate breeze started blowing from the south-east, and with it we sailed up to the entrance of Port Resolution. It was just about sunset when we approached the harbour, and the wind fell very light. We were not able to make out anything but cocoanut and other trees, besides an old house of apparently native build near the water. So we headed seaward again with the intention to stand off for the night and look for a mission house next morning. Some of my readers might think that we acted timidly in not sailing into the harbour to anchor there for the night. To these I wish to point out that the inhabitants of the New Hebrides in former days had a very bad reputation for cannibalism and treacherous manners in their intercourse with whites. Being only two in a little vessel, and neither my mate nor myself disposed to be slaughtered and eaten or to become involved in trouble, we took this precaution. We had just swung the boat round and pointed to the open ocean when we noticed a boat passing the head of the harbour. I took a quick glance through my glasses and distinguished eight fellows, who pulled straight towards us. By that time the wind had completely died out, and it was impossible for us to keep clear of the approaching boat; we therefore at once made our firearms ready for instant use.

The natives drew steadily nearer, and when they were within about four hundred feet we put our rifles to shoulder and taking aim shouted 'Hands up!' At this the steersman immediately swung the boat round and all hands stopped pulling. Thereupon, the former stood up in the stern, and I must confess that I felt somewhat cheap when he called out in fairly good English, 'Are you afraid of us, Captain?'

'Not exactly that,' I answered, 'but we want to know what you are after!'

The man then explained that a missionary had sent them out to tow us into the harbour.

'A missionary,' I said; 'where is the mission house?'

He then pointed to a small opening in the tops of some high trees, just large enough to allow a glimpse of the steeple of the mission church. By that I knew that the man had told us the truth, we laid down our rifles and invited the black strangers to come alongside, which they did. To be friendly with the darkies, I presented each with a small plug of tobacco, and as there was no wind the natives towed us into harbour.

On arrival at the anchorage near the mission house three Europeans came off in a small boat to meet us. When on board one of the gentlemen introduced himself as Mr Watt, missionary of Tanna, and one of his companions as Mr Wilson, a trader, while the third was a young assistant missionary. When the anchor was down, we gave a short explanation as to our visit and cruise. Following Mr Watt's invitation we accompanied the party ashore, where we enjoyed a very nice dinner with him and his wife.

In the course of the ensuing conversation I asked Mr Watt about the habits and customs of the natives, and especially whether cannibalism was still practised. This question was immediately answered by the trader who assured me that they ate a native man there only a few days previously. And Mr Watt added that it was very difficult to stop this horrible custom. Mr Wilson further explained that on the last occasion the younger missionary had gone to the place where the feast had occurred in order to reason with the natives. But instead of taking his advice they had picked up some of the bones and throwing them at the missionary gave him to understand that he had better mind his own business.

From J.C. Voss, *The Venturesome Voyages* of *Captain Voss* (1913).

Animals Lead to Cannibals (i)

Yet if, for heaven's sake, it is really impossible for us to be free from error because we are on such terms of familiarity with it, let us at least be ashamed of our ill doing and resort to it only in reason. We shall eat flesh, but from hunger, not as a luxury. We shall kill an animal, but in pity and sorrow, not degrading or torturing it – which is the current practice in many cases, some thrusting red-hot spits into the throats of swine so that by the plunging in of the iron the blood may be emulsified and, as it circulates through the body, may make the flesh tender and delicate. Others jump upon the udders of sows about to give birth and kick them so that, when they have blended together blood and milk and gore (Zeus the Purifier!) and the unborn young have at the same time been destroyed at the moment of birth, they may eat the most inflamed part of the creature. Still others sew up the eyes of cranes and swans, shut them up in darkness and fatten them, making the flesh appetizing with strange compounds and spicy mixtures.

From these practices it is perfectly evident that it is not for nourishment or need or necessity, but out of satiety and insolence and luxury that they have turned this lawless custom into a pleasure. Then, just as with women who are insatiable in seeking pleasure, their lust tries everything, goes astray, and explores the gamut of profligacy until at last it ends in unspeakable practices; so intemperance in eating passes beyond the necessary ends of nature and resorts to cruelty and lawlessness to give variety to appetite. For it is in their own company that organs of sense are infected and won over and become licentious when they do not keep to natural standards. Just so the art of hearing has fallen sick, corrupting musical taste. From this our luxury and debauchery conceives a desire for shameful caresses and effeminate titillations. These taught the sight not to take pleasure in warlike exercises or gesticulations or refined dances or statues and paintings, but to regard the slaughter and death of men, their wounds and combats, as the most precious sort of spectacle. Just so intemperate intercourse follows a lawless meal, inharmonious music follows a shameful debauch, barbarous spectacles follow shameless songs and sounds, insensitivity and cruelty toward human kind follow savage exhibitions in the theatre. It was for this reason that the godlike Lycurgus gave directions ... that the doors and roofs of houses should be fashioned by saw and axe alone and no other tool should be used – not of course because he had a quarrel with gimlets and adzes and other instruments for delicate work. It was because he knew that through such rough-hewn work you will not be introducing a gilded couch, nor will you be so rash as to bring silver tables and purple rugs and precious stones into a simple house. The corollary of such a house and couch and table and cup is a dinner which is unpretentious and a lunch which is truly democratic; but all manner of luxury and extravagance follow the lead of an evil way of life

As new-weaned foal beside his mother runs.

For what sort of dinner is not costly for which a living creature loses its life? Do we hold a life cheap? I do not yet go so far as to say that it may well be the life of your mother or father or some friend or child, as Empedocles declared. Yet it does, at least, possess some perception, hearing, seeing, imagination, intelligence, which last every creature receives from Nature to enable it to acquire what is proper for it and to evade what is not. Do but consider which are the philosophers who serve the better to humanize us: those who bid us eat our children and friends and fathers and wives after their death, or Pythagoras and Empedocles who try to accustom us to act justly toward other creatures also? You ridicule a man who abstains from eating mutton. But are we, they will say, to refrain from laughter when we see you slicing off portions from a dead father or mother and sending them to absent friends and inviting those who are at hand, heaping their plate?

From Plutarch, *Moralia* (c. 45–120 AD), translated by Harold Cherniss and William C. Helmbold.

A Giant Appetite

Disconsolately we set out to search for food and water, and by good fortune came upon some fruit-trees and a running stream. Here we refreshed ourselves, and then wandered about the island until at length we saw far off among the trees a massive building, where we hoped to pass the night in safety. Drawing nearer, we found that it was a towering palace surrounded by a lofty wall, with a great ebony door which stood wide open. We entered the spacious courtyard, and to our surprise found it deserted. In one corner lay a great heap of bones, and on the far side we saw a broad bench, an open oven, pots and pans of enormous size, and many iron spits for roasting.

Exhausted and sick at heart, we lay down in the courtyard and were soon overcome by sleep. At sunset we were awakened by a noise like thunder. The earth shook beneath our feet and we saw a colossal black giant approaching from the doorway. He was a fearsome sight – tall as a palm-tree, with red eyes burning in his head like coals of fire; his mouth was a dark well, with lips that drooped like a camel's loosely over his chest, whilst his ears, like a pair of large round discs, hung back over his shoulders: his fangs were as long as the tusks of a boar and his nails were like the claws of a lion.

The sight of this monster struck terror to our hearts. We cowered motionless on the ground as we watched him stride across the yard and sit down on the bench. For a few moments he eyed us one by one in silence; then he rose and, reaching out towards me, lifted me up by the neck and began feeling my body as a butcher would a lamb. Finding me little more than skin and bone, however, he flung me to the ground and, picking up each of my companions in turn, pinched and prodded them and set them down until at last he came to the captain.

Now the captain was a corpulent fellow, tall and broad-shouldered. The giant seemed to like him well. He gripped him as a butcher grips a fatted ram and broke his neck under his foot. Then he thrust an iron spit through his body from mouth to backside and, lighting a great fire in the oven, carefully turned his victim round and round before it. When the flesh was finely roasted, the ogre tore the body to pieces with his fingernails as though it were a pullet, and devoured it limb by limb, gnawing the bones and flinging them against the wall. The monster then stretched himself out on the bench and soon fell fast asleep. His snores were as loud as the grunts and gurgles that issue from the throat of a slaughtered beast.

Thus he slept all night, and when morning came he rose and went out of the palace, leaving us half-crazed with terror.

From 'The Third Voyage of Sinbad the Sailor', *Tales from The Thousand and One Nights*, medieval, collected late eighteenth century, and translated by N.J. Dawood.

What Dahmer Did

The burden of Fosdal's evidence was that Jeff Dahmer was odd, but not ill. Prompted by McCann ('He will try to dehumanise Jeff as much as Jeff dehumanised his victims', said a journalist sitting next to me), he depicted a man at once pathetic and cruel. Asked whether he regretted not having a steady lover, Dahmer had told him, 'It might have been nice.' 'What would it have taken to stop you killing?' 'A permanent relationship.' Fosdal painted a sorry picture of the bathhouses, stalked by lonely men looking for the brief comfort of a moment's sex, and a harsh one of the defendant, utterly indifferent to the horror of pouring hot water into Weinberger's head. There was no suggestion of sadism – the doctor accepted that killing was only a means to an end. It was he who told the court that Dahmer had to take a shower with two bodies in the bathtub (possibly decapitated), and he who revealed that Dahmer had prepared six meals with various body parts from his victims.

From Brian Masters, *The Shrine* of *Jeffrey Dahmer* (1993).

Our Daily Bread

There is one universal church of the faithful, outside which no one at all is saved. In this church, Jesus Christ himself is both priest and sacrifice, and his body and blood are really contained in the sacrament of the altar under the species of bread and wine, the bread being transubstantiated into the body and the wine into the blood by the power of God, so that to carry out the mystery of unity we ourselves receive from him the body he himself receives from us.

From a declaration by the Fourth Lateran Council, (1215 AD).

The Mystic Lunch of St Catherine of Siena

Accounts of Catherine's life accentuate not only her food abstention and feeding of others; they also underline her substitution of the filth of disease and the blood of Christ's agony for ordinary food. Several of her biographers report that she twice forced herself to overcome nausea by thrusting her mouth into the putrifying breast of a dying woman or by drinking pus, and the reports stress these incidents as turning points in her developing inedia, her eucharistic craving, and her growing compulsion to serve others by suffering. She told [her biographer Raymond [of Capua]: 'Never in my life have I tasted any food and drink sweeter or more exquisite [than this pus].'

[And] on the night following ... a vision [of Christ with his five wounds] was granted to her as she was at prayer ... 'My beloved,' [Christ] said to her, 'you have now gone through many struggles for my sake ... Previously you had renounced all that the body takes pleasure in ... But yesterday the intensity of your ardent love for me overcame even the instinctive reflexes of your body itself: you forced yourself to swallow without a qualm a drink from which nature recoiled in disgust ... As you then went far beyond what mere human nature could ever have achieved, so I today shall give you a drink that transcends in perfection any that human nature can provide ...' With that, he tenderly placed his right hand on her neck, and drew her toward the wound in his side. 'Drink, daughter, from my side,' he said, 'and by that draught your soul shall become enraptured with such delight that your very body, which for my sake you have denied, shall be inundated with its overflowing goodness.' Drawn close ... to the outlet of the Fountain of Life, she fastened her lips upon that sacred wound, and still more eagerly the mouth of her soul, and there she slaked her thirst.

From that time on, says Raymond, she could not digest ordinary food. But, although she could swallow no corporeal food, she feasted not only on pus but also on the eucharist.

From Caroline Walker Bynum, *Holy Feast and Holy Fast: The Religious Significance of Food to Medieval Women* (1987).

Baby Cakes

Mr Bourne omits the *yule-dough*, (or *dow*) a kind of *baby* or *little image* of *paste*, which our bakers used formerly to bake at this season, and *present* to their *customers*, in the same manner as the chandlers gave *Christmas-candles*. They are called *yule-cakes* in the county of Durham. I find in the ancient calendar of the Romish church, that at Rome, on the vigil of the nativity, *sweet-meats* were *presented* to the *fathers* in the *Vatican*, and that all kinds of *little images* (no doubt of *paste*) were to be found at the confectioners' shops.

There is the greatest probability that we have had from *hence* both our *yule-doughs* and *mince pies*, the latter of which are still in common use at this season. The *yule-dough* has perhaps been intended for an *image* of the *Child Jesus*. It is now, if I mistake not, pretty generally laid aside, or at most retained only by children.

From *Brand's Antiquities* (1810).

Human Sacrifice

In 1521, sixty-two Spanish soldiers, captured in war by the Aztec, were led in procession to one of the temple-pyramids of the capital, Tenochtitlán, now Mexico City. As Aztec prisoners of war, they were to be violently killed and their beating hearts offered to the god. Bernal Díaz del Castillo, a soldier in the army of Cortés, describes the scene: 'Again there was sounded the dismal drum of Huichilobos and many other shells and horns and things like trumpets and the sound of them all was terrifying, and we all looked towards the lofty Cue [temple-pyramid] where they were being sounded, and saw that our comrades whom they had captured when they defeated Cortés were being carried by force up the steps, and they were taking them to be sacrificed. When they got them up to a small square in front of the oratory, where their accursed idols are kept, we saw them place plumes on the heads of many of them and with things like fans in their hands they forced them to dance before Huichilobos, and after they had danced they immediately placed them on their backs on some rather narrow stones which had been prepared as places for sacrifice, and with stone knives they sawed open their chests and drew out their palpitating hearts and offered them to the idols that were there, and they kicked the bodies down the steps, and Indian butchers who were waiting below cut off the arms and feet and flayed the skin off the faces, and prepared it afterwards like glove leather with the beards on, and kept those for the festivals when they celebrated drunken orgies, and the flesh they ate in *chilmole*.'

From Margaret Visser, *The Rituals of Dinner* (1991).

Cannibal Greed

Aroe Tanete, king of Soping and the Bouginese, like the ancient inhabitants of Celebes, was a cannibal, and remarkably fond of human flesh, so that he even use'd to faten his prisoners, and, cuting their heart out alive, ate it raw, with pepper and salt, esteeming it the most delicious morsel of all.

The Andamants, a nation of ilanders in the gulf of Bengal, are such barbarous savageës as to kil all who are unhapy enough to be driveën upon their coast, 'and eat them for food.'

The Anzigues, a nation of Africa, endue'd with many temporal benefits, and abounding with natures blessings, delight in eating mans flesh more than any other food, coveting even their friends, whom they embowel with a greedy delight, saying, they can no way better express true affection than to incorporate their dearest friends and relations into themselves, as in love before, now in body, uniteing two in one. They have, allso, shambles of men and womens flesh, jointed and cut in several pieces, and some, weary of life, voluntarily proffer themselves to the butcher, and are accordingly sold and eaten.

The Zuakins, another nation of this quarter, shew a seeming humanity to such strangers as are shipwreck'd on their coast, allowing them a convenient place to lodge in, with plenty of animal food to eat, and sometimes entertain them with their musick, – 'and then destroy the fatest, as they have occasion to feast on them.'

The negros, from the inland parts, are, allmost, without exception, *anthropophagi*, have a terrible, tiger-like, scarcely human aspect, and pointed or jaged teeth, closeing together like those of a fox. Most of these are so fierce and greedy after human flesh, that they bite large pieces out of the arms or legs of their neighbours, and fellow-slaves, which they swallow with great avidity.

From Joseph Ritson, *An Essay on Abstinence from Animal Food as a Moral Duty* (1802).

An English Cannibal

There is a recent instance of cannibalism in Engleland. At the Lent assizeës for Chester, in 1777, one Samuel Thorley, A BUTCHERS FOLLOWER, was try'd for the murder of Ann Smith, a ballad-singer, about twenty-two years of age. He decoy'd her, lay with her, murder'd her, cut her to pieceës, and ate part of her. The circumstanceës were too shocking to relate. He was convicted [executed], and afterward hung in chains.

From Joseph Ritson, *An Essay on Abstinence from Animal Food as a Moral Duty* (1802).

Relative Values

Let us now leave here and pass on to a kingdom called Dagroian. Dagroian is a separate kingdom on its own, with a king and a language of its own, but forming part of the same island. The people, who profess allegiance to the Great Khan, are out-and-out savages. They are idolaters; and I will tell you of one custom they have which is particularly bad. You must know that, when one of them, male or female, falls sick, the kinsfolk send for the magicians to find out whether the patient is due to recover. And these magicians claim by means of their enchantments and their idols and diabolic art to know whether he is destined to recover or to die. You must not suppose, because I speak of 'diabolic art', that that is their account of the matter: they attribute their knowledge to the power of the gods working through the medium of their art. If they say that he is due to die, then the kinsfolk send for certain men who are specially appointed to put such persons to death. These men come and seize the patient and put something over his mouth so as to suffocate him. When he is dead, they cook him. Then all his kinsfolk assemble and eat him whole. I assure you that they even devour all the marrow in his bones. This they do because they do not want one scrap of his substance to remain. For they say that if any scrap remained then this substance would generate worms, which would thereupon die for want of food. And by the death of these worms they declare that the dead man's soul would incur great sin and torment, because so many souls generated by his substance met their deaths. That is why they eat him whole. After they have eaten him, they take his bones and put them in a handsome casket. Then they carry this and hang it in a huge cavern in the mountains, in some place where no beast or other evil thing can touch it. I assure you further that, if they can get hold of some stranger who is not of their country, they seize him and, if he cannot ransom himself, they kill him and devour him on the spot.

From *The Travels* of *Marco Polo*, early thirteenth century, translated by R.E. Latham (1958).

A Modest Proposal

For Preventing the Children of poor People in Ireland, from being a Burden to their Parents or Country; and for making them beneficial to the Publick

IT is a melancholy Object to those, who walk through this great Town, or travel in the Country; when they see the *Streets*, the *Roads*, and *Cabbin-doors* crowded with *Beggars* of the Female Sex, followed by three, four, or six Children, *all in Rags*, and importuning every Passenger for an Alms. These *Mothers*, instead of being able to work for their honest Livelyhood, are forced to employ all their Time in stroling to beg Sustenance for their *helpless Infants*; who, as they grow up, either turn *Thieves* for want of Work; or leave their *dear Native Country, to fight for the Pretender* in Spain, or sell themselves to the *Barbadoes*.

I THINK it is agreed by all Parties, that this prodigious Number of Children in the Arms, or on the Backs, or at the *Heels* of their *Mothers*, and frequently of their *Fathers*, is *in the present deplorable State of the Kingdom*, a very great additional Grievance; and therefore, whoever could find out a fair, cheap, and easy Method of making these Children sound and useful Members of the Commonwealth, would deserve so well of the Publick, as to have his Statue set up for a Preserver of the Nation.

BUT my Intention is very far from being confined to provide only for the Children of *professed Beggars*: It is of a much greater Extent, and shall take in the whole Number of Infants at a certain Age, who are born of Parents, in effect as little able to support them, as those who demand our Charity in the Streets.

AS to my own Part, having turned my Thoughts for many Years, upon this important Subject, and maturely weighed the several *Schemes of other Projectors*, I have always found them grosly mistaken in their Computation. It is true a Child, *just dropt from its Dam*, may be supported by her Milk, for a Solar Year with little other Nourishment; at most not above the Value of two Shillings; which the Mother may certainly get, or the Value in *Scraps*, by her lawful Occupation of *Begging*: And, it is exactly at one Year old, that I propose to provide for them in such a Manner, as, instead of being a Charge upon their *Parents*, or the *Parish*, or *wanting Food and Raiment* for the rest of their Lives; they shall, on the contrary, contribute to the Feeding, and partly to the Cloathing, of many Thousands.

THERE is likewise another great Advantage in my *Scheme*, that it will prevent those *voluntary Abortions*, and that horrid Practice of *Women murdering their Bastard Children*; alas! too frequent among us; sacrificing the *poor innocent Babes*, I doubt, more to avoid the Expence than the Shame; which would move Tears and Pity in the most Savage and inhuman Breast.

THE Number of Souls in *Ireland* being usually reckoned one Million and a half; of these I calculate there may be about Two hundred Thousand Couple whose Wives are Breeders; from which Number I subtract thirty thousand Couples, who are able to maintain their own Children; although I apprehend there cannot be so many, under *the present Distresses of the Kingdom*; but this being granted, there will remain an Hundred and Seventy Thousand Breeders. I again subtract Fifty Thousand, for those Women who miscarry, or whose Children die by Accident, or Disease, within the Year. There only remain an Hundred and Twenty Thousand Children of poor Parents, annually born: The Question therefore is, How this Number shall be reared, and provided for? Which, as I have already said, under the present Situation of Affairs, is utterly impossible, by all the Methods hitherto proposed: For we can *neither employ them in Handicraft or Agriculture*; we neither build Houses, (I mean in the Country) nor cultivate Land: They can very seldom pick up a Livelihood *by Stealing* until they arrive at six Years old; except where they are of towardly Parts; although, I confess, they learn the Rudiments much earlier; during which Time, they can, however, be properly looked upon only as *Probationers*; as I have been informed by a principal Gentleman in the County of *Cavan*, who protested to me, that he never knew above one or two Instances under the Age of six, even in a Part of the Kingdom *so renowned for the quickest Proficiency in that Art.*

I AM assured by our Merchants, that a Boy or a Girl before twelve Years old, is no saleable Commodity; and even when they come to this Age, they will not yield above Three Pounds, or Three Pounds and half a Crown at most, on the Exchange; which cannot turn to Account either to the Parents or the Kingdom; the Charge of Nutriment and Rags, having been at least four Times that Value.

I SHALL now therefore humbly propose my own Thoughts; which I hope will not be liable to the least Objection.

I HAVE been assured by a very knowing *American* of my

Acquaintance in *London*; that a young healthy Child, well nursed, is, at a Year old, a most delicious, nourishing, and wholesome Food; whether *Stewed*, *Roasted*, *Baked*, or *Boiled*; and, I make no doubt, that it will equally serve in a *Fricasie*, or *Ragoust*.

I DO therefore humbly offer it to *publick Consideration*, that of the Hundred and Twenty Thousand Children, already computed, Twenty thousand may be reserved for Breed; whereof only one Fourth Part to be Males; which is more than we allow to *Sheep*, *black Cattle*, or *Swine*; and my Reason is, that these Children are seldom the Fruits of Marriage, *a Circumstance not much regarded by our Savages*; therefore, *one Male* will be sufficient to serve *four Females*. That the remaining Hundred thousand, may, at a Year old, be offered in Sale to the *Persons of Quality* and *Fortune*, through the Kingdom; always advising the Mother to let them suck plentifully in the last Month, so as to render them plump, and fat for a good Table. A Child will make two Dishes at an Entertainment for Friends; and when the Family dines alone, the fore or hind Quarter will make a reasonable Dish; and seasoned with a little Pepper or Salt, will be very good Boiled on the fourth Day, especially in *Winter*.

I HAVE reckoned upon a Medium, that a Child just born will weigh Twelve Pounds; and in a solar Year, if tolerably nursed, encreaseth to twenty eight Pounds.

I GRANT this Food will be somewhat dear, and therefore very *proper for Landlords*; who, as they have already devoured most of the Parents, seem to have the best Title to the Children.

INFANTS Flesh will be in Season throughout the Year; but more plentiful in *March*, and a little before and after: For we are told by a grave Author, an eminent *French* Physician, that *Fish being a prolifick Dyet*, there are more Children born in *Roman Catholick Countries* about Nine Months after *Lent*, than at any other Season: Therefore reckoning a Year after *Lent*, the Markets will be more glutted than usual; because the Number of *Popish Infants*, is, at least, three to one in this Kingdom: and therefore it will have one other Collateral Advantage, by lessening the Number of *Papists* among us.

I HAVE already computed the Charge of nursing a Beggar's Child (in which List I reckon all *Cottagers*, *Labourers*, and Four fifths of the *Farmers*) to be about two Shillings *per Annum*, Rags included; and I believe, no Gentleman would repine to give Ten Shillings for the *Carcase of a good fat Child*; which, as I have said, will make four Dishes of excellent nutritive Meat, when he hath only some particular Friend, or his own Family, to dine with him. Thus the

Squire will learn to be a good Landlord, and grow popular among his Tenants; the Mother will have Eight Shillings net Profit, and be fit for Work until she produceth another Child.

THOSE who are more thrifty (*as I must confess the Times require*) may flay the Carcase; the Skin of which, artificially dressed, will make admirable *Gloves for Ladies*, and *Summer Boots for fine Gentlemen*.

AS to our City of *Dublin*; Shambles may be appointed for this Purpose, in the most convenient Parts of it; and Butchers we may be assured will not be wanting; although I rather recommend buying the Children alive, and dressing them hot from the Knife, as we do *roasting Pigs*.

A VERY worthy Person, *a true Lover of his Country*, and whose Virtues I highly esteem, was lately pleased, in discoursing on this Matter, to offer a Refinement upon my Scheme. He said, that many Gentlemen of this Kingdom, having of late destroyed their Deer; he conceived, that the Want of Venison might be well supplied by the Bodies of young Lads and Maidens, not exceeding fourteen Years of Age, nor under twelve; so great a Number of both Sexes in every County being now ready to starve, for Want of Work and Service: And these to be disposed of by their Parents, if alive, or otherwise by their nearest Relations. But with due Deference to so excellent a Friend, and so deserving a Patriot, I cannot be altogether in his Sentiments. For as to the Males, my *American* Acquaintance assured me from frequent Experience, that their Flesh was generally tough and lean, like that of our School-boys, by continual Exercise, and their Taste disagreeable; and to fatten them would not answer the Charge. Then, as to the Females, it would, I think, with humble Submission, *be a Loss to the Publick*, because they soon would become Breeders themselves: And besides it is not improbable, that some scrupulous People might be apt to censure such a Practice (although indeed very unjustly) as a little bordering upon Cruelty; which, I confess, hath always been with me the strongest Objection against any Project, how well soever intended.

BUT in order to justify my Friend; he confessed, that this Expedient was put into his Head by the famous *Salmanazor*, a Native of the Island *Formosa*, who came from thence to *London*, above twenty Years ago, and in Conversation told my Friend, that in his Country, when any young Person happened to be put to Death, the Executioner sold the Carcase to *Persons of Quality*, as a prime Dainty; and that, in his Time, the Body of a plump Girl of fifteen, who was crucified for an Attempt to poison the Emperor, was sold to his Imperial *Majesty's prime Minister of State*, and other great *Mandarins* of the Court, *in Joints from the Gibbet*, at Four hundred Crowns. Neither indeed can I deny, that if the same Use were made of several plump young girls in this Town, who, without one single Groat to their Fortunes, cannot stir Abroad without a Chair, and appear at the *Play-house*, and *Assemblies* in foreign Fineries, which they never will pay for; the Kingdom would not be the worse.

SOME Persons of a desponding Spirit are in great Concern about that vast Number of poor People, who are Aged, Diseased, or Maimed; and I have been desired to employ my Thoughts what Course may be taken, to ease the Nation of so grievous an Incumbrance. But I am not in the least Pain upon that Matter; because it is very well known, that they are every Day *dying*, and *rotting*, by *Cold* and *Famine*, and *Filth*, and *Vermin*, as fast as can be reasonably expected. And as to the younger Labourers, they are now in almost as hopeful a Condition: They cannot get Work, and consequently pine away for Want of Nourishment, to a Degree, that if at any Time they are accidentally hired to common Labour, they have not Strength to perform it; and thus the Country, and themselves, are in a fair Way of being soon delivered from the Evils to come.

I HAVE too long digressed; and therefore shall return to my Subject. I think the Advantages by the Proposal which I have made, are obvious, and many, as well as of the highest Importance.

FOR, *First*, as I have already observed, it would greatly lessen the *Number of Papists*, with whom we are yearly overrun; being the principal Breeders of the Nation, as well as our most dangerous Enemies; and who stay at home on Purpose, with a Design to *deliver the Kingdom to the Pretender*; hoping to take their Advantage by the Absence *of so many good Protestants*, who have chosen rather to leave their Country, than stay at home, and pay Tithes against their Conscience, to an idolatrous *Episcopal Curate*.

SECONDLY, The poorer Tenants will have something valuable of their own, which, by Law, may be made liable to Distress, and help to pay their Landlord's Rent; their Corn and Cattle being already seized, and *Money a Thing unknown*.

THIRDLY, Whereas the Maintenance of an Hundred Thousand Children, from two Years old, and upwards, cannot be computed at less than ten Shillings a Piece *per Annum*, the Nation's Stock will be thereby encreased Fifty Thousand Pounds *per Annum*; besides the

Profit of a new Dish, introduced to the Tables of all *Gentlemen of Fortune* in the Kingdom, who have any Refinement in Taste; and the Money will circulate among ourselves, the Goods being entirely of our own Growth and Manufacture.

FOURTHLY, The constant Breeders, besides the Gain of Eight Shillings *Sterling per Annum*, by the Sale of their Children, will be rid of the Charge of maintaining them after the first Year.

FIFTHLY, This Food would likewise bring great *Custom to Taverns*, where the Vintners will certainly be so prudent, as to procure the best Receipts for dressing it to Perfection; and consequently, have their Houses frequented by all the *fine Gentlemen*, who justly value themselves upon their Knowledge in good Eating; and a skilful Cook, who understands how to oblige his Guests, will contrive to make it as expensive as they please.

SIXTHLY, This would be a great Inducement to Marriage, which all wise Nations have either encouraged by Rewards, or enforced by Laws and Penalties. It would encrease the Care and Tenderness of Mothers towards their Children, when they were sure of a Settlement for Life, to the poor Babes, provided in some Sort by the Publick, to their annual Profit instead of Expence. We should soon see an honest Emulation among the married Women, *which of them could bring the fattest Child to the Market.* Men would become as *fond* of their Wives, during the Time of their Pregnancy, as they are now of their *Mares* in Foal, their *Cows* in Calf, or *Sows* when they are ready to farrow; nor offer to beat or kick them, (as it is too *frequent* a Practice) for fear of a Miscarriage.

MANY other Advantages might be enumerated. For instance, the Addition of some Thousand Carcasses in our Exportation of barrelled Beef: The Propagation of *Swines Flesh*, and Improvement in the Art of making good *Bacon*: so much wanted among us by the great Destruction of *Pigs*, too frequent at our Tables, which are no way comparable in Taste, or Magnificence, to a well-grown fat yearling Child; which, roasted whole, will make a considerable Figure at a *Lord Mayor's Feast*, or any other publick Entertainment. But this, and many others, I omit: being studious of Brevity.

SUPPOSING that one Thousand Families in this City, would be constant Customers for Infants Flesh; besides others who might have it at *merry Meetings*, particularly *Weddings* and *Christenings*; I compute that *Dublin* would take off, annually, about Twenty Thousand Carcasses; and the rest of the Kingdom (where probably they will be sold somewhat cheaper) the remaining Eighty Thousand.

I CAN think of no one Objection, that will possibly be raised against this Proposal; unless it should be urged, that the Number of People will be thereby much lessened in the Kingdom. This I freely own; and it was indeed one principal Design in offering it to the World. I desire the Reader will observe, that I calculate my Remedy *for this one individual Kingdom of* IRELAND, *and for no other that ever was, is, or I think ever can be upon Earth.* Therefore, let no man talk to me of other Expedients: *Of taxing our Absentees at five Shillings a Pound: Of using neither Cloaths, nor Houshold Furniture except what is of our own Growth and Manufacture: Of utterly rejecting the Materials and Instruments that promote foreign Luxury: Of curing the Expensiveness of Pride, Vanity, Idleness, and Gaming in our Women: Of introducing a Vein of Parsimony, Prudence and Temperance: Of learning to love our Country, wherein we differ even from* LAPLANDERS, *and the Inhabitants of* TOPINAMBOO: *Of quitting our Animosities, and Factions; nor act any longer like the Jews, who were murdering one another at the very Moment their City was taken: Of being a little cautious not to sell our Country and Consciences for nothing: Of teaching Landlords to have, at least, one Degree of Mercy towards their Tenants.* Lastly, *Of putting a Spirit of Honesty, Industry, and Skill into our Shopkeepers; who, if a Resolution could now be taken to buy only our native Goods, would immediately unite to cheat and exact upon us in the Price, the Measure, and the Goodness; nor could ever yet be brought to make one fair Proposal of just Dealing, though often and earnestly invited to it.*

THEREFORE I repeat, let no Man talk to me of these and the like Expedients; till he hath, at least, a Glimpse of Hope, that there will ever be some hearty and sincere Attempt to put *them in Practice*.

BUT, as to my self; having been wearied out for many Years with offering vain, idle, visionary Thoughts; and at length utterly despairing of Success, I fortunately fell upon this Proposal; which, as it is wholly new, so it hath something *solid* and *real*, of no Expence, and little Trouble, full in our own Power; and whereby we can incur no Danger in *disobliging* ENGLAND: For, this Kind of Commodity will not bear Exportation; the Flesh being of too tender a Consistence, to admit a long Continuance in Salt; *although, perhaps, I could name a Country, which would be glad to eat up our whole Nation without it.*

AFTER all, I am not so violently bent upon my own Opinion, as to reject any Offer proposed by wise Men, which shall be found equally innocent, cheap, easy, and effectual. But before something of that Kind shall be advanced in Contradiction to my Scheme, and offering a better; I desire the Author, or Authors, will be pleased maturely to consider two Points. *First*, As Things now stand, how they will be able to find Food and Raiment, for a Hundred Thousand useless Mouths and Backs? And *secondly*, There being a round Million of Creatures in human Figure, throughout this Kingdom; whose whole Subsistence, put into a common Stock, would leave them in Debt two Millions of Pounds *Sterling*; adding those, who are Beggars by Profession, to the Bulk of Farmers, Cottagers, and Labourers, with their Wives and Children, who are Beggars in Effect; I desire those Politicians, who dislike my Overture, and may perhaps be so bold to attempt an Answer, that they will first ask the Parents of these Mortals, Whether they would not, at this Day, think it a great Happiness to have been sold for Food at a Year old, in the Manner I prescribe; and thereby have avoided such a perpetual Scene of Misfortunes, as they have since gone through; by the *Oppression of Landlords*; the Impossibility of paying Rent, without Money or Trade; the Want of common Sustenance, with neither House nor Cloaths, to cover them from the Inclemencies of Weather, and the most inevitable Prospect of intailing the like, or greater Miseries upon their Breed for ever.

I PROFESS, in the Sincerity of my Heart, that I have not the least personal Interest, in endeavouring to promote this necessary Work; having no other Motive than the *publick Good of my Country, by advancing our Trade, providing for Infants, relieving the Poor, and giving some Pleasure to the Rich*. I have no Children, by which I can propose to get a single penny; the youngest being nine Years old, and my Wife past Child-bearing.

Jonathan Swift (1729).

Your Money or You're Dinner

You must know that the idols of these islands are of the same type as those of Cathay and Manzi. I assure you that the islanders, and the other idolaters as well, have idols with the heads of cattle and of pigs, of dogs and sheep, and of many other sorts. There are some with heads of four faces and some with three heads, one in the right place and one on either shoulder. Some have four hands, some ten, and some a thousand. But these are the best and the ones that command the greatest reverence. When Christians ask them why they make their idols in such a diversity of shapes, they answer: 'It is in these shapes that our forefathers left them to us, and so we shall leave them to our sons and to those who come after us.' The works of these idols are so manifold and of such devilish contrivance that it is not proper to speak of them in our book, since they are no fit hearing for Christians. So we shall say no more of them, but turn to other matters. I will content myself with saying that the idolaters of these islands, when they capture some man who is not one of their friends, hold him to ransom for money. If this is not forthcoming, they send out invitations to their relatives and friends, saying: 'I should like you to come and dine with me at my house.' Then they kill their captive and make a meal of him with their kinsfolk. You must understand that they first cook him; and this human flesh they consider the choicest of all foods.

From *The Travels of Marco Polo*, early thirteenth century, translated by
R.E. Latham (1958).

Animals Lead to Cannibals (ii)

As human sacrifices were a natural effect of that superstitious cruelty which first produce'd the slaughter of animals, so is it equally natural that those accustom'd to eat the brute, should not long abstain from the man: more especially as, when toasted or broil'd on the altar, the appearance, savour, and taste of both would be nearly, if not entirely, the same. But, from whatever cause it may be deduce'd, nothing can be more certain than that the eating of human flesh has been a practice, in many parts of the world, from a very remote period, and is so, in some, at this day. That it is a consequence of the use of animal food there can be no doubt, as it would be impossible to find an instance of it among people who were accustom'd solely to a vegetable diet. The progress of cruelty is rapid. Habit renders it familiar, and hence it is deem'd natural.

The man who, accustom'd to live on roots and vegetables, first devour'd the flesh of the smallest animal, committed a greater violence to his own nature than the most beautyful and delicate female, accustom'd to animal food, would feel in sheding the blood of her fellow-creatures for sustenance; possess'd as they are of exquisite feelings, a considerable degree of intelligence, and even, according to her own religious system, of a liveing soul. That this is a principle in the social disposition of mankind is evident from the deliberate coolness with which seamen, when their ordinary provisions are exhausted, sit down to devour such of their comrades as chance or contriveance renders the victim of the moment: a fact of which there are but too many, and those too wel-authenticated, instances. Such a crime, which no necessity can justify, would never enter the mind of a starving Gentoo, nor, indeed, of any one that had not been previously accustom'd to animal food. Even among the Bedouins, or wandering Arabs of the desert, according to the observation of the enlighten'd Volney, though they so often experience the extremity of hunger, the practice of devouring human flesh was never hear'd of. Content with his milk and his dates, the Bedouin has not desire'd flesh; he has shed no blood; his hands are not accustom'd to slaughter, nor his ears to the crys of suffering creatures; he has preserve'd a humane and sensible heart. The habit of sheding blood, he says, and tearing his prey, has familiarise'd the savage to the sight of death and sufferings. Tormented by hunger he has desire'd flesh; and finding it easy to obtain that of his fellow-creature, he could not long hesitate to kill him, to satisfy the craveings of his appetite. The first experiment made, this cruelty degenerates into a habit; he becomes a cannibal, sanguinary and atrocious, and his mind acquires all the insensibility of his body.

From Joseph Ritson, *An Essay on Abstinence from Animal Food as a Moral Duty* (1802).

I Could Eat You Up

Our teeth began to move slowly, with equal rhythm, and our eyes stared into each other's with the intensity of serpents' – serpents concentrated in the ecstasy of swallowing each other in turn, as we were aware, in our turn of being swallowed by the serpent that digests us all, assimilated ceaselessly in the process of ingestion and digestion, in the universal cannibalism that leaves its imprint on every amorous relationship and erases the lines between our bodies and *sopa de frijoles*, *buachinango a la veracruzana*, and *enchiladas* ...

From Italo Calvino, *Under the Jaguar Sun* (1986), translated by William Weaver.

Ossi Dei Morti

The name of these cookies means 'dead men's bones' and it is not difficult to see why. Thin and brittle, they even rattle like skeletons when they are shaken in the tin! Ossi dei Morti are traditionally made in Italy for All Souls' Day on November 2. Many different shapes are made according to the region. Sometimes they are fashioned into the shape of ears, noses, legs and arms, other times they are simply shaped into small beans, in which case they are known as Fave dei Morti or 'dead men's beans'.

MAKES 30–35

7 tbsps all-purpose flour
$^1/_4$ tsp baking soda
$^1/_2$ cup sugar

$^1/_2$ cup shelled hazelnuts (filberts),
toasted, skinned and finely ground
1 egg white

Preheat the oven to 375°F. Line several baking sheets with nonstick parchment paper.

Sift the flour and baking soda into a bowl, then stir in the sugar and hazelnuts. Beat the egg white until stiff, then beat into the mixture until evenly incorporated to a soft, sticky dough.

Fill a pastry bag fitted with a $^1/_4$ inch plain tube with the mixture. Pipe 2 inch lengths on to the parchment paper, spacing them well apart as the mixture spreads widthwise. Bake in batches (2 baking sheets at a time) for 7–8 minutes or until golden brown. Transfer the cookies on the paper to wire racks and leave to cool (they will harden on cooling).

From Jeni Wright, *Patisserie of Italy* (1988).

A Diner, not a Dish

Somewhere at the back of our minds, carefully walled off from ordinary consideration and discourse, lies the idea of cannibalism – that human beings might *become* food, and eaters of each other. Violence, after all, is necessary if any organism is to ingest another. Animals are murdered to produce meat; vegetables are torn up, peeled, and chopped; most of what we eat is treated with fire; and chewing is designed remorselessly to finish what killing and cooking began. People naturally prefer that none of this should happen to them. Behind every rule of table etiquette lurks the determination of each person present to be a diner, not a dish. It is one of the chief roles of etiquette to keep the lid on the violence which the meal being eaten presupposes.

From Margaret Visser, *The Rituals of Dinner* (1991).

Hungry Men in a Boat

The fourth day came, but not a breath of air,
   And Ocean slumber'd like an unwean'd child:
The fifth day, and their boat lay floating there,
   The sea and sky were blue, and clear, and mild –
With their one oar (I wish they had had a pair)
   What could they do? and hunger's rage grew wild:
So Juan's spaniel, spite of his entreating,
Was kill'd, and portion'd out for present eating.

On the sixth day they fed upon his hide,
   And Juan, who had still refused, because
The creature was his father's dog that died,
   Now feeling all the vulture in his jaws,
With some remorse received (though first denied)
   As a great favour one of the fore-paws,
Which he divided with Pedrillo, who
Devour'd it, longing for the other too.

The seventh day, and no wind – the burning sun
   Blistered and scorch'd, and, stagnant on the sea,

They lay like carcasses; and hope was none,
  Save in the breeze that came not; savagely
They glared upon each other – all was done,
  Water, and wine, and food – and you might see
The longings of the cannibal arise
(Although they spoke not) in their wolfish eyes.

At length one whisper'd his companion, who
  Whisper'd another, and thus it went round,
And then into a hoarser murmur grew,
  An ominous, and wild, and desperate sound,
And when his comrade's thought each sufferer knew,
  'Twas but his own, suppress'd till now, he found:
And out they spoke of lots for flesh and blood,
And who should die to be his fellow's food.

But ere they came to this, they that day shared
  Some leathern caps, and what remain'd of shoes;
And then they look'd around them, and despair'd,
  And none to be the sacrifice would choose;
At length the lots were torn up, and prepared,
  But of materials that much shock the Muse –
Having no paper, for the want of better,
They took by force from Juan Julia's letter.

The lots were made, and mark'd, and mix'd, and handed,
  In silent horror, and their distribution
Lull'd even the savage hunger which demanded,
  Like the Promethean vulture, this pollution;
None in particular had sought or plann'd it,
  'Twas nature gnaw'd them to this resolution,
By which none were permitted to be neuter –
And the lot fell on Juan's luckless tutor.

He but requested to be bled to death:
  The surgeon had his instruments, and bled
Pedrillo, and so gently ebb'd his breath,
  You hardly could perceive when he was dead.
He died as born, a Catholic in faith,
  Like most in the belief in which they're bred,
And first a little crucifix he kiss'd,

And then held out his jugular and wrist.

The surgeon, as there was no other fee,
    Had his first choice of morsels for his pains;
But being thirstiest at the moment, he
    Preferr'd a draught from the fast-flowing veins:
Part was divided, part thrown in the sea,
    And such things as the entrails and the brains
Regaled two sharks, who follow'd o'er the billow –
The sailors ate the rest of poor Pedrillo.

The sailors ate him, all save three or four,
    Who were not quite so fond of animal food;
To these was added Juan, who, before
    Refusing his own spaniel, hardly could
Feel now his appetite increased much more;
    'Twas not to be expected that he should,
Even in extremity of their disaster,
Dine with them on his pastor and his master.

'Twas better that he did not; for, in fact,
    The consequence was awful in the extreme;
For they, who were most ravenous in the act,
    Went raging mad – Lord! how they did blaspheme!
And foam and roll, with strange convulsions rack'd,
    Drinking salt-water like a mountain-stream,
Tearing, and grinning, howling, screeching, swearing,
And, with hyaena laughter, died despairing.

Their numbers were much thinn'd by this infliction,
    And all the rest were thin enough, heaven knows;
And some of them had lost their recollection,
    Happier than they who still perceived their woes;
But others ponder'd on a new dissection,
    As if not warn'd sufficiently by those
Who had already perish'd, suffering madly,
For having used their appetites so sadly.

And next they thought upon the master's mate,
    As fattest; but he saved himself, because,
Besides being much averse from such a fate,

There were some other reasons; the first was,
He had been rather indisposed of late,
    And that which chiefly proved his saving clause,
Was a small present made to him at Cadiz,
By general subscription of the ladies.

Of poor Pedrillo something still remain'd,
    But was used sparingly – some were afraid,
And others still their appetites constrain'd,
    Or but at times a little supper made;
All except Juan, who throughout abstain'd,
    Chewing a piece of bamboo, and some lead:
At length they caught two boobies, and a noddy,
And then they left off eating the dead body.

From Lord Byron, *Don Juan*, Canto II (1819).

Just Desserts?

Meanwhile, however, the murderers had arrived. These were the centurion Herennius and Popillius, an officer in the army, who had in the past been defended by Cicero when he was prosecuted for having murdered his father. They had their helpers with them. They found the doors shut and broke them down; but Cicero was not to be seen and the people in the house said that they did not know where he was. Then, we are told, a young man who had been educated by Cicero in literature and philosophy, an ex-slave of Cicero's brother Quintus, Philologus by name, told the officer that the litter was being carried down to the sea by a path that was under the cover of the trees. The officer took a few men with him and hurried round to the place where the path came out of the woods, and Herennius went running down the path. Cicero heard him coming and ordered his servants to set the litter down where they were. He himself, in that characteristic posture of his, with his chin resting on his left hand, looked steadfastly at his murderers. He was all covered in dust; his hair was long and disordered, and his face was pinched and wasted with his anxieties – so that most of those who stood by covered their faces while Herennius was killing him. His throat was cut as he stretched his neck out from the litter. He was in his sixty-fourth year.

By Antony's orders Herennius cut off his head and his hands – the hands with which he had written the Philippics. (It was Cicero himself who called these speeches against Antony 'the Philippics'; and they have retained the title to the present day.)

When these severed extremities of Cicero's person were brought to Rome Antony happened to be organizing an election. Hearing the news and seeing the sight, he cried out: 'Now let there be an end of our proscriptions.' Then he ordered the head and the hands to be fastened up over the ships' rams on the public platform in the forum. It was a sight to make the Romans shudder. They seemed to see there, no so much the face of Cicero, as the image of the soul of Antony. However, in all this Antony did show one sign of decent feeling. He handed over Philologus to Pomponia, the wife of Quintus. And she, when she had got the man in her power, inflicted all sorts of terrible punishments on him and finally made him cut off his own flesh bit by bit, roast the pieces, and then eat them. This, at least, is the account given by some historians; though Cicero's own ex-slave, Tiro, makes no reference at all to the treachery of Philologus.

From Plutarch, *Life of Cicero* (c. 45–120 AD), translated by Rex Warner.

Strawberry Breasts
(Formula by the Futurist Poet of National Record Farfa)

A pink plate with two erect feminine breasts made of ricotta dyed pink with Campari with nipples of candied strawberry. More fresh strawberries under the covering of ricotta making it possible to bite into an ideal multiplication of imaginary breasts.

From F.T. Marinetti, *The Futurist Cookbook* (1932), translated by Suzanne Brill.

A Reformed Cannibal

We had been but three days in Anaho when we received the visit of the chief of Hatiheu, a man of weight and fame, late leader of a war upon the French, late prisoner in Tahiti, and the last eater of long-pig in Nuka-hiva. Not many years have elapsed since he was seen striding on the beach of Anaho, a dead man's arm across his shoulder. 'So does Kooamua to his enemies!' he roared to the passers-by, and took a bite from the raw flesh. And now behold this gentleman, very wisely replaced in office by the French, paying us a morning visit in European clothes. He was the man of the most character we had yet seen: his manners genial and decisive, his person tall, his face rugged, astute, formidable, and with a certain similarity to Mr. Gladstone's only for the brownness of the skin, and the high-chief's tattooing, all one side and much of the other being of an even blue. Further acquaintance increased our opinion of his sense. He viewed the *Casco* in a manner then quite new to us, examining her lines and the running of the gear; to a piece of knitting on which one of the party was engaged, he must have devoted ten minutes' patient study; nor did he desist before he had divined the principles; and he was interested even to excitement by a type-writer, which he learned to work. When he departed he carried away with him a list of his family, with his own name printed by his own hand at the bottom. I should add that he was plainly much of a humorist, and not a little of a humbug. He told us, for instance, that he was a person of exact sobriety; such being the obligation of his high estate: the commons might be sots, but the chief could not stoop so low. And not many days after he was to be observed in a state of smiling and lop-sided imbecility, the *Casco* ribbon upside down on his dishonoured hat.

From Robert Louis Stevenson, *In the South Seas* (1896).

Eat Me

'All those who have legacies in my will, except for my freedmen, will receive them only on this condition – that they cut up my corpse and eat it in front of the people.'

*

'We know that among certain races the custom of the dead being eaten by their relations is still observed. In fact, sick people are often reproached for causing their flesh to deteriorate. I therefore advise my friends not to shrink from my request, but eat my body in the same spirit as they damned my soul.'

*

The enormous reputation of his money blinded the eyes and hearts of the poor fools.

Gorgias was ready to carry out the terms.

*

'I see nothing to fear in your stomach revolting. It will obey your command if you promise it a lot of luxuries as compensation for one hour's disgust. Just close your eyes and pretend you are eating a million sesterces, not human offal. Then for another thing, we'll find some seasonings to change the taste. After all, no meat is pleasant by itself; it's adulterated in some way and made acceptable to the reluctant stomach. And if you want your determination to be justified by examples, there are the Sanguntines, who ate human flesh when they were hard pressed by Hannibal – and they weren't expecting a legacy. The Petelians did the same in the last stages of a famine and all they were after in eating this dish was to avoid dying of starvation. When Numantia was captured by Scipio, there were some mothers found carrying around with them the half-eaten bodies of their own children.'

From Petronius, *The Satyricon and the Fragments*, first century AD, translated by J.P. Sullivan.

Cannibal Ghosts

Certain presences, called Vehinehae, frequent and make terrible the nocturnal roadside; I was told by one they were like so much mist, and as the traveller walked into them dispersed and dissipated; another described them as being shaped like men and having eyes like cats; from none could I obtain the smallest clearness as to what they did, or wherefore they were dreaded. We may be sure at least they represent the dead; for the dead, in the minds of the islanders, are all-pervasive. 'When a native says that he is a man,' writes Dr. Codrington, 'he means that he is a man and not a ghost; not that he is a man and not a beast. The intelligent agents of this world are to his mind the men who are alive, and the ghosts the men who are dead.' Dr. Codrington speaks of Melanesia; from what I have learned his words are equally true of the Polynesian. And yet more. Among cannibal Polynesians a dreadful suspicion rests generally on the dead; and the Marquesans, the greatest cannibals of all, are scarce likely to be free from similar beliefs. I hazard the guess that the Vehinehae are the hungry spirits of the dead, continuing their life's business of the cannibal ambuscade, and lying everywhere unseen, and eager to devour the living. Another superstition I picked up through the troubled medium of Tari Coffin's English. The dead, he told me, came and danced by night around the paepae of their former family; the family were thereupon overcome by some emotion (but whether of pious sorrow or of fear I could not gather), and must 'make a feast,' of which fish, pig, and popoi were indispensable ingredients.

From Robert Louis Stevenson, *In the South Seas* (1896).

V OBSESSION

ONE of the best-selling books in Britain in the late 1980s was Rosemary Conley's *Hip and Thigh Diet*. Together with its sequel, it has sold more than two million copies. Four more volumes, including a *Hip and Thigh Diet Cookbook*, have been bestsellers, as was Conley's *Whole Body Programme* video. A revised version of the original book, published in 1993, contains testimony from successful slimmers and this explanation from Conley for her continuing popularity: 'It's simply because my diets and exercises work for ordinary, real people.' Beaming from the covers of paperbacks, videos and magazines, Conley has become the instantly recognisable symbol of a multi-million-pound business which embraces such rival theories and methods as Weightwatchers, health farms, manufacturers of low-fat meals and magazines which promote contests to find the 'slimmer of the year'. Most are targeted on women, although government figures released in 1993 show that weight is even more of a problem for English men; the paradox is that as the slimming industry grows in size and profitability, the population's weight problems are becoming proportionately larger instead of smaller. The Health Survey for England in 1993 found that nearly half of women were overweight or obese, with the 55 to 64 age group worst affected; the situation is much the same in Wales, where 47 per cent of the female population fell into one or both categories in the same year.

These figures are nothing to do with perception, with the tendency many women display to have a distorted self-image and complain about non-existent areas of fat. They are based on body-mass index, the widely used measure of obesity which takes into account weight and height; what they suggest is that, regardless of individual successes, the slimming industry is on the whole far better at putting on pounds for its shareholders than taking them off for the women who subscribe to its products. That is why more drastic methods are gaining in popularity: surgical removal of fat or interventions which limit or prevent the intake of solid food. (Some years ago, when I was being interviewed about a subject that had nothing to do with eating on a Los Angeles radio station, our discussion was interrupted two or three times in half an hour by a cheery advert for stomach stapling, in which a reassuring voice-over offered people the opportunity to have half their stomachs sealed off in a Hollywood clinic as an alternative to dieting.) Yet diets, whether their purpose is weight loss or a more healthy way of life, retain their popularity no matter how ineffective they happen to be or contradictory their advice. Some even produce the opposite effect to what their inventors and advocates intend; according to the American food writer Harold McGee, the Zen macrobiotic diet which was claimed to increase life expectancy was responsible for 'a rash of cases of severe malnutrition, ranging from scurvy to anemia'. The French gastronome and food writer Jean-Anthelme Brillat-Savarin recorded an extreme example of the harm done by dieting in Dijon in 1776 when an eighteen-year-old girl, whose friends had teased her about her plumpness, embarked on a regime of fasting combined with drinking a glass of vinegar each morning. Brillat-Savarin wrote in *The Physiology of Taste* that he discovered the cause of her sudden weight loss too late and although doctors were called, she wasted away and died in his arms.

What this suggests is that diets, instead of being a solution, are actually a *symptom* of a very widespread problem with food and eating. This becomes clearer when they are looked at not in terms of stated aims, which vary from getting rid of 'cellulite' (almost certainly a figment of someone's imagination) or living to the age of 120, but of what they have in common; this is, invariably, a set of rules and prohibitions which divide eating and food into lists of 'good' and 'bad' practices. For Conley, fat is the culprit and her diet is designed to eliminate it, as far as is practically possible, from people's lives; her books are full of recipes for melon salad with 'oil-free vinaigrette dressing' and 'dry roast' potatoes and parsnips. There is even a 'forbidden list' which pronounces an ukase on all types of oil, whole milk, milk puddings, egg yolks, fatty meat and fish, all nuts except chestnuts, and a host of other foodstuffs too numerous to list. This is a tough regime but not *too* tough, as Conley hastens to reassure the reader: 'You will probably be very pleasantly surprised at the volume of food you are allowed and how you will feel really quite full after each meal. You will be delighted at how quickly you will begin to lose weight and inches (cm) and how different from previous diets this one proves to be.'

Sounds familiar? 'These menus can be followed with little or no hardship, and you will be amazed at the way the fat rolls off,' promised the pioneer health guru Gayelord Hauser in *The Gayelord Hauser Cook Book*, back in 1955. Hauser, who was nutritional director of Elizabeth Arden's 'beauty farm' in Maine, offered a Seven-Day Painless Reducing Diet which frowned on carbohydrates ('starch') and recommended in their place protein, whose 'dynamic action ... helps burn up unneeded calories'. His menus included plenty of eggs (up to eight a week), fatty fish like halibut and main courses based around meat ('1 large hamburger with lots of chopped parsley and onion'). Hauser was fanatically keen on vitamins, yogurt and vegetable juices, which were the key to his promise that 'you can eat seven years onto your life' – a modest claim compared to that made in the 1990s by Dr Roy L. Walford, a professor of pathology at the UCLA School of Medicine in California, who insists that a nutrient-rich diet with limited calories can extend the human lifespan to between 110 and 150 years.

What all these diet manuals offer is a promise (slimmer thighs, longer life, better looks) based on the renunciation of *something* (fat, carbohydrate) but with the assurance that giving it up isn't too unbearable. This is, in a mild form, precisely what religion has to offer, not forgetting those lists of banned substances which roughly correspond, in the culinary cosmology, to sins. 'All my adult life I had adored foods which were high in fat,' writes Rosemary Conley in the *Hip and Thigh Diet*, exactly in the manner of an evangelist telling potential converts about an earlier existence of unbridled lust or unchecked idolatry. What her list of banned food actually resembles, although the language is more populist, is that section of the Bible in which God hands over a set of dietary rules to Moses. Generally known as the Abominations of Leviticus, the list goes into immense detail about which foods are taboo and which permitted: 'these are the beasts which ye shall eat among all the beasts that are on the earth', it begins, dividing animals and birds into categories of clean and unclean according to a system which has long puzzled both biblical scholars and anthropologists. Why is it all right to eat the bald locust but not the swan, the frog but not the hare? One explanation is that they are no more than sensible rules to do with hygiene; Leviticus bans pork, a notoriously dicey meat in hot regions like the Middle East, especially in the absence of modern methods of refrigeration. But what's striking about the list is its arbitrariness, a characteristic which suggests it is the existence of rules, rather than what they say, which matters. I am reminded here of Freud's observation, in his essay on 'The Taboo of Virginity', that people invent taboos as a way of dealing with something which frightens them; the coincidence that all the major world religions – Christianity, Judaism, Hinduism, Buddhism, Islam – have produced dietary prohibitions along the lines of Leviticus suggests that food has always made people anxious.

What is it, then, that scares us so much? The first and most obvious answer can be summed up in one word: fat. In any society where food intake is not restricted by scarcity or poverty, people overeat. In sophisticated Western countries, they have begun to do so on an epic scale. When Brillat-Savarin, who moved temporarily to New York in the 1790s to escape the worst excesses of the French Revolution, recalled a grotesquely fat man whose girth attracted the stares of amazed passers-by as he sat in the window of his apartment on Broadway, he was deliberately describing a phenomenon. But prosperity has made obesity into an everyday condition in the second half of the twentieth century, so that everyone in the developed world now knows someone who is severely overweight; for millions of people, food is no longer a necessity but an addiction. These are addicts, though, who do not have the option – like smokers or alcoholics – of entirely giving up the substance they crave, which lends an edge of desperation to their search for a solution. It is on this desperation, and a credulous belief in miracle cures, that the whole slimming industry is founded; anyone who dreams up a 'new' regime, no matter how unscientific the theory, and gives it a snappy title, is on to a winner.

Yet widespread obesity – as opposed to an indulgence of the rich – is a recent development. (People forget that Petronius, whose account of a dinner party in the section of the *Satyricon* known as the *cena Trimalchionis* is often cited as proof of Roman gluttony, was actually satirising the behaviour of a small class, the *nouveaux riches*.) Dietary rules existed long before large numbers of people had the opportunity to over-indulge on a regular basis, suggesting that they address a more complex phenomenon than the cycle of craving, satisfaction and guilt set up by eating to excess. One clue to what this might be lies in the language in which they are couched: God's insistence in Leviticus that certain animals are 'unclean' and must be avoided in order to be 'holy', Conley's throwaway remark that she had discovered 'something more than just another diet'. Respondents to Conley's questionnaires on the efficacy of the *Hip and Thigh Diet* wrote that it had changed their lives, making them happier as well as thinner, and one even described her post-Conley condition as 'Absolute Heaven'. There is a strong suggestion here not just of guilt being removed but of dietary prohibitions producing something like a morally superior state; this idea, that food taboos improve not just the body but the mind, becomes overt when you examine the arguments in favour of vegetarianism, a regime whose popularity is increasing dramatically as we approach the *fin de siècle*.

Joseph Ritson, an early and influential polemicist against meat-eating, published a short book in 1802 which cited a range of authorities in an attempt to prove that carnivores were far more 'cholerick, fierce and cruel' than vegetarians. 'I hold that the depravity of the physical and moral nature of man originated in his unnatural habits of life' is the uncompromising opening sentence of Shelley's pamphlet *A Vindication of Natural Diet*, published eleven years later. The poet claimed there was no disease, physical or mental, that could not be mitigated by a vegetable diet; he even suggested that the 'murders and victories' of Napoleon Bonaparte would have been impossible if the 'bile-suffused' tyrant had been a vegetarian. George Bernard Shaw, who converted to vegetarianism after reading Shelley, argued in 1898 that as human beings became more sophisticated, they would turn their backs on eating meat: 'A hundred years hence a cultivated man will no more dream of eating flesh or smoking than he now does of living, as Pepys's contemporaries did, in a house with a cesspool under it.' Shaw suggested that meat-eating turned soldiers into cowards although his appropriation of vegetarianism as 'a fighting diet' makes uncomfortable reading with hindsight. Senior members of the Nazi party in Germany tended to favour vegetarianism; Hitler was famously non-carnivorous while Himmler, who set up the death camps, disliked hunting and admitted he had considered following Hitler's example.

Although there is a clear ethical case for not eating animals, the forcefulness of the language used in vegetarian tracts and their contempt for carnivores is striking; as well as loathing the whole business of slaughterhouses and the frequently inhumane treatment of animals reared for food, there is also a palpable revulsion from the idea of flesh. Shaw talked disgustedly about his refusal to 'batten' on the 'scorched corpses of animals' and vegetarian pamphlets dwell not just on the suffering of cows and sheep but on the physical properties – shape, smell, texture – of blood and guts. Carnivores use different devices, such as buying food in pre-packed packages from supermarkets, to avoid thinking about what animal food consists of although many of them share similar anxieties. Animals are flesh, just like ourselves; eating their corpses threatens our illusion of bodily integrity, our perception of ourselves as discrete from other living creatures. ('What we eat today/Walks and talks tomorrow', according to a Slav proverb quoted by Gayelord Hauser.) This ingestion and incorporation of the recognisable other is simply unbearable for some people, who restrict themselves to eating plants; few of us, after all, identify with a courgette or a green pepper. The rest adopt alternative strategies, such as the distancing mechanism of rules, which may explain why virtually all carnivorous cultures have lists of taboo and non-taboo animals. Accepting communal prohibitions of this sort, no matter how illogically constructed, displaces uncertainty about eating animal corpses at all onto a different question, *which* instead of *whether*; it's worth noting here that Leviticus deals with animals, birds and insects – animate creatures – rather than the wide range of plants on whose edible properties the Israelites might be thought to need guidance. Similarly Rosemary Conley's prohibition on fat places many, though not all, animal products (fatty meat, sausages, poultry skin, lard, milk, cream, butter and cheese, which is permissible only in an attenuated form) out of bounds. Another regime which was extremely popular in its time, Audrey Eyton's *F-Plan Diet*, favours a vegetarian product – fibre – over meat.

The proposition that people have an inborn, unconscious anxiety about food, particularly food of animal origin, helps explain a peculiar feature of recent years: the frequency and persistence of scares. Some of these are expressed in the form of urban myths, stories about a cousin of a friend who ordered raw fish in a Japanese restaurant and ended up with a twenty-foot worm in his gut. But there has also been a response verging on panic to a tiny handful of cases of CJD, a disease in humans similar to the fatal cattle disease, BSE. The condition, popularly known as 'mad cow' disease, is terrifying but there is no proof, at the time of writing, that it has jumped the species barrier from cattle to humans. Indeed the fact that steps have been taken to tighten up hygiene on farms and in abattoirs suggests that the risk is currently lower than it's ever been, yet in

December 1995 schools and other institutions all over Britain rushed to remove beef and beef products from their menus. In March 1996, when a government advisory committee admitted that a small number of CJD cases *might* be associated with the BSE agent in cattle before the introduction in 1988 of a ban on cattle and sheep ingredients in animal feed, beef sales in Britain dropped dramatically; in spite of the committee's clear insistence that there is no direct evidence of a link between CJD and BSE, Britain's EC partners took the extraordinary step of banning British beef exports. Yet all the evidence suggests that, even if there is a connection between the two diseases, the damage to humans was done in the mid to late 1980s. You cannot protect yourself from infection retrospectively by giving up beef now.

It's precisely because we don't recognise that food is frightening (of course: it can make you sick), and our ambiguous relation to it of desire and fear, that we are vulnerable to these melodramatic, probably unnecessary adjustments to our diets. We are also suckers for slimming regimes that don't work – a proposition amply borne out by the statistics – and whose exponents have little or no grasp of the complexity of the problem they are addressing.

Brillat-Savarin spelled it out in a characteristically no-nonsense formulation: 'Tell me what you eat; I will tell you what you are.' But people don't *want* to be told and for centuries it was left to religion and priests to devise rules to defend us from such unwelcome knowledge. In secular societies, that function has passed to gurus with cheesy grins, weight charts and leotards; it's no surprise to learn from a biographical note at the front of the *Hip and Thigh Diet* that its author is a 'committed Christian' (as, by the way, is Britain's most popular cook, Delia Smith). Dieting is a multi-million pound business but it also exhibits many of the characteristics of a religious cult: self-denial, the promise of rewards, and a belief in miracles. The *Hip and Thigh Diet* is no better or worse than any of the others but it's surprising that so many people put their faith in the Abominations of Rosemary Conley. There's a simpler and much less bothersome diet in Muriel Spark's novel, *A Far Cry from Kensington*: eat the same meals but only half the quantity. Even if you don't keep to it, at least you'll enjoy the book.

Causes of Obesity

The first is the natural constitution of the individual. Nearly all men are born with certain predispositions, of which their physiognomy bears the stamp. Out of a hundred persons who die of consumption, ninety have brown hair, long faces, and pointed noses. Out of a hundred obese persons, on the other hand, ninety have short faces, round eyes, and snub noses.

It is certain therefore that there are persons virtually doomed as it were to corpulence, persons whose digestive activities, all things being equal, create more fat than those of their fellows.

This physical truth, of which I am firmly convinced, sometimes influences my way of looking at things in a most unfortunate manner.

When there appears in society a vivacious, pink-cheeked young person, with a pert nose, rounded contours, and short plump hands and feet, everybody is entranced and finds her charming; everyone, that is, but I. For, taught by experience, I look at her with eyes of twelve years hence, see the ravages which obesity will have wrought on those fresh young charms, and groan inwardly over ills so far non-existent. This anticipatory compassion is a painful sensation and furnishes one proof, among a thousand others, that man would be unhappier than he already is, if he could foresee the future.

The second of the chief causes of obesity is the floury and starchy substances which man makes the prime ingredients of his daily nourishment. As we have said already, all animals that live on farinaceous food grow fat willy-nilly; and man is no exception to the universal law.

Starch produces its effect sooner and more surely in conjunction with sugar; sugar and fat both contain hydrogen as a common element; both are inflammable. With this addition, it is the more active in that it pleases the palate more, and because sweet dishes are seldom eaten until the natural appetite has already been satisfied, when only that luxury appetite remains which must be coaxed by the most refined art and the subtlest variety.

Starch is no less fattening when conveyed in drinks, such as beer and other beverages of the same kind. The beer-drinking countries are also those where the biggest bellies are found; and certain

Parisian families which, in 1817, drank beer for reasons of economy, were rewarded with paunches which they scarcely know what to do with.

Continued

A dual cause of obesity results from excess of sleep and want of exercise.

The human body gains a great deal during sleep, and loses very little in the same period, since muscular activity is suspended. It thus becomes essential for the surplus acquired to be reduced by exercise; yet the time for activity is reduced in direct proportion to the time spent in sleep.

By another necessary consequence, heavy sleepers shun everything that promises to be at all tiring; the excess products of assimilation are therefore swept away by the torrent of circulation; they are there charged, by a process of which Nature alone holds the secret, with a little more hydrogen, and fat soon forms, to be deposited by the same agency in the capsules of the cellular tissue.

Continued

A last cause of obesity consists of excessive eating and drinking.

We have had occasion to say that it is one of the privileges of mankind to eat without being hungry and drink without being thirsty; and indeed it cannot be a privilege shared by the animals, for it is born of reflection on the pleasures of the table, and the desire to prolong them.

This dual inclination has been found wherever men exist; and it is well known that savages eat to excess and drink themselves into a stupor whenever an opportunity presents itself.

As for ourselves, the citizens of the two worlds, who believe that we stand at the summit of civilization, it is certain that we eat too much.

I am not speaking of the few who, for reasons of avarice or impotence, live alone and apart; the former gloating over the money they are saving, the latter lamenting their inability to do better; I am speaking of all those who, moving about us, are in turn hosts or guests, politely offering or complaisantly accepting; who, when all their needs are satisfied, eat a dish because it is attractive, or drink a wine because it is new to them: I insist that whether they sit every day in fine dining-rooms or only celebrate Sundays and occasionally Mondays, the vast majority eat and drink too much, and huge quantities of food are absorbed every day without need.

This cause, almost always present, acts differently according to the constitution of the individual; and in the case of those who have bad stomachs, its effect is not obesity, but indigestion.

Anecdote

We have witnessed with our own eyes an example which half Paris had the opportunity of observing.

Monsieur Lang had one of the most luxurious houses in that city; his table especially was excellent, but his stomach was as bad as his gourmandism was extreme. He did the honours perfectly, and himself ate with a courage worthy of a better fate.

Everything would go well until after the coffee; but soon his stomach would refuse to do its duty, pains would begin, and the wretched gastronome would be forced to throw himself down on a sofa and remain there till next day, expiating the brief pleasures he had tasted in prolonged anguish.

The remarkable thing is that he never changed his ways; as long as he lived, he freely accepted this strange alternation; and never allowed the sufferings of the evening to interfere with next day's dinner.

In the case of those whose stomach is in good shape, over-eating acts as described in the previous chapter. Everything is digested and what is not needed for the body's recuperation solidifies and turns into fat.

With the others, chronic indigestion is the rule; their food passes through them without benefiting them, and those who are unaware of the reason are surprised when so many good things fail to produce better results.

It will be seen that I am not dealing exhaustively with the subject; for there are a thousand secondary causes arising out of our habits, occupations, enthusiasms, and pleasures which aid and abet those I have just mentioned.

All of this I bequeath to the successor I planted at the beginning of this chapter, contenting myself with that prelibation which belongs by right to first comers in every sphere.

It is a long time since intemperance first claimed the attention of observers. Philosophers have praised temperance, princes have made sumptuary laws, religion has moralized over gourmandism; but alas, not a mouthful the less has been eaten as a result, and the art of overeating flourishes more and more every day.

Perhaps I shall meet with better luck if I follow a new course; I intend to expose the *physical disadvantages of obesity*; self-preservation will perhaps be a stronger force than morals, more persuasive than sermons, more powerful than laws; for the fair sex, I believe, is quite prepared to open its eyes to the light.

Disadvantages of Obesity

Obesity has an unfortunate effect on both sexes since it injures both strength and beauty.

It injures strength because, while increasing the weight of the mass to be moved, it does not increase the motive power; it is also harmful in that it obstructs breathing, and so makes any work impossible which demands the prolonged use of muscular energy.

Obesity injures beauty by destroying the originally established harmony of proportion; because all parts of the body do not fatten equally.

It also injures it by filling up the hollows which are Nature's shading; thus it is all too common to see faces which were once extremely attractive made almost plain by obesity.

The head of the late government did not escape the effects of this law. He grew extremely fat in the course of his last campaigns; his complexion turned from pale to ashen, and his eyes lost part of their proud fire.

Obesity brings with it a distaste for dancing, walking, and riding, and an inaptitude for every occupation or amusement requiring some degree of agility or skill.

It also opens the way for various diseases, such as apoplexy, dropsy, and ulcers of the legs, and makes all other ailments more difficult to cure.

Examples of Obesity

Of heroes who were corpulent, I can remember none but Marius and John Sobieski.

Marius, who was a short man, became as round as he was long, and it may have been his very enormity which terrified the Cimbrian charged with the duty of slaying him.

As for the King of Poland, his obesity came close to being the end of him; for, being forced to flee from a large body of Turkish cavalry, his breath soon failed him, and he would undoubtedly have been done to death if some of his aides-de-camp had not supported him, half unconscious, in his saddle, while others nobly sacrificed their lives to check the enemy.

If I am not mistaken, the Duc de Vendôme, that worthy son of the great Henri, was also a man of remarkable corpulence. He died at an inn forsaken by one and all, and retained enough consciousness to see the last of his servants snatch the cushion from under his head, just as he was giving up the ghost.

History provides many other instances of monstrous obesity; I shall pass over them, to speak a few words of those I have observed with my own eyes.

Monsieur Rameau, my schoolfellow as a boy and later Mayor of La Chaleur, in Burgundy, was only five feet two inches tall, and weighed five hundred pounds.

Monsieur le Duc de Luynes, beside whom I have often sat at table, became enormous; fat completely ruined his once elegant figure and he spent the last years of his life in a state of almost permanent somnolence.

But the most extraordinary example of this kind I ever saw was a citizen of New York, whom many Frenchmen still alive in Paris may have seen in the street called Broadway, sitting in a huge armchair the legs of which would have supported a church.

Edward was at least five feet ten inches tall, and as fat had blown him out in all directions, he was at least eight feet round. His fingers were like those of that Roman Emperor who used his wife's necklaces as rings; his arms and thighs were tubular, and as thick as an ordinary man's body; and he had feet like an elephant's, half hidden under the flesh of his legs; the weight of fat had drawn his lower eyelids down; but what made him hideous to behold was three spheroidal chins, which hung down for more than a foot over his chest, so that his face looked like the capital of a wreathed column.

In this condition Edward spent his life sitting at the window of a ground-floor room which looked out on to the street, every now and then drinking a glass of ale, a huge pitcher of which was always by his side.

Such an extraordinary figure could not fail to bring passers-by to a halt; but they were not allowed to linger, for Edward soon put them to flight, exclaiming in sepulchral tones: 'What are you staring at me for, like so many wild cats? ... Get along with you, you lazy body ... Be gone, you good for nothing dogs!' and other similar compliments.

I often used to greet him by name, and sometimes stopped for a chat; he assured me that he was neither bored nor unhappy, and that provided death did not disturb him, he would gladly await the end of the world in this fashion.

From what has been said in this chapter it is clear that if obesity is not a disease, it is at least an unfortunate indisposition, into which we nearly always fall through our own fault.

From Jean-Anthelme Brillat-Savarin, *The Physiology of Taste* (1825), translated by Anne Drayton.

Edible Nightmares

Vitellius' ruling vices were extravagance and cruelty. He banqueted three and often four times a day, namely morning, noon, afternoon, and evening – the last meal being mainly a drinking bout – and survived the ordeal well enough by taking frequent emetics. What made things worse was that he used to invite himself out to such meals at the houses of a number of different people on one and the same day; and these never cost his various hosts less than 4,000 gold pieces each. The most notorious feast of the series was given him by his brother on his entry into Rome; 2,000 magnificent fish and 7,000 game birds are said to have been served. Yet even this hardly compares in luxuriousness with a single tremendously large dish which Vitellius dedicated to the Goddess Minerva and named 'Shield of Minerva the Protectress of the City'. The recipe called for pike-livers, pheasant-brains, peacock-brains, flamingo-tongues, and lamprey-milt; and the ingredients, collected in every corner of the Empire right from the Parthian frontier to the Spanish Straits, were brought to Rome by naval captains and triremes. Vitellius paid no attention to time or decency in satisfying his remarkable appetite. While a sacrifice was in progress, he thought nothing of snatching lumps of meat or cake off the altar, almost out of the sacred fire, and bolting them down; and on his travels would devour cuts of meat fetched smoking hot from wayside cookshops, and even yesterday's half-eaten scraps.

From Suetonius (born c. 70 AD), *The Twelve Caesars*, translated by
Robert Graves (1957).

Feeding Time

His heart astir he pushed in the door of the Burton restaurant. Stink gripped his trembling breath: pungent meatjuice, slop of greens. See the animals feed.

Men, men, men.

Perched on high stools by the bar, hats shoved back, at the tables calling for more bread no charge, swilling, wolfing gobfuls of sloppy food. Their eyes bulging, wiping wetted moustaches. A pallid suetfaced young man polished his tumbler knife fork and spoon with his napkin. New set of microbes. A man with an infant's sauce-stained napkin tucked round him shovelled gurgling soup down his gullet. A man spitting back on his plate: halfmasticated gristle: no teeth to chewchewchew it. Chump chop from the grill. Bolting to get it over. Sad booser's eyes. Bitten off more than he can chew. Am I like that? See ourselves as others see us. Hungry man is an angry man. Working tooth and jaw. Don't! O! A bone! That last pagan king of Ireland Cormac in the schoolpoem choked himself at Sletty southward of the Boyne. Wonder what he was eating. Something galoptious. Saint Patrick converted him to Christianity. Couldn't swallow it all however.

– Roast beef and cabbage.

– One stew.

Smells of men. His gorge rose. Spaton sawdust, sweetish warmish cigarette smoke, reek of plug, spilt beer, men's beery piss, the stale of ferment.

Couldn't eat a morsel here. Fellow sharpening knife and fork, to eat all before him, old chap picking his tootles. Slight spasm, full, chewing the cud. Before and after. Grace after meals. Look on this picture then on that. Scoffing up stewgravy with sopping sippets of bread. Lick it off the plate, man! Get out of this.

He gazed round the stooled and tabled eaters, tightening the wings of his nose.

– Two stouts here.

– One corned and cabbage.

[280]

That fellow ramming a knifeful of cabbage down as if his life depended on it. Good stroke. Give me the fidgets to look. Safer to eat from his three hands. Tear it limb from limb. Second nature to him. Born with a silver knife in his mouth. That's witty, I think. Or no. Silver means born rich. Born with a knife. But then the allusion is lost.

An illgirt server gathered sticky clattering plates. Rock, the bailiff, standing at the bar blew the foamy crown from his tankard. Well up: it splashed yellow near his boot. A diner, knife and fork upright, elbows on table, ready for a second helping stared towards the foodlift across his stained square of newspaper. Other chap telling him something with his mouth full. Sympathetic listener. Table talk. I munched hum un thu Unchster Bunk un Munchday. Ha? Did you, faith?

Mr Bloom raised two fingers doubtfully to his lips. His eyes said.
— Not here. Don't see him.
Out. I hate dirty eaters.

He backed towards the door. Get a light snack in Davy Byrne's. Stopgap. Keep me going. Had a good breakfast.
— Roast and mashed here.
— Pint of stout.
Every fellow for his own, tooth and nail. Gulp. Grub. Gulp. Gobstuff.
He came out into clearer air and turned back towards Grafton street. Eat or be eaten. Kill! Kill!

From James Joyce, *Ulysses* (1922).

Breaking for Lunch

[Claudius] gave many splendid banquets, usually in large halls, and at times invited no fewer than 600 guests. One banquet was held close to the debouchment of the Fucine Lake on the day it was emptied; but the water came rushing out in a deluge and almost drowned him. His sons and daughters, like those of other distinguished figures, were always expected to dine with him, sitting in old-fashioned style at the ends of the couches on which their parents reclined. Once, when a guest was believed to have pocketed a golden bowl, Claudius invited him again the next evening, this time setting a small earthenware basin in front of him. Some say that he planned an edict to legitimize the breaking of wind at table, either silently or noisily – after hearing about a man who was so modest that he endangered his health by an attempt to restrain himself.

No matter what time it was or where Claudius happened to be, he always felt ready for food or drink. One day, while he was judging a case in Augustus' Forum, the delicious smell of cooking assailed his nostrils; it was being prepared for the priestly college of the Salii in the adjacent Temple of Mars. He descended from the Tribunal, closed the court, and went up to the place where the priests were, taking his place beside them. It was seldom that Claudius left a dining-hall except gorged and sodden; he would then go to bed and sleep supine with his mouth wide open – thus allowing a feather to be put down his throat, which would bring up the superfluous food and drink as vomit.

From Suetonius (born c. 70 AD), *The Twelve Caesars*, translated by
Robert Graves (1957).

Too Much

More than half of men and almost half of women are overweight, with nearly one in eight of the men and one in six women classified obese, according to government figures yesterday.

Almost 9 out of 10 adults have one or more of the main risk factors for heart disease, which could be reduced by changes in lifestyle.

A survey made in 1993 for the Office of Population Censuses and Surveys found 44 per cent of men and 32 per cent of women were overweight, and a further 13 per cent of men and 16 per cent of women obese. Only one in 10 adults was free from all four main modifiable risk factors of heart disease: smoking, raised blood pressure, raised cholesterol and lack of exercise.

The survey, based on interviews with 16,500 people, is the third in a series, monitoring progress towards the heart disease targets in the Government's Health of the Nation Initiative. It found that a quarter of men and women had been diagnosed as having a cardiovascular disorder or related condition, such as high blood pressure or diabetes, at some time. One in five either had high blood pressure or were taking drugs to control it.

Only one in three adults had a desirable cholesterol level (below 5.2 millimoles of cholesterol per litre of blood), while 6 per cent of men and 8 per cent of women had severely raised levels (7.8mmol/l or more).

Almost one in five adults had taken no moderate or vigorous exercise in the four weeks before interview.

Forty-two per cent of men, compared to 30 per cent of women, had been drunk in the past three months. A fifth of men and 14 per cent of women felt they should cut down their drinking.

Baroness Cumberlege, a junior health minister, said: 'If anyone needed more reasons to give up smoking on National No Smoking Day next Wednesday – March 8 – this survey will surely convince them.'

Chris Mihill, *Guardian* (2 March 1995).

The Jazz Diet

After work, [Duke] Ellington and Strayhorn are likely to go to some Negro all-night spot, if they are in Buffalo, Cleveland, Chicago, New Orleans, Pittsburgh, San Francisco, or some other big town which affords such a luxury. Duke, who is always worrying about keeping his weight down, may announce that he intends to have nothing but Shredded Wheat and black tea. When his order arrives, he looks at it glumly, then bows his head and says grace. After he has finished his snack, his expression of virtuous determination slowly dissolves into wistfulness as he watches Strayhorn eat a steak. Duke's resolution about not overeating frequently collapses at this point. When it does, he orders a steak, and after finishing it he engages in another moral struggle for about five minutes. Then he really begins to eat. He has another steak, smothered in onions, a double portion of fried potatoes, a salad, a bowl of sliced tomatoes, a giant lobster and melted butter, coffee, and an Ellington dessert – perhaps a combination of pie, cake, ice cream, custard, pastry, jello, fruit, and cheese. His appetite really whetted, he may order ham and eggs, a half-dozen pancakes, waffles and syrup, and some hot biscuits. Then, determined to get back on his diet, he will finish, as he began, with Shredded Wheat and black tea.

From *New Yorker* (1944).

A Growing Population

American adults may be more aware of the need to exercise and count calories than they once were, but more of them than ever are overweight.

The number of overweight adults, which had remained stable at about a fourth of the adult population from 1960 through 1980, suddenly jumped to a third of all adults between 1980 and 1991, according to a recent study by the National Center for Health Statistics in the Centers for Disease Control and Prevention.

For purposes of the study, obesity was defined as being 20 per cent or more above a person's desirable weight. That is about 25 pounds for an average 5-feet-4-inch woman and 30 pounds for an average 5-feet-10-inch man.

The increase in obesity rates continues despite a growing awareness that it has a negative effect on health and despite the continued growth of the diet industry, now estimated to have revenues of $40 billion to $50 billion a year.

The study's figures on children were not available last week, but several experts who had seen the data said that obesity among the nation's youth was increasing at an even faster rate than it was among adults.

Although the study confirms what experts have said they suspect, it is the first time the growth of the problem in the 80's has been measured.

The data on American weight patterns have been collected in several Government surveys that began in 1960. The studies are designed to determine the relationship between diet and health and help the Government run its food-assistance programs.

The latest study found that the groups with the highest proportion of overweight people were black non-Hispanic women, at 49.5 percent, and Mexican-American women, at 47.9 percent. Those levels represent increases of 12.2 percent and 15.7 percent, respectively, compared with the 1980 rates.

Although the percentage of white non-Hispanic women who were overweight was lower, 32.4 percent, obesity in that group increased at a much higher rate, 35.6 percent, from 1980 to 1991.

The study offers additional support to health and nutrition professionals who argue that a national campaign to reduce obesity is essential to contain health care costs.

Dr. Philip R. Lee, assistant secretary of health in the Department of Health and Human Services, said on Friday: 'The Government is not doing enough. It is not focused. We don't have a coherent across-the-board policy. We are in the process of developing one.'

On Tuesday, the *Journal of the American Medical Association* will publish an article based on the study's findings about adults. In an editorial that will accompany the article, Dr. F. Xavier Pi-Sunyer, director of the division of endocrinology, diabetes and nutrition at St. Luke's-Roosevelt Hospital Center and a professor of medicine at Columbia University, wrote: 'The proportion of the population that is obese is incredible. If this was about tuberculosis, it would be called an epidemic.'

Dr. Pi-Sunyer added: 'The problem with obesity is that once you have it, it is very difficult to treat. What you want to do is prevent it.'

Despite the relationship between obesity and chronic diseases of the heart and other organs, obesity is usually defined not as a disease, but as a condition that will yield to good old-fashioned willpower.

Neither the Federal Government, insurance companies nor the medical profession devote many resources to preventing obesity. But the food industry spends $36 billion a year on advertising designed to entice people to eat, the Agriculture Department says.

Federal expenditures for nutrition education are minuscule. For example, the Government allots states $50,000 each for nutrition education in schools. The annual advertising budget for Kellogg's Frosted Flakes is twice the budget for the National Cancer Institute's entire '5 a Day' program, which promotes the consumption of fruits and vegetables.

Obesity cost the nation an estimated $68.8 billion in 1990, according to a study by Dr. Graham A. Colditz, an associate professor of medicine at Harvard Medical School. His study which appeared in 1994 in *PharmacoEconomics*, an international journal devoted to evaluations of drug economics and quality, drew its estimates from the costs of medical problems that have been linked to obesity, including cancer, cardiovascular disease, adult-onset diabetes and gall-bladder disease.

Few insurance companies or health maintenance organizations will reimburse the cost of medical or nutritional counseling to help patients lose weight. The health care bills being considered by Congress either do not include preventive nutrition programs and reimbursement for nutrition counseling or make those services optional.

'There is no commitment to obesity as a public health problem,' said Dr. William Dietz, director of clinical nutrition at the New England Medical Center in Boston. 'We've ignored it and blamed it on gluttony and sloth.'

Experts agree that the root causes of obesity in this country – a sedentary life style and an abundance of food – are very difficult to change.

'It's what I call the 3,700-calorie-a-day problem,' said Dr. Marion Nestle, chairwoman of the Department of Nutrition at New York University and managing editor of the 1988 Surgeon General's Report on Nutrition and Health.

The Department of Agriculture reports that the American food supply produces 3,700 calories a day for every man, woman and child in this country. Women need only about half that number of calories, and men need about two-thirds of that. But people are constantly bombarded with advertisements that encourage them to eat far more than they need, Dr. Nestle said. 'Advertising budgets for food that no one needs are astronomical. Compared to what is spent on nutrition education, it's laughable.'

Health experts say the level of physical activity among Americans has decreased because of people watching television and riding in automobiles instead of walking and because of the disappearance of physical education classes from school programs.

'TV-watching figures are shocking,' said Michael Jacobson, executive director of the Center for Science in the Public Interest, a nutrition advocacy group in Washington. 'Adults watch between four and five hours a day; children watch three to four hours a day. Only 36 percent of elementary and secondary schools offer physical education classes.'

Dr. Dietz said television's contribution to obesity was compounded because watching television was often accompanied by eating food, especially snacks that are high in calories and fat. 'Just turn off the television and almost anything you do will be less sedentary,' Dr. Dietz said. 'And if you turn off the television, you are less likely to consume food.'

In the last few years, there has been a tendency to say that since diets do not work, people should give up dieting and that people should be allowed to attain their biologically natural weight. This attitude frustrates researchers in the field.

'We have got to stop saying that diets don't work, that obesity doesn't matter,' said Dr. George Blackburn, an associate professor at Harvard and director of the school's Center for Study of Nutrition and Medicine at Deaconess Hospital in Boston.

'There is an anti-dieting movement out there,' said Dr. Pi-Sunyer. 'But weight is not like body temperature; it keeps climbing. And there are so many mixed messages out there. People are confused.'

The experts agree that it will be difficult to change attitudes. Dr. Jacobson has suggested that a President's Council on Diet and Health be established, and Representative Edolphus Towns, Democrat of Brooklyn, will introduce such legislation on Tuesday.

Dr. Jacobson also said that states should require schools to provide daily physical education classes and that any health overhaul should include community-wide strategies to promote health. He suggested that the Clinton Administration sponsor an annual national 'No-TV Week,' encouraging children and adults to exercise instead of watching television.

'In order for the Public Health Service to address the problems, they have to do more than just educate,' Dr. Nestle said. 'They need to look at more structural changes: restrictions on children's television advertising, major campaigns in schools, some of the same incentives that have been used to get people to stop smoking.'

Marian Burros, *New York Times* (17 July 1994).

Advice for Boys

A good many illnesses come from over-eating or eating the wrong kind of food.

A scout must know how to take care of himself, else he is of no use. He must keep himself light and active. Once he has got the right kind of muscles on he can remain fit without further special exercising of those muscles, provided that he eats the right kind of food.

Eustace Miles, the tennis and racquet champion, does not go into training before he plays his matches; he knows he has got his muscles rightly formed, and he simply lives on plain, light food always, and so is always fit to play a hard game. He never eats meat.

In the siege of Mafeking, when we were put on short commons, those of the garrison who were accustomed to eat very little at their meals did not suffer like some people, who had been accustomed to do themselves well in peace time; these became weak and irritable. Our food there towards the end was limited to a hunk of pounded-up oats, about the size of a penny bun, which was our whole bread-supply for the day, and about a pound of meat and two pints of 'sowens,' a kind of stuff like bill-stickers' paste that had gone wrong.

English people as a rule eat more meat than is necessary, in fact, they could do without it altogether if they tried, and would be none the worse. It is an expensive luxury. The Japanese are as strong as us, but they do not eat any meat, and only eat small meals of other things.

The cheapest and best foods are dried peas, 2d. per lb.; flour, 1s. 4d. per stone; oatmeal, 2d. per lb.; potatoes, $\frac{1}{2}$d. per lb.; hominy, $1\frac{1}{2}$d. per lb.; cheese at 6d. per lb. Other good foods are fruit, vegetables, fish, eggs, nuts, rice, and milk, and one can live on these perfectly well without meat; bananas are especially good food, they are cheap, have no seeds nor pips to irritate your inside, their skin protects them from germs of disease, and their flesh is of a wholesome kind and satisfying.

The natives of the West Coast of Africa eat very little else all their lives, and they are fat and happy.

If you have lots of fresh air you do not want much food; if, on the other hand, you are sitting indoors all day, much food makes you fat and sleepy, so that in either case you are better for taking a little; still, growing boys should not starve themselves, but, at the same time, they need not be like that little hog at the school feast, who when asked, 'Can't you eat any more?' replied, 'Yes, I could *eat* more, but I've no room to *swallow* it.'

A great cause of illness nowadays is the amount of medicine which fellows dose themselves with when there is no reason for taking any medicine at all. The best medicine is open-air and exercise and a big cup of water in the early morning if you are constipated, and a pint of hot water on going to bed.

From Robert Baden-Powell, *Scouting For Boys*, revised edition (1909).

Advice for Girls

How to Grow Big

I am sure that every Brownie would like to make herself strong and healthy. But she can also do more than the Jap or the Ghoorka can do, for she can help herself not only to become strong but to grow big if she tries.

I will tell you some of the things which you can do to make yourself big and strong and healthy.

Good Blood and Plenty of It

The main thing is to keep the blood inside you strong and plentiful. The blood to your body is what steam is to the engine; it makes it go well or badly according to the strength of the steam. But also your blood is food to the body, like water to a plant, it makes it grow: if your body doesn't get enough it remains small and weak and often withers and dies.

You ask: how can I get *good* blood and *plenty* of it when it is all made for me inside me?

Wholesome Food

Well, it is made from the food you take in through your mouth, and to get plenty of it you must take in food that is good for making blood, not acid drops or sweeties, they are no good though they may taste nice, but good healthy meat and vegetables and bread are what make good, healthy blood.

Daily Clear Out

When you have taken in your food and have chewed it well and have swallowed it, it goes down into your stomach, and there the good parts of it go off into the blood, and the useless part of it passes out of you at the other end. If you let this useless part of it stay inside you too long – that is, for more than a day – it begins to poison your blood and so to undo the good of taking in good food.

So you should be very careful to get rid of the poisonous part of your food at least once a day regularly. That is the secret of keeping healthy and well.

From Robert Baden-Powell, *Girl Guiding: The Official Handbook* (1918).

A Doctor Writes

*Maestro Lorenzo Sassoli to Francesco di Marco Datini,
May–June 1404*

I will concede you fowls and partridges, pigeons, veal, mutton, and kid; and with each of these you can make use of the things that promote urination, such as parsley, capers, asparagus, and other things with which vinegar is mixed; for vinegar, in small quantities, encourages urination. The meats which displease me for you are goose, duck, young mutton and pork – especially fresh; and I not only disapprove of these meats, but bid you beware of pies of any meat whatsoever, and of every other dish that coarsens and clogs the blood – such as mixed herbs, fritters, and pastry.

As to the fruit to which you bear so sweet a love, I grant you almonds, both fresh and dried, as many as you like; and nuts, both fresh and dry and well cleaned ... and fresh and dried figs before a meal, and also grapes; but after a meal, beware of them. Take melons, in season, before a meal, and cast not away what is in them, for that is the best and most medicinal part. And I will grant you many cherries, well ripe, before a meal; but by God, after a meal let them be. And I beseech you, since I am so generous in conceding fruit to you according to your mind, be so courteous to me as to cast aside the others which are harmful, such as *baccelli*, apples, chestnuts, and pears.

It is, if you take thought, not only harmful for you but very shameful – at the age you have reached – not to have learned a little restraint. And do not excuse yourself saying, 'The things I want are cheap'; for the theologians and moral philosophers think it a greater

sin to be incontinent in vulgar matters ... Now consider if it is a fine
crown for old age, that a man should be called the slave of his greed!

From Iris Origo, *The Merchant of Prato* (1957).

Flesh and Blood

After all there's a lot in that vegetarian fine flavour of things from the
earth garlic, of course, it stinks Italian organgrinders crisp of onions,
mushrooms truffles. Pain to animal too. Pluck and draw fowl.
Wretched brutes there at the cattlemarket waiting for the poleaxe to
split their skulls open. Moo. Poor trembling calves. Meh. Staggering
bob. Bubble and squeak. Butchers' buckets wobble lights. Give us
that brisket off the hook. Plup. Rawhead and bloody bones. Flayed
glasseyed sheep hung from their haunches, sheepsnouts bloodypa-
pered snivelling nosejam on sawdust. Top and lashers going out.
Don't maul them pieces, young one.

From James Joyce, *Ulysses* (1922).

Dirt, Blood and Guts

The arguments in favour of vegetarianism are fourfold: æsthetic,
sentimental, evolutional and pragmatic.

(i.) 'Animal food is revolting.' Who, walking through a meat
market, has not often felt that? There you see hecatombs of
slaughtered bulls. Their carcases are exposed to the city air with its
dust and fogs and microbes, or to the coats of the passing populace.
The meat is the camping ground of flies, which are hatched in ordure
and repeatedly return thither, spreading filth and disease. When the
meat has to be moved it is man-handled by an artisan Hercules in
greasy overalls, and as the carcases are carried along their fat sides
rub against his curly hair. Underneath the foot is blood, and
throughout the air there permeates an odour, faint, but insistent and
nauseating, of raw meat and incipient corruption. Romantic?
Perhaps when seen in the half light of dawn from the hospital gates
across the way; but in the crude noon glare, nauseating and
repulsive.

(ii.) 'Meat eating is cruel and inhuman.' To sate his lust for flesh man snatches the calf from its mother and the lamb from his ewe; tortures and mutilates the store cattle; drags them miles by train and boat in cruel conditions of crowding; and butchers them in each other's sight in dens reeking of blood and entrails. Even were the life of an animal destined for food that of the hero of a Sunday school novel and his death a euthanasia, the effects on those who direct them, and on the handlers of the carcase, are degrading.

(iii.) 'Man by nature is a frugivorous animal.' According to the Darwinian hypothesis man is descended from monkeys; monkeys live on fruit; therefore man should live on fruit. So runs the syllogism of the vegetarian. Further man's teeth are not carnivorous in type, but herbivorous – or at any rate, frugivorous. He is departing from what Nature intended in killing and eating animals.

(iv.) 'Vegetarianism works.' Every now and then vegetarianism arranges an impressive display of the prowess of its devotees. They win endurance tests, climb mountains, swim torrents, and lift weights against the rest of the world, and for their small numbers produce a disproportionate effect.

Sometimes this display impresses even the sceptical researcher in nutrition. For instance, a boarding school in the West of England, which has a vegetarian house, finds that that house, though numerically and otherwise on a par with the other houses, takes a larger percentage than its share of both the intellectual and athletic prizes of the school. The physique and health of this house are better than those of the other houses. All this can hardly be the result of 'community spirit' – of the feeling that the boys of this house are a 'chosen people' and must do deeds of valour and daring upon the Philistines. The interest of such experiments is so great that they should be further extended and investigated by the Medical Research Council of Great Britain.

From V.H. Mottram, *Food and the Family* (1925).

Vegetarians Are Better People

That the use of animal food disposes man to cruel and ferocious actions is a fact to which the experience of ages gives ample testimony. The Scythians, from drinking the blood of their cattle, proceeded to drink that of their enemys. The fierce and cruel disposition of the wild Arabs is supposed, chiefly, if not, solely, to proceed from their feeding upon the flesh of camels: and, as the gentle disposition of the natives is probabley oweing, in a great degree, to temperance, and a total abstinence from animal food; so the common use of this diet, in the bulk of other nations, has, in the opinion of M. Pagés, exalted the natural tone of their passions; and he can account, he says, upon no other principle for the strong harsh features of the Musulmans and Christians, compare'd with the small trait and placid aspect of the Gentoos. 'Vulgar and uninform'd men,' it is observe'd by Smellie, 'when pamper'd with a variety of animal food, are much more cholerick, fierce and cruel in their tempers than those who live chiefly on vegetables.' This affection is equally perceptible in other animals: 'An officer, in the Russian service, had a bear, which he fed with bread and oats, but never gave him flesh. However, a young hog hapening, one day, to stroll too near his cel, he got hold of it, and pul'd it in; and, after he had once drawn blood, and tasted flesh, he grew so fierce that he became unmanageable, attacking every body that came near him; so that the owner was oblige'd to kil him.' It was not, says Porphyry, from those who live'd on vegetables, that robers or murderers, sycophants, or tyrants, have proceeded, but from flesh-eaters. Prey being allmost the sole object of quarrel among carnivorous animals, while the frugivorous live together in constant peace and harmony, it is evident that, if men were of this last kind, they would find it much more easey to subsist in a state of nature, and have much less occasion to leave it.

The barbarous and unfeeling sports (as they are call'd) of the Engleish, their horse-raceing, hunting, shooting, bul and bear-baiting, cock-fighting, boxing-matches, and the like, all proceed from their immoderate addiction to animal food. Their natural temper is thereby corrupted, and they are in the habitual and hourly commission of crimes against nature, justice, and humanity, at which a feeling and reflective mind, unaccustom'd to such a diet, would revolt; but in which they profess to take delight. The kings of Engleland have from a remote period been devoted to hunting; in which pursuit one of them, and the son of another, lost his life. 'James the first,' according to Scaliger, 'was merciful, except at the chace, where he was cruel, was very angery when he could not catch the stag: God, he say'd, is enrage'd against me, so it is that i shall have him: when he had him, he would put his arm all entire into the belly and entrails of the beast.' This anecdote may be parallel'd with the following, of one of his successours: 'The hunt on Tuesday last' (as stated in *The General Advertiser*, March 4, 1784) 'commence'd near Salthil, and afforded a chace of upward of fifty miles. His majesty was present at the death of the chace near Tring, in Hertfordshire. It is the first deer that has been run to death for many months; and, when open'd, its heart-firings were found to be quite rent, as is suppose'd, with the force of running:' *Siste vero, tandem, carnifex!* The slave-trade, that abominable violation of the rights of nature, is, most probablely, oweing to the same cause; as wel as a variety of violent acts, both national and personal, which are usually attributed to other motives.

From Joseph Ritson, *An Essay on Abstinence from Animal Food as a Moral Duty* (1802).

Animal Crackers

Hearing of their son's collapse, the parents hurried to the hospital. It was a shock for me to realise that their son represented not the first but the second generation of the nose-ringed.

'Duane's always been difficult,' said his mother, a woman who had remained slender on a diet of nicotine.

I should perhaps mention *en passant* that the names Dean, Duane, Lee and Jason provide strong evidence in favour of the doctrine of predestination.

'He can really only communicate with animals,' said his father.

'Yes,' affirmed his mother. 'He's got a seventeen-foot python in his room. Whenever Duane's angry he wants to smash the walls with his fists. You can't do nothing with him, but when he goes into his room and wraps that snake round him, all the anger drains out of him in a second.'

'Is he violent in general?' I asked.

'No, only when he thinks people are being cruel to animals. He's a vegetarian. He can't stand meat.'

'Do you think Duane'll be all right, doctor?' asked his father.

'Oh yes,' I replied.

'Thank you, doctor.'

His parents got up to go. As they reached the door, I asked, 'By the way, what does Duane's python eat?'

'Chickens and rabbits. They have to be live: it won't eat no dead food.'

From Theodore Dalrymple, 'If Symptoms Persist', *Spectator* (25 February 1995).

A Fighting Diet

'Why are you a vegetarian?' I began.

'Oh, come, Mr Blathwayt! That boot is on the other leg. Why should you call me to account for eating decently? If I battened on the scorched corpses of animals, you might well ask me why I did that. Why should I be filthy and inhuman? Why should I be an accomplice in the wholesale horror and degradation of the slaughterhouse? I am a vegetarian, as Hamlet puts it, "after my own honour and dignity". My practice justifies itself. I have no further reasons to give for it.'

'Why is a vegetarian necessarily, apparently, everything else that he shouldn't be?'

'*Is* he?'

'Well, then, is vegetarianism a good thing to fight on, either in the Sudan or Trafalgar Square?'

'You have put your finger on the weak spot in vegetarianism. I regret to say that it is a fighting diet. Ninety-nine per cent of the world's fighting has been done on farinaceous food. In Trafalgar Square I found it impossible to run away as fast as the meat-eaters did. Panic is a carnivorous speciality. If the army were fed on a hardy, healthy, fleshless diet, we should hear no more of the disgust of our coloured troops, and of the Afridis and Fuzzywuzzies at the cowardice of Tommy Atkins. I am myself congenitally timid, but as a vegetarian I can generally conceal my tremors; whereas in my unregenerate days, when I ate my fellow-creatures, I was as patent a coward as Peter the Great. The recent spread of fire-eating fiction and Jingo war worship – a sort of thing that only interests the pusillanimous – is due to the spread of meat-eating. Compare the Tipperary peasant of the potatoes-and-buttermilk days with the modern gentleman who gorges himself with murdered cow. The Tipperary man never read bloody-minded novels or cheered patriotic music-hall tableaux; but he fought recklessly and wantonly. Your carnivorous gentleman is afraid of everything – including doctors, dogs, disease, death and truth-telling; there is no wickedness or cruelty too dastardly for him to champion if only it ends in some dirty piece of witchcraft that promises him immunity from the consequences of his own nasty habits. Don't, in the name of common-sense, talk of courage in connection with the slaughter-house.'

'Let me put you a more personal question. When did you become a vegetarian, and what on earth led you to it?'

'In 1880 or thereabouts. My attention had been called to the enormity of my old habits by the works of Shelley – I am a thorough Shelleyan – but in the seventies the practical difficulties of vegetarian-ism were very great, as the vegetarian restaurant had not then become an institution. A lecture by a journalistic colleague of mine, named Lester, since deceased, brought me to the point. During the last seventeen years I have made half-a-dozen separate reputations; and there is not an ounce of corpse in any of them.'

'There is the question of butchers. How would you compensate them for their calling? What would you do with them?'

'Set them up in business as greengrocers and cornchandlers.'

'Has vegetarianism any real *raison d'être* for the present, or hope for the future?'

'Vegetarianism needs no *raison d'être* any more than life itself does. A hundred years hence a cultivated man will no more dream of eating flesh or smoking than he now does of living, as Pepys' contemporaries did, in a house with a cesspool under it. But I do not believe that vegetarianism, as I practise it, is a final solution of the diet question. Man will end by making his food with more care than he makes anything else. Stock-breeding is an advance on the hunter's promiscuous catching and killing. Gardening and agriculture are advances on stock-breeding; but they still mean taking what you find and making the best of it. The human race has not been a very great success on that system. I do not know what the food of the future will be; but it will not be the food of the pigeon, the elephant or the tiger.'

'Another personal question. How do vegetarianism and dramatic criticism blend?'

'A glance at the columns of the *Saturday Review* will enable you to answer that question for yourself without violence to my modesty. The carnivorous output in criticism is very considerable. Just compare the two. Meat-fed criticism is the best for the managers. The vegetarian article is best for the public.'

From 'What Vegetarianism Really Means: A Talk with Mr Bernard Shaw',
The Vegetarian (15 January 1898).

Nutritional Foods, Past and Present

Salisbury Steak

Dr. James H. Salisbury, in *The Relation of Alimentation and Disease* (1888), proclaimed the discovery that bodily disorders of all sorts are largely caused by starchy foods. And why should bread and vegetables be bad for us? Because 'By structure, man is about two-thirds carnivorous and one-third herbivorous.' According to Salisbury, most of our teeth are 'meat teeth,' and our stomach is designed to digest lean meat; only the small intestine works on plant foods. It follows, then, that 'healthy alimentation would consist in a diet of about one part of vegetables, fats, and fruits, to about two parts of lean meat.' The trouble with even this amount of starch is that, since our digestive enzymes work only gradually on it, it 'ferments' in the stomach and intestine to produce acid, vinegar, alcohol, and yeast: all substances which poison and paralyze the tissues and can cause heart disease, tumors, mental derangement, and especially tuberculosis. Salisbury's cure for all these ills, naturally, is a diet low in starch and high in lean meat, together with lots of hot water to rinse out the products of fermentation. Here is his prescription, or recipe.

Eat the muscle pulp of lean beef made into cakes and broiled. This pulp should be as free as possible from connective or glue tissue, fat and cartilage ... The pulp should not be pressed too firmly together before broiling, or it will taste livery. Simply press it sufficiently to hold it together. Make the cakes from half an inch to an inch thick. Broil slowly and moderately well over a fire free from blaze and smoke. When cooked, put it on a hot plate and season to taste with butter, pepper, and salt; also use either Worcestershire or Halford sauce, mustard, horseradish, or lemon juice on the meat if desired.

So is born the Salisbury Steak, which in its contemporary manifestations often seems to be more glue tissue than muscle pulp.

Kellogg against Meat

Forty years later, one of the pioneers in breakfast cereals, Dr. John Harvey Kellogg, remarked that '"Salisbury steaks" are now seldom seen or heard of': a fact for which Kellogg himself was partly responsible, he being a strong advocate of the vegetarian diet. He did share with Salisbury the belief, first made popular by Sylvester Graham, that diet was the determining factor in health, and said, 'dyspepsia is unquestionably the foundation of the greater share of all chronic maladies,' among which he included rheumatism, gout, tuberculosis, typhoid fever, 'organic diseases of the spine and brain, and even insanity ...' This is how he put the argument for vegetarianism in *The New Dietetics: A Guide to Scientific Feeding in Health and Disease* (3rd edition, 1927).

> Flesh foods are not the best nourishment for human beings and were not the foods of our primitive ancestors. They are secondary or second-hand products, since all foods comes originally from the vegetable kingdom, being the product of the magic of the chlorophyll grain. There is nothing necessary or desirable for human nutrition to be found in meats or flesh foods which is not found in and derived from vegetable products.

Meats are especially unappealing because they necessarily contain the waste products of the animal's last muscular activity, so that 'in the words of Professor Halliburton, the English Chemist, "beef tea bouillon is simply an ox's urine in a tea cup."' And muscle tissue itself, once inside the human intestine, encourages the growth of 'putrefactive and other poison-forming bacteria' which can cause 'auto-intoxication,' or self-poisoning. The remedy, once more, is obvious: change your diet, this time by eliminating all meat.

Hay's Menus: Don't Mix

Striking a balance between Salisbury and Kellogg was Dr. William Howard Hay, who wrote an influential book called *Health Via Food* (1929). Hay thought, with Salisbury, that the fermentation of undigested starch caused poisoning from within, but agreed with Kellogg that meat is not a desirable food. As he put it, 'ideal health cannot be attained with any other line of foods than those outlined by God to Adam and Eve in the Garden of Eden.' Hay's gimmick was to assert that the digestion of starch 'requires alkaline conditions throughout the digestive tract' – an unwarranted extrapolation from the fact that human saliva, which contains a starch-digesting enzyme, is alkaline – and that 'acid at any stage [of starch digestion] will permanently arrest this ...' The arrest of digestion means the onset of fermentation, with disease not far behind. The solution to this dilemma is to avoid acid fruits, and acid-producing meats, in any meal that includes starchy foods: in other words, 'scientific' menu planning.

> All of the foregoing is the result of 24 years of experience in the application to every sort of disease condition of the simple plan of treatment founded on the right selection and combination of foods, wholly without remedies of any kind whatever, the entire object being to arrest the formation of acids of adventitious character in the body ...

Don't eat starchy foods with anything else, and you'll have no need for medicine of any kind. The last two chapter titles in Hay's book indicate the drift of his appeal: 'Everyone His Own Physician' and 'A Medical Millennium.' Hay's theory was quite popular for a while, and several menu books were put out by his disciples.

The Common Fallacies

Notice what the theories of Salisbury, Kellogg, and Hay have in common, aside from being wrong – even laughably so. First, each claims that most chronic diseases are caused by a diet that is faulty in one way or another. Second, each finds its justification in a religious or quasi-rational view of man's 'natural' or proper diet. Hey refers to the biblical Eden, Kellogg to a 'scientific' version of Eden, our primate ancestors, and Salisbury to the numerology of teeth and digestive organs. Finally, the key to health each claims to have found turns out to be a very simple one, a single aspect of diet. A contemporary observer, Alexander Bryce, described this tactic as 'the elevation of some minor detail of eating and drinking into a cult.' Avoid starch, says Salisbury; avoid meat, says Kellogg; avoid mixing starch and meat, says Hay. A simple rationale, a simple prescription, and the promise of a disease-free life: verily a Medical Millennium.

The fallacies of this kind of thinking are fairly obvious. First, while it is true that malnutrition can cause various diseases, it is by no means true that all, or even most diseases are caused by malnutrition. In fact, many necessary nutrients can be harmful when eaten in excessive amounts. Second, the appeal to the distant past for an indication of our 'natural' diet presupposes that at some point the human body and human diet were in perfect coordination, and that over time we have deviated from this ideal state. As the three examples indicate, the choice of this point is more a matter of individual taste than of reasoned argument. And the very notion of such a point is an idealization. Human evolution, like all evolution, is a process of continual adaptation to a continually changing environment, more like compromise than a series of outright victories over circumstance. Third, common sense should tell us that the existence of a panacea – a single substance which will prevent or cure all major disease – is highly unlikely. Both history, which records many claims but no confirmation of any, and our steadily improving knowledge of how the human body works – that is, in an extremely complicated way – are our best guides on this point. Proper nutrition is a matter of the inclusion and balance of many different substances, some of which, notably the vitamins, these early faddists were ignorant of. And no doubt we remain ignorant of some.

So we have come a long way since these Dark and Amusing Ages? Not really.

From Harold McGee, *On Food and Cooking: The Science and Lore of the Kitchen* (1984).

Fletcherism

One of the saner food fads is 'Fletcherism.' This consists in chewing one's food so many times that before it is swallowed it has lost all flavour. The originator and protagonist of the cult maintained that he needed much less food than the normal man because he chewed his food so thoroughly instead of bolting it in a semi-masticated state. Doubtless he pointed to the chewers of history, of whom Gladstone was the most famous. He masticated every mouthful thirty-two times and maintained a physique which enabled him to lead an extremely active and wearing public life and live to the advanced age of eighty-eight. Bolted food is certainly a cause of indigestion, and if such indigestion is serious, undoubtedly less is obtained from the food. As will be shown later, there is a chain of digestive secretions in the alimentary tract, each secretion depending on the preceding link in the chain. To start the chain of reflex secretions a thorough chewing of the food, if not essential, is advisable. Especially is this true of starchy and uncooked vegetable foods (salads, etc.). Fletcherism obtains, then, a mild support from the physiologists and a more strong support from dentists, who believe in the use of crisp food, such as toast, apples and lettuce for their power of cleaning the teeth and in the need of thorough mastication of all foods.

The devotees of Fletcherism, however, carried their claims to extraordinary lengths. Like most people conscious of possessing some of the world's stock of truth, they exalted it above all others. When accurate experiments were made to test its chief claim – that very thorough chewing enabled the experimenters to obtain much more nutriment from their food than the average man – and the experiments threw very grave doubt on this claim, they impudently impugned the doctrine of the conservation of energy. This doctrine is a fundamental doctrine of science, and if it be false all science is false. Consequently, no scientist can accept their claims. Moreover, the protagonist refused to include in his dietary tables the bag of chocolates from which he refreshed himself from time to time throughout the day!

From V.H. Mottram, *Food and the Family* (1925).

Easy Reducing Diets

I had intended this book to be fun, showing how really good food can be prepared in the modern healthful manner. But every day I am besieged by fat ladies and gentlemen who have all sorts of mistaken ideas about reducing – subconsciously they hate to give up their 'smashed potato' diets. So I have decided to give you here a week of menus which will help to build you down, my Seven-Day Painless Reducing Diet. Also, for those who do not need such strenuous reducing, my Be More Beautiful Diet, a one-day house-cleaning regimen.

These menus can be followed with little or no hardship, and you will be amazed at the way the fat rolls off. Follow these menus until you are your own slim self again. Or you can make up your own menus by remembering to have two or three first-class protein foods every day. Proteins have a dynamic action which helps to burn up unneeded calories; and at the same time they keep the skin and muscles firm. This is a principle which must never be overlooked in any reducing diet. Don't use any such extras as gravies, mayonnaise, sugar, and so forth. They are the foods which prevent you from losing weight. Use the reducing dressings on your salads. I find the Vegetable Reducing Dressing most delicious, also the Yogurt Dressing. Mineral-oil dressing, it has been proved, is definitely harmful. Smart people no longer use cream and sugar in their coffee. Try your coffee black for a week and you will never go back to the fattening cream and sugar. But if black coffee doesn't appeal to you, try *café au lait*, which is half coffee and half hot milk, but with no topping of cream.

Here, then, are the menus, in which I have used those foods which are plentiful and easy to get. In just seven days you can be slimmer and trimmer, so get going and good luck. Before you begin, and as you progress, check your weight by the tables on page 297.

My Seven-Day Painless Reducing Diet

Monday

Breakfast
¹/₂ grapefruit
Black coffee

Mid-morning:
Glass of buttermilk, yogurt, tomato juice, or hot broth

Luncheon:
2 hard-cooked eggs
Chopped carrot salad
Beverage

Mid-afternoon:
1 cup tea with lemon, or 1 glass lemonade, or 1 cup clear broth

Dinner:
1 cup clear broth
2 slices lean lamb or beef
Combination salad of cucumbers, tomatoes, and celery

Black after-dinner coffee

Before retiring:
 This is a good time to take your vitamins or 1 tablespoon brewers'
yeast in 1 glass fruit juice, vegetable juice, or yogurt.

Tuesday

Breakfast:
 1 sliced orange
 Black coffee

Mid-morning:
 1 glass buttermilk, yogurt, or tomato juice, or 1 cup hot broth

Luncheon:
 1 large hamburger with lots of chopped parsley and onion
 $^1/_2$ head lettuce sprinkled with lemon juice and vegetable salt
 Beverage

Mid-afternoon:
 1 cup tea with lemon, or 1 glass lemonade, or 1 cup clear broth

Dinner:
 Carrot and celery sticks
 Large slice of lean roast beef
 $^1/_2$ cup spinach
 $^1/_2$ grilled grapefruit
 Black after-dinner coffee

Before retiring:
 This is a good time to take your vitamins or 1 tablespoon brewers'
yeast in 1 glass fruit juice, vegetable juice, or yogurt.

Wednesday

Breakfast:
 Baked apple or apple sauce
 Black coffee

Mid-morning:
 1 glass buttermilk, yogurt, or tomato juice, or 1 cup hot broth

Luncheon:

2 eggs à la mode (2 boiled or poached eggs topped with $^1/_2$ cup stewed tomatoes)
Chopped carrot and apple salad
Beverage

Mid-afternoon:
1 cup tea with lemon, or 1 glass lemonade, or 1 cup clear broth

Dinner:
Fruit salad
2 grilled lean lamb chops
$^1/_2$ cup green beans sprinkled with parsley
Black after-dinner coffee

Before retiring:
This is a good time to take your vitamins or 1 tablespoon brewers' yeast in 1 glass fruit juice, vegetable juice, or yogurt.

Thursday

Breakfast:
$^1/_2$ grapefruit
Black coffee

Mid-morning:
1 glass buttermilk, yogurt, or tomato juice, or 1 cup hot broth

Luncheon:
2 slices grilled liver
Chopped cabbage and green-pepper salad
Beverage

Mid-afternoon:
1 cup tea with lemon, or 1 glass lemonade, or 1 cup clear broth

Dinner:
Vegetable juice cocktail
1 large veal chop
Fresh celery
Apple sauce
Black after-dinner coffee

Before retiring:
This is a good time to take your vitamins or 1 tablespoon brewers' yeast in 1 glass fruit juice, vegetable juice, or yogurt.

Friday

Breakfast:
  Fruit or tomato juice
  Black coffee

Mid-morning
  1 glass buttermilk, yogurt, or tomato juice, or 1 cup hot broth

Luncheon:
  Eggs à la mode (two poached eggs covered with ¹/₂ cup chopped spinach)
  Celery and carrot sticks
  Beverage

Mid-afternoon:
  1 cup tea with lemon, or 1 glass lemonade, or 1 cup clear broth

Dinner:
  1 cup Hauser Broth
  1 large slice grilled fish (sole, whitefish, or halibut)
  ¹/₂ cup stewed tomatoes and celery
  ¹/₂ grapefruit, fresh or broiled
  Black after-dinner coffee

Before retiring:
  This is a good time to take your vitamins or 1 tablespoon brewers' yeast in 1 glass fruit juice, vegetable juice, or yogurt.

Saturday

Breakfast:
  Sliced orange
  Black coffee

Mid-morning:
  1 glass buttermilk, yogurt, or tomato juice, or 1 cup hot broth

Luncheon:
  3 tablespoons cottage cheese mixed with chives or onions on a bed of lettuce
  Raw celery and carrots
  Beverage

Mid-afternoon:
   1 cup tea with lemon, or 1 glass lemonade, or a cup clear broth

Dinner:
   Grilled grapefruit
   2 slices roast lamb
   $^1/_2$ cup spinach, string beans, or broccoli
   Baked apple
   Black after-dinner coffee

Before retiring:
   This is a good time to take your vitamins or 1 tablespoon brewers'
yeast in a glass of fruit juice, vegetable juice, or yogurt.

Sunday

Breakfast:
   2 scrambled eggs
   1 slice whole-wheat toast
   Tea or black coffee

Mid-morning:
   1 glass buttermilk, yogurt, or tomato juice, or 1 cup hot broth

Luncheon:
   Large salad bowl (chopped lettuce, celery, watercress) mixed with
$^1/_2$ cup cold meat or chicken
   Baked apple or apple sauce
   Beverage

Mid-afternoon:
   1 cup tea with lemon, or 1 glass lemonade, or 1 cup clear broth

Dinner:
   1 cup broth
   $^1/_2$ grilled chicken
   $^1/_2$ cup cauliflower
   4 stewed apricots
   Black after-dinner coffee

Before retiring:
   This is a good time to take your vitamins or 1 tablespoon brewers'
yeast in 1 glass fruit juice, vegetable juice, or yogurt.

From Gaylord Hauser, *The Gaylord Hauser Cook Book* (1955).

Luncheon for the Girls

Or Wait Till You Taste Maybelle's Peanut Butter Aspic

Few things are so pleasant as a Ladies' Luncheon, when the ladies meet in some neutral corner like the Carioca Room at the Sherry-Hinterland, or at Harry's Bar and Grill.

There they may relax and swap knitting patterns, serene in the knowledge that they needn't eat anything moulded unless they order it. There, too, a lady can have an honest Scotch-and-soda instead of a medium sherry with no fear of being stripped of her Brownie badge: and not one lady needs to jump up to change plates and miss hearing what Harriet said when Charlotte told her what Thelma said when she saw that awful Henderson woman at the cinema with that boy who used to go around with Eloise's neighbour's niece.

Furthermore, someone else is left to get the lipstick off the napkins.

However, as to the Ladies' Luncheon at home, about the best thing that can be said for it is that – like the whooping crane – it is definitely on the downward path to extinction. More and more ladies are discovering that with only a little fast footwork they can turn a luncheon into a Morning Coffee (with a lot of good little pastries) or an Afternoon Tea (sandwiches and rich cakes) or a Cocktail Affair (see Chapter 8) – any one of which is a lot easier. And when you hate to cook, your agility in this respect is truly remarkable. It is only once in a long long month of Sundays that the woman who hates to cook finds herself stuck with a Luncheon for the Girls.

This, accordingly, is a brief chapter. It consists of six luncheon menus: 1. The Soup-Sandwich; 2. The Soup-Salad; 3. The Salad-Sandwich; and if you are so unlucky as to find yourself on the Patty-Shell Circuit, 4, 5, 6. The Hot Main Dish.

In each menu, only one thing takes any doing. Also, each menu, in its entirety, can be made in advance, which enables you to be with your friends in the living room until a minute or so before you eat. After all, if they're your best friends, you want to be with them; and if they're your second-best friends, you don't dare not.

First, a general word about DESSERT

It is wise to keep in mind that in any group of two or more women, at least one is on a diet, and several others think they ought to be. If you serve them a rich dessert which you spent considerable time making, they will probably eat it, but they will be annoyed with you. If they do *not* eat it, you will be annoyed with them. And, on the other hand, the nondiet-minded ladies will look at you squint-eyed if they have dutifully ploughed through the main part of the luncheon only to find that there's no dessert at all.

This poses a pretty little problem, which is best solved by a fruit dessert (see Menu No. 1, below) *plus* a plateful of shop-bought petit-fours (or other rich little cakes), or a dish of good chocolates, or a bowl of nuts and raisins, or all three, hereinafter known as Oddments.

Everyone can eat the fruit dessert, you see, and you, as hostess, will not be offended if they pass up the rich goodies. After all, you spent no time making them, and, also, there will be more left for you and the family to enjoy when the ladies finally go home.

Remember, too: if your luncheon is reasonably substantial or contains a good deal of fruit anyway, you can even skip the fruit dessert and just bring out the Oddments.

And so to Menu No. 1.

Luncheon Menu No. 1: Soup-Sandwich

Cheese-Chicken Soup
Chicken, Ham or Beef Sandwiches
(or all three)
Honeydew Melon
Oddments
Coffee

Cheese-Chicken Soup

for 6

2 *tins condensed cream of chicken soup*
1½ *small jars tasty processed cheese spread*
parsley

Blend a tin of water with the soup, in the top of the double saucepan. Then stir in the cheese spread, and keep stirring until it's all smooth and hot. You can keep this waiting as long as you like, over hot water. Parsley it with a lavish hand before you serve it.

Luncheon Menu No. 2: Soup-Salad

India Chicken Soup
with slivered almonds
Fresh Fruit Salad
with Chutney Cream Dressing (p. 48)
Hot Rolls
Oddments
Coffee

India Chicken Soup

for 4

1 teaspoon curry powder
1 tin condensed cream of chicken soup
1 chicken-bouillon cube dissolved in ²/₃ tin hot water
1 tin cream

First mix the curry powder with the soup, using the top of the double saucepan. Then add and blend everything else, heat it through, and when you serve it, sprinkle slivered toasted almonds on top.

From Peg Brachen, *The I Hate to Cook Book* (1961)

A New Woman

All my adult life I had adored foods which were high in fat. In fact I had never even imagined life without fat so it was something of a challenge to create a very low-fat diet for myself, first of all, and then for my slimmers – a diet which at the same time as being very low in fat included all the necessary nutrients.

Butter, margarine and oil are obviously high in fat – in fact they are 80–100% fat. Foods like eggs, avocado pears and peanuts are not so easily recognizable. But first let's get everything into understandable perspective.

In the last chapter I said that the average consumption of fat in the Western world is about 130 grams (over 4¹/₂ oz) a day. So, 130 grams of fat is equal to almost 5 oz of butter. 'But I don't eat anywhere *near* that amount of fat in a day,' I hear you say, and of course in the form of butter or pure fat, no doubt you don't. You probably eat only 1 oz (28 g) or even half that! So how do we eat the rest of our daily intake of fat? Of course it's the cheese, milk, eggs, meat, fried foods, cakes, pastries, pies, nuts, cream, ice cream, mayonnaise, sauces ... the list is endless. What foods are left, then, which contain no fat or at least very little? At first it is difficult to think of anything except apples and oranges!

I prepared a diet as free from fat as possible yet incorporating protein, carbohydrate, vitamins and minerals. In formulating the diet I paid particular attention to moisture, realizing that, after all, the inclusion of fat in our daily diet added considerably to its palatability.

I also tried to incorporate a strong element of freedom so that a long-term eating habit could be created. I didn't want anyone to feel that this diet was a 'prison sentence' to be endured for a few weeks or months before old habits could be reintroduced. No, this was a new healthy way of eating that was going to change previous diet failures into long-term success stories. It could also help towards healthier generations in the future. After all, the way we feed our children has a great bearing on how they will eat in later life and in turn, how *they* will feed *their* families in years to come.

I first gave the diet to some of the members at my classes. Not only did they enjoy it but it certainly worked extremely well for those that followed it properly. However, as they had mostly lost significant amounts of weight already and it hadn't occurred to me to ask them to measure their weekly progress in terms of inches (cm), the results, whilst remarkable, were only visual. I still needed evidence in black and white that the inches (cm) really *did* disappear from areas previously impossible to reduce – namely the hips and thighs.

As a regular broadcaster on local radio I went along to Radio Nottingham for one of my phone-ins on slimming. It seemed like a good idea to ask for 'guinea pigs' to test the diet. They were asked to monitor their progress not only with scales but with a tape measure. One hundred ladies kindly volunteered and eight weeks later I asked them to complete a lengthy questionnaire. I received twenty completed record sheets – and a load of very apologetic letters explaining why the remainder had been unable to do justice to the trial. Reasons from holidays, family and work problems, moving house, and so on were given. Nevertheless, the twenty who *did* reply offered most interesting statistics, observations and confirmation of the effectiveness of the diet.

At this stage I felt I had actually discovered something more than just another diet. On the questionnaires there were comments such as: 'It was a very nice diet, the first that has actually worked for me all over my body! I have more confidence and feel good in clothes again. Thank you.' And, 'the "Bum and Thigh" diet *does* work! I shall certainly be interested in carrying on with it as part of my natural diet now. Thank you.' Another said, 'I have been thoroughly happy with this diet, though I must admit I do enjoy bread, fruit and salads in the normal way of things. There was very little inconvenience in leaving out the butter and salad cream, and I have enjoyed the diet even more whilst watching the inches disappear, and enjoying being complimented on how much slimmer I look. Oh, and how lovely to be able to open the wardrobe doors and say "I haven't got anything to wear – they are all *too big*." Absolute Heaven! Very many thanks.'

I was beginning to realize that this diet could in fact be a breakthrough for all those who were still left with the typical 'pear' shape, even after losing weight successfully. However, I felt we still needed more trials so that I could prove without doubt that my inch (cm) loss theory worked.

I was holding a slimming exhibition at the beginning of September at the Holiday Inn, Leicester, and wanted as much publicity as possible to attract visitors. I rang my friends at Radio Leicester and Peter Crankshaw, the producer of the phone-in programme *Cross Talk* said 'Yes' to my suggestion that I mention my exhibition. I also told him about the new hip and thigh diet and said I could do with some more volunteers to try it out. This all seemed ideal from everyone's point of view so the following week I went along.

The programme was being broadcast from Radio Leicester's shop in Leicester's Haymarket shopping precinct. Morgan Cross, the presenter, and I chatted about my new diet and the telephone lines immediately came alive. I discussed the format of the diet with various callers and then one of my members came in to the shop. Di Driver had been coming to my classes for some time and she knew I was appearing on the programme but I had no idea that she planned on paying me a visit 'on air'. In fact I was quite embarrassed by her arrival as I was aware that listeners might think I had invited her. I honestly hadn't. Her visit was spontaneous, she said, and her testimony on air really said it all. She had lost 3 st (19 kg) in four months and had extremely slim hips and thighs to prove it. You would never have believed that she had ever had a problem in that area. Well, volunteers for the diet seemed to be coming out of the woodwork! People were coming over to us out of the shops, pleading to be included in my trials. The phones just didn't stop ringing. We gave my home address on air so that volunteers could send me a stamped, self-addressed envelope so that I could forward them a diet sheet. It was just as well I did request an s.a.e. as over the next ten days I received over five hundred requests!

My husband Mike and I spent the whole of the following week opening mail, printing diet sheets and letters of instruction and stuffing envelopes. The names and addresses of every volunteer had to be entered on to our computer. Our village Post Office had never seen so much activity!

From *Rosemary Conley's Hip and Thigh Diet* (revised edition, 1993).

The Abominations of Leviticus

And the LORD spake unto Moses and to Aaron, saying unto them,

2 Speak unto the children of Israel, saying, These are the beasts which ye shall eat among all the beasts that are on the earth.

3 Whatsoever parteth the hoof, and is clovenfooted, and cheweth the cud, among the beasts, that shall ye eat.

4 Nevertheless these shall ye not eat of them that chew the cud, or of them that divide the hoof: as the camel, because he cheweth the cud, but divideth not the hoof; he is unclean unto you.

5 And the coney, because he cheweth the cud, but divideth not the hoof; he is unclean unto you.

6 And the hare, because he cheweth the cud, but divideth not the hoof; he is unclean unto you.

7 And the swine, though he divide the hoof, and be clovenfooted, yet he cheweth not the cud; he is unclean to you.

8 Of their flesh shall ye not eat, and their carcase shall ye not touch; they are unclean to you.

9 These shall ye eat of all that are in the waters: whatsoever hath fins and scales in the waters, in the seas, and in the rivers, them shall ye eat.

10 And all that have not fins and scales in the seas, and in the rivers, of all that move in the waters, and of any living thing which is in the waters, they shall be an abomination unto you:

11 They shall be even an abomination unto you; ye shall not eat of their flesh, but ye shall have their carcases in abomination.

12 Whatsoever hath no fins nor scales in the waters, that shall be an abomination unto you.

13 And these are they which ye shall have in abomination among the fowls; they shall not be eaten, they are an abomination: the eagle, and the ossifrage, and the ospray,

14 And the vulture, and the kite after his kind;

15 Every raven after his kind;

16 And the owl, and the night hawk, and the cuckow, and the hawk after his kind,

17 And the little owl, and the cormorant, and the great owl,

18 And the swan, and the pelican, and the gier eagle,

19 And the stork, the heron after her kind, and the lapwing, and the bat.

20 All fowls that creep, going upon all four, shall be an abomination unto you.

21 Yet these may ye eat of every flying creeping thing that goeth upon all four, which have legs above their feet, to leap withal upon the earth;

22 Even these of them ye may eat; the locust after his kind, and the bald locust after his kind, and the beetle after his kind, and the grasshopper after his kind.

23 But all other flying creeping things, which have four feet, shall be an abomination unto you.

24 And for these ye shall be unclean: whosoever toucheth the carcase of them shall be unclean until the even.

25 And whosoever beareth ought of the carcase of them shall wash his clothes, and be unclean until the even.

26 The carcases of every beast which divideth the hoof, and is not clovenfooted, nor cheweth the cud, are unclean unto you: every one that toucheth them shall be unclean.

27 And whatsoever goeth upon his paws, among all manner of beasts that go on all four, those are unclean unto you: whoso toucheth their carcase shall be unclean until the even.

28 And he that beareth the carcase of them shall wash his clothes, and be unclean until the even: they are unclean unto you.

29 These also shall be unclean unto you among the creeping things

that creep upon the earth; the weasel, and the mouse, and the tortoise after his kind,

30 And the ferret, and the chameleon, and the lizard, and the snail, and the mole.

31 These are unclean to you among all that creep: whosoever doth touch them, when they be dead, shall be unclean until the even.

32 And upon whatsoever any of them, when they are dead, doth fall, it shall be unclean; whether it be any vessel of wood, or raiment, or skin, or sack, whatsoever vessel it be, wherein any work is done, it must be put into water, and it shall be unclean until the even; so it shall be cleansed.

33 And every earthen vessel, whereinto any of them falleth, whatsoever is in it shall be unclean; and ye shall break it.

34 Of all meat which may be eaten, that on which such water cometh shall be unclean: and all drink that may be drunk in every such vessel shall be unclean.

35 And every thing whereupon any part of their carcase falleth shall be unclean; whether it be oven, or ranges for pots, they shall be broken down: for they are unclean, and shall be unclean unto you.

36 Nevertheless a fountain or pit, wherein there is plenty of water, shall be clean: but that which toucheth their carcase shall be unclean.

37 And if any part of their carcase fall upon any sowing seed which is to be sown, it shall be clean.

38 But if any water be put upon the seed, and any part of their carcase fall thereon, it shall be unclean unto you.

39 And if any beast, of which ye may eat, die; he that toucheth the carcase thereof shall be unclean until the even.

40 And he that eateth of the carcase of it shall wash his clothes, and be unclean until the even: he also that beareth the carcase of it shall wash his clothes, and be unclean until the even.

41 And every creeping thing that creepeth upon the earth shall be an abomination: it shall not be eaten.

42 Whatsoever goeth upon the belly, and whatsoever goeth upon all four, or whatsoever hath more feet among all creeping things that creep upon the earth, them ye shall not eat; for they are an abomination.

43 Ye shall not make your selves abominable with any creeping thing that creepeth, neither shall ye make yourselves unclean with them, that ye should be defiled thereby.

44 For I am the LORD your God: ye shall therefore sanctify yourselves, and ye shall be holy; for I am holy: neither shall ye defile

yourselves with any manner of creeping thing that creepeth upon the earth.

45 For I am the LORD that bringeth you up out of the land of Egypt, to be your God: ye shall therefore be holy, for I am holy.

46 This is the law of the beasts, and of the fowl, and of every living creature that moveth in the waters, and of every creature that creepeth upon the earth:

47 To make a difference between the unclean and the clean, and between the beast that may be eaten and the beast that may not be eaten.

Leviticus: II, Authorised Version.

Fido Food

'She said it looks like Fido food. Ask her.'

'I'd never say a thing like that. You said it.'

'I did not. You did.'

Faced with telling the truth to a reporter about an anti-aging buffet served at Betty Friedan's house in Sag Harbor, L.I., earlier this month, most of the guests took the Fifth.

Those few who spoke too soon begged to withdraw their remarks later.

A conversation between a reporter and Rona Jaffe, the novelist, went like this:

'What do you think of the food?' the reporter asked.

'It has no taste.' Pause. 'Are you interviewing me?'

'Yes.'

'It's wonderful.'

Or: 'I'm a kosher boy. What would I know about this food?' And: 'I can't tell you or I'll never be invited back to Betty's again.'

What caused so much weaseling was a buffet based on a book written by Ms Friedan's guest of honor, Dr Roy L. Walford, a professor of pathology at the UCLA School of Medicine. His daughter, Lisa, created the recipes for *The Anti-Aging Plan* (Four Walls, Eight Windows, $19.95) and supervised their preparation for the buffet.

Dr Walford, who has been studying the effects of diet on aging for almost 30 years, believes that a nutrient-rich diet with limited calories will extend life to between 110 and 150 years and reduce the risk of chronic diseases. Many animal studies have confirmed this theory.

And now there is some good evidence in humans that such a diet does reduce weight, blood pressure and cholesterol. But the findings about extended life spans in animals have not been replicated in humans, and no one alive today will live long enough to know the answer.

Here's part of the problem: If most of the people at the Sunday evening buffet had to eat that kind of food every day, they'd rather die at 80.

Dr Walford's remarks to the crowd were not reassuring. 'This diet has had remarkable effects in mice and rats,' he said. The audience laughed nervously.

Then it was Ms Walford's turn to talk up the food. She makes the waif model Kate Moss look fat. 'The crusts for the pizza are made with wheat germ and sweet potatoes,' she said.

Yum.

'You must have a piece of chocolate cake. It has oat flour, oat bran, cocoa and egg whites. But I'll let the food speak for itself.'

And so it did.

Everything that has ever given healthful food a bad name was summed up in the meal, which harked back to the 1960s' hippie cooks who thought appearance and taste counted for nothing and virtuousness was all. There was cold, soggy 'pizza', mushy, cold 'lasagna', salad dressed with vinegar and 'chocolate' cake that stuck to the roof of your mouth. Sweet potatoes turned up in everything, giving a pasty quality to the food.

Looking at the cookbook, the recipes don't seem so unpalatable, although seasonings, with the exception of garlic, are used sparingly if at all. But much of the food at the buffet seemed to be garlic-free. And salt-free. And taste-free. One guest kept walking around the table muttering: 'It needs garlic. It needs garlic.'

'It's a treatment, not a treat,' said one of the guests who immediately followed up her observation with the caveat of the day: 'I'd prefer not to be quoted, or I'll lose a friend.' She was referring to Ms Friedan.

In presenting Dr Walford to her friends – writers and artists who live in New York and the Hamptons including Linda Wolfe, Daniel Stern, Richard Reeves, Cathy O'Neill, Sherrye Henry and Irwin

Bazelon – she called him a friend who has 'introduced me to performance art and to feminist porn art'.

'He has enriched my life a lot,' she added.

Dr Walford looks as if he has lived an abstemious life: there is not an ounce of fat on his body. His age was a subject of interest to the other guests.

'He's only 70?'

'He looks 10 years older.'

'He's 70? I'm 72 and I look better than he does.'

During the party, Ms Friedan got in a plug for Dr Walford's book, as well as for her own most recent one, *The Fountain of Age*. 'You needed to read my book to appreciate how you could live to be 120,' she said.

Later, she added that when she goes out to dinner with Dr Walford, he doesn't eat the kind of food served at the party. 'He just does it for one meal a day and then he is discreet,' she said.

More than once, Ms Friedan assured her guests that even though Dr Walford was the physician for the Biosphere 2 team, he was legitimate. Biosphere, the enclosed ecosystem in the Arizona desert, was criticized as being more show than science.

In an interview earlier in the day, Dr Walford acknowledged that many criticisms of the project were fair. 'I know Biosphere does not have a good reputation, and it shouldn't,' he said. 'It was not managed incompetently, just not in a good scientific manner.'

There is nothing to indicate that Dr Walford's nutritional experiments with the Biospherians were anything but sound science. This work was reported in the December 1992 issue of the *Proceedings of the National Academy of Sciences*.

There were eight Biosphere subjects, whose diet averaged 1,780 calories a day, with 10 percent of the calories from fat. The diet was largely vegetarian and was dense with nutrients. All the food was grown in the Biosphere: six varieties of fruits, five cereal grains, four varieties of beans and peas, 19 vegetables and greens, white and sweet potatoes and small quantities of goat milk and yogurt, goat meat, pork, chicken, fish and eggs. During this six-month period, the subjects worked the equivalent of three to four hours at manual farming each day.

There was significant weight loss; about 22 pounds. Average blood pressure dropped from 110/70 to 85/55, and average total cholesterol dropped from 198 to 123.

Dr Walford thinks these changes were entirely diet related. He said a person could sit in an armchair all day and achieve the same results. 'I don't want to come out as an anti-exercise person,' he said, 'but you can't drop your cholesterol like this by exercise.'

Because the same changes seen in animals were seen in the Biospherians, Dr Walford thinks that on the diet, humans, like animals, can live much longer than they do now.

The doctor might have made a convert or two at Ms Friedan's party.

'I've been eating Dean Ornish stuff moderately for a year,' said Christopher Cary, director of college relations at Connecticut College. He was referring to a vegetarian diet named for a doctor who has written about ways to reverse atherosclerosis. The Ornish diet is frequently criticized because taste was not a primary consideration when it was developed. But compared with the buffet at Ms Friedan's, the Ornish food is ambrosial.

Mr Cary continued: 'Because of the Ornish diet, I'm prepared to like this food more than I might have before. Your taste buds change. The payoff was going to the doctor who said, "You've lost 10 pounds, your cholesterol is down, your blood pressure is down – you've done a good job with yourself." I walked out of there feeling 10 feet tall.'

But Daniel Stern, a writer, spoke for most of his fellow guests when he said, 'I'll convert when there are more old doctors than old drunks.'

Marian Burros, *New York Times* (20 July 1994).

Good Food for Good Dogs

Right from the start I must confess I haven't fed nearly as many dogs as I have human beings, but with the pets I have had and still have, I have always had good luck.

There was Faust, the handsome police dog, with the fiery eyes and wonderful fur coat. He thrived on his diet until some cruel person ran over him in Chicago.

Ricky, my Sealyham, who travelled with me for years – and is known to thousands – got to be a wise old man (he was more than a dog). He would now be fifteen years old if Lana Turner's Great Dane hadn't bitten him in two.

There were others, more Sealyhams, an Afghan, Sunny the chocolate-brown poodle, and Buster, an uncertain mixture who adopted me and my friend when we were walking in the hills of Beverly. All these pets remained healthy and hearty and I believe one of my secrets is that I never gave any of them anything that I could not eat myself, excepting raw meat.

Dogs are not like pigs and should not be given a pig's diet of a lot of old bread with greasy gravy. I don't even believe that a dog can be at his best when he constantly gets canned or dehydrated foods.

I am convinced that our dogs can live longer and always be in top form if we feed them more intelligently. A veterinary doctor once told me that 90 per cent of all dog diseases could be eliminated if people would stop giving their dogs sweets, too much starch, and instead gave them a balanced diet rich in proteins, minerals, and vitamins.

Here, I believe, is a well proportioned menu for any pet: 60 per cent meat – 20 per cent vegetables – 20 per cent starch.

The meat should be as fresh as possible. Cheap cuts are just as good as expensive ones, but best of all are the organ meats such as heart, kidneys, liver, and tripe. The meat should be ground up or cut in small pieces. Raw meat is best but for variety's sake slightly heat the meat, but do not fry.

The vegetables are best when raw and finely chopped. Chopped carrots are probably the best all-round vegetable for dogs. Carrots have a beneficial effect upon the 'innards' of man and beast. However, all raw chopped vegetables can be used.

The starch should be of the whole variety. Whole wheat, whole rye, or whole corn are favourites. Broken-up bits of whole-wheat bread, rye bread, and corn breads are a good choice. The whole-wheat biscuits, which can be bought in any grocery store and stored, are liked by all dogs.

Mix together the fresh meat, the freshly chopped vegetables, and the whole starch and moisten with some soup stock, broth, milk, or gravy (remove the fat). When well mixed this looks like a nice big hamburger which *you* would want to eat and that is as it should be. If you can't afford such a dish for your Buster then you can't afford to have a dog.

Occasionally add one or two egg yolks, or one or two tablespoons of wheat germ, or one tablespoon of dry vegetable broth, or a clove of garlic.

My prize pet meal can be used for enriching your pet's diet.

Here's how to make it:

1 cup dried brewers' yeast	*1 cup fine bone meal*
1 cup wheat or corn germ	*1 cup dried sea greens*

Mix the four dry ingredients together. Put in a tin can or bottle. Keep dry and covered. Mix 1 or 2 tablespoons of this mixture with the rest of the meal. Mix it up well, the first few times until your pet 'cries for it.' If you have a pampered one, let him go hungry until he will eat it.

Here is what it does: The brewers' yeast and wheat germ are wonderful for his skin and coat, the bone meal furnishes lots of calcium for his teeth, and sea greens (dried vegetables from the ocean) add a little iodine and other minerals necessary for a balanced diet.

One meal a day is best for grown dogs.

From Gaylord Hauser, *The Gaylord Hauser Cook Book* (1955).

Ham 'n' Eggs

I don't eat no ham 'n' eggs
'Cause they're high in cholesterol
Hey, yo, Phife, do ya eat 'em?
No, Tip, do you eat 'em?
Uh-uh, not at all
Again: I don't eat no ham 'n' eggs
'Cause they're high in cholesterol
Jarobi, do ya eat 'em?
Nope
Sha, do ya eat 'em?
Nope
Not at all (hey)

A tisket, a tasket
What's in mama's basket
Some veggie links
And some fish that stinks
Why just the other day
I went to grandma's house
Smelled like she conjured up a mouse

Eggs was fryin'
Ham was smellin'
In ten minutes
She started yellin'
'Come and git it'
And the gettin' looked good
I said, 'I shouldn't eat it'
She said, 'I think ya should'
But I can't
I'm plagued by vegetarians
No cats and dogs
I'm not a veterinarian
Strictly collard greens

And a occasional steak
Goes on my plate
Asparagus tips looked yummy yummy yummy
Candy yams inside my tummy
A collage of good eats
A snack, some nice treats
Applesauce and some nice red beets
This is what we snack on when we're questin'
No second guessin'

I don't eat no ham 'n' eggs
'Cause they're high in cholesterol
I dig it
Hey, yo, Phife, do ya eat 'em?
No, Tip, do ya eat 'em?
Uh-uh, not at all
Come on again
I don't eat no ham 'n' eggs
'Cause they're high in cholesterol
Jarobi, do ya eat 'em?
No, Sha, do ya eat 'em?
Nope, not at all
Bridget

Now drop the beat
So I can talk about my favorite tastings
The food that is the everlasting

See I'm not fasting
I'm gobblin'
Like a doggone turkey
Beef jerkeys, slim jims
I eat sometimes
I like lemon and limes
And if not that
I get the roti and the sour sop
Sit back, relax
Listen to some hip hop
Gum drops and gummy bears
Tease my eyes
A sight for sore ones

And so are pies
And other goodies that are filled with goo
Fried apple hoops
Delectable delights
Controls my appetites
Pa says, 'Boy, eat right'
But I know what I like
Chicken for lunch
Chicken for my dinner
Chicken chicken chicken
I'm a finger-lickin' winner
When breakfast time comes
I don't recognize
Pig in the pan
Or a pair of roguish eyes
Fancy stewed tomatoes
Home-fried potatoes
Or anything with flair
You cook it, I'm in there
Pay attention to the Tribe
As we impose
This is how it goes

I don't eat no ham 'n' eggs
'Cause they're high in cholesterol
Hey, yo Phife, do ya eat 'em?
Hey, Tip, do ya eat 'em?

Uh-uh, not at all
Come and get 'em!
I don't eat no ham 'n' eggs
'Cause they're high in cholesterol
Yo, Jaro', do ya eat 'em?
No, Sha, do ya eat 'em?
No, not at all (Again, again again)
I don't eat no ham 'n' eggs
'Cause they're high in cholesterol
Afrika, do ya eat 'em?
Nope, Pos, do ya eat 'em?
Hell, yeah, all the time
I don't eat no ham 'n' eggs

'Cause they're high in cholesterol
Hey yo Phife, do ya eat 'em?
Nah, Tip, do ya eat 'em?
Uh-uh, not at all
I don't eat no ham 'n' eggs
'Cause they're high in cholesterol
Yo, Jarobi, do ya eat 'em?
Nope, Sha, do ya eat 'em?
Nope, not at all
I don't eat no ham 'n' eggs
'Cause they're high in cholesterol
Afrika, do ya eat 'em?
Nope, Gary do ya eat 'em?
Yeah, all the time

A Tribe Called Quest (1990).

Colour-Coded

The waiter came to take our order. Would Stephen care to try snails?
No, no. What about smoked salmon, smoked eel? No. Pâté? No. An
artichoke? No. Soup, then? Carrot soup?

   'Just tomatoes.'

   'Tomatoes, sir?'

'I think my friend would like a tomato salad. With basil, perhaps, and onions.'

'No onions,' said Stephen. 'Don't require onions.'

Veal and beef and lamb and chicken were not required either. A large bowl of tomatoes was all he wanted. And water.

'Do you always eat so frugally?'

'What's frugally?'

'Well, so little.'

'I asked him for a lot of tomatoes. That's not frugally.'

'You seem to be in a red mood today. Have you chosen tomatoes because they match your clothes?'

He looked at me and smiled briefly. 'Yes,' he replied after a pause. 'Yes. Because. Because I'm different.'

'What do you eat when you're wearing green?'

'Cabbages. Peas. Grapes.'

'And yellow?'

He thought for a minute. 'Squash.'

From Paul Bailey, *Sugar Cane* (1993).

Catholic Tastes

It was with Papa's death that I discovered we had been rich. I learnt this when we suddenly became poor. The second-floor apartment in the rue Vandal with its rare collections of antelope masks from the Ivory Coast, masks with weary, hooded eyes carved of black wood; soap-stone sculptures of old men taking their ease on small chairs; Bundu masks from Sierra Leone with their funny squashed faces and helmets like knights; grave-faced Basuku masks, dreamily sedate faces with wooden birds perched on their heads and great straw beards – all sold from under our feet and the proceeds seized 'pending investigation'. What investigation? And my mother, beside herself with worry (who could blame her?), stole away to England – as if she recognised her status had been diminished.

I was just twelve and at twelve one doesn't have many alternatives. One puzzles, wonders, weeps and perhaps learns the sounds of idiomatic English at the North London Academy for Girls even if the food was so bad that my appetite began to fail. One reads and talks to oneself, and grows up fast.

It was at about this time that I began to depend more and more on chocolates. My tastes are pretty catholic: *Praline*, *After Eights* and *Rolos*, as well as *Lindt Excellence*, *Côte d'Or 'Extra Dry'* and *Cadbury's Bourneville Dark*. I'm not a chocolate snob, I'm a chocolate catholic. It began as a comfort but it became my salvation. Faced by the barbaric custom of feeding children at school which the English adopt, faced by little cow-pats of grey meat between buns; or the minced remainders of yesterday's lunch floating in a greasy soup covered in an elderly thatch of potato and called a 'pie', I turned to the corner shop and there among the racks of chocolate found how to save myself.

From Christopher Hope, *My Chocolate Redeemer* (1989).

The Perfect Sandwich

The secret of sandwiches is this. You have one dry thing and one wet thing. More, and it becomes too complicated. Less, and it becomes one thing between two pieces of bread. Most people disagree with me, and think that a piece of beef between two pieces of good bread is good enough. It is good. It just isn't a sandwich. The wet and dry theory goes, in principle, like this. Soft cheese (dry) and grapes (wet). Tuna (dry) and cucumber (wet). Beef (dry) and peach (wet). It isn't infallible.

From Philip Hensher, *Other Lulus* (1994).

Sucking Oranges

However, it so fell out that Fanny had to leave; and Miss Matilda begged me to stay and 'settle her' with the new maid; to which I consented, after I had heard from my father that he did not want me at home. The new servant was a rough, honest-looking country-girl, who had only lived in a farm place before; but I liked her looks when she came to be hired; and I promised Miss Matilda to put her in the ways of the house. The said ways were religiously such as Miss Matilda thought her sister would approve. Many a domestic rule and regulation had been a subject of plaintive whispered murmur to me, during Miss Jenkyns's life; but now that she was gone, I do not think that even I, who was a favourite, durst have suggested an alteration. To give an instance: we constantly adhered to the forms which were observed, at meal times, in 'my father, the Rector's house'.

Accordingly, we had always wine and dessert; but the decanters were only filled when there was a party; and what remained was seldom touched, though we had two wine glasses apiece every day after dinner, until the next festive occasion arrived; when the state of the remainder wine was examined into, in a family council. The dregs were often given to the poor; but occasionally, when a good deal had been left at the last party (five months ago, it might be), it was added to some of a fresh bottle, brought up from the cellar. I fancy poor Captain Brown did not much like wine; for I noticed he never finished his first glass, and most military men take several. Then, as to our dessert, Miss Jenkyns used to gather currants and gooseberries for it herself, which I sometimes thought would have tasted better fresh from the trees; but then, as Miss Jenkyns observed, there would have been nothing for dessert in summer-time. As it was, we felt very genteel with our two glasses apiece, and a dish of gooseberries at the top, of currants and biscuits at the sides, and two decanters at the bottom. When oranges came in, a curious proceeding was gone through. Miss Jenkyns did not like to cut the fruit; for, as she observed, the juice all ran out nobody knew where; sucking (only I think she used some more recondite word) was in fact the only way of enjoying oranges; but then there was the unpleasant association with a ceremony frequently gone through by little babies; and so, after dessert, in orange season, Miss Jenkyns and Miss Matty used to rise up, possess themselves each of an orange in silence, and withdraw to the privacy of their own rooms, to indulge in sucking oranges.

From Mrs Gaskell, *Cranford* (1853).

Go to Work on an Egg

Indeed, in everything that is seen of his can be discerned a spirit set apart and very different from other painters, and with a penetrating subtlety in the investigation of certain subtle secrets hidden deep in

Nature, without regard to time or effort, but only for his own delight and for pleasure in the art. And it could not be otherwise, for having fallen in love with painting, he cared nothing for his creature comforts and reduced himself to eating only boiled eggs which, to economize on fire, he used to cook whenever he was boiling glue, not six or eight, but fifty at a time, keeping them in a basket and eating them one by one.

Piero di Cosimo, from Giorgio Vasari, *Lives of the Artists*, vol. II (1568),
translated by George Bull.

Frugal Habits

In this character sketch I need not omit his eating habits. [Augustus] was frugal and, as a rule, preferred the food of the common people, especially the coarser sort of bread, small fishes, fresh hand-pressed cheese, and green figs of the second crop; and would not wait for dinner, if he felt hungry, but ate anywhere. The following are verbatim quotations from his letters:

> I had a snack of bread and dates while out for my drive today ...

and:

> On the way back in my litter from the Regia, I munched an ounce of bread and a few hard-skinned grapes.

and again:

> My dear Tiberius,
> Not even a Jew fasts so scrupulously on his sabbaths as I have done today. Not until dusk had fallen did I touch a thing; and that was at the baths, before I had my oil rub, when I swallowed two mouthfuls of bread.

This failure to observe regular mealtimes often resulted in his dining alone either before or after his guests, and touching nothing while the meal was in progress.

Augustus was also a habitually abstemious drinker. During the siege of Mutina, according to Cornelius Nepos, he never took more than three drinks of wine-and-water at dinner. In later life his limit was a pint; if he ever exceeded this he would deliberately vomit. Raetian was his favourite, but he seldom touched wine between meals; instead, he would moisten his throat with a morsel of bread dunked in cold water; or a slice of cucumber or the heart of a young lettuce; or a sour apple either fresh or dried.

From Suetonius (born c. 70 AD), *The Twelve Caesars*, translated by
Robert Graves (1957).

Re-embracing Flesh

It happened overnight. Abruptly, I stopped talking to foodie friends about the best Marcella Hazan recipe for lamb and turned into a timorous nibbler of vegetables.

This was a dramatic rejection of my carnivorous past. I tried not to think about the Paris restaurant where I used to eat steak melting with Roquefort, or about roast guinea-fowl in Gubbio and lamb *cous-cous* in Fez. Instead, I resigned myself to a diet of pasta, vegetables and more pasta.

'I don't mind,' I insisted to dismayed and disbelieving friends. 'After all, I never really liked meat that much.' They groaned, complained about the awkwardness of producing vegetarian meals and compromised by serving endless quantities of poached salmon, my remaining concession to flesh.

I don't even *like* fish, so I should have known something was wrong. Towards the end of this ludicrous period, I began to cheat: a sliver of *prosciutto* here, a hunk of *luganega* there, as though Italian meat was somehow in a different category. Then, on the evening of my birthday last year, I went with friends to an Italian restaurant in Chelsea and ordered a huge plate of *fegato alla veneziana* – calves' liver with onions. No starter, no pudding, just meat: I abandoned vegetarianism as wholeheartedly, though not as impulsively, as I had embraced it.

I half expected a hostile reaction, assuming that such a large and unaccustomed quantity of offal might be an unwelcome shock to my gastric juices. But the next day, I felt exceptionally well and incredibly cheerful; over the next few weeks I binged on Toulouse sausages, venison paté, pork with dried *porcini* and juniper berries.

I completed the re-entry process by spending New Year's Eve at a hotel in Burgundy that served a nine-course meat extravaganza – one of those French feasts which seem expressly designed to challenge the whimsical notion that any part of an animal could possibly be inedible.

I don't really approve of such fanatical carnivorousness, but it did bring home the fact that I had engaged in a major act of self-deception: I love meat and the event which apparently prompted my vegetarianism – a sighting of a terrified fox with the local hunt in pursuit – was actually a cover for a much more arcane motivation.

This strange conversion happened at one of the lowest points in my life: I was writing a book which was not going well, I was so physically run-down I caught every cold that passed through Oxfordshire, and I was very, very unhappy. I am far too greedy to become anorexic but, like many women writers and artists, I fell into the trap of making a sinister deal with myself: if I gave up something I really liked, I would be able to go on working.

I am not elevating myself to the level of Emily Brontë or Gwen John, two prime exponents of creative self-starvation. But I had unknowingly joined those women whose tortured relationship with food is inextricably linked with their gnawing need for self-expression. Vegetarianism, like anorexia, brings with it an illusion of control, turning every mealtime into a ritual of calculation, denial and self-congratulation.

I am surprised at how long I allowed this absurd state of affairs to continue. What is now obvious is that, as I began to get my life back under some sort of control and my writer's block evaporated, my pretence at being a committed vegetarian became more and more untenable.

As I finished my last novel, completing the final chapters with my private life in turmoil but enjoying the writing more than anything I had ever done, I realised I would soon start eating meat again. But I needed to understand why I had taken such an unaccountable decision in the first place.

The link with my writing was the easy bit. As I wrote with greater confidence than before, I thankfully accepted that I no longer had to make self-punishing deals with myself. But the other part of the puzzle involved a more painful realisation which centred on the double meaning of the word 'flesh'. It finally dawned on me, as I considered this earthier, more carnal synonym for meat, that in my case the decision to become vegetarian had been a side-effect of feeling miserably and involuntarily cut off from my sexuality.

It embarrasses me to think I ever imagined I was going without meat out of concern for animals; I am soft-hearted about fur, paws and tails, but that did not stop me eating meat for the greater part of my life. And I have always been relatively unsqueamish about handling meat, baulking at only the most grisly jobs like chopping the feet off pheasants (dead ones, I hasten to add).

This is not to deny that many people become vegetarians and even vegans for purely ethical reasons. Leonardo da Vinci and Piero di Cosimo liked animals too much to eat them; George Bernard Shaw wrote of 'the enormity of eating the scorched corpses of animals', a phrase I often quoted in my vegetarian period.

I understand their revulsion but it no longer has sufficient force to make me turn down a dish of tender lamb with apricots. I have re-embraced flesh and, like Piaf, I have no regrets.

Joan Smith, *Observer* (8 May 1994).

Eat Half (i)

Combe Florey, 29 September 1843

You are, I hear, attending more to diet than heretofore. If you wish for anything like happiness in the fifth act of life, eat and drink about one-half what you *could* eat and drink. Did I ever tell you my calculation about eating and drinking? Having ascertained the weight of what I could live upon, so as to preserve health and strength, and what I did live upon, I found that, between ten and seventy years of age, I had eaten and drunk forty four-horse waggon-loads of meat and drink more than would preserve me in life and health! The value of this mass of nourishment I considered to be worth seven thousands pounds sterling. It occurred to me that I must, by my voracity, have starved to death fully a hundred persons. This is a frightful calculation, but irresistibly true; and I think, dear Murray, your waggons would require an additional horse each!

From Sydney Smith (1771–1845) *Selected Letters*, edited by Nowell C. Smith.

Eat Half (ii)

Milly, like everyone else in the house or in my office, never used my first name. Although I was a young woman of twenty-eight I was generally known as Mrs Hawkins. This seemed so natural to me and was obviously so natural to those around me that I never, at the time, thought of insisting otherwise. I was a war-widow, Mrs Hawkins. There was something about me, Mrs Hawkins, that invited confidences. I was abundantly aware of it, and indeed abundance was the impression I gave. I was massive in size, strong-muscled, huge-bosomed, with wide hips, hefty long legs, a bulging belly and fat backside; I carried an ample weight with my five-foot-six of height, and was healthy with it. It was, of course, partly this physical factor that disposed people to confide in me. I looked comfortable. Photographs of the time show me with a moon-face, two ample chins and sleepy eyes. These are black-and-white photos. Taken in colour they would have shown my Rubens quality of flesh, eyes, skin. And I was Mrs Hawkins. It was not till later, when I decided to be thin, that right away I noticed that people didn't confide their thoughts to me so much, neither men nor women. As an aside, I can tell you that if there's nothing wrong with you except fat it is easy to get thin. You eat and drink the same as always, only half. If you are handed a plate of food, leave half; if you have to help yourself, take half. After a while, if you are a perfectionist, you can consume half of that again. On the question of will-power, if that is a factor, you should think of will-power as something that never exists in the present tense, only in the future and the past. At one moment you have decided to do or refrain from an action and the next moment you have already done or refrained; it is the only way to deal with will-power. (Only under sub-human stress does will-power live in time present but that is a different discourse.) I offer this advice without fee; it is included in the price of this book.

From Muriel Spark, *A Far Cry from Kensington* (1988).

VI LA DOLCE VITA

IN May 1928, on her first visit to the Middle East, Freya Stark arrived in the Syrian village of Resas. She found her hosts, a Druze family called Atrash, living in tents, a circumstance for which they apologised profusely. They were not nomads like the Bedouin, they explained, but their houses had recently been destroyed by the French in retaliation for their part in the Arab revolt. Even in these makeshift conditions they were able to produce a 'splendid' dinner of chicken on rice, beans, rice pudding and coffee which Stark gratefully recorded in her book, *Letters From Syria*. Sixty-six years later, in the spring of 1994, I visited Resas and was welcomed by the same family, including an old lady who had been photographed by Freya Stark as a baby. We sat in the upstairs living-room of their imposing house, making polite conversation while the women, in their stiff embroidered dresses, worked for a good couple of hours in the kitchen. Eventually the women re-appeared, struggling under the weight of a round plate at least four feet across and heaped with rice and chicken – exactly the same dish that their great-grandmothers had prepared for Stark nearly seventy years before. The rice had been cooked to a delicate fluffy texture, coloured with saffron and studded with slivers of almonds while the chicken quarters were coated in a simple sauce whose exact ingredients I was unable to discover (the friend who had driven me to Resas was by now being bombarded with questions from the women: how old was I, did I have a husband, what did I think of Syria?). I half-listened as I heaped chicken on my plate, still trying to identify the spices which were rapidly becoming one of my lasting impressions of the country; as I walked through the centre of Damascus at dusk the previous evening, on my way to dinner in someone's apartment, the warm breeze had been heavy with their scent as people cooked with their windows wide open or out of doors. I was also aware of an unexpected connection, through the food and the setting, with the past: not my own past, which is what happened to Proust's narrator when he tasted a madeleine, but with fleeting images (drawn, I'm sure, from photographs) of that earlier English traveller, making her way across the scorching desert in dusty old-fashioned clothes as Arabia plotted to throw off its colonial oppressors.

For people who regard eating as a not very interesting necessity of life, this reaction to a few mouthfuls of fragrant rice will no doubt seem inexplicably intense. But food is like sex in its power to stimulate imagination and memory as well as those senses – taste, smell, sight – on which its impact is most direct. The most powerful writing about food rarely addresses the qualities of a particular dish or meal alone; it almost always contains elements of nostalgia for other times, places and companions, and of anticipation of future pleasures. In a *New Yorker* profile of Duke Ellington published in 1944, the jazz musician reeled off a catalogue of places he had played, each of them fixed in his mind by a fabulous meal: Chicago for a restaurant where he had eaten barbecued ribs, the Ile-de-France for its *crêpes Suzette*, the Café Royal in The Hague for the 'best hors d'ouevres in the world' (eighty-five different kinds, all of which he claimed to have sampled). Henry James, rather more sedately, recalled the town of Bourg-en-Bresse in eastern France for its combined visual and alimentary impact: 'late Gothic sculpture and *tartines*'. In Myra Schneider's poem 'The Mango', biting into the succulent yellow flesh of the tropical fruit momentarily transports an old woman from a dull English cathedral city to the Caribbean: 'I'm feeding/body and mind on mellowed sun'. Proust's lyrical (and unparalleled) description in *Swann's Way* of the shape and colour of uncooked asparagus, with crumbs of soil still clinging to the base of the stalks, frankly and pleasurably anticipates an effect which many people recall only with mild embarrassment: the way in which it perfumes human urine.

What these passages have in common is a refreshing absence of self-consciousness about the pleasure of eating, even though an unsympathetic onlooker might – especially in the case of Duke Ellington – condemn it as greed. There is a puritan notion that simple food, consumed in moderate quantities, is better than a feast, but this overlooks the uncomfortable fact that some people *enjoy* eating to excess. (Pretending this isn't the case is rather like the bewildered reaction of governments and law enforcement agencies to the use of recreational drugs; the simple answer to the question 'Why do they do it?' is that they like it.) According to Boswell, Dr Johnson's single-minded passion for food was so great that the veins of his forehead bulged as he ate, to the disgust of dining companions with more delicate constitutions; Johnson was not, wrote Boswell, 'a *temperate* man either in eating or drinking', but he certainly looked forward to dinner. At a time when millions of people have an anguished relation to food, locked into a cycle of bingeing and dieting, it is hard not to warm to a shady character in *Buddenbrooks*, Thomas Mann's novel about the decline of a bourgeois banking family, as he eats his way with unfeigned enjoyment through a *ragoût* of shellfish, julienne soup, fried soles, roast veal with creamed potatoes and cauliflower, maraschino pudding and pumpernickel with roquefort. The American feminist Alix Kates Shulman, whose autobiographical book *Drinking the Rain* reveals her austere 1950s beatnik attitude to material possessions, nevertheless dissolves into rapture as soon as she gets on to the subject of food. The first person in her family to visit Europe, Shulman admits to an almost evangelical mission to introduce her friends and relatives in America to all the pleasures they had missed: blood oranges, snails, squash flowers and fennel. 'I wanted to share the thrill', she writes, 'of the flavors of French, German, and Italian food that had taken me completely by surprise.'

Shulman's childhood, like mine a few years later, revolved around meals which were too unimaginative to stimulate curiosity or even appetite. She recalls broiled steak dinners and spaghetti swimming in tomato sauce; I remember ungarnished lamb chops and frozen cod steaks in parsley sauce. Such sensory deprivation is, with hindsight, a blessing; it means you never quite lose a feeling of wonder as the world opens up to your adult gaze and, more to the point, your astounded taste buds. Shulman's account of her transition from an indifferent to a passionate eater is the same journey I embarked on in my early twenties, endowing me with an impetuous openness towards unfamiliar dishes such as sweetbreads in Burgundy, virulently hot chicken jalfrezi in Dhaka, raw reindeer tongues stuffed with sour cream in Stockholm, brain fritters in Damascus. In this we are children of our time, emerging from the spartan post-war years when rationing was still a recent memory into an age in which food from all over the world is available on the street corner. The American polemical writer Camille Paglia dates her blissful discovery of Indian food ('my substitute for LSD') to 1973, about a year before

I overcame my own inherited suspicion of it; now, within walking distance of my house in West London, I am able to eat French, Chinese, Italian, Indian, Thai, Greek and Japanese food, most of it of very high quality.

I'm also able to buy anything from wild mushrooms to venison and wild boar sausages in my local shops. Simone de Beauvoir, in a rather unexpected passage in *The Second Sex*, wrote about food shopping as a species of contest between the 'housewife' and the shopkeeper, whom she has to outwit in order to acquire a substantial cabbage or a ripe Camembert. 'Buying is a profound pleasure, a discovery, almost an invention,' she suggested, a description which seems somewhat fanciful when applied to the majority of such transactions. In the same way, de Beauvoir's eulogy on cooking, which characterises it as alchemy, sorcery, the transmutation of substances, is so hopelessly romantic that the reader can't help wonder whether she ever cooked anything herself or ate anywhere other than in cafés. For the pleasure of cooking lies not in some mystical realm but in its intensely physical qualities – handling and preparing sometimes messy ingredients, enjoying their smell and texture, looking forward to sharing the finished product with friends. De Beauvoir's writing about food misses the point that cooking is a *sensual* experience; it is a consciousness of this fact, expressed in a delighted appraisal of each ingredient or dish, which informs the best writing about food from Proust to Elizabeth David. The latter's wonderful essay 'Para Navidad' published in 1964 when the Spanish fruit and vegetables she was writing about would have been unfamiliar to most of her readers, is a classic of its kind: revelling in the characteristics of different types of figs, olives, almonds and dates (some of them in 'tortoiseshell-cat colours'), David's assured prose attempts no less than to import the unfamiliar Mediterranean world into chilly, xenophobic Britain. Great cooks and cookery writers are sensualists who know that food is entitled to its place, along with sex, as an essential constituent of *la dolce vita*.

Heavenly Creatures (i)

Eating was as close to heaven as my mother ever came. (In our day we have a name for a passion as disordered as hers.)

And almost as heavenly as eating was the making – how she gloried in it! Every last body on this earth has a particular notion of paradise, and this was hers, standing in the murderously hot back kitchen of her own house, concocting and contriving, leaning forward and squinting at the fine print of the cookery book, a clean wooden spoon in hand.

It's something to see, the way she concentrates, her hot, busy face, the way she thrills to see the dish take form as she pours the stewed fruit into the fancy mold, pressing the thickly cut bread down over the oozing juices, feeling it soften and absorb bit by bit a raspberry redness. Malvern pudding; she loves the words too, and feels them dissolve on her tongue like a sugary wafer, her tongue itself grown waferlike and sweet. Like an artist – years later this form of artistry is perfectly clear to me – she stirs and arranges and draws in her brooding lower lip. Such a dish this will be. A warm sponge soaking up color. (Mrs. Flett next door let her have some currants off her bush; the raspberries she's found herself along the roadside south of the village, even though it half kills her, a woman of her size walking out in the heat of the day.)

She sprinkles on extra sugar, one spoonful, then another, then takes the spoon to her mouth, the rough crystals that keep her alert. It is three o'clock – a hot July afternoon in the middle of Manitoba, in the middle of the Dominion of Canada. The parlor clock (adamantine finish, gilded feet, a wedding present from her husband's family, the Goodwills of Stonewall Township) has just struck the hour. Cuyler will be home from the quarry at five sharp; he will have himself a good cheerful wash at the kitchen basin, and by half-past five the two of them will sit down at the table – this very table, only spread with a clean cloth, every second day a clean cloth – and eat their supper. Which for the most part will be a silent meal, both my parents being shy by nature, and each brought up in the belief that conversing and eating are different functions, occupying separate trenches of time. Tonight they will partake of cold corned beef with a spoonful of homemade relish, some dressed potatoes at the side, cups of sweet tea, and then this fine pudding. His eyes will widen; my father, Cuyler Goodwill, aged twenty-eight, two years married, will never in his life have tasted Malvern pudding. (That's what she's preparing for – his stunned and mild look of confusion, that tender, grateful male mouth dropping open in surprise. It's the least she can do, surprise him like this.) She sets a flower-patterned plate carefully on top of the pudding and weights it with a stone.

From Carol Shields, *The Stone Diaries* (1993).

The Mango

lies cool in the palm of my hand,
egg of a mythical bird. It's reddened
like a path over the Caribbean Sea
I tried to catch in the camera's box.
Cutting into this fruit tonight

I'm slicing the sun. Its gorgeous flesh
is yellow and boned by a stone flat
as an oar. I hold up a sliver – it shines
Juice drips from elbow and chin.

'You must eat a mango in the bath,'
said the old lady shut in a dim
upstairs flat in a cathedral city
in England, after a lifetime
of Trinidad's sprawling heat.

The pulp is more generous than peach,
rich as laughter, carries a trace
of jasmine, melts my mouth. I'm feeding
body and mind on mellowed sun.
If this were religion I'd believe it!

From Myra Schneider, *Exits* (1995).

The Measure of My Powers

The first thing I cooked was pure poison. I made it for Mother after my little brother David was born, and within twenty minutes of the first swallow she was covered with great itching red welts. The doctor came, soda compresses were laid on, sedatives and mild physic were scattered about, and all subsided safely ... except my feeling of deep shock and hurt professional pride. As the nurse, Miss Faulck, pointed out, I should have been content to let well enough alone.

The pudding was safe enough: a little round white shuddering milky thing I had made that morning under the stern eyes of Miss Faulck and whoever it was that succeeded mad Ora in the kitchen. It had 'set' correctly. It was made according to the directions for Invalid Cookery in Mother's best recipe book, and I had cleaned my fingernails until tears filled my eyes before I touched so much as the box of cornstarch.

Then, in the middle of the afternoon, when the pudding slid with a chill plop into the saucer, I knew that I could not stand to present it, my first culinary triumph, in its naked state. It was obscenely pure, obscenely colorless.

A kind of loyalty to Ora rose in me, and without telling Miss Faulck I ran into the back yard and picked ten soft ripe blackberries. I blew off the alley-dust, and placed them gently in a perfect circle around the little pudding. Its cool perfection leaped into sudden prettiness, like Miss America when the winning ribbon is hung around her high-breasted symmetry.

And even a little while later, when Mother lay covered with compresses and Miss Faulck pursed her lips and David howled for a meal he couldn't have because he might drink hive-juice, Mother smiled at my shocked anxious confusion, and said, 'Don't worry, sweet ... it was the loveliest pudding I have ever seen.'

I agreed with her in spite of the despair.

I can't remember ever learning anything, that is, I don't hear Mother's voice saying to me, 'Now this is a teaspoon, and this is the way you sift flour, and warm eggs won't make mayonnaise ...' But evidently I loved to cook, and she taught me several things without making them into lessons, because in the next few years I knew how to make white sauce, and cup cakes with grated orange rind in them. (Father was always very complimentary about them, and Anne and I loved to save ours until the rest of the family had left the table, and then cover them with cream and sugar and eat them with a spoon.)

I could make jelly rolls, too, which seems odd now; I don't think I've ever tasted one since I was about ten, much less had any interest in putting one together.

I loved to read cookbooks (unlike my feeling for jelly roll that passion had grown stronger with the years), and inevitably I soon started to improve on what I had read. Once I made poor Anne share my proud misery with something I called Hindu Eggs. I was sure I had read about it in Fanny Farmer; all you did was add curry powder to a white sauce and pour it over sliced hardboiled eggs.

When Mother said she and Father would be away one night, and I might get supper alone, I hid the gleam in my eye when she told me to put the sauce and the eggs in a casserole, and be sure to drink milk, and open a jar of plums or something for dessert.

'Yes, Mother, I know I can do it,' I said smoothly, and the word *Hindu* danced sensuously in my mind, safely unsaid until Mother was out of the house.

The casserole was handsome, too, when Anne and I sat down to it in exciting solitude at the big table. Anne admired me, there was no doubt of it ... and I admired myself. The rich brown sauce bubbled and sent out puffs of purely Oriental splendor. I sat in Father's place, and served each of us generously.

The first bite, and perhaps the next two or three, were all right; we were hungry, and in a hurry to feel the first warmth in our little bellies. Then Anne put down her fork. She beat me to it, so I continued to hold mine, determined like any honest cook to support my product.

'It's too hot, it burns,' my little sister said, and gulped at her milk.

'Blow on it,' I instructed. 'Mother's not here.'

We blew, and I ate three more bites to Anne's dutiful one. The heat seemed to increase. My influence over Anne must have been persuasive as well as autocratic in those far days, because she ate most of what was on her plate before the tears started rolling down her round brown cheeks.

I ate all mine, proudly, but inside I was cold with the new knowledge that I had been stupid. I had thought I remembered a recipe when I didn't, and I had used curry without knowing anything about it, and when the sauce looked boringly white I had proceeded to make it richly darker with probably five tablespoonfuls of the exotic powder.

I ate all I could, for fear Father would see how much we threw into the garbage pail, and then after my sweet forgiving little sister helped me straighten the kitchen we went upstairs and, with the desperate intuition of burned animals, sat on the edge of the bath-tub for a long time with our mouths full of mineral oil. She never said anything more about it, either; and the next morning there were only a few blisters, just inside our lips.

When I was eleven we all moved to the country. We had a cow, and chickens, and partly because of that and partly because Grandmother had died we began to eat more richly.

We had chocolate puddings with chopped nuts and heavy cream. The thought of them makes me dizzy now, but we loved them. And lots of butter: I was good at churning, and learned very well how to sterilize the wooden churn and make the butter and then roll it into fine balls and press it into molds. I liked that. And we could have mayonnaise, rich yellow with eggs and oil, instead of the boiled dressing Grandmother's despotic bowels and stern palate called for.

Mother, in an orgy of baking brought on probably by all the beautiful eggs and butter lying around, spent every Saturday morning making cakes. They were piled high with icings. They were filled with crushed almonds, chopped currants, and an outrageous number of calories. They were beautiful. Saturday afternoons they sat cooling, along with Mother and the kitchen after the hectic morning, and by Sunday night they were already a pleasant if somewhat bilious memory.

After about a year of this luscious routine, Mother retired more or less permanently to the front part of the house, perhaps with half an eye on the bathroom scales, but before she gave up cooking, I learned a lot about cakes from her. The fact that I have never made one since then – at least, the kind with many layers and fillings and icings and all that – has little to do with the gratitude I have often felt for knowing how to measure and sift and be patient and not be daunted by disappointment.

Mother, like all artists, was one-sided. She only cooked what she herself liked. She knew very little about meats, so I gradually learned all that myself. She hated gravies, and any sauces but 'white sauce' (probably a hangover from Grandmother's training), so I made some hideous mistakes with them. And there was always an element of surprise, if not actual danger, in my meals; the Hindu eggs had larned me but not curbed my helpless love of anything rare or racy.

But in spite of all that, I was the one who got dinner on the cooks' off-night. I improved, there is no doubt about it, and it was taken for granted that I would step into the kitchen at the drop of a hat.

Perhaps Anne would have liked a chance at having all the family's attention for those few hours. If so she never got it. The stove, the bins, the cupboards, I had learned forever, make an inviolable throne room. From them I ruled; temporarily I controlled. I felt powerful, and I loved that feeling.

I am more modest now, but I still think that one of the pleasantest of all emotions is to know that I, I with my brain and my hands, have nourished my beloved few, that I have concocted a stew or a story, a rarity or a plain dish, to sustain them truly against the hungers of the world.

From M.F.K. Fisher, *The Gastronomical Me* (1943).

Tasting the Past

Many years had elapsed during which nothing of Combray, except what lay in the theatre and the drama of my going to bed there, had any existence for me, when one day in winter, on my return home, my mother, seeing that I was cold, offered me some tea, a thing I did not ordinarily take. I declined at first, and then, for no particular reason, changed my mind. She sent for one of those squat, plump little cakes called 'petites madeleines,' which look as though they had been moulded in the fluted valve of a scallop shell. And soon, mechanically, dispirited after a dreary day with the prospect of a depressing morrow, I raised to my lips a spoonful of the tea in which I had soaked a morsel of the cake. No sooner had the warm liquid mixed with the crumbs touched my palate than a shiver ran through me and I stopped, intent upon the extraordinary thing that was happening to me. An exquisite pleasure had invaded my senses, something isolated, detached, with no suggestion of its origin. And at once the vicissitudes of life had become indifferent to me, its disasters innocuous, its brevity illusory – this new sensation having had the effect, which love has, of filling me with a precious essence; or rather this essence was not in me, it *was* me. I had ceased now to feel mediocre, contingent, mortal. Whence could it have come to me, this all-powerful joy? I sensed that it was connected with the taste of the tea and the cake, but that it infinitely transcended those savours, could not, indeed, be of the same nature. Where did it come from? What did it mean? How could I seize and apprehend it?

From Marcel Proust, *Swann's Way* (1913), translated by C.K. Scott Moncrieff and Terence Kilmartin, revised by D.J. Enright.

Just Another Slice

And he came. He came in a not quite new-fashioned, rather wrinkled, but still handsome bell-shaped frock coat which gave him a solid, respectable look. He was rosy and smiling, his scant hair carefully parted, his whiskers curled and scented. He ate a ragout of shell-fish, julienne soup, fried soles, roast veal with creamed potatoes and cauliflower, maraschino pudding, and pumpernickel with roquefort; and he found a fresh and delicate compliment for each fresh course. Over the sweet he lifted his dessert-spoon, gazed at one of the tapestry statues, and spoke aloud to himself, thus: 'God forgive me, I have eaten far too well already. But this pudding –! It is too wonderful! I must beg my good hostess for another slice.'

From Thomas Mann, *Buddenbrooks* (1902), translated by H.T. Lowe-Porter.

Inviting a Friend to Supper

Tonight, grave sir, both my poor house and I
Do equally desire your company:
Not that we think us worthy such a guest,
But that your worth will dignify our feast
With those that come; whose grace may make that seem
Something, which else could hope for no esteem.
It is the fair acceptance, sir, creates
The entertainment perfect, not the cates.
Yet shall you have, to rectify your palate,
An olive, capers, or some better salad
Ushering the mutton; with a short-legged hen,
If we can get her, full of eggs, and then
Lemons, and wine for sauce; to these, a cony

Is not to be despaired of, for our money;
And though fowl now be scarce, yet there are clerks,
The sky not falling, think we may have larks.
I'll tell you of more, and lie, so you will come:
Of partridge, pheasant, woodcock, of which some
May yet be there; and godwit, if we can;
Knat, rail and ruff, too. Howsoe'er, my man
Shall read a piece of Virgil, Tacitus,
Livy, or of some better book to us,
Of which we'll speak our minds, amidst our meat;
And I'll profess no verses to repeat;
To this, if aught appear which I not know of,
That will the pastry, not my paper, show of.
Digestive cheese and fruit there sure will be;
But that which most doth take my Muse and me
Is a pure cup of rich Canary wine,
Which is the Mermaid's now, but shall be mine;
Of which had Horace or Anacreon tasted,
Their lives, as do their lines, till now had lasted.
Tobacco, nectar, or the Thespian spring
Are all but Luther's beer to this I sing.
Of this we will sup free, but moderately;
And we will have no Poley or Parrot by;
Nor shall our cups make any guilty men,
But at our parting we will be as when
We innocently met. No simple word
That shall be uttered at our mirthful board
Shall make us sad next morning, or affright
The liberty that we'll enjoy tonight.

Ben Jonson (1616).

Never Mind What She Does in Her Spare Time

She is a little square woman, between fifty and sixty, with a ruby button of a nose and hair, that oil and age has robbed of its brilliant red, drawn smoothly back into a tight screw at the back of her broad head. Her eyes are a fishy green grey, the left eyelid droops; when she thinks you are not looking, a sly elusive gleam brightens them, her pursed lips loosen, and if you happen to see it, you think that there may be something after all in the stories the gossips whisper of Marie Larsen. Her dress is exquisitely neat, her apron snowy. No one in the district can make such a *suprême* of fish as Marie; no one beat her at roasting a capercailzie and serving it with sour cream sauce; or brew such caudles and possets for a lying-in, or bake such meats for a funeral-feast. And what if there be an old-time tale of a brat accidentally smothered? And what if the Amtmanden (superior magistrate), he who had the sickly wife, did send Marie to Germany to learn cooking? Well, he had money to spare and was always freehanded. And if Nils Pettersen did write home and say that he saw her in Hamburg at a trade – well, other than cooking – sure Nils Pettersen was a bit of a liar anyhow, and good cooking covers a multitude of frailties.

From George Egerton, 'Under A Northern Sky', *Keynotes* (1893).

A Happy Glutton

At supper this night [Dr Johnson] talked of good eating with uncommon satisfaction. 'Some people (said he,) have a foolish way of not minding, or pretending not to mind, what they eat. For my part, I mind my belly very studiously, and very carefully; for I look upon it, that he who does not mind his belly will hardly mind anything else.' He now appeared to me *Jean Bull philosophe*, and he was, for the moment, not only serious but vehement. Yet I have heard him, upon other occasions, talk with great contempt of people who were anxious to gratify their palates; and the 206th number of his *Rambler* is a masterly essay against gulosity. His practice, indeed, I must acknowledge, may be considered as casting the balance of his different opinions upon this subject; for I never knew any man who relished good eating more than he did. When at table, he was totally absorbed in the business of the moment; his looks seemed rivetted to his plate; nor would he, unless when in very high company, say one word, or even pay the least attention to what was said by others, till he had satisfied his appetite, which was so fierce, and indulged with such intenseness, that while in the act of eating, the veins of his forehead swelled, and generally a strong perspiration was visible. To those whose sensations were delicate, this could not but be disgusting; and it was doubtless not very suitable to the character of a philosopher, who should be distinguished by self-command. But it must be owned, that Johnson, though he could be rigidly *abstemious*, was not a *temperate* man either in eating or drinking. He could refrain, but he could not use moderately. He told me, that he had fasted two days without inconvenience, and that he had never been hungry but once. They who beheld with wonder how much he eat upon all occasions when his dinner was to his taste, could not easily conceive what he must have meant by hunger; and not only was he remarkable for the extraordinary quantity which he eat, but he was, or affected to be, a man of very nice discernment in the science of cookery. He used to descant critically on the dishes which had been at table where he had dined or supped, and to recollect very minutely what he had liked. I remember, when he was in Scotland, his praising 'Gordon's palates,' (a dish of palates at the Honourable Alexander Gordon's) with a warmth of expression which might have done honour to more important subjects. 'As for Maclaurin's imitation of a *made dish*, it was a wretched attempt.' He about the same time was so much displeased with the performances of a nobleman's French cook, that he exclaimed with vehemence, 'I'd throw such a rascal into the river;' and he then proceeded to alarm a lady at whose house he was to sup, by the following manifesto of his skill: 'I, Madam, who live at a variety of good tables, am a much better judge of cookery, than any person who has a very tolerable cook, but lives much at home; for his palate is gradually adapted to the taste of his cook; whereas, Madam, in trying by a wider range, I can more exquisitely judge.' When invited to dine, even with an intimate friend, he was not pleased if something better than a plain dinner was not prepared for him. I have heard him say on such an occasion, 'This was a good dinner enough, to be sure; but it was not a dinner to *ask* a man to.' On the other hand, he was wont to express, with great glee, his satisfaction when he had been entertained quite to his mind. One day when we had dined with his neighbour and landlord in Bolt-court, Mr Allen, the printer, whose old housekeeper had studied his taste in every thing, he pronounced this eulogy: 'Sir, we could not have had a better dinner had there been a *Synod of Cooks*.'

From James Boswell, *The Life of Samuel Johnson* (1791).

Breakfast, Lunch, Dinner: Eating the Day Away

But the impatient reader may ask, how, in this year of grace 1825, must a meal be contrived in order to combine the conditions which procure the pleasures of the table in the highest degree?

That question I am about to answer. Compose yourselves, readers, and pay attention; Gasterea inspires me, the prettiest of all the Muses; I shall be clearer than an oracle, and my precepts will go down the ages.

'Let the number of guests be not more than twelve, so that the talk may be constantly general;

'Let them be chosen with different occupations but similar tastes, and with such points of contact that the odious formalities of introduction can be dispensed with;

'Let the dining-room be well lighted, the cloth impeccably white, and the atmosphere maintained at a temperature of from sixty to seventy degrees;

'Let the men be witty without being too pretentious, and the women charming without being too coquettish;*

'Let the dishes be few in number, but exquisitely choice, and the wines of the first quality, each in its class;

'Let the service of the former proceed from the most substantial to the lightest, and of the latter, from the mildest to the most perfumed;

'Let the progress of the meal be slow, for dinner is the last business of the day; and let the guests conduct themselves like travellers due to reach their destination together;

'Let the coffee be piping hot, and the liqueurs chosen by a connoisseur;

'Let the drawing-room be large enough to allow a game at cards to be arranged for those who cannot do without, yet still leave space for postprandial conversations;

'Let the guests be detained by the charms of the company and sustained by the hope that the evening will not pass without some further pleasure;

'Let the tea be not too strong, the toast artistically buttered, and the punch mixed with proper care;

'Let retirement begin not earlier than eleven o'clock, but by midnight let everyone be in bed.'

Whoever has been present at a meal fulfilling all these conditions

---

* I am writing this in Paris, between the Palais-Royal and the Chaussée-d'Antin.

may claim to have witnessed his own apotheosis; and for each of them which is forgotten or ignored, the guests will suffer a proportionate decrease of pleasure.

I have said that the pleasures of the table, such as I have described them, can be of quite lengthy duration; I am going to prove this by giving the true and detailed history of the longest meal I have ever eaten; this is a sweet I am putting in the reader's mouth, as a reward for his kindness in reading my book.

At the lower end of the Rue du Bac there used to live a certain family composed as follows: the doctor, aged seventy-eight; the captain, aged seventy-six; and their sister Jeannette, aged seventy-four. They were relatives of mine, and always welcomed me very kindly when I went to see them.

'Dammit!' Doctor Dubois said to me one day, raising himself on tip-toe to slap me on the back, 'you are always boasting of your *fondues* (scrambled eggs with cheese), till our mouths water at the thought of them; we cannot stand it any longer. One of these days we are coming to breakfast with you, the captain and I, to find out what they are like.' (It was about 1801, I think, that he teased me like this.)

'By all means,' I replied; 'and you shall have one in all its glory, for I'll make it myself. Your proposal fills me with joy. Come round tomorrow, at ten o'clock, military time.*

At the appointed hour my two guests appeared, newly shaved and carefully combed and powdered; two little old men, still hale and hearty.

They smiled with pleasure when they saw the table ready, a white cloth, three places laid, and in each place two dozen oysters, with a bright golden lemon in their midst.

A tall bottle of Sauterne stood at each end of the table, carefully wiped except for the corks, which indicated in no uncertain manner that a long time had passed since it had been drawn.

Alas for the countless gay breakfasts of old, when oysters were swallowed by the thousand! I saw the end of those breakfasts, for they went out with the abbés, who always ate at least a gross of oysters, and the chevaliers, who went on eating them for ever. I regret them, but philosophically; if time can change governments, what powers it must have over mere customs!

---

* Whenever a rendezvous is announced in this way, the first dish must be served up as the clock strikes, and all late comers are regarded as deserters.

After the oysters, which proved admirably fresh, came broiled kidneys, a jar of truffled *foie gras*, and the *fondue*.

The ingredients were all ready in the saucepan which was placed on the table over a spirits-of-wine burner. I officiated on the field of battle, and none of my movements escaped my cousins' notice.

They went into raptures over the dish, and asked me for the recipe, which I promised to give them, meanwhile telling them two anecdotes on the subject which the reader may perhaps encounter elsewhere.

After the *fondue* came fresh fruit and preserves, a cup of real Mocha made *à la Dubelloy* (a method which was then beginning to be known), and finally two different kinds of liqueur, a detergent spirit and a soothing oil.

When breakfast was well and truly over, I proposed a little exercise, in the form of a tour of my apartment, which, though far from elegant, is both vast and comfortable, and where my friends felt all the more at home in that the ceilings and gilding date from the middle of the reign of Louis XV.

I showed them the clay original of the bust of my pretty cousin, Madame Récamier, by Chinard, and her portrait in miniature by Augustin; they were both so impressed that the doctor pressed his thick lips to the portrait, while the captain made so free with the bust that I was obliged to chastise him; for if all the admirers of the original were to do likewise, that voluptuously rounded bosom would soon be reduced to the condition of Saint Peter's toe at Rome, which the faithful have worn away with their kisses.

Next I showed them a few casts after the best sculptors of antiquity, some pictures which are not without merit, my guns and musical instruments, and some fine editions of French and foreign authors.

In the course of this polymathical excursion, they did not forget my kitchen. There I showed them my economical stock-pot, my Dutch oven, my clockwork turn-spit, and my steamer. They examined everything with minute attention, all the more astonished in that their own kitchen had remained unaltered since the days of the Regency.

We had just returned to the drawing-room when the clock struck two. 'Botheration!' exclaimed the doctor, 'it is dinnertime, and my sister Jeannette will be waiting for us. We must go home at once. Not that I feel at all hungry, but I must have my soup for all that. It is such an old habit of mine that whenever I let a day go by without taking it, I say with Titus: *Diem perdidi*.'

'My dear doctor,' I replied, 'why go so far in search of what is close at hand? I will send word to your sister that you are staying with me, and that you are going to give me the pleasure of your company at dinner; though I must ask for your indulgence towards the meal which will not have all the merit of an *impromptu* composed at leisure.'

The two brothers held an ocular deliberation over my invitation, and then formally accepted it. I promptly dispatched a *volante* to the Faubourg Saint-Germain, and had a word with my master cook; and within a very short space of time, drawing on his own resources and those of neighbouring restaurateurs, he served us up a very neat and appetizing little dinner.

I was filled with satisfaction when I saw the alacrity with which my two friends sat down, pulled their chairs up to the table, spread out their napkins, and prepared for action.

They met with two surprises which I had not realized would be novelties to them; for I gave them Parmesan with their soup, and a glass of dry Madeira after it. Both had been recently imported by Monsieur le Prince de Talleyrand, the greatest of diplomats, to whom we are indebted for so many profound and witty sayings, and who, whether in power or in retirement, has always commanded the interest of the nation.

The dinner went very well, with respect to both its essential substance and its necessary accessories, and my friends contributed as much indulgence as gaiety to the meal.

After dinner, I proposed a game of piquet; but the captain said they preferred the *far niente* of the Italians, so we drew our chairs up to the fire.

Despite the charms of the *far niente*, I have always thought that nothing makes conversation easier than some occupation of a trivial kind, so I suggested we should take tea.

Tea was something quite novel to Frenchmen of the old school; nevertheless, they agreed to try it. I made it in their presence, and they drank a few cups of it, with all the more pleasure in that till then they had never regarded it as any thing but a form of medicine.

Long experience had taught me that one surrender leads to another, and that he who once sets out on the path of acceptance soon forgets how to refuse. So it was in an almost dictatorial tone that I talked of ending up with a bowl of punch.

'But you will kill us!' said the doctor.

'But you will make us drunk!' said the captain.

My only reply was to call for sugar, lemons, and rum.

I mixed the punch, and in the meantime toast was made, thin, delicately buttered, and salted to perfection.

This time I met with some opposition. My cousins declared that they had eaten quite enough, and that they would not touch the toast. But knowing the charm of that simple preparation, I replied that my only anxiety was that there might not be sufficient. Sure enough, it was not long before the captain took the last slice, and I caught him looking to see if any was left, or if more was being made; so I ordered more straight away.

Meanwhile time had not stood still, and the hands of my clock had passed the eighth hour.

'We must fly,' said my guests; 'we really must go and eat a little salad with our poor sister, who hasn't set eyes on us all day.'

This time I made no objection; and, mindful of the courtesy due to two such charming old men, I saw them to their carriage and watched them drive away.

The reader may ask whether so long a sitting was not marred by a few tedious moments.

I shall answer in the negative; my guests' interest was maintained by the making of the *fondue*, the tour of my apartment, a few novelties at dinner, the tea, and above all the punch, which they had never tasted before.

Moreover, the doctor was acquainted with the genealogy and reputation of everyone in Paris; the captain had spent part of his life in Italy, both in the army and as an envoy to the court of Parma; and I have travelled a great deal myself; we conversed without pretension, and listened when it was our turn. This was more than enough to make the time pass smoothly and swiftly.

Next morning I received a letter from the doctor in which he was kind enough to inform me that the little debauch of the day before had had no evil after-effects; on the contrary, he said, after a good night's rest they had risen wonderfully refreshed and ready to begin all over again.

From Jean-Anthelme Brillat-Savarin, *The Physiology of Taste* (1825), translated by Anne Drayton.

Eating like a King

I was about three months hedging in the first piece, and till I had done it I tethered the three kids in the best part of it, and used them to feed as near me as possible to make them familiar; and very often I would go and carry them some ears of barley, or a handful of rice, and feed them out of my hand; so that after my enclosure was finished, and I let them loose, they would follow me up and down, bleating after me for a handful of corn.

This answered my end, and in about a year and a half I had a flock of about twelve goats, kids and all; and in two years more I had three and forty, besides several that I took and killed for my food. And after that I enclosed five several pieces of ground to feed them in, with little pens to drive them into, to take them as I wanted, and gates out of one piece of ground into another.

But this was not all for now I not only had goat's flesh to feed on when I pleased, but milk too, a thing which indeed in my beginning I did not so much as think of, and which, when it came into my thoughts, was really an agreeable surprize. For now I set up my dairy, and had sometimes a gallon or two of milk in a day. And as nature, who gives supplies of food to every creature, dictates even naturally how to make use of it; so I that had never milked a cow, much less a goat, or seen butter or cheese made, very readily and handily, tho' after a great many essays and miscarriages, made me both butter and cheese at last, and never wanted it afterwards.

How mercifully can our great Creator treat His creatures, even in those conditions in which they seemed to be overwhelmed in destruction! How can He sweeten the bitterest providences, and give us cause to praise Him for dungeons and prisons! What a table was here spread for me in a wilderness, where I saw nothing at first but to perish for hunger!

It would have made a stoick smile to have seen me and my little family sit down to dinner; there was my majesty the prince and lord of the whole island; I had the lives of all my subjects at my absolute command; I could hang, draw, give liberty, and take it away, and no rebels among all my subjects.

Then to see how like a king I dined too, all alone, attended by my servants. Poll, as if he had been my favourite, was the only person permitted to talk to me. My dog, who was now grown very old and crazy, and had found no species to multiply his kind upon, sat always at my right hand, and two cats, one on one side the table, and one on the other, expecting now and then a bit from my hand, as a mark of special favour.

From Daniel Defoe, Robinson Crusoe (1719).

Food for Thought

In all the four years I worked in the fields, I never worked one hour under cover of a barn, and only once did we have a meal in a house. And I shall never forget that one meal or the woman who gave us it. It was a most terrible day. The cold east wind (I suppose it was an east wind, for surely no wind ever blew colder), the sleet and snow which came every now and then in showers seemed almost to cut us to pieces. We were working upon a large farm that lay half-way between Croyland and Peterborough. Had the snow and sleet come continuously we should have been allowed to come home, but because it only came at intervals, of course we had to stay. I have been out in all sorts of weather but never remember a colder day. Well, the morning passed along somehow. The ganger did his best for us by letting us have a run in our turns, but that did not help us very much because we were too numbed with the cold to be able to run much. Dinner-time came, and we were preparing to sit down under a hedge and eat our cold dinner and drink our cold tea, when we saw the shepherd's wife coming towards us, and she said to our ganger, 'Bring these children into my house and let them eat their dinner there.' We went into that very small two-roomed cottage, and when we got into the largest room there was not standing room for us all, but this woman's heart was large, even if her house was small, and so she put her few chairs and table out into the garden, and then we all sat down in a ring upon the floor. She then placed in our midst a very large saucepan of hot boiled potatoes, and bade us help ourselves. Truly, although I have attended scores of grand parties and banquets since that time, not one of them has seemed half as good to me as that meal did.

From *Life as We Have Known It*, edited by Margaret Llewelyn Davies (1931).

Worth the Wait

(*Resas, 16 May 1928*)

We were being eaten alive meanwhile, and were very languid for food: ten hours since the last meal, and it was 9.30 and the talk going round to the Divinity of Christ; I felt the words wandering from me in a mist; it had gone on solidly for three hours. Lucky Venetia who could be silent, drooping in the shadow of her hat; and 'Arif, who just curled himself on the floor and slept! Venetia says that the first three mouthfuls of dinner gave my voice quite a different ring! It was a splendid dinner: chicken on rice, beans, rice pudding, coffee, the delicious coffee freshly made which we shall miss so often.

From Freya Stark, *Letters from Syria* (1942).

A Lucullan Banquet

Captain Carey Ashburn's useless arm was hurting him again and moreover he was depressed by the thought that his courtship of Scarlett was at a standstill. That had been the situation ever since the news of Ashley Wilkes' capture, though the connection between the two events did not occur to him. Scarlett and Melanie both were thinking of Ashley, as they always did when urgent tasks or the necessity of carrying on a conversation did not divert them. Scarlett was thinking bitterly, sorrowfully: 'He must be dead or else we would have heard.' Melanie, stemming the tide of fear again and again, through endless hours, was telling herself: 'He can't be dead. I'd know it – I'd feel it if he were dead.' Rhett Butler lounged in the shadows, his long legs in their elegant boots crossed negligently, his dark face an unreadable blank. In his arms Wade slept contentedly, a cleanly picked wishbone in his small hand. Scarlett always permitted Wade to sit up late when Rhett called because the shy child was fond of him, and Rhett oddly enough seemed to be fond of Wade. Generally Scarlett was annoyed by the child's presence, but he always behaved nicely in Rhett's arms. As for Aunt Pitty, she was nervously trying to stifle a belch, for the rooster they had had for supper was a tough old bird.

That morning Aunt Pitty had reached the regretful decision that she had better kill the patriarch before he died of old age and pining for his harem which had long since been eaten. For days he had drooped about the empty chicken-run, too dispirited to crow. After Uncle Peter had wrung his neck, Aunt Pitty had been beset by conscience at the thought of enjoying him, en famille, when so many of her friends had not tasted chicken for weeks, so she suggested company for dinner. Melanie, who was now in her fifth month, had not been out in public or received guests for weeks, and she was appalled at the idea. But Aunt Pitty, for once, was firm. It would be selfish to eat the rooster alone, and if Melanie would only move her top hoop a little higher no one would notice anything and she was so flat in the bust anyway.

'Oh, but Auntie, I don't want to see people when Ashley –'

'It isn't as if Ashley were – had passed away,' said Aunt Pitty, her voice quavering, for in her heart she was certain Ashley was dead. 'He's just as much alive as you are and it will do you good to have company. And I'm going to ask Fanny Elsing, too. Mrs Elsing begged me to try to do something to arouse her and make her see people –'

'Oh, but Auntie, it's cruel to force her when poor Dallas has only been dead –'

'Now, Melly, I shall cry with vexation if you argue with me. I guess I'm your auntie and I know what's what. And I want a party.'

So Aunt Pitty had her party, and, at the last minute, a guest she did not expect, or desire, arrived. Just when the smell of roast rooster was filling the house, Rhett Butler, back from one of his mysterious trips, knocked at the door, with a large box of bonbons packed in paper lace under his arm and a mouthful of two-edged compliments for her. There was nothing to do but invite him to stay, although Aunt Pitty knew how the doctor and Mrs Meade felt about him and how bitter Fanny was against any man not in uniform. Neither the Meades nor the Elsings would have spoken to him on the street, but in a friend's home they would, of course, have to be polite to him. Besides, he was now more firmly than ever under the protection of the fragile Melanie. After he had intervened for her to get the news about Ashley, she had announced publicly that her home was open to him as long as he lived and no matter what other people might say about him.

Aunt Pitty's apprehensions quieted when she saw that Rhett was on his best behaviour. He devoted himself to Fanny with such sympathetic deference she even smiled at him, and the meal went well. It was a princely feast. Carey Ashburn had brought a little tea, which he had found in the tobacco-pouch of a captured Yankee en route to Andersonville, and everyone had a cup, faintly flavoured with tobacco. There was a nibble of the tough old bird for each, an adequate amount of dressing made of corn meal and seasoned with onions, a bowl of dried peas, and plenty of rice and gravy, the latter somewhat watery, for there was no flour with which to thicken it. For dessert, there was a sweet potato pie followed by Rhett's bonbons, and when Rhett produced real Havana cigars for the gentlemen to enjoy over their glass of blackberry wine, everyone agreed it was indeed a Lucullan banquet.

From Margaret Mitchell, *Gone With the Wind* (1936).

A Culinary Joke

2 June 1660

All the afternoon with two or three captains in the Captain's cabin, drinking of white wine and sugar and eating pickled oysters – where Capt. Sparling told us the best Story that ever I heard; about a gentleman that persuaded a country fellow to let him gut his oysters or else they would stink.

From *The Diary of Samuel Pepys*, edited by Robert Latham and William Matthews (1985).

Gobbling Up the World

I'd never liked to shop. From the time I fled Ohio in the early Fifties for my beatnik apprenticeship in New York City, embracing mind and eschewing 'things' had been my self-defining strategy, one that, through the mysterious imperatives of culture, deemed sensual pleasures (good) and material possessions (bad) mutually exclusive. Even after I relinquished bohemia for family life, when Stevie and Amy were little I ordered the family clothes from the Sears catalogue, though we were right there in the middle of Manhattan surrounded by boutiques. Food shopping I liked better, with all the ethnic specialty shops and neighborhood markets in New York City, and when a farmers' market opened nearby on Union Square I looked forward to the pleasures of squeezing vegetables and sampling fruits on Saturday mornings. But there were none to squeeze at the island store.

That was a pity for someone as passionate about food as I. In fact, it was through food that I'd first learned to gobble up the world after a childhood as an indifferent eater. To this day my memories of a transforming student year in Europe, when my husband was a Fulbright and I a 'halfbright,' as wives were called, are as dense with the taste of food – my first artichoke, my first celery-root salad with my first rémoulade sauce, my first weisswurst and prosciutto – as with images of pissoirs along the grand Parisian boulevards, the bombed-out streets of Munich, flamenco dancers on the outskirts of Spanish villages, the young wolves representing Remus and Romulus pacing their Roman cage on Michelangelo's Campidoglio. Other people show snapshots and slides when they come home, but I, returning to New York in 1957, with missionary zeal taught myself to cook in order to make monthly European feasts for friends not lucky enough to have gone abroad in those days when transatlantic travel was prohibitively expensive, when a broiled steak dinner represented the pinnacle of celebration, when Italian food meant spaghetti swimming in tomato sauce. The first person in my family to cross the ocean going east, I felt a calling to introduce my compatriots to such wonders of nature as blood oranges, snails, squash flowers, and fennel. To me food was part of the great postwar cultural adventure: mind-expanding and sensual, titillating and educational, like atonal music, or experimental sex, or marijuana, or a new language, only more readily accessible, and I wanted to share the thrill of the flavors of French, German, and Italian food that had taken me completely by surprise. As Marco Polo had brought back noodles from China to Italy, so I brought spaghetti alla carbonara from Rome to provincial young New Yorkers.

Returning home every evening from my editorial job to cook dinner for my graduate-student husband was a comedown after the adventure of cooking in Europe. I missed the excitement of setting off of a morning to fill my string bag with each new offering of the butcher, the baker, the greengrocer, the sausage-maker of München–Obermenzing, often returning home with the grocer's personal recipe. Then one happy day I discovered the long stretch of Greek, Italian, and Middle Eastern markets in Hell's Kitchen on Ninth Avenue, collectively called Paddy's Market, where I immediately took to spending my precious Saturdays grocery shopping. Strolling before the pushcarts and laden windows felt something like being in another country: Syrian bakeries displayed baklava in pans made of the empty film cans discarded by the documentary-film industry that shared the neighborhood; greengrocers sold kale, chard, mustard, turnip, dandelion, and other unnamed greens, unobtainable in those days at the A&P but redolent of the mysterious wild 'field salads' I had so recently enjoyed in Europe. One butcher shop sold veal chops with the kidney attached, another displayed lamb's heads, sweet-breads, trotters, and small round organs which my youthful eye had already identified as some poor creature's testicles. Pointing, I asked the butcher in my most innocent voice, 'What're those?' The butcher smiled, summoned two of his colleagues with a wave of his hand, and answered as innocently, 'Mountain oysters.' 'Oysters?' I asked incredulously. 'Really? How do I cook them?' Grinning now for his buddies: 'You just slice them up, dip them in a little egg, coat them in bread crumbs or flour' – clapping imaginary slices between almost floury palms – 'fry them up in a little butter. Salt and pepper, maybe some chopped garlic – but better not tell your boyfriend.' 'I'll take a dozen,' I said, barely able to hide my glee, already planning new hors d'oeuvres for that weekend's lucky guests.

From Alix Kates Shulman, *Drinking the Rain* (1995).

The Alchemy of Cooking

The preparation of food, getting meals, is work more positive in nature and often more agreeable than cleaning. First of all it means marketing, often the bright spot of the day. And gossip on doorsteps, while peeling vegetables, is a gay relief for solitude; to go for water is a great adventure for half-cloistered Mohammedan women; women in markets and stores talk about domestic affairs, with a common interest, feeling themselves members of a group that – for an instant – is opposed to the group of men as the essential to the inessential. Buying is a profound pleasure, a discovery, almost an invention. As Gide says in his *Journal*, the Mohammedans, not knowing gambling, have in its place the discovery of hidden treasure; that is the poetry and the adventure of mercantile civilizations. The housewife knows little of winning in games, but a solid cabbage, a ripe Camembert, are treasures that must be cleverly won from the unwilling storekeeper;

the game is to get the best for the least money; economy means not so much helping the budget as winning the game. She is pleased with her passing triumph as she contemplates her well-filled larder.

Gas and electricity have killed the magic of fire, but in the country many women still know the joy of kindling live flames from inert wood. With her fire going, woman becomes a sorceress; by a simple movement, as in beating eggs, or through the magic of fire, she effects the transmutation of substances: matter becomes food. There is enchantment in these alchemies, there is poetry in making preserves; the housewife has caught duration in the snare of sugar, she has enclosed life in jars. Cooking is revelation and creation; and a woman can find special satisfaction in a successful cake or a flaky pastry, for not everyone can do it: one must have the gift.

From Simone de Beauvoir, *The Second Sex* (1949), translated by H.M. Parshley.

Dropping Curry

My substitute for LSD was Indian food, to which Fessenden introduced me and which became a constant theme of our exchanges. It began in 1973 during a short visit to Bennington by the brilliant British philosopher Gillian Rose, the last woman Fessenden (as a graduate student) had dated. She concocted a fantastic Indian soup, golden-mustard in color and silty with twelve fresh-ground spices. It packed a wallop: I was hung over for two days. In New York, Fessenden took me to his favorite restaurant, the hole-in-the-wall Bit of Bengal on upper Broadway, where I had my first ultra-hot lamb vindaloo, a seductive culinary rut I have never escaped, no matter how resolutely I scan the rest of the menu. There Fessenden, languorous as Lewis Carroll's hookah-smoking caterpillar, ordered my first ambrosial, rust-red mulligatawny soup and educated me about its proper ceremonious consumption. '*Really*, Camille,' he thundered, as I gulped it down. Obscure Indian restaurants all over New York became the scene of my spice-triggered psychedelic 'trips' with Fessenden. After our mammoth feasts, I would smoke a cigar as, gorged and happy, we strolled the streets.

From Camille Paglia, *Vamps and Tramps: New Essays* (1995).

Steak à la Lautrec

At the time [Toulouse-Lautrec] commented on the event almost as an afterthought: 'My poster was put up today on the walls of Paris, and I'm going to make another one,' was all he wrote to his mother in a letter otherwise devoted to Alph's bout of influenza and instructions to Adèle about shipping him fowl and truffles. 'On re-reading my letter,' Henry commented, 'I find it has a gastronomic character.' Thirteen lines were devoted to food and only two to the hanging of the poster which made him famous.

Henry, following in his father's footsteps, took pride in his gastronomic *finesse*, both in the preparation of good food and in the recognition of fine quality ingredients. He liked to cook for friends and did so often enough for Maurice Joyant to begin collecting the recipes he used. Several anecdotes refer to Henry's arriving in a friend's kitchen armed with all the ingredients for some complicated dish, like lobster *à l'Armoricaine*. However, as such preparations required the drinking of large quantities of alcohol in the kitchen, his impromptu dinners received a mixed welcome. One legendary recipe which persisted in Henry's family as having been invented by him was 'Steak à la Lautrec': 'You grill three of them, one stacked on top of another (on a fire made of grapevine wood, naturally) copiously covered with pepper and mustard – but you only serve the one in the middle, which is the only one which is cooked perfectly.'

From Julia Frey, *Toulouse-Lautrec: A Life* (1994).

Almond Tarts

Poised on steady legs
First your poet begs
Several eggs.
Froth them to a mousse,
And then introduce
Lemon juice.
Shimmering like silk,
Aromatic milk
Of almonds will
come next, and next prepare

Pastry light as air
To coat with care
Each pretty pastry mould.
Which sweetly will enfold
The liquid gold.
Smile, a father, fond,
Wave your fiery wand,
Bake till blond.
Melting mouths and hearts,
Mmmmmm, saliva starts –
Almond tarts.

From Edmond Rostand (1868–1918), *Cyrano de Bergerac*, translated by
Anthony Burgess.

Dinner as Anti-Depressant

Just back from L.'s speech at Brighton. Like a foreign town: the first
spring day. Women sitting on seats. A pretty hat in a teashop – how
fashion revives the eye! And the shell encrusted old women, rouged,
decked, cadaverous at the tea shop. The waitress in checked cotton.

No: I intend no introspection. I mark Henry James's sentence:
Observe perpetually. Observe the oncome of age. Observe greed.
Observe my own despondency. By that means it becomes serviceable.
Or so I hope. I insist upon spending this time to the best advantage. I
will go down with my colours flying. This I see verges on
introspection; but doesn't quite fall in. Suppose, I bought a ticket at
the Museum; biked in daily & read history. Suppose I selected one
dominant figure in every age & wrote round & about. Occupation is
essential. And now with some pleasure I find that its seven; & must
cook dinner. Haddock & sausage meat. I think it is true that one
gains a certain hold on sausage & haddock by writing them down.

Last night I analysed to L. my London Library complex. That
sudden terror has vanished; now I'm plucked at by the H. Hamilton
lunch that I refused. To right the balance, I wrote to Stephen & Tom:
& will write to Ethel & invite myself to stay; & then to Miss Sharp
who presented me with a bunch of violets. This to make up for the
sight of Oxford Street & Piccadilly which haunt me. Oh dear yes, I
shall conquer this mood. Its a question of being open sleepy, wide

eyed at present – letting things come one after another. Now to cook
the haddock.

Entry for Saturday, 8 March 1941, from *The Diary of
Virginia Woolf*, Vol. 5, 1936–41, edited by Anna Olivier Bell,
assisted by Andrew McNeillie.

Juan's Feast

Great things were now to be achieved at table,
   With massy plate for armour, knives and forks
For weapons; but what Muse since Homer's able
   (His feasts are not the worst part of his works)
To draw up in array a single day-bill
   Of modern dinners? where more mystery lurks
In soups or sauces, or a sole ragout,
Than witches, b—ches, or physicians brew.

There was a goodly 'soupe à la *bonne femme*,'
   Though God knows whence it came from; there was too
A turbot for relief of those who cram,
   Relieved with dindon à la Parigeux;
There also was – the sinner that I am!
   How shall I get this gourmand stanza through? –
Soupe à la Beauveau, whose relief was Dory,
Relieved itself by pork, for greater glory.

But I must crowd all into one grand mess
   Or mass; for should I stretch into detail,
My Muse would run much more into excess,
   Than when some squeamish people deem her frail.
But though a 'bonne vivante,' I must confess
   Her stomach's not her peccant part: this tale
However doth require some slight refection,
Just to relieve her spirits from dejection.

Fowls à la Condé, slices eke of salmon,
   With sauces Genevoises, and haunch of venison;
Wines too which might again have slain young Ammon –

A man like whom I hope we shan't see many soon;
They also set a glazed Westphalian ham on,
    Whereon Apicius would bestow his benison;
And then there was Champagne with foaming whirls,
As white as Cleopatra's melted pearls.

Then there was God knows what 'à l'Allemande,'
    'A l'Espagnole,' 'timballe,' and 'Salpicon' –
With things I can't withstand or understand,
    Though swallow'd with much zest upon the whole;
And 'extremets' to piddle with at hand,
    Gently to lull down the subsiding soul;
While great Lucullus' (*Rôbe triumphal*) muffles –
(*There's blame*) – young Partridge' fillets, deck'd with truffles.

What are the *fillets* on the victor's brow
    To these? They are rags or dust. Where is the arch
Which nodded to the nation's spoils below?
    Where the triumphal chariots' haughty march?
Gone to where victories must like dinners go.
    Further I shall not follow the research:
But oh! ye modern heroes with your cartridges,
When will your names lend lustre even to partridges?

Those truffles too are no bad accessaries,
    Follow'd by 'Petits puits d'Amour' – a dish
Of which perhaps the cookery rather varies,
    So every one may dress it to his wish,
According to the best of dictionaries,
    Which encyclopedize both flesh and fish;
But even sans 'comfitures,' it no less true is,
There's pretty picking in those 'petits puits.'

The mind is lost in mighty contemplation
    Of intellect expended on two courses;
And indigestion's grand multiplication
    Requires arithmetic beyond my forces.
Who would suppose, from Adam's simple ration,
    That cookery could have call'd forth such resources,
As form a science and a nomenclature
From out the commonest demands of nature?

The glasses jingled, and the palates tingled;
　　The diners of celebrity dined well;
The ladies with more moderation mingled
　　In the feast, pecking less than I can tell;
Also the younger men too; for a springald
　　Can't like ripe age in gourmandise excel,
But thinks less of good eating than the whisper
(When seated next him) of some pretty lisper.

Alas! I must leave undescribed the gibier,
　　The salmi, the consommé, the purée,
All which I use to make my rhymes run glibber
　　Than could roast beef in our rough John Bull way:
I must not introduce even a spare rib here,
　　'Bubble and squeak' would spoil my liquid lay;
But I have dined, and must forego, alas!
The chaste description even of a 'Becasse,'

And fruits, and ice, and all that art refines
　　From nature for the service of the goût, –
Taste or the *gout*, – pronounce it as inclines
　　Your stomach! Ere you dine, the French will do;
But *after*, there are sometimes certain signs
　　Which prove plain English truer of the two.
Hast ever *had* the *gout*? I have not had it –
But I may have, and you too, Reader, dread it.

The simple olives, best allies of wine,
　　Must I pass over in my bill of fare?
I must, although a favourite 'plat' of mine
　　In Spain, and Lucca, Athens, every where:
On them and bread 'twas oft my luck to dine,
　　The grass my table-cloth, in open air,
On Sunium or Hymettus, like Diogenes,
Of whom half my philosophy the progeny is.

Amidst this tumult of fish, flesh, and fowl,
　　And vegetables, all in masquerade.
The guests were placed according to their roll,
　　But various as the various meats display'd:
Don Juan sat next an 'à l'Espagnole' –

No damsel, but a dish, as hath been said:
But so far like a lady, that 'twas drest
Superbly, and contained a world of zest.

From Lord Byron, Canto XV, *Don Juan* (1823).

Down with Great Soles

Most of our food is fish, I remember. There is a local industry, called
sperling. Cut open a round fish, flatten it, dry him bone-white for
days on a rock of wire netting, smoke him, boil him in milk. Not
bad, tasting like dull veal. The local people are lovers of sperling,
though, and taste more in them than I do. Then there are baby soles,
four-inch things too small for sale in the city with the adult soles.
They are fried and delicious. Down with great soles henceforward.

From *Selected Letters of T.E. Lawrence*, edited by David Garnett (1938).

Waiting for William

He was coming at Christmas for five days. There had never been such
preparations. Paul and Arthur scoured the land for holly and
evergreens. Annie made the pretty paper hoops in the old-fashioned
way. And there was unheard-of-extravagance in the larder. Mrs
Morel made a big and magnificent cake. Then, feeling queenly, she
showed Paul how to blanch almonds. He skinned the long nuts
reverently, counting them all, to see not one was lost. It was said that
eggs whisked better in a cold place. So the boy stood in the scullery,
where the temperature was nearly at freezing-point, and whisked and
whisked, and flew in excitement to his mother as the white of egg
grew stiffer and more snowy.

'Just look, mother! Isn't it lovely?'
And he balanced a bit on his nose, then blew it in the air.
'Now, don't waste it,' said the mother.
Everybody was mad with excitement. William was coming on
Christmas Eve. Mrs Morel surveyed the pantry. There was a big
plum cake, and a rice cake, jam tarts, lemon tarts, and mince-pies –

two enormous dishes. She was finishing cooking – Spanish tarts and cheese-cakes. Everywhere was decorated. The kissing bunch of berried holly hung with bright and glittering things, spun slowly over Mrs Morel's head as she trimmed her little tarts in the kitchen. A great fire roared.

There was a scent of cooked pastry. He was due at seven o'clock, but he would be late. The three children had gone to meet him. She was alone. But at a quarter to seven Morel came in again. Neither wife nor husband spoke. He sat in his armchair, quite awkward with excitement, and she quietly went on with her baking. Only by the careful way in which she did things could it be told how much moved she was. The clock ticked on.

From D.H. Lawrence, *Sons and Lovers* (1913).

The Poetry of Butter

One asks oneself how all this decoration, this luxury of fair and chiselled marble, survived the French Revolution. An hour of liberty in the choir of Brou would have been a carnival for the image-breakers. The well-fed Bressois are surely a good-natured people. I call them well-fed both on general and on particular grounds. Their province has the most savoury aroma, and I found an opportunity to test its reputation. I walked back into the town from the church (there was really nothing to be seen by the way), and as the hour of the midday breakfast had struck, directed my steps to the inn. The table d'hôte was going on, and a gracious, bustling, talkative landlady welcomed me. I had an excellent repast – the best repast possible – which consisted simply of boiled eggs and bread and butter. It was the quality of these simple ingredients that made the occasion memorable. The eggs were so good that I am ashamed to say how many of them I consumed. 'La plus belle fille du monde', as the French proverb says, 'ne peut donner que ce qu'elle a'; and it might seem that an egg which has succeeded in being fresh has done all that can reasonably be expected of it. But there was a bloom of punctuality, so to speak, about these eggs of Bourg, as if it had been the intention of the very hens themselves that they should be promptly served. 'Nous sommes en Bresse, et le beurre n'est pas mauvais,' the landlady said with a sort of dry coquetry, as she placed

this article before me. It was the poetry of butter, and I ate a pound
or two of it; after which I came away with a strange mixture of
impressions of late gothic sculpture and thick *tartines*.

From Henry James, *A Little Tour in France* (1884).

Oberon's Feast

SHAPCOT, *to thee the faery state*
I with discretion dedicate;
Because thou prizest things that are
Curious, and unfamiliar.
Take first the feast: these dishes gone,
We'll see the faery court anon.

A little mushroom table spread,
After short prayers they set on bread:
A moon-parched grain of purest wheat,
With some small glittering grit, to eat
His choice bits with; then in a trice
They make a feast less great than nice.
But all this while his eye is served,
We must not think his ear was sterved:
But that there was in place, to stir
His spleen, the chirring grasshopper;
The merry cricket, puling fly,
The piping gnat for minstrelsy.
And now, we must imagine first
The elves present to quench his thirst
A pure seed-pearl of infant dew,
Brought and besweetened in a blue
And pregnant violet; which done,
His kitling eyes begin to run
Quite through the table, where he spies
The horns of papery butterflies,
Of which he eats, and tastes a little
Of that we call the cuckoo's spittle.
A little fuzzball pudding stands
By, yet not blessed by his hands,

That was too coarse; but then forthwith
He ventures boldly on the pith
Of sugared rush, and eats the sag
And well bestrutted bee's sweet bag;
Gladding his palate with some store
Of emmet's eggs: what would he more,
But beards of mice, a newt's stewed thigh,
A bloated earwig, and a fly;
With the red-capped worm that's shut
Within the concave of a nut,
Brown as his tooth. A little moth,
Late fattened in a piece of cloth:
With withered cherries; mandrakes' ears;
Moles' eyes; to these, the slain stag's tears;
The unctuous dewlaps of a snail;
The broke heart of a nightingale
O'ercome in music; with a wine
Ne'er ravished from the flattering vine,
But gently pressed from the soft side
Of the most sweet and dainty bride,
Brought in a dainty daisy, which
He fully quaffs up to bewitch
His blood to height; this done, commended
Grace by his priest: *The feast is ended.*

Robert Herrick (1648).

Around the World in Eighty Meals

Duke [Ellington] seemed to feel that the conversation had taken too
sombre a turn and he began speaking of his appetite, documenting
his claim that it is national, even international, in scope. 'I have
special places marked for special dishes,' he said. 'In Taunton,
Massachusetts, you can get the best chicken stew in the United States.
For chow mein with pigeon's blood, I go to Johnny Cann's Cathay
House in San Francisco. I get my crab cakes at Bolton's – that's in
San Francisco, too. I know a place in Chicago where you get the best
barbecued ribs west of Cleveland and the best shrimp Creole outside
New Orleans. There's a wonderful place in Memphis, too, for

barbecued ribs. I get my Chinook salmon in Portland, Oregon. In Toronto I get duck orange, and the best fried chicken in the world is in Louisville, Kentucky. I get myself a half-dozen chickens and a gallon jar of potato salad, so I can feed the sea gulls. You know, the guys who reach over your shoulder. There's a place in Chicago, the Southway Hotel, that's got the best cinnamon rolls and the best filet mignon in the world. Then there's Ivy Anderson's chicken shack in Los Angeles, where they have hot biscuits with honey and very fine chicken-liver omelets. In New Orleans there's gumbo filé. I like it so well that I always take a pail of it out with me when I leave. In New York I send over to the Turf Restaurant at Forty-ninth and Broadway a couple of times a week to get their broiled lamb chops. I guess I'm a little freakish with lamb chops. I prefer to eat them in the dressing room, where I have plenty of room and can really let myself go. In Washington, at Harrison's, they have devilled crab and Virginia ham. They're terrific things. On the Ile-de-France, when we went to Europe, they had the best crêpes Suzette in the world and it took a dozen at a time to satisfy me. The Café Royal, in The Hague, has the best hors d'oeuvres in the world – eighty-five different kinds, and it takes a long time to eat some of each. There's a place on West Forty-ninth Street in New York that has wonderful curried food and wonderful chutney. There's a place in Paris that has the best octopus soup. And, oh, my, the smorgasbord in Sweden. At old Orchard Beach, Maine, I got the reputation of eating more hot dogs than any man in America. A Mrs. Wagner there makes a toasted bun that's the best of its kind in America. She has a toasted bun, then a slice of onion, then a hamburger, then a tomato, then melted cheese, then another hamburger, then a slice of onion, more cheese, more tomato, and then the other side of the bun. Her hot dogs have two dogs to a bun. I ate thirty-two one night. She has very fine baked beans. When I eat with Mrs. Wagner, I begin with ham and eggs for an appetizer, then the baked beans, then fried chicken, then a steak – her steaks are two inches thick – and then a dessert of applesauce, ice cream, chocolate cake, and custard, mixed with rich, yellow country cream. I like veal with an egg on it. Monseigneur's, in London, has very fine mutton. Durgin-Park's, in Boston, has very fine roast beef. I get the best baked ham, cabbage, and corn bread at a little place near Biloxi. St. Petersburg, Florida, has the best fried fish. It's just a little shack, but they can sure fry fish. I really hurt myself when I go there.'

Duke's audience seemed awed at his recital, and he looked rather impressed himself. 'Gee,' he said admiringly, 'I really sent myself on that, didn't I?'

Some of the passengers wanted to ask more questions, but Duke had worked himself up to the point of having to go to the diner.

From *New Yorker* (1944).

Heavenly Creatures (ii)

At the hour when I usually went downstairs to find out what there was for dinner, its preparation would already have begun, and Françoise, a commanding officer with all the forces of nature for her subalterns, as in the fairy-tales where giants hire themselves out as scullions, would be stirring the coals, putting the potatoes to steam, and, at the right moment, finishing over the fire those culinary masterpieces which had been first got ready in some of the great array of vessels, triumphs of the potter's craft, which ranged from tubs and boilers and cauldrons and fish kettles down to jars for game, moulds for pastry, and tiny pannikins for cream, through an entire collection of pots and pans of every shape and size. I would stop by the table, where the kitchen-maid had shelled them, to inspect the platoons of peas, drawn up in ranks and numbered, like little green marbles, ready for a game; but what most enraptured me were the asparagus, tinged with ultramarine and pink which shaded off from their heads, finely stippled in mauve and azure, through a series of imperceptible gradations to their white feet – still stained a little by the soil of their garden-bed – with an iridescence that was not of this world. I felt that these celestial hues indicated the presence of exquisite creatures who had been pleased to assume vegetable form and who, through the disguise of their firm, comestible flesh, allowed me to discern in this radiance of earliest dawn, these hinted rainbows, these blue evening shades, that precious quality which I should recognise again when, all night long after a dinner at which I had partaken of them, they played (lyrical and coarse in their jesting like one of Shakespeare's fairies) at transforming my chamber pot into a vase of aromatic perfume.

From Marcel Proust, *Swann's Way* (1913), translated by C.K. Scott Moncrieff and Terence Kilmartin, revised by D.J. Enright.

A Surprise Dinner

To my great surprize [Dr Johnson] asked me to dine with him on Easter-day. I never supposed that he had a dinner at his house; for I had not then heard of any one of his friends having been entertained at his table. He told me, 'I generally have a meat pye on Sunday: it is baked at a publick oven, which is very properly allowed, because one man can attend it; and thus the advantage is obtained of not keeping servants from church to dress dinners.'

I supposed we should scarcely have knives and forks, and only some strange, uncouth, ill-drest dish: but I found every thing in very good order. We had no other company but Mrs Williams and a young woman whom I did not know. As a dinner here was considered as a singular phænomenon, and as I was frequently interrogated on the subject, my readers may perhaps be desirous to know our bill of fare. Foote, I remember, in allusion to Francis, the *negro*, was willing to suppose that our repast was *black broth*. But the fact was, that we had a very good soup, a boiled leg of lamb and spinach, a veal pye, and a rice pudding.

From James Boswell, *The Life of Samuel Johnson* (1791).

A Picnic Lunch

In a far corner a woman was sitting with her four children around a large dish piled with *mujaddarah** and pickled turnips, their preoccupation with their meal rendering them completely oblivious to what was going on around them in the baths. When the dish had been emptied of food the mother took from a basket by her side a large cabbage. Gripping its long green leaves, she raised it up and then brought it down hard on the tiled floor, until it split apart and scattered into fragments. The children tumbled over each other to snatch them up and greedily devoured them, savoring their fresh taste.

From Ulfat al-Idilbi, 'The Women's Baths', *Modern Syrian Short Stories*, translated by Michael Azrak (1988).

* A Syrian dish of rice, lentils, onions, and oil.

A Culinary Virgin

When I was six my mother consulted her GP, complaining that my diet consisted almost exclusively of chocolate-coated digestive biscuits and glasses of milk. He observed sensibly that I would grow out of it, although I doubt whether he realised how long it would take. By the time I was eighteen my diet had expanded to include bacon sandwiches (streaky, not back), raw rhubarb stalks dipped in icing sugar, Jacob's Cream Crackers and, to persuade my still-anxious mother I was getting enough protein, the odd slice of processed cheese.

The chief result of this regime was that my weight in my teens hardly ever rose above seven stone, prompting frequent and irritating (since they merely stated the obvious) exclamations of 'Isn't she thin!' It wasn't that I was anorexic, bulimic or suffering from any other identifiable eating disorder; I simply hadn't learned to like food. My mother's cooking was plain and sensible, prepared in deference to her stomach ulcer and her absolute aversion, which she shared with my father, to foreign food.

They shuddered at the thought of curry, picturing the damage it would do to their sensitive English digestive tracts, and walked quickly past the Chinese restaurant which bravely opened its doors in the concrete wasteland of Basingstoke. At fourteen I began to haunt travel agents, fingering brochures and trying to persuade my parents of the delights of Belgium – I would have gone anywhere in the Western World, so great was my desire to go abroad – but most of our summer outings were to windswept south coast resorts or to north Wales.

The food in the guest houses we frequented was usually an inferior version of what my mother cooked at home, served at a fixed time in a cramped dining room where we exchanged restrained greetings with the other residents. Meat arrived sodden with gravy, puddings were invisible under a thick blanket of custard, and the notion of a serving dish from which you could *help yourself* was entirely unknown. Some of these occasions were not even proper holidays, for my father took us with him each year to the conferences he attended as a parks superintendent – keeping up to date with new ways of laying out football pitches and landscape design for municipal cemeteries.

One year, the delegates turned up at the civic reception laid on by a grateful town council looking distinctly green about the gills, having just returned from an outing to the local crematorium. I do not recall much about the food at these municipal banquets, but one of them was enlivened by the presence of a stripper or belly dancer – I have expunged the detail from my memory – who came to our table and perched on my father's knee. I fled to my room where a packet of chocolate digestives was waiting.

By the time I arrived at university my attitude to the food I had heard about but never tasted – French, Indian, Chinese, Italian – was very much like my idea of sex. I longed to try them both but needed time to overcome years of hostile propaganda (if there was one thing my mother disapproved of more than foreign food, it was sex). In the end I shook off both sets of inhibitions together, losing my virginity and going to an Indian restaurant for the first time in the same month, I'm not sure in which order.

Then I became a journalist and entered what now seems a rather promiscuous phase (I'm talking about food here, not sex). I ate my way indiscriminately through every cuisine I encountered on my travels, ignoring the sensible rule of eating what the locals did; I stuffed myself with satay in Berlin, stifado in Thornton Cleveleys and a series of dreadful Cantonese meals in Dhaka.

I had no sooner tasted something I liked than I wanted to cook it myself. Somewhere along the line I acquired a severely puritan attitude to ingredients, which meant that I wasted several years of my life pestering puzzled shop assistants in suburban shopping centres for fresh lemon grass, tahini paste and genuine harissa. All these things are easily available now but they weren't in 1976; by the time I tracked them down I was often too exhausted to do anything with them.

Then, in the Eighties, I fell hopelessly and permanently in love. Having discovered my consuming passion, Italian food, I abandoned fruitless searches for obscure Thai ingredients in favour of simpler pleasures: grilled porcini slithering voluptuously on the tongue, the crunch of courgette flowers fried in batter, prosciutto slices crumpled on a plate with over-ripe figs (I write the latter with some embarrassment as I am, nominally at least, a vegetarian).

I began to cook from Marcella Hazan, Giuliano Bugialli and Elizabeth David's *Italian Food*; I learned how to roast garlic and sun dry my own tomatoes; I ate polenta on the shores of Lake Garda, black pasta in Sardinia and ribollita in Certaldo. The contrast with my childhood eating habits was puzzling and intense, until one day the purpose of those long years of culinary deprivation became clear.

Without nostalgic memories of holidays in France, of sun-drenched summers on the shores of the Mediterranean, I had nothing to look back on and compare, to its detriment, with the present. My childhood, precisely because it wasn't pre-lapsarian, was the perfect preparation for the flavours and smells of Italy, for my entry into a cuisine and culture which represents for me, quite simply, Paradise Found.

Joan Smith, Harpers & Queen (August 1993).

Para Navidad

It is the last day of October. Here in the south-eastern corner of Spain the afternoon is hazy and the sun is warm, although not quite what it was a week ago. Then we were eating out-of-doors at midday, and were baked even in our cotton sweaters. The colours of the land are still those of late summer – roan, silver, lilac, and ochre. In the soft light the formation of the rock and the ancient terracing of the hills become clearly visible. In the summer the sun on the limestone-white soil dazzles the eyes, and the greens of June obscure the shapes of the ravines and craggy outcroppings. Now there are signs of autumn on the leaves of some of the almond trees. They have turned a frail, transparent auburn, and this morning when I awoke I devoured two of the very first tangerines of the season. In the dawn their scent was piercing and their taste was sharp. During the night it had rained – not much, nothing like enough to affect the parched soil – but all the same there was a sheen on the rose bricks and grey stones of the courtyard. The immense old terra-cotta oil jar in the centre was freshly washed, and over the mountains a half-rainbow gave a pretty performance as we drank our breakfast coffee.

At midday we picked small figs, dusty purple and pale jade green. On the skins is a bloom not to be seen on midsummer figs. The taste, too, is quite different. The flesh is a clear garnet red, less rich and more subtle than that of the main-crop fruit, which is of the *vernal* variety, brilliant green. Some of the figs have split open and are half dried by the sun. In the north we can never taste fruit like this, fruit midway between fresh and dried. It has the same poignancy as the black Valencia grapes still hanging in heavy bunches on the vines. These, too, are in the process of transforming themselves – from fresh grapes to raisins on the stalk as we know them. Here the bunches have been tied up in cotton bags.

The two ancients who tend the almond trees (this is Valencia almond country, and it has been a bad season. If the rain fails, next year's crop may prove to be another disaster) and who have known the estate of La Alfarella all their lives, were hoping that the grapes could be cut late and hung in the storeroom until Christmas. Their plans have been foiled by the wasps. This year there has been a fearsome plague of the persistent and destructive brutes. They have bitten their way through the protecting cotton, sucked out the juice of the fruit, and left nothing but husks. Here and there where a bunch has escaped the marauders, we have cut one and brought it back to the house in a basket with the green lemons and some of the wild thyme that has an almost overpowering scent, one that seems to be peculiar to Spanish thyme. It is perhaps fanciful, but it seems to have undertones of aniseed, chamomile, hyssop, lavender.

My English host, who has re-created this property of La Alfarella out of a ruin and is bringing its land back to life after twenty years of neglect, is at the cooking pots. He seizes on the green lemons and grates the skins of two of them into the meat mixture he is stirring up. He throws in a little of the sun-dried thyme and makes us a beguiling dish of *albóndigas*, little *rissoles* fried in olive oil. He fries them skilfully and they emerge with a caramel-brown and gold coating reflecting the glaze of the shallow earthenware *sartén*, the frying dish in which they have been cooked and brought to the table. All the cooking here is done in the local earthenware pots. Even the water is boiled in them. They are very thick and sturdy, unglazed on the outside, and are used directly over the Butagaz flame, or sometimes on the wood fire in the open hearth. As yet there is no oven. That is one of next year's projects.

Surprisingly, in an isolated farmhouse in a country believed by so many people to produce the worst and most repetitive food in Europe, our diet has a good deal of variety, and some of the produce is of a very high quality. I have never eaten such delicate and fine-grained pork meat, and the cured fillet, *lomo de cerdo*, is by any standard a luxury worth paying for. The chicken and the rabbit that go into the ritual paella cooked in a vast burnished iron pan (only for paella on a big scale and for the frying of *tortillas* are metal pans used) over a crackling fire are tender, possessed of their true flavours. We have had little red mullet and fresh sardines *à la plancha*, grilled on primitive round tin grill plates made sizzling hot on the fire. This is the utensil, common to France, Italy, Spain, and Greece, that also produces the best toast in the world – brittle and black-barred with the marks of the grill.

To start our midday meal we have, invariably, a tomato and onion salad, a few slices of fresh white cheese, and a dish of olives. The tomatoes are the Mediterranean ridged variety of which I never tire. They are huge, sweet, fleshy, richly red. Here they cut out and discard the central wedge, almost as we core apples, then slice the tomatoes into rough sections. They need no dressing, nothing but salt. With the roughly cut raw onions, sweet as all the vegetables grown in this limestone and clay soil, they make a wonderfully refreshing salad. It has no catchy name. It is just *ensalada*, and it cannot be reproduced without these sweet Spanish onions and Mediterranean tomatoes.

In the summer, seventeen-year-old Juanita asked for empty wine bottles to take to her married sister in the village, who would, she explained, preserve the tomatoes for the winter by slicing them, packing them in bottles, and sealing them with olive oil. They would keep for a year or more, Juanita said. Had her sister a bottle we could try? No. There were only two of last year's vintage left. They were to be kept *para Navidad*, for Christmas.

Yesterday in the market there were fresh dates from Elche, the first of the season. They are rather small, treacle-sticky, and come in tortoiseshell-cat colours: black, acorn brown, peeled-chestnut beige; like the lengths of Barcelona corduroy I have bought in the village shop. Inevitably, we were told that the best dates would not be ready until *Navidad*. That applies to the oranges and the muscatel raisins: and presumably also to the little rosy copper medlars now on sale in the market. They are not yet ripe enough to eat, so I suppose they are to be kept, like Juanita's sister's tomatoes, and the yellow and green Elche melons stored in an *esparto* basket in the house, for *Navidad*. We nibble at the candied melon peel in sugar-frosted and lemon-ice-coloured wedges we have bought in the market, and we have already torn open the Christmas-wrapped *mazapan* (it bears the trade name of El Alce, 'the elk': a sad-faced moose with tired hooves and snow on its antlers decorates the paper), which is of a kind I have not before encountered. It is not at all like marzipan. It is very white, in bricks, with a consistency reminiscent of frozen sherbet. It is made of almonds and egg whites, and studded with crystallized fruit. There is the new season's quince cheese, the *carne de membrillo*, which we ought to be keeping to take to England for *Navidad* presents, and with it there is also a peach cheese. How is it that one never hears mention of this beautiful and delicious clear amber sweetmeat?

There are many more Mediterranean treats, cheap treats of autumn, like the newly brined green olives that the people of all olive-growing countries rightly regard as a delicacy. In Rome, one late October, I remember buying new green olives from a woman who was selling them straight from the barrel she had set up at a street corner. That was twelve years ago. I have never forgotten the fresh flavour of the Roman green olives. The *manzanilla* variety we have bought here come from Andalucía. They are neither green nor black, but purple, rose, lavender, and brown, picked at varying stages of maturity, and intended for quick home consumption rather than for export. It is the tasting of familiar products at their point of origin (before they are graded, classified, prinked up, and imprisoned in bottles, tins, jars, and packets) that makes them memorable; forever changes their aspect.

By chance, saffron is another commodity that has acquired a new dimension. It was somewhere on the way up to Córdoba that we saw the first purple patches of autumn-flowering saffron crocuses in bloom. On our return we called on Mercedes, the second village girl who works at La Alfarella, to tell her that we were back. Her father was preparing saffron – picking the orange stigmas one by one from the iridescent mauve flowers heaped up in a shoe box by his side and spreading them carefully on a piece of brown paper to dry. The heap of discarded crocus petals made a splash of intense and pure colour, shining like a pool of quicksilver in the cavernous shadows of the village living room. Every night, during the six-odd weeks that the season lasts, he prepares a boxful of flowers, so his wife told us. The bundle of saffron that she took out of a battered tin, wrapped in a square of paper, and gave to us must represent a fortnight's work. It is last year's vintage because there is not yet enough of the new season's batch to make a respectable offering. It appears to have lost nothing of its penetrating, quite violently acrid-sweet and pungent scent. It is certainly a handsome present that Mercedes' mother has given us, a rare present, straight from the source, and appropriate for us to take home to England for *Navidad*.

An even better one is the rain. At last, now it is real rain that is falling. The ancient have stopped work for the day, and most of the population of the village is gathered in the café. The day the rain comes the village votes its own fiesta day.

Elizabett David, *Spectator* (27 November 1964).

Perfection

Luncheon was laid on bare pink marble under a trellis of mulberry.

There was a loaf of butter on a leaf, the bread was on a board; there was a dish of lemons, and there were wooden mills for black pepper and grey pepper and the salt; the china was eighteenth-century Moustier and the wine stood, undecanted, in a row of thick green cool unlabelled bottles. Julius drew the corks himself; poured, held up, handed glasses. Below the olive trees they could see the valley, the linear terraced hill, and the other slope, soft again, in full sunlight now, feathery with mimosa.

'How good,' said Sarah.

'When it is like this, it is like this,' said Julius.

'After six days of mistral.'

'*Der Süden* ...'

'I could never live anywhere else,' said Julius.

'I have never been before,' said Mélanie.

The sea-urchins came heaped in a great armorial pile, sable and violet, tiered on their burnished quills, like the unexplained detail on the hill by the thistles and the hermitage of a quattrocento background, exposing now inside each severed shell the pattern of a tender sea-star.

'With a spoon,' Julius said. 'Like this.'

Presently he struck a match and set fire to the next course. The flames, fed by rosemary and fennel, crackled, aromatic, invisible almost in the brilliant air.

'Like plum-pudding!'

'So over-rated,' said Julius. In a flash of silver blades he laid bare the nut-white fish inside the charred, bark-like crust.

Mélanie looked for the sauce-boat. There seemed to be no potatoes.

Julius helped her to a few drops of limpid oil.

'Perfection, Jules,' said Sarah.

From Sybille Bedford, *A Legacy* (1956).

EPILOGUE: THE RAW AND
THE COOKED

Peperoni Arrostiti

6 large red, green and yellow
  capsicum peppers
3 fat garlic cloves

1 tbsp fresh capers (optional)
extra virgin olive oil

Heat the oven to 200°C (gas mark 6). Wash the peppers and arrange them whole on a baking tray. Place them in the middle of the oven and bake until they begin to collapse and the skins are blackened (this will take at least half an hour, depending on the size of the peppers). Remove them from the oven and allow to cool (vital if you wish your fingers to emerge intact). Place a cooled pepper on a plate or chopping board and pull gently on the stalk; the seeds should come away as well and be discarded. Peel off the blackened skin, flatten the pepper out and trim it into edible strips. Arrange them on a plate and do the same for the remaining peppers, alternating the three colours. Peel and thinly slice the garlic, arranging the raw slices on top of the peppers. Add the capers, if you like them, and pour over a liberal quantity of olive oil, which will pick up the flavour of the vegetables. Allow to stand for at least an hour before eating, and serve with slices of *ciabatta* bread to mop up the oil.

Frittata con le Cipolle

1 lb very fresh onions, either
   Italian red or the translucent
   white variety
olive oil
6 eggs

freshly grated parmesan
a handful of basil leaves,
   roughly torn
black pepper
butter

Peel and thinly slice the onions, leaving them in rings. Heat a generous quantity of olive oil in a heavy frying pan and add the onions. Turn the heat down as soon as they begin to wilt, and continue cooking until they are limp and sweet; this may take anything up to 40 minutes. Break the eggs into a bowl and beat briskly with a fork. Add the grated cheese, the basil and the black pepper. Mix well. Lift the onions from the frying pan with a slotted spoon, allowing them to drain well. Add to the egg mixture. Drain most of the olive oil from the frying pan, add a little butter and warm over a medium heat. Pour in the egg mixture and cook until it is almost set. Place the *frittata* under a pre-heated grill to brown the top. Slide on to a plate, cut into wedges and serve at once. A green salad is a good accompaniment, dressed with extra virgin olive oil and balsamic vinegar, and topped with parmesan shavings.

Note: this recipe also works well with thinly sliced courgettes instead of the onions. They need a far shorter frying time, no more than two or three minutes, but the rest of the instructions remain the same.

Spinach, Avocado and Pine Nut Salad

fresh spinach leaves
1 ripe avocado
pine nuts

extra virgin olive oil
balsamic vinegar
a touch of mustard

Wash and dry the spinach. If you are using large leaves, tear them into more manageable pieces and arrange in a deep bowl. Peel and slice the avocado and add to the spinach. Heat a heavy skillet and toast the pine nuts to a golden-brown colour. Tip them into the bowl with the other salad ingredients and mix thoroughly. Pour the olive oil into a jar, add a dash of balsamic vinegar and the mustard. Close the jar and shake well. Pour the dressing over the salad and toss. Serve with *ciabatta* bread to mop up the oil and nuts at the bottom of the bowl.

Fegato alla Veneziana

1lb red or white onions
olive oil

thin slices of calves' liver (2 per person)

Heat the olive oil in a heavy frying-pan and add the thinly sliced onions. Cook until soft and sweet. Add the liver and cook gently until it is no longer pink, turning each slice once. Serve on its own or with a simple vegetable such as wilted spinach or green beans.

Couscous with Lamb and Apricots

stewing lamb cut into pieces, with most of the fat removed
olive oil
1 onion, roughly chopped
1 clove of garlic, roughly chopped
1 tbsp tomato paste
1 inch-long piece fresh ginger, peeled and thinly sliced
2 or 3 different vegetables: carrots, green beans, mange-
touts, parsnips, baby sweetcorn
meat stock or water
whole dried apricots (preferably those sold in vacuum packs which do not need to be reconstituted)
couscous
ground cinnamon
harissa paste

Place the lamb, olive oil, onion, garlic, ginger, tomato paste and vegetables in a heavy pan, preferably a *couscoussière*. Add enough stock or water to cover and cook over a medium heat until the lamb is tender, then put in the apricots (how many is a matter of taste). Cook on a low heat. In the meantime, pour boiling water over the couscous and add a little oil. When the water has been absorbed, tip the couscous into a fine-holed colander or the top half of the *couscoussière* and place on top of the stew. Cover with a lid or a large plate and cook gently until the couscous is light and fluffy.

Turn the couscous on to an elegant warmed dish and sprinkle with cinammon. Make a well in the centre and add the meat and vegetables, leaving most of the liquid behind. Add a couple of teaspoons of harissa to the meat juice (depending how hot you like it) and pour the liquid into a jug. Guests help themselves to the couscous, lamb and apricots, then pour over the sauce to taste. For people who like it really hot, a small bowl of harissa can be served on the side.

Pasta with Tuna, Tomato and Lemon Sauce

dried pasta of your choice or, if you can get it, fresh squid-ink pasta
olive oil
1 onion
1 clove of garlic, crushed

tinned Italian tuna
fresh capers (optional)
1 small tin chopped tomatoes
black pepper
1 lemon

Put a large pan of salted water on to boil and add 1 tspn olive oil. Fry the chopped onion and garlic gently in olive oil, then crumble the tuna into it. Add the capers, if using. When the mixture is soft, add the chopped tomatoes and a couple of grindings of black pepper. Meanwhile, when the water comes to the boil, add the pasta, carefully noting the cooking time (a couple of minutes if it's fresh, otherwise check the packet). You can turn off the tuna and tomato mixture if the pasta needs to catch up.

When the pasta is almost ready, make sure the tuna and tomato sauce is really hot, then add the juice of the lemon and some more black pepper. Drain the pasta, toss with a little olive oil, and serve.

Baked Garlic

1 head of plump garlic per person

olive oil

Tidy the heads of garlic by removing all but the inner layer of paper, but leave them whole. Plunge them into boiling water for no more than a minute, then arrange in a heat-proof dish. Sprinkle olive oil over them and place the dish in a hot oven (220°C, gas mark 7). Leave to cook for an hour, then serve either as a starter, with bread, or as a vegetable accompaniment to a main course. The trick is to break off each clove and suck out the pulp – sounds unlikely, I know, but the result is heavenly.

Cipolline in Agrodolce

1 lb of small onions or shallots   *balsamic vinegar*
extra virgin olive oil

Peel the onions, leaving them whole. Heat the olive oil in a heavy frying pan or casserole, add the onions. Brown them, then turn down the heat and cook for 45 minutes. Stir occasionally, taking care not to push the onions out of shape. At the very end of cooking, when the onions are soft and sweet, add a dash of good-quality balsamic vinegar. Serve as anti-pasti, with slices of oiled, grilled aubergines, or as an unusual vegetable with the meat course.

Purea di Fava con Spinace

fresh spinach
freshly shelled or tinned broad
  beans
1 carrot
1 onion

1 potato, peeled
black pepper
fresh nutmeg
extra-virgin olive oil

Prepare the spinach by placing it in a pan and cooking it until it wilts. Place in a colander and leave to drain. Put the broad beans in a heavy saucepan with the roughly chopped carrot, onion and potato. Add water to cover and boil until the ingredients are very soft. Tip away any surplus water and place the bean mixture in a liquidiser. It should emerge as a smooth green paste (tinned beans need a longer cooking and liquidising time to soften the skins). Arrange several tbsps of cold bean purée on one half of a plate. Place an equal amount of spinach next to it. Sprinkle both with black pepper, then grate a little nutmeg on to the spinach. Pour liberal quantities of extra-virgin olive oil on both, then serve.

Home from the Hunt Lunch

a mixture of wild mushrooms –
  porcini, chanterelles, pieds de
  mouton, trompettes de mort
olive oil

2 cloves garlic, peeled
a dash of Calvados (optional)
luganega or wild boar sausages
fresh coriander

Clean the mushrooms, brushing or wiping off any soil, and check carefully for maggots. Slice the *porcini* into strips. Heat the oil in a heavy frying-pan and sauté the crushed garlic. Add the mushrooms and cook over a medium heat, taking care not to burn them. Pour over the Calvados, if using, and cook till it evaporates. Meanwhile prick the sausages and place them under a hot grill, turning them a couple of times until they're brown all over. Sprinkle chopped coriander over the mushrooms and arrange them on a large warm plate. Place the sausages on top and serve.

Chicken Breasts with Coriander

olive oil
unsalted butter
four boned and skinned
  chicken breasts, 1 per person

juice of 2 lemons
fresh coriander, roughly
  chopped

Heat some oil and butter in a heavy frying-pan. Put in the chicken breasts and cook gently for 4 or 5 minutes. Remove them and put aside. Add more oil and butter to the pan and when melted add the lemon juice. Turn up the heat and allow the contents of the pan to sizzle. Now turn the heat down again and add the chicken breasts and coriander. Cook gently until the chicken is done and the coriander is just beginning to turn crisp. Serve, making sure each chicken breast has a generous helping of sauce.

Panettone al Forno con Lamponi

2 tbsps raisins
Marsala wine
1 medium plain panettone (dry
   Italian sponge cake)
butter
fresh raspberries

3 eggs
3 tbsps sugar
10 fl oz milk
8 fl oz double cream
vanilla essence

Place the raisins in a bowl and cover them with Marsala. Allow to stand until raisins are soft, at least an hour. Cut the *panettone* into chunks, heat some butter in a frying-pan and fry the pieces until golden. Arrange in a shallow oblong or oval serving dish with the fresh raspberries and the soaked raisins sprinkled in between. Pour the wine from the bowl over the *panettone*. Break the eggs into a bowl and beat until frothy. Add the sugar, milk, cream and vanilla essence. Pour over the *panettone* and bake uncovered for 30 minutes at 180°C (gas mark 4). The pudding is ready when the custard is just beginning to turn golden-brown. This summery version of bread and butter pudding should be served at once; the leftovers are delicious eaten cold the next day.

Tiramisu

3 tbsps brandy or Marsala
1 espresso cup of coffee
a bar of good dark chocolate
3 eggs
3 tbsps sugar

500 g Mascarpone
Savoiardi (Italian sponge
   fingers)
chocolate-covered coffee beans

Mix together the brandy or Marsala and the coffee. Grate the chocolate. Separate the eggs and whisk the whites until stiff. Add the sugar to the yolks and beat well with a fork, then slowly add the mascarpone. Fold in the egg whites. Arrange a layer of Savoiardi in the bottom of a dish and soak them with the coffee and brandy. Cover with the mascarpone/egg mixture and sprinkle with grated chocolate. Continue like this until you have three layers, finishing with grated chocolate. Cover with a plate or foil and place in the fridge for at least 4 hours. Before serving, decorate with some chocolate-covered coffee beans.

Mont Blanc

a large tin of chestnut purée   *3 tbsps rum*
4 tbsps milk   *1 tbsp sugar*
4 ozs grated chocolate   *half pint of whipping cream*

Put the chestnut purée in a saucepan with the milk. Cook on a low heat, stirring frequently, until it reaches the consistency of a soft paste. Add the grated chocolate and the rum. Mix well and remove from heat. Cover the bowl and put it in the fridge until it is really cold.

Using a food mill, pass the chestnut mixture through a disc with large holes, allowing it to fall onto a decorative plate. Try to move the mill in decreasing circles, creating a mountain effect on the plate. Whip the cream and sugar until it is in stiff folds, then slowly spoon the cream on top of the chestnut mixture, allowing it to slip down the sides like snow. Serve.

ACKNOWLEDGEMENTS

The editor and publishers grateful acknowledge permission to reprint copyright material as follows:

Aitken & Stone Ltd for excerpts from UNDER THE JAGUAR SUN and T ZERO by Italo Calvino, translated by William Weaver, and ALIVE: THE STORY OF THE ANDES SURVIVORS by Piers Paul Read; Berger-Levrault Communication S.A. for an excerpt from LES SECRETS DES FERMES AU COEUR DE LA FRANCE, translated by Anthea Bell (1982); Blackwell Publishers for an excerpt from THE CONDITION OF THE WORKING CLASS IN ENGLAND by Friedrich Engels, translated by W.O. Henderson and W.H. Challenor; British Broadcasting Corporation for PANORAMA interview with Princess Diana (BBC1 on 20 November 1995); to Bloomsbury Publishing for excerpts from THE MAN WHO WASN'T MAIGRET: A PORTRAIT OF GEORGES SIMENON by Patrick Marnham, and DRINKING THE RAIN by Alix Kates Shulman, to Curtis Brown Ltd for THE GAYELORD HAUSER COOKBOOK by Gayelord Hauser (Faber, 1955); Carcanet Press Ltd for excerpts from COLLECTED POEMS by Robert Graves; Harper Collins Publishers for excerpts from LA DOULEUR by Marguerite Duras, translated by Barbara Brey, CHRISTIE MALRY'S OWN DOUBLE ENTRY by B.S. Johnson, MEMORIES, DREAMS, REFLECTIONS by C.G. Jung, translated by Richard and Clara Winston, and ON FOOD AND COOKING: THE SCIENCE AND LOVE OF THE KITCHEN by Harold McGee (also by permission of Scribner, a Division of Simon & Schuster); Harper Collins Publishers (Canada) Ltd for excerpts from THE RITUALS OF DINNER by Margaret Visser; Leo Cooper Ltd for an excerpt from DEKHO! INDIA THAT WAS by Elizabeth Crawford Wilkin, Andre Deutsch Ltd and McClelland & Stewart Inc, Toronto,

V.H. Mottram; Jill Norman on behalf of the estate of Elizabeth David for 'Para Navidad' (*The Spectator*, 27 November 1964), and an excerpt from MEDITERRANEAN FOOD; Michael O'Mara Books Ltd for an excerpt from DIANA: HER TRUE STORY by Andrew Morton; Susie Orbach for FAT IS A FEMINIST ISSUE; Orion Pictures Corporation for THE SILENCE OF THE LAMBS by Thomas Harris; Orion Publishing Group Ltd for excerpts from A LEGACY by Sybille Bedford (Weidenfeld), and TOULOUSE LAUTREC: A LIFE by Julia Frey (Weidenfeld, 1994); Oxford University Press for excerpts from THE MISFORTUNES OF VIRTUE by the Marquis de Sade, translated by David Coward (World's Classics), THE ROMANCE OF THE ROSE by Guillaume de Lorris and Jean de Meun, translated and edited by Frances Horgan (World's Classics), and JANE AUSTEN'S LETTERS, edited by Deirdre Le Faye; Penguin Books Ltd for excerpts from FROM THE PHYSIOLOGY OF TASTE by Jean-Anthelme Brillat-Savarin, translated by Anne Drayton, DE BELLO GALLICO by Julius Caesar, translated by S.A. Handford, TALES FROM THE THOUSAND AND ONE NIGHTS, translated by N.J. Dawood, THE SECOND SEX by Simone de Beauvoir, translated by H.M. Parshley, THE FEMININE MYSTIQUE by Betty Friedan, OTHER LULUS by Philip Hensher, BENITO MUSSOLINI: THE RISE AND FALL OF IL DUCE by Christopher Hibbert, EPODES by Horace, translated by W.G. Shepherd, LES MISERABLES by Victor Hugo, translated by Norman Denny, THE TRAVELS OF MARCO POLO, translated by R.E. Latham, IF THIS IS A MAN by Primo Levi, translated by Stuart Woolf, UTOPIA by Thomas More, translated by Paul Turner, THE MERCHANT OF PRATO by Iris Origo, VAMPS AND TRAMPS: NEW ESSAYS by Camille Paglia, THE GHOST by Plautus, translated by E.F. Watling, HOW THE OTHER HALF DIES by Susan George, CARMINA BURANA, translated by David Parlett, THE SATYRICON OF PETRONIUS, translated by J.P. Sullivan, THE LIFE OF CICERO by Plutarch, translated by Rex Warner, THE SECRET HISTORY by Procopius, translated by G.A. Williamson, A FAR CRY FROM KENSINGTON by Muriel Spark, FLESH AND BLOOD by Reay Tannahill, LIVES OF THE ARTISTS by Vasari, translated by George Bull, THE RITUALS OF DINNER by Margaret Visser, and NANA by Emile Zola, translated by George Holden; Murray Pollinger (Literary Agent) for excerpts from SOMEONE LIKE YOU (Michael Joseph/Penguin Books) by Roald Dahl; Quartet Books Ltd for an excerpt from WOMEN OF SAND AND MYRRH by Hanan Al-Shaykh, translated by Catherine Cobham; Random House UK Ltd for

INDEX